The Oil Road

The Oil Road

Journeys from the Caspian Sea to the City of London

James Marriott and Mika Minio-Paluello

VERSO

London • New York

First published by Verso 2012
© James Marriott and Mika Minio-Paluello 2012

1 3 5 7 9 10 8 6 4 2

Verso
UK: 6 Meard Street, London W1F 0EG
US: 20 Jay Street, Suite 1010, Brooklyn, NY 11201

www.versobooks.com

Verso is the imprint of New Left Books

ISBN-13: 978-1-84467-646-0

British Library Cataloguing in Publication Data
A catalogue record for this book is available from the British Library

Library of Congress Cataloging-in-Publication Data
Marriott, James.
The oil road : travels from the Caspian to the city / James Marriott and Mika Minio-Paluello.
p. cm.
Includes bibliographical references and index.
ISBN 978-1-84467-646-0 (hardback : alk. paper) – ISBN 978-1-84467-927-0 (ebook)
1. Petroleum industry and trade–Azerbaijan–Baku. 2. Petroleum industry and trade–Europe. 3. Caspian
Sea. I. Minio-Paluello, Mika. II. Title.
HD9575.A943B356 2012
338.2'7282094754–dc23
2012019763

Typeset in Minion Pro by Hewer Text UK, ltd, Edinburgh
Printed and bound in the US by Maple Vail

What has its roots in the sea, its trunk in the mountains,
and its branches in the cities?

CONTENTS

PART III: THE SHIP

PART IV: THE ROAD

PART V: THE FACTORY

LIST OF MAPS

FOREWORD AND ACKNOWLEDGEMENTS

The Oil Road is a travelogue in pursuit of oil. Rising from the Caspian Sea, we tracked BP's pipeline westwards over the Caucasus Mountains and Anatolian plateau before it descends to the Turkish coast. As the oil was carried onwards aboard tankers and through further pipes, so our journey continued, across the Mediterranean and the Alps, to Bavaria and London. From the revolutionary Futurism of 1920s Baku to the unblinking capitalism of our city, the drive to control oil reserves – and hence people and events – has shattered nature and shaped societies. The stupendous wealth of Azerbaijani crude has long inspired dreams of a world remade. Thus this book travels through both time and space, exploring a landscape of power, resistance and profit.

While the narrative portrays a particular journey made in 2009, it refers back to stories we gathered on travels made to the places described since 1998. All of the conversations portrayed are based on recordings or notes taken at the time. Very occasionally names have been changed to avoid putting individuals at risk. Several of the main characters in the book have kindly read and checked the final text.

The Oil Road passes through the lands of ten major languages, and we have tried to draw out this richness in the story, using the orthography particular to these languages where possible. Transcribing Azeri, Georgian, Kurdish and Turkish names into English can be challenging, and we apologise for our mistakes and shortcomings.

The pipeline systems that we travel also have their own tongue, conventionally described in the numerical language of engineering. We have used this numbering pattern in the headings of sections that take place directly on the route itself, giving both the length of each pipeline section to that location, its 'kilometre point' or 'KP', and the distance travelled along the entire Oil Road. Hence a section title such as:

BTC KP 484 – 671 km – Krtsanisi, Georgia

We have used the measurement of the sea, nautical miles, to describe the passage of the tanker. Those locations not directly on the route of the oil – such as Baku itself – are without numbers.

This book would have been impossible without the close collaboration of friends who we worked with over the past decade as Platform and our allies scrutinised and challenged the industrial project and the governments behind it. We would particularly like to thank some remarkable people – brave, skilled and determined: Mayis Gulaliyev, Zardusht Alizade, Manana Kochladze, Kety Gujaraidze, Ferhat Kaya, Ali Kurdoğlu , Mehmet Ali Uslu, Mustafa Gündoğdu, Kerim Yıldız , Elena Gerebizza, Antonio Tricarico, Greg Muttitt, Mark Brown, Nick Hildyard and Hannah Griffiths.

There are many others who have engaged in the issues in the book with perseverance and brilliance, but whom we have been unable to mention in the text, including Mirvari Gahramanli, Rochelle Harris, Petr Hlobil, Martin Skalsky, Yuri Urbansky, Sebastien Godinot, Doug Norlen, Regine Richter, Piotr Trzaskowski, Greig Aitkin, Andrea Baranes, Pippa Gallop, Carol Welch, Karen Decker, Steve Kretzman, Wilimijn Nagel, Paul de Clerk, Clive Wicks, Hannah Ellis, Rachel Bernu, Andy Rowell, Michael Gillard, Nick Rau, Tony Juniper, Foye Hatton, Alexandra Woodsworth, Steve, Catriona Vine, Sally Eberhardt, Andrew Barry, Kate Hampton, Rob Newman, Anke Stock, Mark Thomas, Kate Geary and Anders Lustgarten.

In addition to those mentioned above, we are extremely grateful for the time and assistance given to us during our travels by a number of dedicated individuals, including Arzu Abdullayeva, Mehdi Gulaliyev, Ramazi Lomsadze, Marzia Piron, Simone Libralato, Bruno Lisjak, Rudi Remm, Guy Chazan, Ülkü Güney, Guney Yildiz, Yaprak Yildiz, Can Gündüz, Oktay Ince, 'Mali' Mehmet Ali Uzelgun, Idil Soyseckin and Tennur Baş.

We would particularly like to thank the people who live along the route of the pipelines, for inviting us into their homes, trusting us with their stories and sharing their fears and frustrations, despite the repression and the fact that we sound and look like the many others from the cities who brought the pipelines with them. We could only write this book because of the freedom that we – unlike many of the people we met – have to travel, move across borders and access people. The book is also a product of our particular set of privileges, which also frame what we see and experience and what we don't.

The research and travel for this book was graciously funded by the Amiel and Melburn Trust and the Charles Stewart Mott Foundation. Early research was funded from a fellowship given by the Environment Foundation awarded by John Elkington. We have also been financially supported by the Arts Council England, the Joseph Rowntree Charitable Trust, the Roddick Foundation and the Sigrid

Rausing Trust. We would particularly like to thank Gordon Roddick, Sandra Smithey, Theodoros Chronopoulos and Stephen Pittam for their understanding of the value of this work. We also relied on the patience and support of close allies such as Charlie Kronick and Lorne Stockman.

We are extremely grateful for the encouragement, advice and patience of three editors at Verso – Tom Penn, Dan Hind and Leo Hollis; and to Andrea Scaringella and Helen Sheehan for allowing us to use their photographs, Sophy Newton and the Cotesbach Educational Trust for discovering the Marriott photographs, Elena Gerebizza and Marzia Piron for helping source the image from Muggia, Thames & Hudson for allowing us to reprint the photograph of the *Symphony of Factory Sirens*, Dominic Latham and Jimmy Edmondson at UHC for producing the Carbon Web diagram, and John Jackson for the excellent maps.

We would especially like to thank our colleagues at Platform, and our trustees, for all their support and for bearing with us over the years: Ben Amunwa, Mel Evans, Anna Galkina, Dan Gretton, Tanya Hawkes, Sarah Legge, Adam Ma'anit, Mark Roberts, Kevin Smith and Jane Trowell, as well as past colleagues including Benjamin Diss, Mehmet Ali Uslu and Greg Muttitt. Neither of us can imagine a better place to work than Platform – an organisation that truly values creativity, political purpose and collaboration.

In the writing of the text we were immeasurably assisted by the support of friends who read, researched and commented on drafts, or listened to us talk for hours about revolutionary labour in 1905 Baku, shipping lanes in the Mediterranean, or the oil texture of London: John de Falbe, Gareth Evans, Anna Galkina, Kelly Bornshlegel, Nick Robins, Dan Gretton, Greg Muttitt, Maddy Evans, Jane Trowell, Ory Rose and Cameron Lee.

This was a collaborative project, and we have benefited from much good advice and support. However, any remaining mistakes or omissions are either ours, or due to the lack of transparency around oil politics.

The politics and struggles described in this book are live, constantly unfolding and expanding in the geography we describe and beyond. As this book goes to print, Ferhat Kaya in Ardahan is facing a prison sentence on charges widely seen as a pretext for punishment of his activism around the pipeline. For updates on Ferhat and other characters in the book, as well as on the future of the Oil Road itself, see theoilroad.com.

GLOSSARY

ACG – Azeri– Chirag–Gunashli oilfield in Caspian
ADR – Azerbaijan Democratic Republic (1918–20)
AIOC – Azerbaijan International Operating Company
AKP – Justice and Development Party (Turkey)
AWP – Adria–Wien Pipeline
BIL – BOTAŞ International Ltd
BNITO – Batumi Oil Refining and Trading Company
BOTAŞ – Turkish State Pipeline Corporation
BTC – Baku–Tbilisi–Ceyhan pipeline
BTC Co. – Baku–Tbilisi–Ceyhan Pipeline Company
CIP – Community Investment Programme
CRBM – Campagna per la Riforma della Banca Mondiale
DEHAP – Democratic People's Party (Turkey)
DTP – Democratic Society Party (Turkey)
EBRD – European Bank for Reconstruction and Development
ECGD – Export Credit Guarantee Department (now renamed UK Export
    Finance)
EITI – Extractive Industries Transparency Initiative
ERM – Environmental Resources Management
Expro – Exploration and Production
FCO – Foreign and Commonwealth Office
GOGC – Georgian Oil and Gas Corporation
IKL – Ingolstadt–Kralupy–Litvinov pipeline
IST – Integrated Supply and Trading
METU – Middle East Technical University (Ankara)
MHP – Nationalist Movement Party (Turkey)
MTN – Ministry of National Security (Secret Police of Azerbaijan)
NKVD – People's Commissariat for Internal Affairs (Secret Police of Soviet
    Union)

OECD – Organisation for Economic Cooperation and Development
OSI – Open Society Institute
PKK – Kurdistan Worker's Party
RBS – Royal Bank of Scotland
SCP – South Caucasus Gas pipeline
SOCAR – State Oil Company of Azerbaijan Republic
SOFAZ – State Oil Fund of Azerbaijan
SPC 2888 – Speciality Polymer Coatings pipeline coating number 2888
TAL – Transalpine pipeline
USAID – United States Agency for International Development

MAP I: OVERVIEW OF THE CASPIAN–BAVARIA ROUTE

Pipeline route by land
Route by sea
Oil refinery

TAL – Transalpine Pipeline
AWP – Adria–Wien Pipeline
IKL – Ingolstadt–Kralupy–Litvinov Pipeline

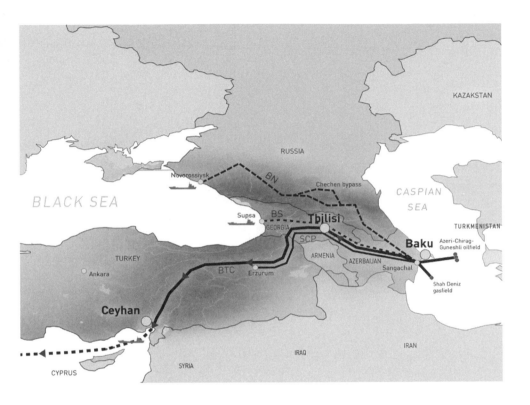

BTC – Baku–Tbilisi–Ceyhan Pipeline   BN – Baku–Novorossiysk Pipeline
BS– Baku–Supsa Pipeline   SCP – South Caucasus Pipeline

PROLOGUE: THE OIL CITY

OLD BROAD STREET, THE CITY, LONDON

28 January 2009. After several weeks of juggling dates we have finally fixed a meeting with Rory Sullivan, Director of Investor Responsibility at Insight Investment. We have an hour to present our critique of BP's Canadian tar sands projects and explain why they pose not only environmental and social risks, but financial ones too. It is potentially a matter of concern for institutional investors, for one in six of the equities held by UK pension funds are shares in BP.

We come in from the street of roaring traffic to an atrium of glass and light. The receptionist takes names, issues passes, and ushers us into a beige, windowless room at the centre of the building. Insight is the world's sixth-largest shareholder in BP, and Rory has been in Socially Responsible Investment for a decade. He is the chair of the United Nations Environment Programme Finance Initiative, so we are keen to influence him.

He appears after a few minutes. He is long-limbed and energetic, with bright blue eyes. Before we begin our presentation, we settle in with a few introductions. Rory interrupts with a touch of impatience: 'Yeah, yeah, I know Platform. I remember your involvement in the debates over BP and the BTC pipeline . . . it's finished now . . . it's a done deal.'

For months after, that comment echoes in our minds. We can recall little else about the meeting except the line: 'It's a done deal.'

BUTLERS WHARF, LONDON

We undertook the journey that forms the core of this book the following spring, but we had already travelled to most of these places several times over the previous eleven years. The Baku–Tbilisi–Ceyhan pipeline, BTC, has been a highly political piece of industrial infrastructure since its inception. Together with a number of individuals and non-governmental organisations in Azerbaijan, Georgia, Turkey, Italy, Germany, the Czech Republic, England and elsewhere, we have scrutinised and questioned its construction, financing and operation since 2001.

In a café just across the River Thames from the City of London, we meet with three friends involved in that coalition: Hannah Griffiths, who worked at Friends of the Earth; Nick Hildyard of The Corner House; and Greg Muttitt, who was at Platform. Seated outside in the cold sunshine, we look back over the long public campaign around the pipeline and discuss the strands of work that continue. We began our collaboration when rigs were already extracting oil from the Caspian Sea, but at that time the BTC pipeline only existed in engineering plans, legal agreements and financial spreadsheets. Now, eight years on, it has been constructed over the Caucasus Mountains and Anatolian plateau, and it pumps nearly a million barrels of oil a day to the port of Ceyhan on the Mediterranean. From there the crude is shipped by tankers to terminals around the world, much of it to a port in northern Italy and from there through a second, older pipeline across the Alps to refineries in Austria, Germany and the Czech Republic.

From our current position we can now recognise that BTC was already under construction throughout the twelve years prior to the public campaign. Any industrial project of this scale takes decades to realise and is built in phases, many of them overlapping. It is constructed in politics and law, in public finance and private finance, in engineering design and social-impact studies. Much of this work runs concurrently with the building of oil platforms at sea, and the laying of the pipelines across the steppe and through the forests. Surrounding all of this is the constant construction of what is known in the industry as the 'social licence to operate', through actions such as the sponsorship of museums, or the financing of community investment programmes.

Our experience, gained over years of researching BTC, has taught us that such a massive project is not carried out by one company, BP, but rather by a network of bodies, which we have come to call the Carbon Web. Around the oil corporation are gathered institutions that enable it to conduct its business. These include public and private banks, government ministries and military bodies, engineering companies and legal firms, universities and environmental consultants, non-governmental organisations and cultural institutions. All of these make up the Carbon Web that drives forward the extraction, transportation and consumption of fossil fuels. In our attempt to explore and unravel this network, we will not only travel through the landscape of the pipelines, but also investigate the topography of the bodies most responsible for this contemporary Oil Road.

The infrastructure of the oil platforms and the pipelines has immense geopolitical importance. Much of the impetus behind its creation came from the desire in Washington, echoed in London and Brussels, to create an 'energy corridor' that would bypass Russian territory, running westwards from the Caspian. The governments in these capitals aim to guarantee the supply of oil and gas to their economies by asserting control over supply routes and ensuring that hydrocarbons enter a global market economy.

In the years before the pipes were laid in the ground, as battle raged over the provision of public finance for the project, BP went to extraordinary lengths to assure all concerned that this pipeline would be different. Unlike oil projects in the previous century, this would be carried out to the highest social and environmental standards. Once completed – to quote their strapline – it would be 'safe, silent and unseen'. This public relations campaign was largely successful, and helped underpin the sense that the pipeline was 'a done deal'; that this project, which was supposed to represent a new future, was now the past.

Part of the purpose of our forthcoming travels will be to explore the current reality of this infrastructure, and how it continues to be contested years after oil began to be pumped through it. The term 'energy corridor' implies a space of calm orderliness, whereas, in reality, much of the geography covered is scarred by repression and turbulence. During the single year of 2008 there was a near disaster on the oil platforms in the Caspian, and the pipeline was blown up in Turkey and bombed by Russian fighter planes in Georgia. By consigning this infrastructure to a completed past, there is a tacit assumption that its future over the next forty years is assured. However, like so many parts of the oil and gas industry, the future of this Oil Road is highly insecure. Besides the threat of decline in both the supply and demand for oil, it faces the immense challenge of climate change.

Time is drawing on. Nick and Greg have to hurry off, though not before sending their wishes to friends in the Caucasus – Mayis in Baku, Manana in Tbilisi, and Ferhat in Ardahan. We stay talking for a while with Hannah about all the work that she and colleagues did, coordinating public pressure on various government departments and organising protests, such as the pipeline they built out of cloth, running all the way down Bishopsgate to the headquarters of BP in Finsbury Circus.

ROCKOLDING, BAVARIA, GERMANY

It is a busy morning at the Aral petrol station on the outskirts of the village of Rockolding. Trucks and cars come and go on the forecourt, filling up just off Highway 16. We hang around among the racks of sweets, magazines and motor oil, watching the woman at the till serve her customers with routine indifference. Two guys in work dungarees lean on a bar at the back of the room drinking alcohol-free beers. A leaflet at the counter explains that Aral's parent company, BP, has an initiative called Target Neutral that will help every driver cut back on their carbon dioxide emissions. We buy chocolate and saunter out. The air is damp and filled with the familiar, delicious smell of petrol. An articulated lorry revs its engines as it pulls onto the road, driven forward by the constant rhythm of explosions in its piston chambers. Fumes rise from its exhaust pipe, the geology of elsewhere disappearing into air.

How does this stuff get to Rockolding? Where does the oil that drives our cars and trucks, planes and factories, come from? How is it transferred from those distant elsewheres to its central position in our lives?

Just across the road from the petrol station is an industrial estate; beyond it, a line of poplar trees along a ditch and a patch of scrubland. Beneath this ground, a couple of metres down, is the Transalpine Pipeline, a steel tube a metre in diameter, through which pulses a constant flow of black crude oil: 100 per cent of the oil used in Bavaria.

To the north, above the roofs of the village, are the distant chimneys of the Vohburg Refinery. The pipeline feeds this plant and two others on the outskirts of the city of Ingolstadt, before heading on to refineries at Karlsruhe in Baden-Württemberg, and at Kralupy and Litvinov in the Czech Republic.

The pipeline has come from the south, running along the valley of the River Ilm from the deep green of the forests of the Hallertau. Mentally tracing the crude in reverse, we know that beyond the limits of our view it has travelled across Bavaria, tunnelled through the Austrian Alps and risen up from north-eastern Italy. The Transalpine pipeline begins at the oil terminal in Muggia, on the outskirts of the city of Trieste. There the white cylinders of the depot overlooking the blue Adriatic are filled with crude pumped from the tankers in the bay. These ships bring oil from countries such as Libya and Algeria, Gabon and Nigeria, but the largest portion of cargoes comes from the Caspian region that was once in the Soviet Union.

Before docking here, these mammoth vessels have steamed north up the Adriatic through Croatian and Albanian waters, after rounding the Peloponnese and passing the archipelagos of the Greek Aegean. The crude carriers have travelled west along the Turkish Turquoise Coast, from gathering their loads at the oil terminal of Yumurtalik, close to the city of Ceyhan. The tanks of this depot, which mirror those in Muggia, have been filled with oil that has already passed over the high plateaus of eastern Turkey and woven its way through the Caucasus Mountains of Georgia.

The Baku–Tbilisi–Ceyhan pipeline starts its journey at the terminal of Sangachal, just south of the city of Baku, on the coast of the Caspian Sea in Azerbaijan. But the crude comes from further east, via an undersea pipeline running from the platforms far offshore, where oil is drawn up from rocks five kilometres below. The BTC pipeline, among the longest in the world, is a machine built to transport Azeri geology westwards across hills and valleys, forests and plains, orchards and fields.

It takes approximately twenty-two days for the oil to be transported the 5,000 kilometres from beneath the Caspian to Bavaria. It is this Oil Road that has led us through the Caucasus, across the Mediterranean and over the Alps, to the forecourt of the petrol station at Rockolding.

This route is only one of many that supply fossil fuels to Europe, but it runs along the line of one of the oldest Oil Roads, a pathway of pipe, rail and ship that has carried both crude and kerosene. Over a century ago, oil was transported from Baku across the Transcaucasian Province of the Tsarist Russian Empire to tankers at Batumi on the Black Sea, from where it was shipped to ports such as Fiume. This terminal, now Rijeka in Croatia, was once part of the Austro-Hungarian Empire and fuelled its twin capitals of Budapest and Vienna. The profits from the drilling, extraction, refining and transport of oil accrued to companies and families such as the Russian Nobels, the French Rothschilds and the Anglo-Dutch company, Shell. In the nineteenth century, the oil wells and 'gushers' of Baku were the subject of international excitement, featuring in news reports and early motion pictures within only five years of the invention of film. An advertising flyer from Baku read:

> On Sunday, August 2, 1898, Alexander Mishon will show some motion pictures that he has taken with a Lumière movie camera. These films of the Caucasus and Central Asia have been prepared for the forthcoming International Paris Exhibition and will be presented only once in Baku at the V. I. Vasilyev-Vyatski Circus Theater. The following films will be shown: Fire resulting from an oil gusher at Bibi-Heybat oil field, the departure ceremony of His Excellency the Amir of Bukhara in the *Grand Duke Alexei* steamship, a folk dance of the Caucasus, and scenes from the comedy, 'So, You Got Caught,' which was performed recently in one of Baku's parks.[1]

These 'gushers', produced by a violent collision of technology and nature, made the fortunes of whoever owned the oil leases that were drilled. The crude that was pumped to the metropolises underpinned the making of the 'Modern Age'. This extraordinary source of energy fuelled Europe's social visions, wars and political transformations. Our journey along the Oil Road passes through the crucibles of Bolshevism and fascism, Futurism and social democracy, through the furnaces of an industrial continent.

Raw materials have been carried across every landmass and sea from source to places of manufacture and use for the past 10,000 years. Trade routes have been fundamental since the Neolithic Revolution, and they underpinned cities such as ancient Athens, classical Rome and renaissance Venice. The Oil Road that we travel echoes a medieval route between Asia and Europe, named by a nineteenth-century German scholar as the 'Silk Road'.

From the fifth century BCE, Greek mariners were travelling out from the Aegean, through the Bosphorus and into the Black Sea. Exchanging wine and pottery for fish and corn, they established trading posts as far east as Bathys, in the kingdom of

---

1   A. Kazimzade, 'Celebrating 100 Years in Film, not 80', *Azerbaijan International* 5: 3 (Autumn 1997), pp. 30–5.

Colchis.[2] That town is now the city of Batumi, on the coast of Georgia.

Colchis was the source of the myth of Prometheus. The giant who stole fire from the gods and shared it with humankind was punished for this gift of technology. Zeus bound Prometheus to a rock for eternity and sent a great eagle to feast daily on his liver. Being immortal, the giant's organs regrew each night, only to be devoured again the following day.

The rock to which he was chained was at the peak of Mount Kazbegi, the highest mountain in Georgia, which now overlooks the westward-bound Oil Road from Azerbaijan, whose name means 'the land of fire'.

---

2   N. Ascherson, *Black Sea*, Hill & Wang, 1996.

Part I THE WELLS

MAP II WESTERN CASPIAN AND AZERBAIJAN

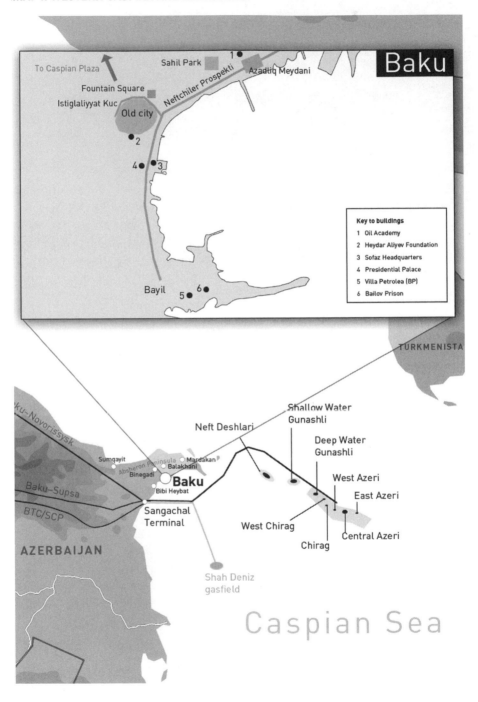

1 IT HAS TO BE THE CASPIAN

0 KM[1] – CENTRAL AZERI, ACG, AZERBAIJAN

Frazer dangles on a rope from the rig high above the steel-blue swell. Below him, three of his six-man team abseil off the platform, checking for corrosion. The strengthening sun makes Frazer's red overalls tight and irritating. His tattooed arms and back run with sweat. To make the work a little less routine, he gently pulls on the rope of his colleague below, and then lets go. The body beneath jerks suddenly; there is a gasp, and a stream of expletives rises up towards Frazer. He laughs.

It is shortly after dawn. Activity on the oil platform slowly increases before the real heat of the day. Over 100 kilometres east of Baku, but only 10 from the territorial waters of Turkmenistan, Frazer is at work over the treasure house of Azerbaijan: the Azeri–Chirag–Gunashli oilfield, known as ACG. A few metres above his head is the 16,000-tonne steel deck of the Central Azeri no. 1 platform, covering an area of several football pitches. Built on top of it are six storeys of utilities and living quarters, piled nearly 30 metres over the sea. The drill tower, like the spire of a cathedral, rises far into the air. Shooting out from the side of the main deck, an arm raised in salute, is the flare stack, burning off the gas, a roaring burst of orange flame, brilliant both in brightest day and darkest night. The fire from beneath the sea.

Shift follows shift, day in, day out; this mine never rests. The staff on the platform come here from all corners of the globe, flying in to Baku's Heydar Aliyev International Airport before being shuttled out to Central Azeri by helicopter. This labour force operates a platform that, although in Azeri waters, abides by the habits and culture of the Western oil companies, following practices largely

---

1   Each section is titled with the location of the places through which we journey. The numbers describe the accumulated distance travelled in kilometres, and in most cases also the kilometre point (KP) of the specific pipeline we are following. These digits exactly describe the passage of this infrastructure in its own numerical language.

evolved in the North Sea.[2] English is the language, and dollars the currency, on this Scots offshore island.

Central Azeri is one of seven platforms in the ACG oilfield. Looking north-west, Frazer can see the lights of the twin structures of Deep Water Gunashli, ten kilometres away. Between them and him rise the solo towers of Chirag 1 and West Azeri, while away to the south-east lies the lone East Azeri. All but one of these seven mountains of steel were built on a more or less identical model. The one that stands distinct is Chirag, which was partially constructed by the Soviet oil industry in the 1980s and only completed by BP and other Western companies in 1997.

The main platforms were manufactured in ready-made sections in Norway. They were transported down the Volga Canal by barge and across the Caspian Sea to Azeri rig yards south of Baku. Here the sections were assembled and then towed out to sea, guided to their precise locations by satellites. Each pair of support legs was tipped and lifted by cranes mounted on barges, until they stood upright in 120 metres of water. Seven hundred thousand tonnes of components – gas turbines, valves, cables, pumps and linepipe – were transported here by ship, train, truck and plane. With 3,000 orders from around the world, it was like building a space station in orbit.[3] Now complete, these monuments – weathered by the sun and sea – have to be checked by Fraser and 'his boys' for rust.

At the heart of Central Azeri, as with the other platforms, is the drilling unit, from which the drill itself plunges to the floor of the Caspian and then down another five kilometres to the oil-bearing rocks of the Lower Pliocene sandstone layer. Through a complex web of valves on the seabed, the seven platforms operate sixty oil wells in the ACG field, drawing up Azeri Light crude formed between 3.4 and 5.3 million years ago.[4]

The hydrocarbons are made from plankton and plants that thrived long before *Homo sapiens* evolved. These organisms stored the energy of sunlight from the Tertiary period; now their fossilised and compressed remains are penetrated by the drills and, under immense geological pressure, rush up through the risers to the platforms. The oil industry is built on the extraction of these long-dead ecosystems, and the Oil Road is constructed to distribute ancient liquid rocks so that our one species may live beyond the limits of the ecosystems of our times.

This extraction and distribution of geology is a high-risk process. Oil always

2   'North Sea Style Development Eyed for Pair of Oil Fields off Azerbaijan', *Oil & Gas Journal* 92: 9 (1994).

3   H. Campbell, 'Shipshape in the Caspian', *BP Magazine* 1 (2009), pp. 11–17; and H. Campbell, 'Scale of the Century', *Horizon Magazine* 1 (2009), pp. 38–9.

4   K. Choi, M. Jackson, G. Hampson, A. Jones and A. Reynolds, *Predicting the Impact of Sedimentological Heterogeneity on Gas-Oil and Water-Oil Displacements: Fluvio-Deltaic Pereriv Suite Reservoir, Azeri–Chirag–Gunashli Oilfield, South Caspian Basin*, Department of Earth Science and Engineering, Imperial College, London, 2011.

comes from the deep mixed with natural gas – known as associated gas – which can be as unpredictable as the sea that thunders against the platform's legs. Gas can accumulate in the risers in great bursts that strain the steel structure. And it can leak, so that one chance ignition turns a platform into an inferno. Early in the morning of 17 September 2008, the alarms on Central Azeri blared and the air was filled with the thunder of helicopters.[5] Sensors had detected a gas leak below the installation, and when workers looked down at the sea they noticed bubbles on the surface. It was a potential disaster. All the 210 personnel were evacuated, and the platform was shut down. Extraction in the ACG field fell from 850,000 barrels of oil per day to 350,000, incurring a daily loss of $50 million in income. How would it have been if the platform had blown, like BP's Deepwater Horizon rig in the Gulf of Mexico a year and a half later? The spill from that disaster would have covered much of the Caspian.

As morning work starts on the oil platforms we are standing at the dockside in Baku, squinting at the eastern sea. The view is clear, but Central Azeri is far beyond the horizon.

We study a map obtained from a former diver on ACG, despite the restrictions on information and data about the oil installations. It shows a demarcated zone, roughly rectangular, approximately forty-two kilometres long by eight kilometres wide. This is the PSA Area, the sea space defined by the 1994 Production Sharing Agreement, promoted as the 'Contract of the Century', signed by the Azeri government and the private-sector Azerbaijan International Operating Company led by BP. This is the area of the wells, just over 330 square kilometres of designated industrial zone far out in the wildness of the Caspian. Azeri territory under the control of a foreign oil consortium.

We have come to Baku by train and bus to start upon the Oil Road from the Caspian to Germany. Many places along the way are familiar from past visits over the last twelve years, but now we want to travel the route in a continuous journey. Our few days in this city will be filled with a round of interviews that will help illustrate how the oil wells at the beginning of this road were sunk in this country.

It has long been our desire to start with an exploration of the offshore platforms. We have considered it from every angle. But there is no ferry that travels to the area, and to hire a vessel for the130 kilometres out to sea and back would be immensely tricky. Trying to charter a boat would arouse suspicions with the authorities, and we have little doubt that we would be arrested if we approached the platforms. Only those few Azeris employed by the oil companies visit this zone, which is widely understood to be the goldmine of the nation. More than 65 per cent of the country's oil production comes from here.[6]

---

5   T. Bergin, *Spills and Spin: The Inside Story of BP*, Random House, 2011, p. 131.
6   H. Campbell, 'Shipshape in the Caspian', *BP Magazine* 1 (2009), p. 14.

The Azeri–Chirag–Gunashli oilfield is not shown on maps of Azerbaijan. There is no trace of the installations and flares as we search on Google Earth. We have less than thirty photographs of it on our laptop, and all of these are promotional images published by BP. Each one is either a distant photo of a gleaming white platform rising from a calm blue sea, or a closer shot of some unidentified steel structure with men working in orange or red jumpsuits, BP logo on their breasts, wearing white hard hats with an AIOC logo on the crown.[7] These are photos from some other place, of clean orderliness, of uniformed men in a machine world. Like images of a space station rather than an oil well.

Like many places on our journey, the wells lie in a forbidden zone to which only our imaginations can travel. We met Frazer on the train from Baku to Tbilisi a while back, heard his stories of the platforms, and, through careful research, have tried to build the truest picture that we can. We know we will have to do the same for other places on this route, places that impact heavily on the lives of so many people, but are hidden from the world.

The countries through which we are travelling are portrayed in books and music, film and websites – they exist in the world's imagination. Yet the route we are following is obscure. It is described only in technical manuals and industry journals, data logs and government memos.

The journey along this Oil Road echoes those along the Silk Road. The passage through Central Asia was passed to the Western European mind by the likes of the Venetian merchant, Marco Polo. The fantastical things that he reported fed centuries of debate about the authenticity of his travels. Following in Polo's footsteps, there are places that we long to visit and yet are beyond the realm of the possible, places of which we have to construct images from the tales of others, such as Frazer.

So, keen sailors that we are, frustrated at the Baku dockside, we set about describing a journey by boat from the Central Azeri platform to the point where we stand. Tracing our fingers across the map from the diver and a sea chart, we work out the narrative of our passage.

If we were to sail from beneath the platform, a rising north-easterly wind could drive us west-north-west, and the waves would pick up as we pushed against the prevailing current. After seven kilometres we would cross an invisible line and begin to leave the PSA area. To our starboard we would see the outline of Deepwater Gunashli, the last of the platforms to come onstream, in April 2008.

*   *   *

---

7   AIOC is the Azerbaijan International Operating Company, of which BP is the dominant shareholder.

Before these platforms could be built, the political, legal and financial conditions for their creation had to be established. From initial meetings in May 1989, it took nineteen years to reach the point when oil was extracted from ACG at the rate that was planned. In the five years after the first meetings, competition for contracts for the oilfield was dominated by a number of businesses, mainly from Britain (BP and Ramco) and the US (Amoco, Unocal and Pennzoil). Eventually the signing of the 1994 'Contract of the Century' brought these actors into the alliance of the Azerbaijan International Operating Company, a consortium of eleven corporations including BP, Amoco, Lukoil of Russia, and the State Oil Company of the Azerbaijan Republic (SOCAR).

It is this consortium that controls the forbidden zone and the platforms. The membership of the AIOC has fluctuated over time as fortunes have changed. When the contract was signed, BP held a 17.1 per cent stake. Within a few years, after merging with Amoco, the combined company owned a controlling 34.1 per cent. Since the project's outset, BP has been the main player, known as the Operator. BP Exploration Caspian Sea Ltd oversees the corporation's endeavours in Baku. The president of BP Azerbaijan, Bill Schrader, is also the president of AIOC.

From the dockside we gaze at the city around the curve of the bay. To the south, we can see buildings clustered on the headland of Bayil. Hidden among them is Villa Petrolea, the headquarters of BP in Azerbaijan, where Schrader's office is located. The steel structures offshore in the Caspian did not rise from the seabed by some force of nature but through the actions of people – mostly men – and through a myriad of decisions taken over a twenty-year period. The construction of the platforms was driven by geopolitical power and capital, and these forces engulf individuals such as Frazer or Schrader; although that is not to say that those individuals could not have acted differently, or made different decisions that would have altered the course of events. Our intention as we journey along the Oil Road is to meet those who have helped to create it. But, as with the platforms in the forbidden zone, it is difficult to gain access to some of these actors, so we will build a picture of their role in events through newspaper reports, company publications, memoirs, histories and official documents obtained through Freedom of Information requests.

Central among those who helped create the road was John Browne, chief executive of BP. His autobiography describes his first visit to the Azeri capital in July 1990:

> I drew back the thin curtains in a grim Baku hotel room to watch the sun rise over the grey Caspian Sea. Hundreds of feet below that still water, in a stretch called the Absheron Sill, lay the promise of billions of barrels of premium oil. Azerbaijan had been lost behind the Iron Curtain for many years. Many assumed Caspian resources

had dried up because the Soviets had abandoned drilling almost completely. I had come to find out how BP could secure a deal to extract what promised to be a sizable prize. I had little idea what twists and turns the venture would take. And I would become embroiled in the formation of a strategic East–West energy corridor: even Washington would become involved. The venture would even loosely inspire a James Bond film.[8]

The previous year, in March 1989, Browne, then chief executive of US BP subsidiary SOHIO, was promoted. He was moved to BP's head office in the City of London, becoming chief executive of Exploration and Production – the most profitable wing of the company. With him came trusted lieutenants, including Tony Hayward, who would later lead BP into the Deepwater Horizon spill disaster.

By the time of this appointment, Browne was already renowned as an 'eighteen hours a day man', and had built up a strong reputation as a financial mind in a company dominated by engineers. As commercial manager at BP North Sea in Aberdeen, he had marked himself out as exceptionally talented by overseeing a tax coup that gained the company a windfall of £200 million at the expense of the British government. Between 1984 and 1986 he was BP group treasurer, during which time he established BP Finance, known as 'the bank within the company'. Later the former CEO, David Simon, said 'Browne . . . is very strong on the numbers side, financially extremely astute, but the same also goes for the technological side. He understands geopolitics and has got a nose for a deal.'[9]

On arriving in his new post at Head Office, Browne was at the helm of an exploration division facing severe challenges. In the aftershocks of the 1973 oil crisis, OPEC oil regions previously vital to the West had finally been nationalised, following decades of Western control of resource extraction. Increasingly, the private oil companies were relying on a dwindling number of 'safe' fields in home countries.

The situation was particularly acute for BP, which had become known as 'a two-pipeline company', reliant on its North Sea and Alaskan fields. So Browne engaged geologist Tom Hamilton, an old colleague from the US, to make a study of the entire 130-year history of global oilfield discoveries and to suggest new opportunities. Hamilton's team concluded that BP was following a doomed strategy, with its daily extraction rate of 1.5 million barrels in danger of halving in coming years. Browne proposed that the corporation needed a being halved plan to break into 'frontier zones' – those that were politically or technologically difficult to reach.

---

8 J. Browne, *Beyond Business*, Wiedenfeld & Nicholson, 2010, p. 151.
9 'The Andrew Davidson Interview – John Browne', *Management Today*, December 1999, p. 60.

While Hamilton's team was at work, Browne met Margaret Thatcher, then British prime minister. Thatcher had been engaged in a long round of dialogues with the Soviet Union and had concluded that 'we can do business together' with Mikhail Gorbachev. She urged Browne to 'start some investment rolling' in the Soviet Union. He in turn instructed Hamilton's subordinate, Rondo Fehlberg, 'to get to Moscow and make something happen'.[10]

Soon after, BP and Chevron became the first Western oil majors to expand into the Soviet Union since the late 1920s, although their initial target was not Azerbaijan. Fehlberg, a Mormon all-in wrestler, began work on the Soviet Oil Ministry in Moscow, but increasingly focused on key politicians in the Soviet Socialist Republic of Kazakhstan, east of the Caspian.

Eventually BP was outplayed in Kazakhstan by a team from Chevron, but the Oil Ministry in Moscow softened the blow, suggesting that Fehlberg turn his attention to Baku. Several important lessons had been learned by BP from the Kazakh experience: that the Soviet Union was rapidly disintegrating, and the tension between the increasingly independent states and Russia could be exploited; that the distinctions between the Soviet nationalised industrial structure and the Western private model would allow for a fluidity in which great gains could be made; that the Soviet industry, like the USSR itself, was starved of capital; and that Westerners could impress officials with the technological capabilities of the oil majors. BP had taken a team from the Soviet Oil Ministry to visit rigs in the North Sea, and another group from Kazakhstan to see its Alaskan fields. Both events showed BP that these ministers and officials were open to inducements, and some were planning for what life might be like after the Soviet Union.[11]

When, in July 1990, Browne made his first visit to Baku and peered out of his hotel window, Azerbaijan and Armenia were at war over the region of Nagorno-Karabakh, the city was under curfew, and Soviet armoured personnel carriers patrolled the streets. Accompanied by Fehlberg, he visited the Azerneft Oil Ministry, on the Baku seafront, to meet Qurban Abbasov, the oil minister of what was still the Soviet Socialist Republic of Azerbaijan.

Abbasov – nicknamed 'Neftci Qurban' or 'Oily Qurban' – was a legend in Baku. He had begun working in the industry at the age of eighteen, forty-six years previously, and was involved in the pioneering offshore Neft Dashlari project, where he earned a Stalin Prize First Class and a Hero of Socialist Labour award Gold Star. By the time he met Fehlberg he had been a director general within the Azeri state oil companies for ten years.

In 1980 Soviet engineers had discovered four extensive offshore fields and,

---

10   S. Levine, *The Oil and the Glory: The Pursuit of Empire and Fortune on the Caspian Sea*, Random House, 2007.

11   Browne, *Beyond Business*.

following geological surveys, named them '28th April', 'Chirag', '26 Commissars' and 'October Revolution'. All of these fields were interlinked and effectively formed one large reservoir, the Absheron Sill. Thus the Soviets had already completed the geological mapping of the oilfields long before the West arrived. By the late 1980s Azerbaijan's oil industry had stagnated due to limited investment, and Abbasov was eager to rebuild it. He was prepared to negotiate, but with the Soviet Union collapsing, his bargaining position was weak.

BP was most interested in the '26 Commissars' field, named after the Baku Soviet leaders executed in 1918 with the collusion of a British expeditionary force. As discussions progressed, Fehlberg felt confident enough to raise the idea that BP investors might be unhappy about the name. Abbasov obliged, and the field was renamed 'Azeri'. It was a significant gesture towards the company, but also a move that fed the mood of late-Soviet nationalism, a trend that BP seemed keen to stimulate.

By October 1990, Fehlberg had made such progress that Hamilton came to join him in Baku. A month later, it appeared that they had won BP an exclusive deal for the Azeri field, with no competitive bidding process. Details would be negotiated later, but BP's success would be announced at the First Baku Oil Exhibition, opening in November. In August the Armenian parliament had passed a resolution declaring itself a sovereign republic within the USSR; in October Kazakhstan passed a similar resolution, and it was clear that Azerbaijan would follow suit. With the Oil Exhibition and the deal on the offshore field, the Azeri state was asserting its growing independence by opening its arms to the Western oil companies.

But, contrary to what both Fehlberg and Browne expected, what was announced at the exhibition was not a deal but a competition. Fehlberg loudly protested, but the American corporation Amoco had the ear of Azeri President Mutalibov. The slow disintegration of the Soviet Union made for a political fluidity in Baku in which the Western oil companies alternated between fragile alliances and bitter competition. Browne stepped up the pressure, dispatching BP executive Eddie Whitehead to the Caspian and further strengthening the team by signing up Steve Remp's tiny Ramco Energy. Remp had been the first Western oil man in Baku since the 1920s. He had arrived in the city to explore for deals in May 1989, and consequently had very good connections.

After six months of bids and negotiations, in June 1991 the announcement came that Amoco had now won exclusive rights to negotiate terms on the Azeri field for a full year. The BP staff who had been fighting for the contract were shattered, and gathered in a meeting at Heathrow Airport to consider the news. Through Whitehead, Browne insisted: 'If we don't have a deal in three months, we're out of [the Soviet Union].' Possibilities of getting something easier in West Siberia were discussed, but that was not the real prize. 'That's not good enough', declared Whitehead. 'It has to be the Caspian.'[12]

Two months later, the August 1991 failed coup attempt against President Gorbachev left Boris Yeltsin firmly in power in Moscow, and the USSR drew to a close. Azerbaijan declared independence from the Soviet Union two months after the coup failed. Qurban Abbasov was replaced as oil minister. But Browne was still determined to try to forge ahead in Azerbaijan, and his hand was strengthened in September when he was appointed managing director of BP Group, gaining a place on the board.

On the dockside, only a few hundred metres from the old Intourist Hotel that Browne must have stayed in on his first visit to Baku, we study the sea maps and consider the history that led to the construction of those invisible towns in the Caspian where Frazer and his colleagues work.

50 KM – NEFT DASHLARI, AZERBAIJAN

The heat of the day is coming on, so we settle down at one of the many tables under the trees in Bulvar Park, which runs along the dockside. A waiter appears with a chrome tray loaded with small glasses and sells us tea sweetened with sugar lumps.

Unfolding the maps, we begin our narrative again, progressing along the first 187 kilometres of the Oil Road. For running along the seabed are the four pipelines that come from the ACG platforms to the terminal at Sangachal, on the coast south of Baku. They are part of a skein of pipes from the wellheads, 829 kilometres in all, that are like train tracks laid from the coal mines to the metropolis. The hidden veins of the oil economy.

Were we sailing, the horizon before us would be punctuated by Soviet rigs built in the 1970s and 1980s: Shallow Water Gunashli, producing 120,000 barrels of oil a day for SOCAR. And the sea would be becoming shallower – 150 metres deep, 100 metres, 50 metres. Soon the famed Neft Dashlari would come into view.

Operational since 1951 and a source of engineering pride in the Soviet Union, Neft Dashlari still manages 400 working wells. Standing on steel stilts above the water are high-rise tenements that accommodate 5,000 shift workers. This immense industrial installation has 200 kilometres of roads, a cinema, a bakery and a park named after President Heydar Aliyev.

It had long been understood that there were oil seepages on the seabed of the Caspian. In 1949, as part of the USSR's 4th Five Year Plan, workers began to construct the world's largest offshore oil installation. Seven ships were towed out and sunk to create a reef. Platforms were built upon them to provide the structures for the drilling rigs. A generation of Soviet engineers, such as Qurban Abbasov, was trained at Neft Dashlari. Khoshbakht Yussifzadeh, vice-president of

---

12   Levine, *The Oil and the Glory*, p. 159.

SOCAR from the mid 1990s, began his career here: 'For us, it was a brave new era. We were pioneers, explorers. After work we went to the cinema or bars. There were also many women who worked in the laboratories or the canteen. Then I was allowed to go to the university, and . . . I earned 2,900 roubles, with benefits even 5,000 roubles. At the time, that was fantastic!'[13]

When Neft Dashlari was inaugurated, on the thirty-second anniversary of the October Revolution, the Soviet Union, Great Britain and America were no longer the Allies they had been in World War II, and General Secretary Joseph Stalin was no longer 'Uncle Joe'. Winston Churchill had declared that an Iron Curtain had fallen between Gdansk and Trieste, and the West had placed an embargo on technical equipment exports to the USSR. The Soviets innovated, despite this isolation. They not only built offshore platforms, but created a 'turbo-drill' which dramatically increased the speed of sinking oil wells. This enabled 'horizontal drilling' to take place – a technique that the West would only catch up with twenty years later.

Throughout the 1950s and 1960s oil extraction around Baku steadily climbed, reaching a peak in 1969. At the same time Azerbaijan underwent a fundamental energy shift. Gas became the main fuel for all domestic heating. Of all the countries in Europe, Azerbaijan's economy became the most intense user of gas.[14] The entire Soviet Union was experiencing an economic boom, and Nikita Khrushchev, who succeeded Stalin as general secretary, promised that the planned economy would deliver an age of plenty in which Communism would beat Capitalism at its own consumerist game.

Khrushchev visited Neft Dashlari in 1960, and a banquet was held on Platform 408. According to legend, the general secretary became drunk and ordered the construction of a nine-storey apartment block on the platform to reflect the stature of the project. It was duly built, and housed 2,500 workers. In Baku itself he declared of the new Soviet apartments that were being constructed: 'Don't worry, these are only temporary homes! In twenty-five years, when the Soviet Union is the richest country in the world, these buildings will be torn down and replaced with real palaces for working people.'[15]

But as we look up from the café table at the skyline of Baku, we can see *Khrushchevki*, as the apartment blocks were nicknamed, still lining the horizon.

110 KM – ABSHERON PENINSULA, AZERBAIJAN

After sixty kilometres of sailing from Central Azeri, we would round the point of Suiti Barnu. The swell of the open sea would begin to ease as we entered the

---

13   L. Kleveman, *The New Great Game: Blood and Oil in Central Asia*, Atlantic Books, 2004, pp. 19–21.

14   S. Pirani, ed., *Russian and CIS Gas Markets and Their Impact on Europe*, OUP, 2009, p. 205.

15   F. Alakbarov, 'Baku's Architecture', *Azerbaijan International* 9: 4 (2001).

shelter of the Absheron Peninsula – a long low purple landmass to starboard. On a beam reach with a constant breeze, we would relax a little as we headed for Baki Buxtasi – Baku Bay, the finest natural harbour on the western side of the Caspian, sheltered from the prevailing wind by the peninsula.

Shaped like an eagle's beak protruding into the sea, Absheron continues the line of the Greater Caucasus Mountains out towards the east. Despite the barrier that it provides, Baku is still renowned for its winds. The city's name may be derived from the ancient Farsi *bad kube*, 'blown by winds', or *bad kiu*, 'town of winds'. There are two blasts that batter the town – the Khazri from the north, and the Gilavar from the south. Although many curse the dusty heat or the bitter cold that they bring into the city, these forces have been the motive energy for millennia of seafaring on the Caspian. We think of the ships that headed to and from Baku, struggling with storms or becalmed in the exhausting heat.

Baku is jammed between the sea and the desert, drawing sustenance from both. Like Venice, it was built as a point of transition between water and land – between boats and camel trains, between the ships of the sea and the ships of the desert. The city has long been dependent upon what comes in from the water and what passes out through the land.

Passage, trade and war by water on the Caspian may have begun 10,000 years ago. The Mesolithic petroglyphs carved on the rocks of the Gobustan National Park, sixty kilometres south of Baku, include an image of a reedboat. In the mid-seventh century CE, the troops of the Umayyad Caliphate swept through the Caucasus and Arab ships sailed to Baku. The Scandinavian Rus pillaged along the western coast of the Caspian, venturing up the River Kura in 943 CE, into the midst of what is now Azeri territory.

We look out from the park at the shimmering waters of Baku Buxtasi and watch an oil service vessel bound for the distant platforms. In the lethargic haze we imagine it to be a vessel of the Tsarist Caspian flotilla, seizing this Persian city for the Russian Empire. Or Ludvig Nobel's *Zoroaster*, the world's first oil tanker. Or the steamship *Nicholas I*, boarded by Bolshevik activists in Baku harbour. Or the steamer *Kursk*, commandeered by the British Expeditionary Force in 1918. Or one of the seven ships sunk to create Neft Dashlari.

For centuries the Absheron Peninsula was a place of pilgrimage, a shrine of fire. Burning gas had leaked from the ground since the last Ice Age. This was the most sacred site of Zoroastrianism which, prior to Islam, was the dominant faith in the region. The oil-bearing rocks drew people to this place, not to extract petroleum and carry it off to some other site of burning, but to worship it here in the sheets of flame among the rocks. As other faiths arrived – Sunni and Shia Islam, Russian Orthodoxy, Marxism and Capitalism – the holy fire of this peninsula was transformed into a material to be extracted and exported.

150 KM – BIBI HEYBAT, AZERBAIJAN

It is now punishingly hot as we drink more tea and think of those Zoroastrian pilgrims, headed for Baku by ship and camel train. Suddenly, out of nowhere, comes the thundering sound of a helicopter heading towards the horizon and the platforms of ACG.

The final stretch of our journey by boat into Baki Buktasi would bring us past the shallow-water oil structures of Dash Zina, built in the early 1950s – a maze of pipelines, pump stations and drilling towers on wooden stilts, stretching far out into the sea. As we entered the final tack towards this Baku dockside, to our west we would see the headland of Bibi Heybat.

In 1848 the world's first mechanically drilled oil well was sunk on this rocky shore, in what was then the Transcaucasian province of the Russian Empire. It was eleven years before Colonel Drake drilled for oil in Pennsylvania, although Drake is now claimed to have begun the Oil Age. Despite the head start, Azerbaijan is eclipsed in industrial history by the US, in part because allocation of capital for exploration was slow. Development accelerated after December 1872, when Tsar Alexander II ordered oil-bearing land to be auctioned off to entrepreneurs and investors. The declaration marked the arrival of finance capital.

Five technologies transformed Baku: drilling, which enabled wells to be sunk far deeper than anything dug by hand; refining, which created a fuel for lighting called kerosene; and, most importantly, the oil tanker, the railway and the pipeline, which enabled the distribution of vast quantities of crude and refined products. To generate profit, markets needed to be created for the sale of kerosene, of oil as a source of light. Across the world, in cities, towns and villages, from London to Shanghai, kerosene was promoted as the wonder fuel of the hurricane lamp. Replacing whale blubber, distilled alcohol and tallow, a global product had been created.

After the auctioning of the Tsar's land there was frenzied speculation. Hundreds of oil derricks were constructed on the hills around Baku. Steam-driven drilling wells quickly proliferated. The toxic fumes from a multitude of small refineries were so polluting that the Baku authorities decreed that all the plants should be gathered in a new suburb east of the city that became known as Black Town.

To a city of merchants, craftsmen and labourers came a new industrial class of oil workers – peasants who had only recently been released from serfdom on the land.[16] To the new streets of the Outer Town, built around the Old City, came Russians, Jews, Georgians, Armenians and 'Tartars' – as Muslim Azeri-speakers were then labelled.[17] The population quadrupled in a decade.

---

16 Although the reform that freed serfs was passed in Russia in 1861, it was only enacted in Azerbaijan and Armenia in 1870–73.

17 Many Azeri speakers came from either side of the Russian–Persian border.

In the late nineteenth century Baku became one of the great multicultural melting pots of the world economy. A visitor from Britain was struck by the vibrancy of the place, and wrote at the time: 'One might almost fancy oneself in an American city out west. There is the same air of newness about everyone, the same sanguine atmosphere. Everyone is hopeful.' [18]

From the city arose another new class – the plutocracy of the Oil Barons, who quickly acquired staggering wealth, expressed in mansions built in the Outer Town in a myriad of styles: Arabic, Byzantine, Venetian and Gothic. Many of the Oil Barons were incomers like Ludvig Nobel, but among them were locals, the most famous of whom was Haji Zeynalabin Taghiyev. Born in Baku in 1823, the son of an illiterate shoemaker, Taghiyev initially worked as a stonemason, and slowly moved into trading. In the December 1872 auction he managed to obtain leases on land at the village of Bibi Heybat, considered to be of little oil value.

Fourteen years of futile prospecting followed, during which Taghiyev's Armenian co-investor sold out, but on 27 September 1886 a gusher burst seventy metres into the air. A Baku newspaper described the resulting rain and rivers of crude: 'A colossal pillar of smoke, from the crest of which clouds of oil sand detached themselves and floated away a great distance without touching the ground . . . Most of this was lost for want of storage accommodation. The oil simply poured into the Caspian Sea, and was lost forever to mankind.' [19]

Taghiyev became one of Baku's wealthiest citizens, investing profits in a fleet of tankers and barges to take oil north across the Caspian and up the River Volga to Moscow. He built himself a fifty-room mansion in the Outer Town and developed a resort for the rich away from the city at the village of Mardakan, on the north-eastern shore of the Absheron Peninsula.

With his capital he financed the opening of a school of agriculture and an opera house modelled on the Casino et les Jardins in Monte Carlo. [20] Despite his background of limited education, he persuaded Tsar Nicholas II to allow the foundation of a secular girls' school, one of the first in the Muslim World. In all these acts Taghiyev was creating a culture of a new Russian–Tartar *haute bour-geoisie*, developing a vision of a new city. Baku was beginning to resemble the metropolises to which its resource was now marketed – the Belle Epoque cities of European Russia and Western Europe.

T. Swietochowski, *Russian Azerbaijan, 1905–1920: The Shaping of National Identity in a Muslim Community*, CUP, 1985.

18   Quoted in T. Reiss, *The Orientalist: Solving the Mystery of a Strange and a Dangerous Life*, Random House, 2006, p. 12.

19   J. D. Henry, *Baku: An Eventful History*, Constable, 1905, pp. 104–5.

20   T. de Waal, *Black Garden: Armenia and Azerbaijan through Peace and War*, NYU Press, 2004, p. 99.

160 KM – BAKU, AZERBAIJAN

We hear music coming from the trees beyond the café. So we fold the maps and wander over to discover a band of four players seated under a clump of Corsican Pines. One man plays a *saz*, a long-necked lute, while another holds an electric Yamaha keyboard that drones beneath the melody. We sit mesmerised for an hour. The band pays little regard to any audience – and indeed there is no real audience, just people drinking tea and playing *nard*, a Persian game similar to backgammon. At the water's edge, fishermen watch their rods and lines. Nothing stirs and the sea seems heavy, viscous, the surface covered in a petroleum sheen. The heat is passing on our first day of acclimatising ourselves to the Caspian shore, and we begin to prepare to walk through the town.

As we turn our backs to the water, we can survey the city laid out on gently rising ground. Baku itself, with a population of nearly 2 million, feels quiet. A rocky bluff overshadows the İçəri Şəhər, the Old City, and the nineteenth-century grid of streets that spreads out from it, the Outer Town. As within a tree, the rings of the city show the growth of Baku: the Persian core, the Tsarist town, the early Soviet and the late Soviet city, punctuated everywhere by the recent towers of the new capitalist metropolis. The crags in the distance speak of the desert that lies beyond, stretching out south, north and west.

2 YOU CAN SEE WHERE THE PRESIDENT GETS HIS IRON GLOVES

NEFTÇILƏR PROSPEKTI, BAKU, AZERBAIJAN

'Emporio Armani.' 'Dior.' 'Bulgari.' 'D&G.' 'Versace.' We count off the fashion stores along Neftchilər Prospekti – 'Oil Workers Avenue'. Facing out to sea, the grand nineteenth-century mansions have all had their façades scrubbed. Ground floors glisten with plate-glass windows. We've walked this street many times in the past decade, and the change is astounding. From a dusty post-Soviet boulevard, it has become the very image of a twenty-first-century oil-rush city.

Construction is underway everywhere: new shopping malls alongside hotels and luxury flats. Billboards promising a transformation into Dubai surround cranes and open craters. A new Hilton is coming, and soon after a Four Seasons. Mercedes and Porsche SUVs, black with tinted windows, cruise the avenue.

Through an underpass of polished stone that leads to pavements embedded with bright ribbons of lights, we make our way into the body of Baku. Down another street of pristine shop fronts we come to a square where, under the shade of trees, refurbished fountains play in the floodlights. Even now, beyond midnight, well-dressed families and young couples relax in the bars and cafés of Fəvvarələr Meydan, 'Fountain Square'. The tables on the pavements are full, and children hurtle across the piazza on tiny electric-powered quad bikes.

At the double Şamaxi Gate in the city wall, we are about enter the İçəri Şəhər, the Old Town. The sandstone archway brings to mind a passage from *Ali and Nino*, the novel by Kurban Said set in Baku before World War I:

I went up to the flat roof of the house. From there I could see my world, the massive wall of the town's fortress and the ruins of the palace, Arab inscriptions at the gate. Through the labyrinth of streets camels were walking, their ankles so delicate that I want to caress them. In front of me rose the squat Maiden's Tower, surrounded by legends and tourist guides. And behind the tower the sea began, utterly faceless, leaden, unfathomable, the Caspian Sea, and beyond the desert

– jagged rocks and scrub: still, mute, unconquerable, the most beautiful landscape in the world.[1]

The book was published in Vienna in the 1930s, and it is filled with nostalgia for
a Persian Baku which was by then rapidly being rebuilt as a Soviet city.[2]

We enter the citadel, and even here, amid the narrow passages, construction is
underway. Despite this quarter's UNESCO status, hotels are rising on fourteenth-
century foundations. The winding streets take us back to the seafront and
Neftchilər Prospekti. Past the yacht club and the empty marina, we reach a large
hole in the ground surrounded by fencing, jutting out into the sea. Posters on
billboards portray the forthcoming $250 million Full Moon Hotel like a futuristic
skyscraper on the Persian Gulf. Just inland stand the Sports Palace and the Dalga
Plaza Business Centre. The latter's twelve floors of glass rise above the busy street,
with ornamental white marble pillars reaching halfway up the building. The
owners of the tower proudly announce on their promotions that 'during dark
time of days the building looks especially majestic', and that this office block
'makes the President proud'.

The tower is the headquarters of SOFAZ, the State Oil Fund of Azerbaijan. This
national revenue fund receives much of Azerbaijan's hydrocarbon income, and
was established to save the wealth for future generations while 'sterilising' investment so that the local economy would not overheat. In theory, revenues from
Azeri oil sold today are invested in assets abroad, and the income from these
investments will be spent later – gradually – on programmes that diversify the
economy and increase development. SOFAZ has made substantial purchases of
property and equities in countries such as Germany.[3] But things are not what
they seem. In 2010, income to SOFAZ was $7.2 billion. However, predicted
expenditure was $6.6 billion, leaving less than 10 per cent of the income to be
salted away for future generations. Of that planned expenditure, 80 per cent is
allocated for government spending, covering items such as the military, the police
and the construction boom.[4]

---

1   K. Said, transl. Jenia Graman, *Ali and Nino*, Robin Clark, 1990 [1937].
2   Kurban Said was a pseudonym, and the identity of the author continues to be
hotly debated. Tom Reiss's biography, *The Orientalist* (Random House, 2006), makes
a case that Kurban Said was Lev Nussimbaum, who fled from Baku with his father
during the Bolshevik Revolution. However, some have questioned Reiss's scholarship,
and more recently a long research project concluded that the primary author was in
fact Yusif Vəzir Çəmənzəminli. Whatever the truth, the mystery around the novel
adds to its romance.
3   *Annual Report 2008*, State Oil Fund of the Republic of Azerbaijan, 2008.
4   K. Aslanli, 'Oil and Gas Revenues Management in Azerbaijan', *Caucasus
Analytical Digest* 16 (2010).

Although analysts were initially optimistic that it would be well managed, they soon started to recognise that the establishment of the Oil Fund might have been 'designed only for external political consumption – particularly for claiming fiscal responsibility and spending transparency'.[5]

While SOFAZ is the administrative centre for the oil revenues, the fundamental decisions about what income to keep for the future and what to spend on the present are not made in this building. We cross the road and peer through the railings of a park in which lie the Gulustan Palace and the Presidential Palace, the latter presenting a great white stone façade punctuated by over 300 windows. This is where the real power over the oil wealth is located – in the hands of the Aliyev dynasty.

Heydar Aliyev was born in Naxçivan, a mountainous, semi-autonomous region in south-west Azerbaijan, beyond the disputed Nagorno-Karabakh. In 1939, at the age of sixteen, he arrived in Baku to study at the Oil Academy.[6] This was the main academic institute in one of the Soviet Union's most modern cities, where workers on the drilling rigs were hailed as heroes of socialist labour. When the Nazis invaded the USSR two years later, Aliyev avoided being sent to the front by becoming a lieutenant in the NKVD, the Soviet internal security apparatus and the force behind Stalin's Great Terror. Towards the end of the war, and in the following years, the Terror included the mass deportations of Pontic Greeks, Chechens and Meshkheti Turks from the Caucasus.[7] Only with Stalin's death, in March 1953, did the Terror grind to a halt.

Despite Khrushchev's 'de-Stalinisation' process, Aliyev's rise in the now-renamed KGB was not slowed.[8] By 1967 he was head of the Azeri KGB, and two years later the USSR's general secretary, Leonid Brezhnev, appointed him head of the Communist Party of Azerbaijan, the most senior Soviet official in the state. Having reached the pinnacle of power in his home country, he quickly purged the ranks of government and academia, sacking six of his seven ministers. Claiming these as anti-corruption measures, Aliyev replaced those fired with allies from Naxçivan and the KGB. The boy from the mountains was to remain the most powerful man in Azerbaijan for the better part of the next thirty-four years.

Persistent allegations of corruption emerged, but supporters would allow no discussion. When the Azeri prosecutor Gamabai Mamedov raised concerns in

---

5   S. Asfaha, *National Revenue Funds*, IISD, 2007.

6   In the 1930s it was titled the Azerbaijan Industrial Institute, but was later renamed.

7   Ascherson, *Black Sea*, p. 188.

8   *Heydar Aliyev and the National Security Agencies*, Ministry of National Security (Azerbaijan), 2009.

parliament, he was shouted down: 'Who are you speaking against? If you believe in God, you might say that before us stands God himself in the person of [Aliyev].'[9] Evidence was suppressed, the prosecutor fled to Leningrad, and in 1982 Aliyev was promoted to join the Politburo of the Soviet Union.

Aliyev aspired to be general secretary of the USSR, but he was denounced in the Moscow press as exemplifying corruption, on account of his close connections to what were known as 'the oil mafia' and 'the caviar mafia', and because of stories of his giving Brezhnev a bejewelled sword and a huge ring embedded with precious stones. He was ejected from the Politburo as an anti-Glasnost hardliner, opposed to Mikhail Gorbachev's socialist reform movement. In 1987 he was stripped of his position in the Central Committee and his Moscow dacha.

Recognising the changing times, Aliyev shifted direction. In the days following the 1990 Black January massacre in Baku of over a hundred Azeri civilians, he publicly denounced the Soviet forces, and told reporters: 'The absolute majority of the population is behind the Popular Front.'[10] It was a remarkable statement for someone so recently at the pinnacle of Soviet power, and marked his transition to becoming an anti-Soviet nationalist. In retrospect Aliyev's very dismissal from the politburo ultimately enabled him to sidestep the turbulent first years of Azeri independence, returning to power in Baku only three years later with his KGB networks intact.[11]

In the spring of 2009, we are standing as close as we can to the Presidential Residence, from which the eighty-year-old Aliyev ruled up until shortly before his death in December 2003. For six decades his career had been intertwined with the politics of this oil province, and he was an undisputed architect of the Oil Road.

James was here before, in 1998, five years after Aliyev had taken up residence. Wandering nearby armed with a camera, he was foolishly trying to capture the view over the wide Baki Buxtasi. Predictably enough, two presidential guards appeared, guns at the ready, and he was frogmarched to the basement of the Residence. After long, nervous hours and the gutting of his pre-digital camera, James was ejected into the anxious night.

THE OIL ACADEMY, BAKU, AZERBAIJAN

When Heydar Aliyev withdrew from the 2003 presidential elections due to ill health, few doubted that his family would ensure power remained within the

9   Quoted in Levine, *The Oil and the Glory*, p. 176.

10   B. Keller, 'Upheaval in the East: A Former KGB Chief Champions Azerbaijanis', *New York Times*, 26 January 1990.

11   J. Hemming, *The Implications of the Revival of the Oil Industry in Azerbaijan*, Centre for Middle Eastern and Islamic Studies (Durham), 1998.

clan, but there was some hope that his son, Ilham, would be a reformer. As expected, Ilham Aliyev won 76.8 per cent of the votes, but the elections were widely recognised as fraudulent and were followed by mass arrests and repression of journalists.[12]

Despite the crackdown, the opposition continued to organise against the regime. With increased international attention on Azerbaijan accompanying the launch of the export pipeline, a demonstration was called for 21 May 2005. The mayor of Baku refused permission for the protest, claiming that it 'would interfere with preparations for the official opening ceremony of the Baku–Tbilisi–Ceyhan oil pipeline, which will take place on 25 May'.[13] Police raided homes and rounded up forty opposition leaders, and although the organisers boldly pronounced that thousands would attend the rally, privately they knew that most people would be too frightened to participate.[14]

In this context, the fact that people turned out at all was astonishing. Several hundred protestors gathered between the Oil Academy, where the older Aliyev had once studied, and the Kappelhaus, the German Cultural Centre. Mostly middle-aged men and women, they represented the opposition Musavat Party, the Popular Front, and the Democratic Party. We have come to where they gathered, and look along the street that they had intended to march down, six blocks of 28th May Street and Bulbul Prospekti.

Few could have believed that they would make it far, as armoured trucks blocked their route and a dense formation of black-clad riot police and Ministry of Interior troops encircled the crowd at a distance. Nobody moved. Then a chant started up: 'Free elections! Free elections!' At once the tight phalanxes of police charged, batons banging on shields to create a deafening din. As the two groups collided, the crunch of truncheons on bodies and the sound of screaming spread fear and panic through the crowd. Caught on all sides, those who fell were bludgeoned and kicked. The protest leaders were cornered, beaten and hauled off. Others who managed to escape into side-streets were flushed out with water-cannons and imprisoned.

Soon the space that we stand in was empty of life. The unconscious bodies of two women lay where they had fallen, alongside a ripped flag. Abandoned shoes, torn hats and smashed placards littered the concrete; this street was spattered with blood.

Despite the demonstration taking place fifty kilometres from the Sangachal

---

12   *OSCE/ODIHR Election Observation Mission Report: Republic of Azerbaijan – 15 October 2003*, OSCE/ODIHR, Warsaw, November 2003; *The Azerbaijan 'Elections' – October 15th 2003*, Institute for Democracy in Eastern Europe, Baku, October 2003.

13   A. Abdullayeva, N. Jafarova, S. Gojamanli and S. Bananyarli, *Report on Monitoring During the Protest Rally Held by Opposition Parties on May 21, 2005*, Monitoring Group of Human Rights Organizations, 2005.

14   'Police Breaks up Opposition Rally', *AssA-Irada*, 21 May 2005.

Terminal – the nearest point that the pipeline comes to Baku – the BBC accepted the regime's description of the events when covering the celebrations at the opening of BTC four days later. The British broadcaster explained: 'Some demonstrators were beaten and arrested last Saturday, with Azeri authorities saying that they acted because the protest was too close to the pipeline.'[15]

ISTIGLALIYYAT STREET, BAKU, AZERBAIJAN

We are climbing up a wide, dilapidated staircase. Not more than a few hundred metres from the Presidential Palace, this dusty Belle Epoque brick building is the address we have for Arzu Abdullayeva. Active in Azerbaijan's Social Democratic movement throughout the late 1980s and 1990s, Arzu opposed both Soviet rule and the newly created nationalist parties. Since the Aliyevs' return to power she has been a staunch campaigner for human rights, and is co-chair of the International Helsinki Citizens' Assembly. We have come to get an update on the current levels of repression, and to discuss how oil helps the Aliyevs stay in control.

The steps become more decrepit the higher we get, and we are wondering whether we are in the wrong building. At the top of the staircase is an open door. Entering, we find a warren of offices with high ceilings, bustling with young people writing, reading and filing. There is no receptionist, but one of the activists – who, it strikes us, are all women – points us to Arzu's room.

Arzu is neatly dressed in a black jersey with a silver brooch. Her sombre colours are offset by pink lipstick, and hair dyed purple and red. After welcoming us, she immediately launches into a summary of the deteriorating human rights situation across the Caucasus. She feels that in Azerbaijan the primary problem is freedom of expression, as without that freedom it is impossible to assess what is happening with other rights. Some newspapers are banned and others face punitive libel prosecutions. 'Our journalists are particularly persecuted – intimidated, imprisoned and even killed when they write critically. Those in prison are all wonderful guys, very respectable correspondents. But not all are allowed to live.'

'Two months before BTC was launched in 2005, the newspaper editor Elmar Husseinov was murdered.' Arzu is close to tears at the memory. 'After he was killed, a list of further targets emerged including rights activists, opposition politicians and independent writers.' 'Were you on the list?' we ask. 'Yes, unfortunately me too.' She laughs ruefully and sighs. It seems that the state authorities are prepared to go to any lengths to silence critical voices, frequently using fabricated charges of drugs and terrorism to imprison journalists, poets and bloggers.[16] With such intense pressure to remain silent, the community of those

---

15   'Giant Caspian Oil Pipeline Opens', BBC News, 25 May 2005.
16   'Amnesty Condemns Jailing of Azerbaijan Social Media Activist on "Bogus Drug Charges"', Associated Press, 6 May 2011.

activists who continue to raise concerns is understandably small; we are scheduled to meet many of them during our days in Baku.

'We have no freedom of assembly', Arzu continues. Although the constitution guarantees this right, in practice permission is needed from the mayor for any public events. On the rare occasions when requests are approved, the restrictions and amendments – insisting on very short protests in outlying suburbs – make the gathering pointless.

'So sometimes we and others organise non-sanctioned pickets. But this is very dangerous and risky. Large numbers of riot police appear immediately, with their sticks ready. Frequently, they will just begin to beat people cruelly, without saying anything or asking questions.' Arzu and her friends try to grab back people who have been arrested, but usually fail. When in 2003 Ilham Aliyev was made president following the fraudulent election, protests led to over 1,000 arrests and many people being tortured.

In a situation where any type of public dissent is rapidly quashed, trade union rights have suffered. Many have not received formal recognition, with the government, oil companies and subcontractors creating various obstacles to union activities.[17] Arzu recounts numerous stories of people losing their jobs for even daring to mention unionisation.

She agrees with our research that repression and the centralisation of authority under both Aliyevs have allowed the oil companies to operate in a highly profitable environment. The lack of autonomous state institutions asserting a different perspective from that of the president is seen as a blessing. The concentration of power has meant that the corporations have felt little need to be accountable to diverse government departments, nor to consider that there is any opposition to the Aliyevs.[18] In an extraordinary twist of language, a business think tank described how, in Azerbaijan, 'oil projects sidestep many potential administrative pitfalls and delays ... Environmental and labour laws, for example, can prove elastic.'[19] Arzu points out that the benefits flow both ways. BP and the other corporations played a crucial role in enabling Aliyev's regime to strengthen its grip over Azeri society, achieving what the companies describe as 'stability'. We discuss how oil revenues can entrench a stagnant political system, for the elite can draw its wealth from resources rather than citizens' taxes, and thus remain deaf to calls for reform. By setting the rules of the game for oil contracts, the Azeri elite – much of which ruled in the Soviet era – captured the active support of foreign investors in concentrating

17   *2007 Annual Survey of Violations of Trade Union Rights: Azerbaijan*, International Trade Union Confederation, 2007.

18   O. Bayulgen, 'Foreign Investment, Oil Curse, and Democratization: A Comparison of Azerbaijan and Russia', *Business and Politics* 7 (2005).

19   D. Hoffman, 'Azerbaijan: The Politicization of Oil', in R. Ebel and R. Menon, *Energy and Conflict in Central Asia and the Caucasus*, Rowman & Littlefield, 2000.

their power. Each contract signed helped entrench Aliyev further.[20] Arzu adds, 'From my side, I can say that BP doesn't do anything for human rights. Especially as BP is a great cooperator with our regime, I am dissatisfied; they are not helping us build our democracy. It's great that they train some journalists to write articles professionally – but this is minor compared to their support for the repression.'

As we get ready to leave, wondering how Arzu manages to continue in the face of such an entrenched system, she says goodbye with a last thought: 'You see, Europe, the US and the companies wanted more oil. Heydar Aliyev offered to give them control over our oil and its export route, and in return got unlimited rights to rule this country as he wanted. We're living under a dictatorship, but do you see criticism from Britain or the US? Barely a whisper. We ask them not to sell our democracy for oil. But do you think they're listening?'

CASPIAN PLAZA, CƏFƏR CABBARLI KUÇ, BAKU, AZERBAIJAN

We leave the pre–World War I Outer Town, heading towards the Caspian Plaza. This tower, like the offices of SOFAZ, has been constructed within the last ten years, and is a similar monument in glass and steel to Baku's new identity. On the ground floor, a stationery shop sells Moleskine diaries next door to a travel agent promoting business-class seats to London, İstanbul and Moscow. In the offices above, consultants rub shoulders with firms of foreign architects and an assortment of NGOs.

While Arzu gave us an overview of the importance of oil and BP in the Azeri body politic, we have come here to understand the economic context better, by meeting a researcher working for a non-profit organisation focused on tracking government revenues. Emil Omerov is of the younger generation that was educated after the collapse of the Soviet Union. His training is capitalist, not Marxist. Lean, excitable and energetic, he says with a laugh: 'Did you see our big policemen on the streets, with their long sticks? They take up six per cent of our national budget. Six per cent! Then a further 10 to 15 per cent goes to the army. You can see where the president gets his iron gloves.' He explains that lower oil prices will cause the budget to fall by 8.8 per cent in the coming year. Yet, somehow, all the resulting cutbacks are to be passed on to the social services, agriculture and transport, while the police and army will get another 5 per cent raise.[21] Meanwhile, an ever larger share of the SOFAZ money is being transferred into the state budget. We learn that this flow of finance began in 2004, shortly after Ilham Aliyev succeeded his father, and has since increased rapidly: one billion, two billion, now five billion dollars. Forty per cent of this money – meant for future generations – is pumped into construction. 'One bridge alone cost a billion dollars

20   Bayulgen, 'Foreign Investment, Oil Curse, and Democratization'.
21   Aslanli, 'Oil and Gas Revenues Management in Azerbaijan'.

– more than our entire national budget in 2002.' The budget cuts due to the global recession have put a hold on new construction, but there are still around 1,000 unfinished projects waiting to be completed. Apparently, tracking economic impacts is difficult as you cannot rely on official government figures. 'They claim that the global crisis hasn't affected us, and that 700,000 new jobs were opened this year. But this is bullshit. So many people have lost their jobs and become unemployed.'

Ilham Aliyev has announced that the state is diversifying the economy and moving away from oil. Yet Azerbaijan's dependence on crude and petrol-related exports is only increasing. By 2008, 97 per cent of all exports were oil-related. The remaining 3 per cent were agricultural – 'our cucumbers and tomatoes!' Emil jokes. Other sectors that have grown, such as hotels or oil-pipe manufacturers, are all highly dependent on the oil industry.

Massive sales of crude by any state tend to push up the local currency, undermining the competitiveness of other exports. This process, whereby a national currency appreciates due to the export of natural resources, is called 'Dutch Disease', and is one of the reasons that oil-rich economies tend to become more, rather than less, dependent on oil over time. In 2005 the *Economist* reported that 'Dutch Disease has already struck' in Baku.[22] The SOFAZ oil fund created in 1999 had been intended to help ward off this problem, but spending the money on a construction boom does exactly the opposite – it stimulates short-term inflation.

Our interview concludes with Emil telling us that the first oil boom, in the late nineteenth century, created a couple of Azeri and Russian millionaires who built beautiful mansions, while generally it didn't benefit people that much. Then during the second oil boom, in the 1930s and '40s, Azeri crude fuelled four out of five tanks that defeated the Nazis. But again, people didn't benefit locally, in terms of development. More recently, we were promised that Baku would become the Dubai of the Caucasus. And the construction boom gave people optimism for the future – after all, Dubai has many skyscrapers. But now, when people hear that the oil production will peak next year, they ask where the benefits have gone. On the streets, you can see fancy cars. Cars made in German factories in Bavaria will be seen here before they are seen in Munich. But it is only a small part of our society that is living in luxury, while many remain in poverty.

BINƏGƏDI, BAKU, AZERBAIJAN

There is an air of sullen dustiness on the bus that takes us north-east from the Caspian Plaza along Azadliq Prospekti – Freedom Avenue, one of the great arteries of Baku – towards the tower blocks of the Late Soviet city. We are in search of

---

22   'The Oil Satrap', *Economist*, 31 October 2005.

the legendary Billion Dollar Bridge that everyone in Baku is talking about. Stepping off the bus with commuters heading home in the evening, we look around for a spectacular homage to the new Azerbaijan; instead, we see a grey overpass. It has lots of cars on it, and it is pretty large, yet far from monumental. Unsure if we have come to the right place, we ask around, and end up visiting another new overpass nearby, which is still under construction. It looks pretty similar, but is this really what they were talking about?

On reflection we realise that expecting something else was wrong-headed. The bridge was intended merely to ease congestion, not as a major city landmark. This piece of infrastructure began to gain its notoriety and name as the Billion Dollar Bridge only after it had been completed and its true cost became known. Budget inflation for construction projects seems to be the norm. We have been told of a road to the airport that cost $20 million per kilometre, and classrooms built for $70,000 that should have cost $10,000.[23]

It is not just bad project management that is at fault. Purposeful price inflation enables someone to cream off the difference between the bid price and the actual cost, and divert public funds to private bank accounts. Setting up various front companies that do actually deliver the promised building – albeit late and with poor materials – has become the Azerbaijani elite's preferred way of enriching itself, and has helped drive the massive construction boom.

As we wait for a bus, we remember a Soviet joke that a friend shared. 'The Romanian minister of transport visits his counterpart in Russia. He is surprised to see the luxurious house and his rich lifestyle, much more than one would expect for a party member of his rank.

'How do you manage?' he asks.

The Russian minister takes him to the window and asks:

'Do you see that bridge over there?'

'Yes.'

'Well, that bridge cost 100 million roubles. And from such a large sum a little bit comes my way . . .'

A few years later the Russian minister returns the visit. The Romanian minister has an even more lavish lifestyle. The Russian asks:

'How do you manage?'

'You see that bridge over there?'

'What bridge?'

'Well, that bridge too cost 100 million lei.'

Azerbaijan is saturated with corruption at all levels. Police extortion of motorists

---

23　See also M. Gahramanli, V. Rajabov and A. Kazakhov, *Report on Corruption in Azerbaijan Oil Industry Prepared for EBRD and IFC Investigation Arms*, Bankwatch and Committee of Oil Industry Workers' Rights Protection, 2003.

for nonexistent traffic offences is routine. When we travel in private cars, we are repeatedly pulled over and asked to pay. Criticising these traffic charges is politically acceptable in Azerbaijan, and the search for a remedy has received international attention. According to the World Bank, 32 per cent of companies believe that, to get anything done at state level, you need to pay a bribe.[24]

But documenting major corruption and the murky construction deals happening in this 'boom city' is much more dangerous. Evidence implicating the president is especially taboo. Arzu had warned us that those who discover such cases soon end up in the notorious Bayil Prison.

Rumours of corruption over the major oil contracts abound. Almost everybody we speak to – who doesn't work for BP or the government – feels that the company would not have been allowed to drill without paying bribes. BP, needless to say, denies that its activities in Azerbaijan involved any wrongdoing – although what constitutes corruption is apparently a matter of definition. Rondo Fehlberg, BP's chief negotiator in the early 1990s, explained that to call something 'bribery' was a Western oversimplification:

> It's more complex than that. In their culture, with the old Middle Eastern customs that include friendship and baksheesh with a veneer of communism, there is a mix that is difficult to understand. But their culture has a clear morality to it. For me to be befriended by a senior minister and have him work for me and bust his tail to make it happen, in their culture he is entitled to something.[25]

Exactly why a senior minister of the Azerbaijan government was busting his tail for BP – and in what capacity – remains unclear.

More above-board, all the oil contracts between 1992 and 1994 involved legal 'signing bonuses' amounting to $390 million.[26] Rumours circulate about parallel demands for illicit payments running into the hundreds of millions of dollars.[27]

As we trundle back into town, we try and unpick what we have seen. Some of the income from the oil extracted by BP comes to the Azeri state at SOFAZ. However, under the direction of the president much of this is not invested abroad, as is advised, but used to fund current government spending, including construction projects. The Azeri elite owns the companies that carry out these projects, and through price inflation they acquire huge personal wealth, much of which they invest abroad – buying mansions in London, for example. So, even if BP and the other foreign oil companies did not participate in any bribery themselves,

---

24   *Enterprise Surveys*, World Bank, 2009, at enterprisesurveys.org.

25   Quoted in S. Levine, *The Oil and the Glory*, Random House, 2007, p. 164.

26   September 1992: $90 million; July 1993: $70 million; September 1994: $230 million. Total: $390 million.

27   Levine, *The Oil and the Glory*, pp. 183–5.

they are big players in an environment where much, if not most, of the income from oil is being siphoned off by those in power.

A journalist and long-term oppositionist, Zardusht Alizadeh, had described to us several years earlier how the Aliyevs, father and son, had recreated the same type of regime of control, relying on clan corruption, that had existed in the non-Russian Soviet republics through the 1970s – 'the oil mafia' and 'the caviar mafia' that Heydar Aliyev was accused of being involved in. In this 'clan model', around the president sit a group of ten to twenty people. Each of these has a circle of ten, who in turn is surrounded by a further ten. Most of these are either individuals from Heydar Aliyev's native Naxçivan region or former colleagues from the KGB.

But challenging the poor governance and corruption in today's Baku in isolation, as powerful outside agencies such as the World Bank and British Embassy do, is akin to examining Heydar Aliyev's embezzlement of public resources in the 1970s without a critique of the consequences of Soviet power.[28] What we are witnessing in Baku is its transformation into a resource colony for Western energy demands and a profit centre for oil companies, at the expense of the Azeri people's future. This is also corruption – the corruption of state power.

---

28   Other actors focusing on corruption without a structural assessment of power include the IMF and the European Union.

3 THEY ALONE CAN LIGHT FOR US THE ROAD TO THE PROMISED LAND

SUMQAYIT, BAKU, AZERBAIJAN

Thirty Years Ago

The Caspian
Still looks as heavy
as molten lead,
but now we've planted
oil trees
in wells at the bottom of the sea.
The barren place called Sumqayit
with its bone-dry earth
hadn't become a green city
with factories and a hundred thousand people.
Poetry was found in Azerbaijan,
but not Samet's.
The moon was up there,
but all alone –
no little brother yet.

Nazim Hikmet, October 1957, Moscow–Baku[1]

If only Sumqayit had remained the 'green city' described by the Turkish poet Nazim Hikmet. Lying nearly twenty kilometres north of Baku, beyond Binəgədi, is the city that was famous for *gazovka* – the smog that hung above it and suffused everything and everyone. Sumqayit, with its petrochemical pollution levels and the appalling conditions in which its population of 250,000 lived, has become a byword for Soviet environmental destruction.

---

1   N. Hikmet, transl. R. Blasing and M. Konuk, *Poems of Nazim Hikmet*, Persea Books, 1994.

Decades of poor regulation allowed thirty-two chemical and metal plants to spew out 120,000 tonnes of waste annually.[2] Poisonous materials, including DDT and lindane, were manufactured and exported, but not before their by-products had been released into the air, soil and water.[3] Local residents complained that the smell was so bad it could wake you up. 'The pollution enters your brain, it makes you want to throw up. You can't focus or do anything.' There were countless stories of deaths from cancer, and reports of children born with abnormal bodies. Infant mortality rates in Sumqayit were immense, at three times the Soviet average, borne out by the city's large dedicated children's cemetery. In an echo of filmmaker Andrei Tarkovsky's masterpiece *Stalker*, one Moscow documentary-maker called Sumqayit 'the dead zone'.

Sixty years previously, Sumqayit had been a small fishing village on the northern shore of the Absheron Peninsula. In 1935, the people's commissar of heavy industry for the USSR, a Georgian named Sergo Orjonikidze, was promoting the diversification of the oil industry in Baku. He selected the place as a site for petrochemical plants. At this 'barren place', as Hikmet wrote, a new industrial city was to be built, with its promise of modernity.

In the decades after Sumqayit's foundation, the population rose rapidly. Within fifty years, the village of 6,000 had become a petropolis of 350,000. Over time, in parallel with the rising death toll from heart defects and cancer, Sumqayit became unruly. During the 1963 celebrations marking the October Revolution, a crowd from the pipe-rolling factory broke away from the festive march through the city. Workers stormed the podium where local Party leaders were standing and ripped down a vast portrait of Khrushchev that covered the façade of the Palace of Culture. Police battered the protestors with truncheons, but disturbances continued into the night. The residents planned a repeat demonstration on the tenth anniversary – by which time Heydar Aliyev was head of the Communist Party of Azerbaijan – but were foiled by the KGB.[4]

By the late 1980s, across the Soviet Union nationalism had become the primary channel used to express dissent. Both Azeri and Armenian dissidents showed their opposition to the USSR by making territorial demands – primarily competing claims over the mountainous enclave of Nagorno-Karabakh. Attached to the Soviet Republic of Azerbaijan in 1920, this region was populated predominantly by citizens who were increasingly identifying themselves as Armenians. Tragically, the famed mountains, songs and orchards of Nagorno-Karabakh held a renewed importance in the evolving national mythologies of both Azerbaijan and Armenia.

---

2   D. Biello, 'World's Top 10 Most Polluted Places', *Scientific American* 17 (2007), p. 6.

3   K. Ismayilova, 'With More Jobs, More Smog', *Eurasianet*, November 2007.

4   T. de Waal, *Black Garden*, NYU Press, 2004, p. 32.

In 1987 nationalist demonstrations took place in Yerevan, the capital of the Soviet Socialist Republic of Armenia, as well as in Baku and smaller cities, followed by attacks on Azeris in both Armenia and Nagorno-Karabakh. Azeri refugees fled east, arriving in Sumqayit during the winter. In early 1988 violence broke out in the town, this time with the Azeri majority targeting Armenian residents. The attacks began on 28 February 1988; by the following evening martial law was being enforced by Soviet marines, and 5,000 Armenians had taken shelter in the Palace of Culture. The numbers are disputed, with some estimates that twenty-six Armenians and six Azeris had been killed, and 4,000 people arrested. Almost all 14,000 Armenian residents fled.[5]

The deadly clashes in the Soviet Union's petrochemical city marked a watershed in the history of the USSR and the future Azerbaijan. As Armenian militias gradually asserted their control of Nagorno-Karabakh between 1988 and 1994, ethnic Azeris were forced off their land and moved east. Many settled in the empty homes of Sumqayit, which had been vacated by the city's fleeing Armenians. The continued violence between Armenia and Azerbaijan created a chaotic context in which oil corporations could demand highly profitable terms for investment in the Caspian. The new Oil Road was built in the midst of this conflict.

As elsewhere in the former Soviet Union, the political collapse of the early 1990s saw levels of toxic pollution drop in Sumqayit. This was due not to increased environmental regulation in the new market economy, but to rapid de-industrialisation as the planned economy came to an abrupt end. By 1998, only 10 per cent of the chemical plants were still operating. Residents said that the air was cleaner for a while.

In the early twenty-first century the pollution has started to rise again. The residents of Sumqayit feel that if the country's increased oil extraction revives associated industries, as it threatens to do, emissions will once more increase and the dumping of waste will recommence. The *gazovka* is returning, as a resident says: 'We're going back to the old days. We can feel the bad air, smell the bad air, the city stinks after six o'clock.'[6]

BALAKHANI, BAKU, AZERBAIJAN

Two roads lead from Sumqayit to Baku – the main highway and the byroad that winds through Binəgədi and the neighbouring suburb of Balakhani on the northern shore of Boyuk Şor Lake. Unlike Sumqayit, Balakhani was never intentionally singled out for urbanisation and transformation into an industrial city. Yet the forces of modernity swept over this community sixty years before Orjonikidze became a Soviet commissar.

---

5   de Waal, *Black Garden*, p. 37.
6   S. Huseynova, 'Azerbaijan: Sumgayit Becomes One of the World's Most-Polluted Cities', *RFE/RL*, September 2007.

Today, the nineteenth- and twentieth-century oil industry ruins that scar this place make it an utterly alien environment. The ancient oil derricks and puddles of crude are harsh on the eye, the sour air coats you, lining your mouth and throat. This is the premier destination for photojournalists visiting Baku in search of images of oil pollution and destruction. A deathscape of rubbish fires, rusting 'nodding donkey' pumps and collapsed concrete. The rotting remains of street dogs and other scavengers lie alongside abandoned oil pipes, all besmeared with black crude.

Balakhani had already been part of the pre-industrial oil economy for a 1,000 years – with crude extracted from hand-dug pits around the village – when it became a centre of mechanised drilling in the 1870s.[7] Early photographs show it as a zone sacrificed to the extraction of oil. Like Bibi Heybat, it too had its gushers, such as the well named Vermishevsky that blew in June 1872, spouting 2,600 barrels every day for thirteen days. 'All surrounding terrains were covered in oil', and several oil lakes formed.[8]

The frenzy of speculation resulting from this and other gushers attracted capital to Balakhani from far afield. The Swedish–Russian Nobel brothers arrived within the year, quickly establishing a dominant position in this Tsarist province by snapping up assets from smaller competitors. Ludvig Nobel became head of the newly founded Council of Oil Extractors Congress – the oil barons' club. In 1889, the English foreign correspondent Charles Marvin called Nobel 'the Oil King of Baku'.[9]

The Nobels were able to draw capital from elsewhere in Russia to finance the new Branobel oil company. This gave them the power to create new industrial structures. The transportation of crude eight miles from Balakhani to the refineries in the Black Town had for decades been conducted by *arba* – workers using mule- or camel-drawn carts. These workers insisted on certain conditions of labour, such as the observation of Muslim holidays, conditions that the Nobels were determined to break. After observing the methods of John Rockefeller in the US, they began constructing a pipeline from Balakhani to the refineries in Black Town. In the face of fierce local resistance to the pipeline, which involved disruption of construction sites, the company brought in Cossack troops to provide security; in effect, the Nobels hired a paramilitary force.[10] Eventually the Glasgow-manufactured pipes were laid, and by 1900 the Nobels had constructed a network of 326 pipelines across the Absheron Peninsula.

---

7   M. Mir-Babayev, 'Azerbaijan's Oil History – A Chronology Leading up to the Soviet Era', *Azerbaijan International* 10: 2 (2002), pp. 34–40.

8   I. Zonn, A. Kosarev, M. Glantz and A. Kostianoy, *The Caspian Sea Encyclopedia*, Springer, 2010.

9   C. Marvin, *The Region of the Eternal Fire: An Account of a Journey to the Petroleum Region of the Caspian in 1883*, W. H. Allen & Co, 1884.

10   J. Henry, *Baku: An Eventful History*, A. Constable, 1905.

Ludvig Nobel also determined to drive down the price of exporting oil across the Caspian and up the Volga to cities in western Russia. The costs lay in the wooden barrels and the dock handling: oil was transported in barrels stowed on ships, in the same way that Rockefeller exported US products to Europe. So in 1878 Nobel commissioned the *Zoroaster*, a vessel with container tanks built into the ship's hull – the world's first tanker. The Nobels had transformed Baku's oil industry, placing it at the forefront of technological innovation.

The tankers returning from the Volga shipped water as ballast, which was then used to irrigate the trees and shrubs that Nobel had planted around his mansion above the Black Town. Named Villa Petrolea, his residence became the social epicentre for Baku's new plutocracy, and on Wednesdays and Saturdays 'the entire colony' would gather at the Villa Petrolea to play billiards and dance.[11]

The boom city began to draw in capital from far beyond European Russia. The French branch of the Rothschild Bank arrived and financed the building of a railway across the Caucasus to the Black Sea port of Batumi. Taghiyev sold out his holdings to James Viashnau of London, and between 1898 and 1903 British companies invested 60 million roubles in the Baku industry.[12] Alfred Lyttelton Marriott, a great-great-uncle of James's, visited the area in 1901 and wrote:

> I was shown over the work of an English Company purchased by them a few years ago for 5 million roubles and now said to be worth more than ten times that amount. These works owing to their isolated position, escaped damage in the late fires which caused immense destruction and loss of life. The wonder is that there are not more fires, as in all directions there are large open reservoirs of the highly inflammable naphtha or crude petroleum, into which the oil is pumped up before being refined.[13]

Western European capital was integral to the rapid development of an industrial working class. Workers flooded into Balakhani, Bibi Heybat and Baku, and, further afield, into the distant Georgian oil port of Batumi and all the towns along the Baku–Batumi Railway. Lenin described the transformation of the Caucasus in the 1890s: a country 'sparsely populated, inhabited by highlanders and staying aloof from the development of the world economy, aloof even from history was becoming transformed into a country of oil industrialists, wine merchants, grain and tobacco manufacturers'.[14]

---

11   Letter from Ludvig Nobel, quoted in B. Asbrink, 'The Dream of a Small Paradise . . .', branobelhistory.com; R. Tolf, *The Russian Rockefellers*, Hoover Press, 1982.

12   Equivalent to £6 million at the time, and between £600 million and £3 billion today.

13   A. L. Marriott, *Persian Journal*, unpublished manuscript, 1901.

14   I. Deutscher, *Stalin: A Political Biography*, OUP, 1967, p. 39.

The process of industrialisation and the demands of foreign capital to generate maximum returns soon ran up against social resistance. From the 1890s onwards, labour unrest took place in all sections of these new oil structures, inspiring radical organisers and thinkers. Joseph Djugashvili, a son of an illiterate shoemaker, like the oil baron Taghiyev, would later become the most renowned of these organisers.[15] Four years after Djugashvili was born, in 1878, the Baku–Batumi Railway was completed. Rothschild and Nobel rail tankers, rumbling and grinding though the Georgian town of Gori, must have shaken the shack in which he lived. Djugashvili became a key actor in the history of the Oil Road well before he took the name of Stalin.

In August 1898, the nineteen-year-old Djugashvili joined a clandestine socialist organisation in Tbilisi and started to read *Das Kapital*. Soon after, he was expelled from his Tbilisi theological seminary for 'propagating Marxism' to the oil railway workers. Two years later he aligned himself politically with Lenin's grouping within the Russian Social Democratic Party, becoming an '*Iskra*-man' and distributing Lenin's paper across the Caucasus. *Iskra* – 'the spark' – was published in Stuttgart, then, as Lenin fled the Tsarist secret police, in Geneva, and finally at Clerkenwell Green in London. This vessel of radical analysis was conveyed to Batumi and Baku on Nobel's tankers and along the Rothschilds' oil railway. As oil flowed out of the Caucasus, ideas flowed in from distant cities, combining with already fervent labour struggles.

Djugashvili, now known by his *nom de guerre* of Koba – 'The Indomitable' – arrived in Baku in December 1904, after organising strikes in Batumi and escaping from exile in Siberia. A general strike had been launched, and he hurried to join other activists such as Sergo Orjonikidze, the future commissar of heavy industry and founder of Sumqayit, and Stepan Shaumian, the future head of the Baku Soviet. In previous strikes employers had refused the workers' demands point blank, and sent in troops to break the pickets. This time the demonstrations were larger, and workers besieged oil owners inside their offices. In less than three weeks the employers were forced to negotiate, establishing a nine-hour working day, four paid days off per month and a raise in wages.[16]

---

15   Stalin was by no means the central activist in the Caucasus during this period. But he is the best documented, given his later rise to power, his personality cult, and the purges. Formal records of many others were lost or destroyed. These include the independent labour movement in Baku, the 'Balakhany and Bibi-Eibat Workers Organisation', founded in 1904 by Lev and Ilya Shchendrikov, which focused on the economic grievances of the local proletariat. T. Swietochowski, *Russian Azerbaijan, 1905–1920*, CUP, 1985.

16   J. Stalin, 'The December Strike and the December Agreement', in *Works*, Foreign Languages Publishing House, 1954.

Proclaiming victory, the Caucasian Union of Social Democrats issued a statement written by Koba:

Russia is like a loaded gun, at full cock, ready to go off at the slightest concussion . . . We should not forget for even a single moment that only the party committees can lead us in a worthy manner, that they alone can light for us the road to the Promised Land that is called a Socialist World.[17]

The successful Baku strike shook the empire, and unrest spread across Russia. The next month, 1,000 protestors were gunned down in front of the Tsar's Winter Palace in St Petersburg on Bloody Sunday: the spark that ignited the 1905 Revolution. In Baku, however, Tsarist forces provoked communal clashes between the Muslim and Armenian communities, undermining workers' unity and distracting them from shared grievances against the regime.[18] One witness later recalled: 'Thousands of dead lay in the streets and covered the Christian and Mussulman cemeteries, the odour of the corpses stifled us. The whole city was in flames and even the waves of the Caspian Sea, covered in oil from the burning wells, spat fire like a dragon.'[19]

Despite mass support, the Tsar suppressed the Revolution across the empire, and a period of reaction was enforced. But the situation in Baku had changed. The oilfields had been badly damaged, and foreign investors were shaken by the radicalism of the workforce. Unsure of the long-term security of their assets, they stopped financing rig developments and well maintenance. Oil extraction in Baku began to decline. By 1914, Baku had fallen from being the world's largest producer to generating a mere 9 per cent of global crude. The Rothschilds, perhaps nervous after the bloodbath, merged their company into a Royal Dutch Shell trust.

Revolutionary organising continued, and now included expropriations to finance political activity. Kidnappings of oil barons and other raids became more common and high profile, including the capture of the ship *Nicholas I* in Baku harbour. Koba's star was rising among the Bolsheviks. In May 1907 he travelled from Baku to London for the Fifth Congress of the Russian Social Democratic Workers' Party, held in Hackney. 'Two years of revolutionary work among the oil workers of Baku', he later wrote, 'hardened me as a practical fighter. In contact with advanced workers of Baku . . . in the storm of the deepest conflicts between workers and

17   Deutscher, *Stalin*, p. 85.
18   T. Swietochowski, *Russian Azerbaijan, 1905–1920*, CUP, 1985, pp. 40–4; R. Suny, *Revenge of the Past*, Stanford University Press, 1993, p. 168.
19   Ohanian, quoted in Reiss, *Orientalist*, p. 14.

oil industrialists . . . I first learned what it meant to lead big masses of workers.'[20]

Organising among the oil labourers posed immense challenges. The workforce in Balakhani and elsewhere around Baku was deeply divided between different trades and distinct communities. Workers in the refineries at Black Town and the mechanical workshops tended to be Russians and Armenians, while those toiling in the oilfields were the lowest paid, mostly Muslim 'Tartars' from both Persia and the Russian Empire. Arriving from villages and frequently illiterate, they were looked down upon by others; contemporary writers like Essad Bey called them 'savage labourers'.[21] Koba and fellow activists lived among them in the cramped shanties of the Balakhani fields, trying to build a self-identified proletariat making strong demands. The Bolsheviks aimed to build a union that bridged the skilled and unskilled workers, and that would overcome the religious, ethnic, linguistic and national patchwork that was Baku in the first decades of the twentieth century.

On the Absheron Peninsula, amid the squalor of the oilfields, a radical social vision took root: one that looked beyond better working conditions and demanded the transformation of society as a whole – not only society in Baku and the Caucasus, but across Russia, and indeed the world. Amid the chaos of the oil rush and the gushers of Balakhani grew a vision of a new order, 'the Promised Land that is called a Socialist World'.

MIRGASIMOV STREET, GƏNCLIK, BAKU

Not far from the southern shores of the polluted Boyuk Şor Lake lies the Gənclik quarter of Baku. The cold wind hurls desert sands against the blocks of post-war flats and surrounding bungalows. Entering a side road we dodge washing lines strung out onto the street and the men mending cars on the pavement, and make our way to the offices of the Green Party of Azerbaijan and Mayis Gulaliyev.

'Feminism, decentralisation, ecological vision. You see Green Party ideology is the future political mindset for the whole Caucasus region.' Mayis's enthusiasm is unbounded. It warms us from the wind and lifts the shadows of Sumqayit and Balakhani. He believes a more ecological and socially just approach will rid Azerbaijan of its military conflicts, resolve local health disasters, restore the country's capacity to grow its own food, rescue the Caspian Sea from pollution and offer Azeris ways to deal with water scarcity. 'That's why we started the party in 2006. People aren't quite ready for it yet, but we're getting there.'

'On almost every issue, we need to come at it from the side, and there we can

---

20   Deutscher, *Stalin*, p. 108.

21   E. Bey, *Blood and Oil in the Orient*, Simon & Schuster, 1932, p. 4. Essad Bey is a pseudonym, and the author is understood to be Lev Nussimbaum.

find a solution. Decentralisation offers a way to talk to the Armenians about Nagorno-Karabakh without one side "winning" and the other "losing". The solution to the unsustainable extraction of oil and gas – from both an economic and an environmental perspective – is simple: stop drilling for oil and gas. The regime makes all the profits anyway. Of course, if I was actually elected, the CIA would try to throw me out, saying I'm a Kurdish agent or an Armenian agent.'

Mayis is an intriguing character. Born in rural eastern Azerbaijan, he is a compact man of forty-eight, immaculately turned out, dapper in suit and tie. He resembles a middle-aged Robert DeNiro – good-looking, heavy eyebrows, hair greying at the temples, and often smiling.

A physicist in Kazakhstan, then a post-Soviet 'biznesman' in the Ukraine, Mayis returned to Azerbaijan in the late 1990s. Joining the democracy movements campaigning against repression, he took a growing interest in environmental issues. 'But for me justice was always the central issue – combining human rights, ecology and freedom.' As politics and finance increasingly focused on oil and the proposed Baku–Tbilisi–Ceyhan pipeline after 2000, Mayis started raising major concerns about the real impacts on Azerbaijan. 'Everybody kept talking about how we would become Dubai, and that the pipeline would bring freedom and riches. But it was a pipedream! This is a phrase in English, no?' He giggles at his own joke. 'Instead we just get an ugly bridge that cost one billion dollars!'

Being outspoken about the pipeline was a courageous step, especially for someone without a long-running political party or major NGO to back him up. Pretty much everybody in Baku 'civil society' was forcefully enthusiastic about the Western oil developments, with newspapers across the board denouncing anyone who was critical as a foreigner or a traitor. Even those opposed to the regime supported the pipeline, arguing it would boost Azerbaijan's prospects against Armenia and bring greater employment and freedom. The powerful knew they would become richer, while the poor hoped they would get one of the promised jobs. Searching for allies, Mayis made contact with those raising critiques in Georgia, Turkey and beyond; so began our friendship with him. On this journey, Mayis will be our guide in Azerbaijan as we travel beyond Baku.

He no longer lives in the bungalow that is the Green Party offices, but with his wife and children outside the city. He explains how his garden makes him happy. 'I have sixty trees, including apricots. Every morning I rise at six so I can spend an hour in my garden, working, before I come to work. I'm here at the office at nine. And each evening, I leave at six so I can spend an hour in my garden before dinner. I think all people need to have possibility to touch the soil, touch the earth.'

Indeed, Mayis looks blissfully happy in a photograph Mika took in autumn 2005 in Turkey: pitch-forking hay in a meadow, smiling broadly, still smartly dressed. 'These rich oil people don't know what it's like to work with your hands from six in the morning until ten at night. But I'm from a village, not from Baku. My manner is not of the city.'

Mayis's office is reminiscent of dissidents' homes in 1980s Eastern Europe: the wooden floor, painted a deep brown, and covered with a mass-produced Persian rug; the walls lined with a grubby brown patterned wallpaper and, along one side, a large Formica dresser stacked two-deep with books in Russian, Azeri and English.

'I feel for the refugees from the green fields of Nagorno-Karabakh who have been squatting in Binəgədi for fifteen years. They are from the countryside, and now they are stuck in poverty and terrible conditions in this city.' Mayis explains that in the early 1990s thousands of refugees from the war zone settled across Baku in uncompleted concrete structures and decaying tenements without walls. Many communities, still without connections to electricity or gas mains, run their own cables from local electricity substations to their rooms, and cook on electric heaters. Ever resourceful and recognising they are not one of the ruling elite's priorities, the refugees have also constructed their own pipes to siphon sewage and refuse out of their 'apartments' and into the basements. Even when piped water was installed, the networks still often did not work, and many are forced to buy supplies from water trucks.[22]

Despite government claims of a booming economy, Mayis insists that between 20 and 25 per cent of the population remain below the poverty line. 'The government and state institutions point to growing GDP levels as an indicator of falling poverty. Yes, average income has increased, but so have prices.' Overall, there has been no improvement in the real incomes or social welfare level of the population.[23] The scarcity of jobs and resources also exacerbates tensions between the refugees and longer-term Baku residents.[24]

Mayis explains how 'cement trucks and architects came to Binəgədi to build luxurious houses for the new rich. The refugees' homes ruined their view, so the police began to evict people, but they resisted.' Later, after our visit, when the authorities displaced more refugees to make way for a new underground station as part of the gentrification process, the refugees protested. They demonstrated outside the president's Palace and fifty of them were taken away by the police in special buses.[25]

---

22   *Azerbaijan: IDPs Still Trapped in Poverty and Dependence*, Internal Displacement Monitoring Centre (Geneva), 2008.

23   Aslanli, 'Oil and Gas Revenues Management'.

24   A. Balayev, 'Oil Producing Villages: Ethnography, History and Sociology', in L. Alieva, *The Baku Oil and Local Communities: A History*, CNIS (Baku), 2009, p. 203.

25   'Residents of Binagadi Staged Protest Action in Front of the Presidential Administration, azerireport.com, 30 August 2010.

Mayis leans forward on his desk and concludes, 'But despite everything, people haven't given up. The history of oil in Baku shows that things change. This city has been at the forefront of history before, inspiring people, so who says that won't happen again?'

SAHIL PARK, BAKU, AZERBAIJAN

We have arrived here several months too late. In January 2009, the park in central Baku that we are standing in was a building site, as Baku City Authority workers demolished its stone and ceramic centrepiece, the 'Memorial to the Twenty-Six Commissars'. The monument, with its eternal flame fuelled by a natural gas vent, had gained an iconic status in the Soviet Union: visited by foreign dignitaries and school classes, adorned with flowers by newlyweds. The corpses of the commissars, killed with the collusion of the British Army, had been reburied here six months after the city fell to the Red Army in 1920. The poet Vladimir Mayakovsky boldly wrote: 'The blood of the twenty-six shall never cool – never!'

Yet 'never' came to pass; as the USSR disintegrated the memorial was vandalised, and the flame snuffed out. Now, nineteen years after Azerbaijan declared independence, the monument has been broken up and the skeletons excavated amid a blizzard of contradictory reports. Azeri nationalists claimed that the remains of only twenty-two corpses were found, and that these bones showed that the commissars of Armenian descent were never present, including the leader of the Baku Commune: Stepan Shaumian.

A week after the 1917 October Revolution in Petrograd, the Baku Commune seized power, led by Shaumian. The oilfields were quickly nationalised, for the Soviet was eager to put the vast resources controlled by the Nobels, Rothschilds and Shell, and by other oil barons, at the disposal of the worker's state. It was the world's first nationalisation of an oil industry.

The Tsarist Empire, which had ruled Baku for over a century, had imploded, and everything was in flux. The Bolsheviks struggled to hold the city, but were perceived to be aligned with the Armenians and Christians against the Muslims and Azeris. After the Bolsheviks disarmed some Muslim cavalry troops returning to Baku on the ship *Evelina* in March 1918, a vicious conflict broke out in which thousands of Muslim civilians were killed by Bolshevik and Armenian forces.

World War I was still raging, and the German and Ottoman empires were desperate to obtain Baku's oil. Following the October Revolution, the Tsarist Front in Turkey collapsed, and the sultan's Ottoman army advanced towards Baku. But the British were determined to stop the oil from reaching German hands, and themselves had designs on the Caspian oil industry. In London, the War Cabinet decided to deploy a British expeditionary force from Persia, in a seaborne attack on Baku. In the summer of 1918, British troops – known as

'Dunsterforce' after their commander Major General Lionel Dunsterville – briefly backed the anti-Soviet Centro-Caspian Dictatorship that had overthrown Shaumian's Baku Soviet, and imprisoned the commissars.[26]

It was now, with Baku under temporary British control, that the twenty-six commissars escaped from prison, taking a ship across the Caspian to Turkmenistan. But this region was also nominally under British control, and when the twenty-six were executed the Bolsheviks blamed the British. As Fitzroy Maclean reported while spying in 1938, 'the Soviet authorities have never ceased to do everything they could to keep alive the memory of the Allied intervention, and while I was in Baku elaborate preparations were being made for the celebration of the twentieth anniversary of the death of the Twenty-six Commissars'.[27] By the 1990s, generations of Baku children had learned about Britain's imperial aggression in the region. Throughout the country, the martyred commissars were memorialised in statues, streets and the names of oilfields. But now Britain has returned, the '26 Commissars' offshore field has been renamed 'Azeri', and the monument dismantled.

We turn and walk through the streets of high buildings that echo Bucharest or Paris, thinking of the world before those chaotic years at the end of World War I – the world described in *Ali and Nino*:

> Outside the Old wall was the Outer Town, with wide streets, high houses, its people noisy and greedy for money. This Outer Town was built because of the oil that comes from our desert and brings riches. There were theatres, schools, hospitals, libraries, policemen and beautiful women with naked shoulders. If there was shooting in the Outer Town it was always about money.[28]

James begins to tell a story of a set of photographs that he has seen, which left a strong impression on him. The images show a military parade in Tbilisi, Georgia, in February 1919. The marching troops must be the forces of the Menshevik Republic of Georgia, and there are soldiers among the crowd wearing British uniforms. The pictures were taken by his grandfather. In August 1917 Rowland Marriott signed up to fight in the army of the king and empire. He was the youngest of five brothers. Fred and Digby had already been killed at Ypres in France. Rowley never thought he would outlive the war.

However, against expectations, he was not sent to the trenches of the Western Front, but to the relative calm of the southern Balkans. The night before the Allies' 'big push', the Bulgarian Army mutinied, and the sky lit up as they

---

26   See L. C. Dunsterville, *Adventures of Dunsterforce*, Edward Arnold, 1920.
27   F. Maclean, *Eastern Approaches*, Jonathan Cape, 1949, p. 34.
28   Said, *Ali and Nino*, p. 24.

detonated their ammunition dumps. A few days later, Ottoman and British forces signed an armistice. But the war was not entirely over. Rowley's battalion was ordered to head east.

Forty thousand troops steamed across the Black Sea to Batumi, and then boarded trains on the oil railway to Tbilisi. Rowley passed that winter, spring and summer in the Caucasus, before returning to his widowed and bereaved mother in Leicestershire. It is a military expedition almost forgotten in England, but our Georgian friends know it well. All that remains in James's family are the photographs.

It is likely that Rowley was in Tbilisi on 23 July 1919, when Lance Corporal Stell wrote to his own mother: 'Dear Mother, hope this card finds you in the very best of good health as I am at present . . . We are cleaning and polishing all day long. We are not here to put down Bolshevism, but to guard British capital sunk in the oil fields.'[29]

Minutes from ministerial meetings in Whitehall show that Lance Corporal Stell was right. The eastern committee of the War Cabinet was intent on securing the British military's energy interests – after all, the Allies were seen as having floated to victory on a wave of oil.[30] Notes from a meeting in December 1918 show Lord Curzon insisting: 'The idea that the Azerbaijanis, the Armenians or the Bolsheviks could permanently hold Baku and control the vast resource there is one that cannot be entertained for a moment.' Others in the committee suggested that Baku should be given to the French, but a paper by the General Staff declared: 'From the military point of view it would be most undesirable for the approaches to India . . . which converge at Batum, to be placed at the disposal of an ambitious military power [France] which, although friendly to us at the moment, is our historical world rival.'[31]

In a subsequent meeting, Foreign Secretary Arthur Balfour and Lord Curzon planned the future of the Caucasus:

Mr Balfour: 'Of course the Caucasus would be much better governed under our aegis than it would be under French aegis. But why should it not be mis-governed?'

Lord Curzon: 'That is the other alternative – let them cut each other's throats.'

Mr Balfour: 'I'm in favour of that. We will only protect Batum, Baku, the railway between them and the pipeline.'[32]

---

29   Stell documents in Imperial War Museum, Misc 204, Item 2972, quoted in M. Hudson, *Intervention in Russia, 1918–1920: A Cautionary Tale*, Leo Cooper, 2004, p. 129.
30   F. Venn, *Oil Diplomacy in the Twentieth Century*, Palgrave Macmillan, 1986, p. 35.
31   Quoted in Hudson, *Intervention in Russia*, p, 130.
32   Ibid.; S. Abilov, 'Historical Development of the Azerbaijan Oil Industry and the Role of Azerbaijan in Today's European Energy Security', *Journal of Eurasian Studies* 2: 3 (2010).

ISTIGLALIYYAT STREET, BAKU, AZERBAIJAN

The traffic flows thick and fast along the dusty street of Istiglaliyyat – Independence – that arcs around the walls of the Old Town, past the Baki Soveti metro station. We are looking for the building that housed the parliament of the original Azerbaijani Democratic Republic in 1919. We have a black-and-white image of the interior showing men in dark suits, most with a moustache and fez, and a window. Precisely what the outside of the building looked like is hard to determine, but we know it is in this area.

While the debates in Whitehall ebbed and flowed, things moved rapidly in the Caucasus. Less than three weeks after the Turkish Armistice, British troops under Major General William Thompson occupied Baku on 17 November 1918, four months after Dunsterforce retreated. Thompson proclaimed martial law and declared himself military governor. He privatised the oil and shipping industries that had been nationalised by the Baku Soviet and set up a labour control office, using his soldiers to break a general strike.

Political authority was informally divided between the British command and the Musavat government of the Azerbaijani Democratic Republic, which espoused a secular Muslim, Azeri nationalist and socialist politics and introduced universal suffrage ten years before Britain. Yet, in reality, Baku was controlled by Britain, a country that neither recognised Azerbaijan's independence nor was sympathetic to its claims.[33]

When the parliament tried to open in December 1918, Thompson sent his soldiers to blockade the very building we are searching for. Britain continued to intervene in the shaping of the Azeri economy: when the Azeri government invited US corporation Standard Oil to pitch for a contract to control six months of oil shipments from Baku, Thompson intervened to derail the deal in favour of the British–Dutch company Royal Dutch Shell.

Despite the limitations on their governing power, the Musavat leaders were supportive of the British military presence in Baku. For even as they took control over their capital in May 1918, the Azeri nationalists faced a diverse population of Russian, Armenian and Muslim workers, many of whom had undergone a long socialist education, participating in the strikes and struggles of 1904 and beyond. Bolshevism, with its role in past victories for workers' rights, had deep roots in Baku. This meant that Musavat was never fully secure in the city, and relied on foreign powers – first the Ottomans and then the British – 'to back them against the Reds'.[34]

In London the fate of Azerbaijan was wrapped up in the wider debate over the British intervention against the Bolsheviks. The White Russian armies with which Britain was allied suffered repeated defeats and the intervention, coming so soon

---

33   C. King, *The Ghost of Freedom*, OUP, 2008, p. 168.
34   R. Suny, *Revenge of the Past*, Stanford University Press, 1993, p. 42.

after the Great War, was unpopular in England. The discussion over the Caucasus was finally resolved, and in August 1919 British troops evacuated Baku, withdrawing up the railway line to Batumi. They left the Musavat government barely clinging to power for another eight months, before it capitulated to the Red Army's invasion in April 1920.

The oilfields were transferred back into public control, and the oil barons and bourgeoisie fled to İstanbul, Paris or Berlin – among them Lev Nussimbaum and his father. There was a revolutionary ecstasy of redistribution in Baku, with its vision of the downfall of the rich and the meek reclaiming what was theirs. From it was born the first permanently nationalised oil industry, and a state claiming to act in the name of the workers.

With its vital strategic resource, its long radical history and its large industrial proletariat, Baku was extremely important in the early Soviet Union. The fifth anniversary of the October Revolution, on 7 November 1922, was celebrated in spectacular style. Arseny Avraamov's *Symphony of Factory Sirens* was performed across the city, using the foghorns of the entire Soviet Caspian fleet, all the factory sirens of Baku, artillery guns, seaplanes, bus horns and a huge cast of choirs. Conductors stood on specially built towers signalling the different sound units with coloured flags and pistol shots. A 'steam-whistle machine' and enormous bands pounded out the 'Internationale' as noisy trucks raced across Baku for a gigantic sound finale.

Shell, Standard Oil and the Anglo-Persian Oil Company were outraged to lose control over their investments in Baku. They tried a number of legal and political strategies to regain their expropriated assets but, despite a desperate need for foreign currency, the Soviet government held fast. The only concrete deals between the Soviets and the Western industry were similar to present-day 'technical service contracts' – agreements whereby private companies complete specific projects but do not gain control over the oil resources themselves. These kinds of deals were absolutely not what was desired by the major corporations, for whom ownership rights over oilfields were fundamental to their *raison d'être*.

Following the interruptions of the war and revolution, the Oil Road was gradually re-established. The oil wells of Baku were repaired, a new Baku–Batumi pipeline was put into service and refined product was sold on to the world market so successfully that it could compete with Western corporations in their home countries. The Soviet marketing company sold £500,000 of fuel in Britain in 1924, and by 1929 it was selling eight times that amount. By May 1932, Basil Jackson of Anglo-Persian wrote that the market for oil in Europe 'had during the past 12 months been taken away entirely from the American companies by the Russians and the Rumanians'.[35]

---

35   J. Bamberg, *The History of the British Petroleum Company, Volume 2: The Anglo-Iranian Years, 1928–1954*, CUP, 1994, p. 113.

The Soviet nationalisation of one of the key oil-producing regions in the world marked a paradigm shift in the industry. For the first time since mechanical wells had been drilled at Bibi Heybat and Pennsylvania, a substantial section of the oil industry was to be run not for private profit but for the benefit of the state. Not only was the political world divided in two, between socialism and capitalism, between a new East and a new West; so too was the oil industry, between one focused on generating income for private investors and another focused on generating income for the state.

This division within the industry has outlived the division within political ideology. Whereas the number of self-proclaimed socialist states has dwindled since 1989, the percentage of global oil reserves in the hands of state companies has rapidly increased. Yet the person who led the first government to nationalise an oil industry, Stepan Shaumian, is now almost forgotten, even in his home city of Baku.

NACAFQULU RAFIYEV STREET, BAKU, AZERBAIJAN

After looking for the 1918 parliamentary building, we catch a taxi and hurry across the city towards the former Black Town, past the terminal for ferries to Turkmenistan and along Nobel Prospekti. For we have a meeting with 'the invisible father of the BTC pipeline', and are keen to learn more about the motivations of Azerbaijan in offering its oil to Western companies in the early 1990s. There are some echoes in the negotiations between the Azeri government and Shell and of those with Standard Oil in 1919. Will events pre-dating the Soviet Union shed light on events following it?

Sabit Bagirov led the State Oil Company of Azerbaijan, SOCAR, through the negotiations with the Western oil companies in 1992 and 1993, and now works for foreign corporations through his consultancy, the FAR Centre for Economic and Political Research. He has invited us to meet him in his office on the first floor of a shabby house on Nacafqulu Rafiyev Street. We find ourselves amid shelves piled high with neatly ordered books and files, cramming the corridor and several rooms.

A secretary brings us tea as we sit round a table and listen to Sabit's story. He tells us how negotiations began in 1989, when Azerbaijan was still part of the Soviet Union. Moscow felt more investment was needed to exploit the oil in the depths of the Caspian, and the foreign companies were eager – excited about perestroika, the developed local oil infrastructure and large offshore resources.

Gorbachev's waning power led inexorably to the official end of the USSR on 31 December 1991. Azerbaijan was by now independent, and the last head of the Azeri Communist Party, Ayas Mutalibov, had become its first independent president since 1920. Despite John Browne's threat in June 1991 – 'If we don't have a deal in three months, we're out of there' – BP had stayed on. But negotiations were slow, and the battles between the oil corporations were ferocious. BP tried to woo officials with a trip to London, and in a visit to Baku by British Foreign Office minister Douglas Hogg in March 1992, the UK agreed to formal diplomatic relations. Rival companies tried similar tactics: Unocal took the Azeris to California and then Bangkok, where they were given 'a couple of days to get their legs out from under them' before seeing Unocal's Thailand fields.[36]

Sabit picks up the narrative, describing how negotiations accelerated after the now-nationalist Popular Front came to power in June 1992. Mutalibov had been ousted in a coup led by the Azeri 'Grey Wolves', which took control of the parliament and the state radio and television building. Three months later Abulfaz Elchibey of the Popular Front was elected president. Sabit himself became the new head of SOCAR, due to his role in the Popular Front and his understanding of the oil sector, having worked as an engineer for a machinery company.

With the new government in place, BP needed to make moves to outstrip its commercial rivals. In July 1992 Sir David Simon, the new CEO, met Prime Minister John Major to ask for British government support. With more oil companies beginning to muscle in on Baku's oil wealth, BP was worried about being pushed out. An important strategy involved visibly aligning the company with the British government. Although Britain had established diplomatic relations with Azerbaijan, there was at this point no British embassy in Baku, with most matters being dealt with via Moscow. With spare space in its newly acquired downtown offices, BP partitioned off an area to be used by British government representatives, and raised a British diplomatic flag outside. Although BP was then a private company, Browne claimed that it 'was essential for us to be closely aligned with the UK government, as post-Soviet countries still found it easier to understand and accept government-to-government dealings'.[37]

Sabit is clearly proud of the role he played in SOCAR, but seems impatient with our questions, spinning his glasses on the red felt tablecloth, until we ask whether he was in office when Margaret Thatcher came to town in September 1992. His eyes light up, and he becomes animated. 'Yes, I met her. I even have a picture with her. But I won't show it to you. I was informed by the BP representative in Baku about her visit. Then I informed President Elchibey.' Thatcher was being brought in to witness the signing of a memorandum of understanding between SOCAR and BP on the Chirag oil and Shah Deniz gas field.

Thatcher's brief visit was the first by such a senior Western politician to Baku. Twenty years later it is hard to appreciate how much this meant to the young Azeri government. No matter that she had resigned as prime minister nearly two years previously and was no longer even a member of parliament. The British Foreign

36 Levine, *The Oil and the Glory*, p. 159.
37 Browne, *Beyond Business*, p. 156.

Office had proposed that the then trade minister, Michael Heseltine, should attend the signing ceremony, but the Azeris were unimpressed. Thatcher, however, was a different proposition. Browne later explained that in order to get President Elchibey to favour BP over other companies, BP invited Margaret Thatcher. 'Fiercely anti-communist, she was delighted to be asked.'[38] Browne's advisor Nick Butler was sent to accompany her on a flight from Hong Kong to Azerbaijan, and as they approached Baku she told him 'in straightforward terms that if [the Azeris] weren't ready to sign [the deal] she wouldn't leave [Baku]'.[39]

As Thatcher handed Elchibey two cheques totalling $30 million, Browne achieved his aim, impressing the Azeris such as Sabit and thereby sealing the first contract.[40] An FCO internal memo two weeks later titled 'The Baroness in Baku' celebrated the trip as a success: 'BP has done very well in securing exclusive rights . . . Our efforts in organizing Lady Thatcher's visit at such short notice were clearly worthwhile – with proper programming/targeting Lady Thatcher clearly remains a formidable foreign policy weapon for UK Ltd!'[41]

The letter describes how President Elchibey not only admired Thatcher, 'but seems something of a groupie! From what she told me of their private talk they spent most of the time talking about freedom and the fight against communism.' Thatcher promised numerous scholarships to Britain, and support in regaining national treasures from Moscow – causing her British diplomatic escort some embarrassment. The memo concludes, with names redacted, 'When she was in full flood I whispered to BLANK that BLANK could hardly have made the point better. He kindly offered me £5.00 if I would repeat this comment to Lady Thatcher afterwards.'[42]

This initial contract was not published at the time, nor were its details ever released, apart from a $30 million payment by BP to an Azeri government then at the height of its war with Armenia. Thus we are more than a little surprised when Sabit adds proudly: 'As president of SOCAR, I signed the Memorandum. John Browne signed it for BP. I kept it in case I'd need to refer to it in the future. The pdf is on my computer. You can see it, but I won't give it to you, as I might publish it in a book sometime.'

To our eager nods, Sabit passes his laptop across the table. And there it is: BP and Statoil's first contract with Azerbaijan. Mika skim-reads it quickly, trying to

---

38 Ibid.

39 N. Butler, 'Energy: The Changing World Order', bp.com, 5 July 2006.

40 D. Morgan and D. Ottaway, 'Azerbaijan's Riches Alter the Chessboard', *Washington Post*, 4 October 1998.

41 FCO, 'Letter: The Baroness in Baku – AGI/FOI 10', 24 September 1992, obtained through FOIA.

42 FCO, 'With the Baroness in Baku – AG1/FO1 9', September 1992, obtained through FOIA.

memorise as much as possible. A four-page memorandum, it details initial development plans, a promise to construct an export pipeline, and the companies' exclusive right to negotiate future contracts. Just above the signatures, it reads: 'In the British tradition of supporting development of democracy and as appreciation of the recent democratic achievement of the Government of Azerbaijan', BP 'will pay $90 million' to the Azeri government. So it seems that the $30 million cheque was just an initial payment.

Sabit explains that, with the Popular Front leadership desperate to bring in foreign companies, signing a major contract like this was his main priority at SOCAR. The war was devastating the Azeri budget, and contract 'bonuses' were seen as a key source of quick income, while deals with foreign oil companies were a means of building strategic alliances. Across the former Soviet Union, budget problems, instability and high inflation were causing non-payment of wages and pensions, which in turn fuelled political unrest. Developing the giant offshore fields at speed looked to require significant capital and technology not available locally.

Sabit, however, does not draw conclusions about the oil corporations' use of their negotiating strengths and the tactics employed by Browne. From November 1990 until Thatcher's visit two years later, Azeri governments tried to settle on a contract with a foreign company that would not be biased in the company's favour. But three months into the Elchibey presidency, the war, the collapse of the Soviet Union, and perhaps that extra British diplomatic pressure meant that, as the FCO internal memo noted, 'By any normal commercial standards BP has done very well in securing exclusive rights.'[43]

It was a perfect illustration of the use of the British foreign policy machinery by a private oil corporation – echoing Shell and General Thompson's close cooperation in 1919. Notes of a 1993 meeting between Foreign Secretary Douglas Hurd and BP directors sum up the relationship neatly: '[Hurd] emphasised that there were some parts of the world, such as Azerbaijan and Colombia, where the most important British interest was BP's operation. In those countries he was keen to ensure that our efforts intertwined effectively with BP's.'[44] With Thatcher's visit, a 'British' company had beaten the American oil companies to it, just as it had back in 1919.

But BP's lead position was not as secure as it seemed. Amoco still had some hold on the Azeri field and, after a year of pushing, the Americans made headway with their demand for 'unitising' the offshore fields. In May 1993 SOCAR,

43   FCO, 'Letter: The Baroness in Baku – AGI/FOI 10', 24 September 1992, obtained through FOIA.
44   FCO, 'Minutes: Call on the Secretary of State by the Chairman and Chief Executive of British Petroleum – HF/FOI 68', 2 December 1993, obtained through FOIA.

under Sabit, demanded that the Azeri, Chirag and Gunashli fields should be considered as one unit – called ACG. Deals pending for the three distinct areas held by BP, Amoco and Pennzoil were to be subsumed under a new arrangement for a single field. Now the struggle would be over who held the largest percentage share.

On 11 June Elchibey initialled a deal to develop ACG with the consortium of BP, Statoil, Amoco, TPAO, Unocal, McDermott and Pennzoil. He also agreed a 'signing bonus' of $210 million, with an initial payment of $70 million to be transferred before the official ceremony scheduled to be held in London on 30 June. On behalf of the Azeri state, SOCAR received a 30 per cent share in ACG – substantially worse than the 50/50 split that had been proposed in the bid for the Azeri field submitted by BP in March 1991, over two years before.

But the process was still not over. As Sabit explains, 'Just as we were coming very close to signing the final contract and Elchibey was to travel to London, there was a new coup. The Popular Front was overthrown. Heydar Aliyev became the new leader of the country and suspended the negotiation process.'

An armed uprising in Gəncə, Azerbaijan's second city, had given Heydar Aliyev the opportunity he needed. This, according to official government rhetoric, is when Aliyev 'saved the nation'; the date is celebrated with an annual public holiday: Salvation Day. In the space of ten days, he faced down the rebellion in Gəncə, was elected speaker of parliament, and awarded himself 'extraordinary powers' over Azerbaijan.[45] As Browne later wrote, 'I was in Baku at the time and events were dramatic . . . Troops were within a few miles of Baku at one point.'[46] As the threat of conflict loomed, Browne and other oil executives fled to Turkey, and then agonised as to whether to pay the planned initial 'signing bonus'. Desperate to ensure the contract was signed, they did so, even though they did not know who would get the money. But Aliyev cancelled the contract and scrapped the ceremony. The $70 million were never seen again.[47]

Browne described how Aliyev's coup made him even more focused on winning the prize. 'The risks of investing in Azerbaijan were clear. But so too was the size of the prize. If there was going to be a deal, BP had to be the participant with the largest share.'[48] The *Sunday Times*, apparently relying on a Turkish secret service report, even went so far as to allege that BP had backed the coup. 'As a result of our intelligence efforts, it has been understood that two petrol giants, BP and Amoco, British and American respectively . . . are behind the coup d'état carried out against Elchibey in 1993.' A Turkish agent apparently described how he had met

---

45   de Waal, *Black Garden*, pp. 293–4.
46   Browne, *Beyond Business*, p. 158.
47   Levine, *The Oil and the Glory*, pp. 172–3.
48   Browne, *Beyond Business*, p. 158.

with BP executives to discuss an 'arms-for-oil' deal. He said the company had contact with intermediaries who arranged for the supply of arms to Heydar Aliyev.[49] But the story did not stand up – BP denied any involvement, and the article was removed from the *Sunday Times* website.

Following the coup and the cancelling of the deal with Elchibey, negotiations resumed between the companies and the state. The Azeri team had changed. As Sabit recalls, 'I resigned as the head of SOCAR, as I didn't think I could work under Heydar. After bringing in some European consultants at first, he took a closer grip on the issue himself and appointed his son Ilham as the vice-president of SOCAR.'

The oil companies were concerned that Heydar Aliyev would be loyal to his Soviet roots. But they soon recognised in him a skilful and wily politician who brought the 'stability' they desired.[50] After three years of negotiating amid an array of different social forces – the president, political parties, SOCAR officials and popular movements – it suited Western business to have one concentrated centre of power with whom to deal: Heydar Aliyev. A 'one-stop shop' had been established.

Aliyev's priority, like Elchibey's, was to bind Azerbaijan into a web of political alliances that could ensure its independence and bring about an end to the war with Armenia, using the ACG contract and foreign visits to bolster this position. In February 1994, BP pressure helped ensure that he was in the UK meeting Prime Minister John Major and Foreign Secretary Douglas Hurd, and signing a 'declaration on friendship and cooperation' between Azerbaijan and Great Britain.[51]

By early 1994 the oil companies had consolidated their forces, and were negotiating in unison across the table from Heydar's son Ilham Aliyev. By May the final details were being hammered out on the fifth floor of Amoco's Houston offices over late-night pizza. Whatever the truth of the rumours of bribes and support for coups, when the contract was finally signed in September 1994, BP and Amoco shared equal largest stakes, with BP chosen to head the consortium as Operator. Meanwhile SOCAR's share had dropped again – down to 20 per cent. Those five years of haggling since May 1989 had seen the Azeri state's slice of the oil developments drop from half to one-fifth.[52]

---

49   *Sunday Times*, 26 March 2000 – no longer available on website, but referenced at network54.com.

50   J. Hemming, *The Implications of the Revival of the Oil Industry in Azerbaijan*, Centre for Middle Eastern and Islamic Studies, University of Durham, 1998.

51   BP had been encouraging the Foreign Office to invite Aliyev since Chairman David Simon had met Foreign Secretary Douglas Hurd three months earlier.

52   N. Sagheb and M. Javadi, 'Azerbaijan's "Contract of the Century" Finally Signed with Western Oil Consortium', *Azerbaijan International* 2: 4 (1994).

The grandiose title given to the deal, the 'Contract of the Century', suited all the signatories. It is still used today, yet few ask for *whom* it was the contract of the century – for the Azeri people, for the Aliyev clan, or for the oil corporations who had signed an immensely profitable deal and gained control over a major new resource base?

The backdrop to these negotiations was harrowing. While oil executives were meeting in Baku hotels, the Azeri army was retreating across the fields and Baku was filling with a flood of refugees from the fighting in Nagorno-Karabakh.

The Armenian forces achieved dominance, establishing a land corridor between Armenia proper and the conflict zone. Massacres were committed by both sides. By 1993, the Armenian military established a so-called 'buffer zone' much larger than Nagorno-Karabakh, occupying some 20 per cent of Azerbaijan, from which over a million local residents were forcibly expelled. But by spring 1994 the fighting had reached a stalemate, with Azeri forces unable to drive back the entrenched Armenians.[53]

The war is generally described through the lens of inevitability and 'ethnic conflict', both by local and foreign commentators. Yet it did not start because one ethnic group decided to attack another. It was more about controlling territory, and leaders advancing their personal ambitions, than about 'questions of history, identity or national destiny'.[54] Either way, it had a profound effect on the oil negotiations.

By the time the 'Contract of the Century' was signed in September 1994, a shaky ceasefire had been in place for only eighteen weeks, and Azerbaijan had effectively lost one-fifth of its officially recognised territory. Aliyev announced that oil would provide the means to recover the lost lands. Revenues would be channelled towards building up and modernising the Azeri army until it was able to defeat the occupying Armenian forces.

Sabit remains a supporter of the oil-extraction plan, and is clearly proud of his part in having made it a reality – despite the fact that by the time it was signed he had been moved to an academic position. He argues that when Aliyev agreed to the contract, the increased risks enabled the companies to 'put forward more tight claims', due to the unstable political situation.[55]

But these 'tight claims' do not matter to Sabit, who says 'the main thing was that the deal was signed', and that what matters is 'how the oil profits are handled,

---

53   de Waal, *Black Garden*, p. 237.

54   King, *Ghost of Freedom*, p. 219.

55   This is backed up by other analysts, who point out that Heydar Aliyev prioritised securing strong international allies and a ready source of hard currency, intertwining foreign commercial and state interests with Azerbaijan's fate. See, for example, Hoffman, 'Azerbaijan: The Politicization of Oil'.

not our share of oil'. In other words, the contract should be supported because of its geopolitical role, not because it was necessarily a 'fair deal' over its thirty-year lifetime. In a historical parallel with the Musavat government's reliance on the British in 1918, the new Azeri regime was again mortgaging itself to foreign powers to maintain its existence.

4 LOTS OF EMPTY SKYSCRAPERS THAT WE CAN'T KEEP CLEAN

VILLA PETROLEA, BAYIL, BAKU, AZERBAIJAN

Finally, we are on our way to meet BP at their Azerbaijan headquarters. Running south beyond the president's Palace and SOFAZ in its dark glass tower, Neftçilər Prospekti follows the Caspian shore towards Bayıl. Set apart from the body of the city and perched on a rocky promontory jutting out into Baki Buxtasi, this district has its own distinct history as a naval dockyard and a prison quarter.

After the long walk through the dust and trucks of the main road, we are in need of a cup of coffee before our meeting, so we stop off at the Cottage Café which, as its English name suggests, is the preserve of expats: its menu lists shepherd's pie and fish and chips.

Across the road, behind a high wall and a spartan courtyard with carefully tended plants, stands Villa Petrolea. This is not Ludvig Nobel's estate with the watered shrubs above Baku's Black Town, but the current home of BP Azerbaijan, named after Nobel's nineteenth-century residence. This symbolism of corporate inheritance is evoked repeatedly. The inaugural meeting of the Azerbaijan International Operating Company in 1995 was held in the mansion built by the oil baron Zeynalabin Taghiyev. There is a strong underlying narrative here: the Western companies have returned to what is rightfully theirs after a seventy-year Soviet usurpation.

An armed guard stands at the entrance, above which fly the BP and Azeri flags. Much of the conquest of the Caspian seabed, and the accompanying restructuring of the Azeri economy and society over the past decade, has been directed from inside these walls. While government institutions appear ostentatious or intimidating, the oil company's headquarters in Azerbaijan are surprisingly discreet.

In the lobby, we watch a stream of staff and contractors flow through the turnstile, clean-shaven men in shirtsleeves and chinos. Placards mounted on the walls announce various 'employees of the month', alongside a sign advertising puppies for sale. The plasterwork on the stucco ceiling has a relief of hammers and sickles, which gives credence to the story that this was once a building connected to the

Soviet navy. A previous visitor commented: 'On the walls behind the security barrier, official Soviet five-year plan announcements have been replaced by BP advertisement posters.'[1]

ST JAMES'S SQUARE, LONDON, ENGLAND

To build the infrastructure of the Azeri–Chirag–Gunashli platforms, to suck crude from deep beneath the Caspian and to ship it to consumers across the world is a monumental undertaking. This shifting of matter around the planet takes place fundamentally for one reason: not social development, but profit. Ultimately BP, like the enterprises of Taghiyev or Nobel, is engaged in the extraction of crude only because the company can generate major returns on the capital invested. If BP could not make money out of oil they would not search for it, extract it and sell it.

Like all British public limited companies, the holders of BP's capital are its stockholders, who invest in the company by purchasing shares. BP's size and track record are such that it represents about 9 per cent of all shares traded on the London Stock Exchange, and thus is found in most broad-based investment portfolios. According to UK company law, BP's directors must aim to maximise the long-term return on their shareholders' investment. This is the directors' primary obligation. Although a recent British law states that this should be done 'with regard to' the interests of employees, communities and the environment, the stockholders' interests come first. For BP cannot function without the support of its shareholders. If the latter were all to sell their investments, the share price would crash. On the other hand, if the company were to fail and the shares became valueless, shareholders would lose their capital. So the company and its stockholders are locked in a tight embrace of mutual dependence.

BP is a global company. But although its 19 billion shares are held across the world, the bulk of them are controlled by a mere 150 institutions in just a few cities. These institutions are the asset owners – they own the asset of BP. They then entrust the decisions over their shares to firms of 'asset managers'. Just twelve of these asset management firms oversee the dominant portion of BP's stock, and all but one of the twelve are based in London. They include three pension funds, two insurance companies, a bank and five unit trusts.[2] In each of these firms only a handful of

---

1   Kleveman, *The New Great Game*, p. 65.
2   Data from Thomson's – December 2008. In the UK: 1. Legal and General Invest Management, Ltd, 2. M&G Invest Management, Ltd, 3. Capital World Investors, 4. Barclays Global Investors (UK), 5. Scottish Widows Investment Partnership, Ltd, 6. Insight Investment Management (Global), Ltd, 7. Standard Life Investments, Ltd, 8. Capital Research Global Investors, 9. AXA Investment Managers UK, Ltd, 10. Threadneedle Asset Management, Ltd, 11. Aviva Investors Global Services, Ltd; and in the US: 12. State Street Global Advisors (US).

managers are engaged with thinking about the oil industry. Perhaps less than fifty people across the world are involved with the key decisions around BP's shares at any one time. These managers are theoretically bound by their own obligations to maximise the interests of the millions of savers, pension fund beneficiaries and insurance policy holders whose money they are investing.

The asset managers in these institutions have to make judgements on a wide array of stocks and shares, and so are guided by internal advisors. For example, at Insight Investment, the asset managers might ask for advice on social issues from Rory Sullivan, Insight's director of investor responsibility, whom we met on Old Broad Street in The City. They are also guided by external analysts, specialists in the London oil markets. These analysts are mostly attached to banks, and advise the asset managers on whether to 'buy', 'sell' or 'hold' BP shares. They claim to watch the company like hawks, observing its successes and failures, and in particular studying the financial data that it publishes every three months – the Quarterly Results.

These Quarterly Results are presented to the investors and the financial press by BP's chief financial officer. Four times a year, the CFO gives a half-hour talk, keenly followed by asset managers and oil analysts sitting in BP's head offices in St James's Square in London, or listening to it on the webcast.

In spring 2009, the chief financial officer is Byron Grote. This thin American is a heavyweight on the BP board. He has been head of finance since 2002, a long tenure compared to his predecessors. A close colleague of Browne's since they worked together in Cleveland in 1986, Grote became part of Browne's 'clan' and followed him to London alongside Tony Hayward. Grote was central to the negotiations behind the 'Contract of the Century', and in encouraging investors to support BP's plans to invest $29.5 billion into Azeri offshore platforms and the export pipeline.[3] After such an expenditure of capital it is not surprising that BP designated the country a flagship 'BP Profit Centre', or that it has had an important place in Grote's PowerPoint presentations for much of the past decade. Indeed, Grote could be called, like Sabit, one of the 'invisible fathers' of this Oil Road.

Grote knows deeply the importance that the asset managers and oil analysts have for the company's financial Carbon Web. Although they are generally trusting of BP's management, without their support the company could not have made its advance into Baku. They operate in parallel with the foreign energy policy machinery of departments and embassies that we met earlier. Just as BP drew on the government ministers in the Carbon Web to win the contract in Azerbaijan, the company's advance into Baku would have been impossible without the support of financial institutions.

---

3   'BP Sinking Cash into Azerbaijan', upi.com, 2 September 2010.

At the First Quarter Results presentation of April 2009, the audience will, as ever, be keen for reassurance. We might assume that they will be concerned about Azerbaijan, for in the preceding six months all has not been well in this profit centre. In September 2008 the blowout at Central Azeri only narrowly avoided disaster, when workers spotted gas bubbling on the surface of the sea and were rapidly evacuated by helicopter. The crisis happened barely four months after full oil-extraction targets for the ACG fields were finally reached. The news of the narrow escape by all of the platform's personnel would have sent a shockwave through Villa Petrolea. In the boardroom senior staff must have gathered in an emergency conference call with directors in London – Bill Schrader, president of BP Azerbaijan, reporting via video link to CEO Tony Hayward and Grote sitting in St James's Square. Oil production on ACG was slashed by 500,000 barrels of crude per day, causing a weekly loss to income of $350 million.[4]

At the Quarterly Results presentation in St James's Square it will be Grote's task to field any questions from investors on this issue. But none will be forthcoming, as the company has downplayed the crisis on Central Azeri. An investigation by miniature submarine on the seabed found that the leak had resulted from badly executed cementing around the well head. Although this would have been crucial information to the analysts, the company kept it secret in order to maintain investors' faith in BP.[5] A year later it was precisely such bad cementing that caused the Macondo blowout in the Gulf of Mexico, leading to the destruction of 40 per cent of BP's share value in just two months.

VILLA PETROLEA, BAYIL, BAKU, AZERBAIJAN

As we wait in the lobby of Villa Petrolea, we flick through a magazine from the table beside us – the recent issue of *Horizon: The Global Publication for BP People*. There is an article celebrating ACG, entitled 'Scale of the Century': 'In Azerbaijan, aside from oil revenues, ACG has created and sustained, over six years, jobs for 15,000 Azerbaijani nationals, training them to international standards . . . The intent of the "contract of the century" was to develop the country as well as the oil.'[6]

A smartly dressed woman calls us from across the lobby. This must be Irina of the BP Azerbaijan Community Investment Programme – the CIP. She signs us in at the reception desk and we pass through the turnstile.

---

4   J. Herron, 'BP: Azeri Oil Field Partially Restarted', Dow Jones Newswires, 24 December 2008.

5   T. Bergin, *Spills and Spin: The Inside Story of BP*, Random House, 2011, p. 131.

6   H. Campbell, 'Scale of the Century', *Horizon* 1 (2009), p. 39.

We climb up three floors. The stairway is wide and airy, light pouring through large windows giving a sense of the sea nearby. Framed photographs of pipeline construction, smiling children in villages and gleaming platforms have been hung on the walls. Soon we are in a corridor on the top floor, among the offices of the senior managers. This is the space where the board of BP Azerbaijan planned and directed construction of both the later phases of those offshore edifices and the Baku–Tbilisi–Ceyhan oil pipeline. We were not expecting to have our meeting up here.

At one end of the corridor is the office of BP Azerbaijan's president, Bill Schrader. His windows look south over the dark waters of the Caspian, towards the jack-up rigs just offshore. His predecessor, David Woodward, was described as 'arguably the most powerful man in the "BP Country" of Azerbaijan. BP's position is so dominant that hardly any important government decision concerning oil is made without Woodward's (albeit unofficial) consent.' A BP spokesman once claimed that, if the company pulled out of Baku, the country would collapse overnight.[7]

Eight doors away, next to a coffee machine, is the office of Tamam Bayatly. For over a decade she has directed BP Azerbaijan's press and communications strategy, both in the country and abroad. Press, external affairs and community investment offices are all on this corridor. Their proximity to the president illustrates their importance in maintaining BP's position within Azerbaijan – what companies call their 'social licence to operate'.

Next to Schrader's office is the entrance to a conference room; beside it, a heavy steel blast-door that can be swung into place. We are joined by Irina's colleague, Aydin Gasimov. We sit across the large U-shaped table from the two of them, with our backs to the windows. Microphones and communications tech fill the table; wall-mounted display screens and clocks show the time in London, Houston, Ankara and Baku. We are in the boardroom where that emergency conference call in September 2008 must have taken place.

Irina starts into an account of BP's Community Investment Projects along the route of the pipeline and near the Sangachal terminal. As she runs through the description of objectives and outcomes, it is clear she has done this presentation many times before, her black patent three-inch heels tapping insistently against the table leg.

'We conducted a socio-economic survey to find out what the key problems are and where we could see future development interests. Then we started to lay foundations – most of these communities had never seen any development interventions before.' The programmes were outsourced to international NGOs like Save the Children and International Rescue Committee, eager to take BP's contracts. Irina explains that these aid agencies focused on 'mobilising

---

7   Kleveman, *The New Great Game*, p. 65.

communities: making them understand what community groups can do – how they can solve problems. This was about bringing people together, not constructing physical infrastructure.' Later, micro-projects included rehabilitating healthcare facilities, renovating schools and constructing kindergartens. Most of these details we have read in BP Azerbaijan's Sustainability Reports, but Irina is upfront about the company's motivations behind the CIP projects: 'The ultimate goal of community investment is to have good relations with communities – ultimately to secure BP's assets.' Like the rest of BP's investments, it is driven by Byron Grote's fiduciary duty to the shareholders.

After exploring details around pipeline monitoring and the investment programmes, we try to see if we can address some wider issues, with Aydin responding to our questions. He says that the explosion on the BTC pipeline in Turkey in August 2008 did not result in BP making financial losses. 'No, the large available storage capacity at Sangachal means that we can just export later.' But we know that if BP cannot export oil via its pipelines, then within a short period they run out of storage at the terminal and have to stop production on the platforms offshore. And if the company is unable to export its crude, it incurs further losses. We ask whether BP routed crude through Russia that month, after its second pipeline through Georgia was shut down due to the war over South Ossetia. The response is firm: 'I cannot say, I don't know – I'm not prepared to answer that one.'

When we ask about the blowout of September 2008, Aydin refers to it as a 'gas release'. We question him further about the other partners in the consortium, such as ExxonMobil and Statoil: Did they fault BP as Operator for this major technical failure? Apparently not, as 'offshore drilling is very difficult. You are drilling 5 kilometres down and you don't know what is going to happen. When something happens, it is deep underground – in the oil industry these difficult circumstances sometimes happen. But our partners understand this, so it had no impact on relationships.'[8]

Maybe sensing that we can see the gaps in his story, Aydin has become visibly more agitated, and pronounces: 'During our telephone conversation, I said we would talk about the Community Investment Projects. I did not say that we could talk about these political issues.' It is clear that neither he nor Irina are happy to stray beyond the matters covered in the Sustainability Reports. As with Grote and the investors, the company tightly controls what information it wishes to release, and what to withhold.

---

8   A year after our meeting, we discovered through the Wikileaks release of US cables that BP's partners were actually extremely critical and upset about how the company 'sought to limit information flow about this event'. US Embassy, 'Azerbaijan Income Takes a Hit as Now Short-Term Fix', 26 September 2008, released by Wikileaks and guardian.co.uk on 15 December 2010.

Rising from our chairs, we turn to look out the windows behind us before following Aydin and Irina out. The sea glimmers beneath sullen clouds. Much closer, below us, lie several rectangular grey courtyards surrounded by walls and piles of razor-wire. Two men hobble across a yard in shackles, followed by a pair of prison guards.

BAILOV PRISON, BAYIL, BAKU, AZERBAIJAN

To the Caspian

It's past midnight once again,
And again I cannot sleep, I'm restless.
It's the waters of the Caspian,
So frightening in the darkness that won't calm down.

Break down this tower with your waves –
This tower that imprisons us behind these walls.
Drown it with your waves,
This tower that keeps us behind this unbreakable spell.

What is our guilt? What have we done?
You pose the question, for they give me no right to speak.
What did we do to be ashamed of?
You pose the question, for they give me no right to speak.

Ummugulsum Sadigzade, 1937, Bailov Prison[9]

Ummugulsum, a mother of four, wrote these verses inside Bailov prison. Her husband had been rounded up and executed several months earlier, during Stalin's Great Terror. As his wife, Ummugulsum was also arrested by the NKVD. During her first four months inside Bailov she managed to collect scraps of paper to document the inhumane conditions of thirty-six women crammed into one cell, and their attempts at resistance. 'We are continuing our hunger strike. My knees are shaking when I stand up, and green and red flash before my eyes. No one listens to our complaints. No one cares about our grief.' Finally, though, 'we decided to eat because, otherwise, we would lose the only thing we had – ourselves.'

It took a further seven years for NKVD prison and labour camps to extinguish Ummugulsum's life. During her last three years of imprisonment, a young Heydar

---

9 U. Sadigzade, 'Our Eyes Full of Tears: Our Hearts Broken', *Azerbaijan International* 14: 1 (2006), pp. 46–7.

Aliyev began his steady rise through the ranks of Stalin's security police. Whether he worked in the prison or not is secret.

Ummugulsum's treatment in the 1930s and 1940s was not exceptional, but part of a century of state repression directed towards maintaining tight control over Baku's oilfields. Before coming to power and using the prison for his own ends, Stalin had himself been a prisoner in Bailov – captured thirty years earlier, in 1908, by Tsar Nicholas II's Okhrana. The prison was intensely overcrowded, with 1,500 people sharing cells built for 400.

Stalin – then known as Koba – and his fellow street-organiser Sergo Orjonikidze protested against the conditions so effectively that the authorities sent a company of soldiers to beat up the politicals. Forced to run the gauntlet, 'Koba walked, his head unbowed, under the blows of the rifle-butts, book in his hands.'[10]

The seven months, from March to September 1908, spent waiting for deportation orders to Siberia were filled with intense political debates on revolutionary tactics, the oil industry and visions for the future. Imprisoned in filth and degradation, Koba learned Esperanto and passed the time playing backgammon with Sergo. The politics of the following decades means that we know something about Koba and Sergo's resistance inside Bailov, while most of their fellow prisoners were consigned to historical oblivion.

Twelve weeks have passed since police cars surrounded Salur Alizade's vehicle as he drove home in January 2009. Officers pulled him onto the street and handcuffed him, before 'producing' drugs from his car. Now he is in Bailov Prison, awaiting sentencing. Salur knows he stands no chance in court: the judicial system follows orders from above, and the police routinely plant narcotics on individuals to send them down. His court date is due in four days. Three years is his expected sentence, for a crime he did not commit.

'My son was arrested in mid-January. The police claimed it was drugs, as they often do in such cases. Even if Salur did drugs, which he doesn't, he's too smart to take any in his car when his father is a targeted dissident,'[11] Zardusht Alizade explains to us. Two months before Salur's arrest, Zardusht had spoken publicly to European parliamentarians in Brussels, describing how in Azerbaijan an 'organised criminal ruling class uses oil money to assert its authority over the population'. The Azeri ambassador was present, and did not approve.

Then the BBC interviewed Zardusht on the nineteenth anniversary of the massacre of Azeri protestors by Soviet troops on 20 January 1990. He explained that, in hindsight, it had become clear that this event was less about the independence of Azerbaijan than about saving Heydar Aliyev and promoting his interests.

---

10   S. Sebag Montefiore, *Young Stalin*, Weidenfeld & Nicolson, 2007, p. 214.
11   For similar instances, see azerireport.com.

Gorbachev had ordered Aliyev's arrest for corruption and crimes committed while he was first secretary of the Azeri Communist Party. 'By precipitating the disaster, Aliyev saved his skin – whereas we lost many activists, leaders and the relationship with Moscow.'

The next day, the secret police sent Zardusht a message by pulling over his son's car. 'He's not even political – he paints cars. For my speaking out, he is being made to pay the price.' Zardusht has ensured he has a good lawyer, but knows it will make no difference. 'The MTN, the new KGB, knows that this is more effective than sending me to prison myself.'

Koba, Ummugulsum, Salur. All were imprisoned on trumped-up or unfair charges by the secret police in its various incarnations: the Tsar's Okhrana, Stalin's NKVD and Ilham Aliyev's MTN. Both Ummugulsum and Salur were imprisoned not because of their own actions, but in order to put pressure on their relatives, a husband and a father. For the last hundred years, this prison by the sea has helped Baku's rulers keep a tight grip on both the residents of this city and the money from oil beneath the ground.

Leaving the front courtyard of Villa Petrolea, we take Xoşginabi Kuç and head east, searching out the building that the windows of the BP conference room overlook.

Today, Bailov Prison is surrounded by a six-metre-high wall covered in peeling yellow paint, topped with razor-wire. A chain-link fence crowned with barbed wire encircles the whole, and armed wardens patrol the roofs. Besides the guards, there is no sign of life from inside. The street is deserted, apart from two large German Shepherd dogs and a Doberman fighting over and attacking a tin can. James jumps as they run past, and is eager to move on. A lone boy scurries past, carrying bread home, head down, not giving us so much as a glance.

At the prison's main entrance, two soldiers in fur hats are repairing an official-looking black car. Both peer under the bonnet clutching spanners while an officer revs the engine impatiently. Once the car is fixed, the white barrier across the entrance, which looks like it should be automatic, is physically swung open by hand. Salur is still sitting inside this gate, punished for his father's bravery.

We think of the proximity of this cold grey street to the Villa Petrolea, with its lobby, offices and canteen – a world away and yet intimately connected. We think of the lines in *Horizon* magazine: *The intent of the 'contract of the century' was to develop the country as well as the oil.*[12]

AZADLIQ MEYDANI, BAKU, AZERBAIJAN

Back in town, we step off our bus into the vast space of Azadliq Meydani, or Freedom Square. Looming over this expanse of open ground is the massive bulk

---

12   Campbell, 'Scale of the Century', p. 39.

of the Dom Soviet, the 1950s government building of Soviet Azerbaijan. With its ten storeys, arches, pillars, and crown of finials, it is an iconic piece of Stalinist architecture, reminiscent of buildings in Moscow and Warsaw. We wander in its shadow, following the path of a military parade that took place in June 2008 to mark the ninetieth anniversary of a 1918 display by the troops of the Azerbaijani Democratic Republic.

High on a podium stood all the senior military figures of today's Azerbaijan: the defence and national security ministers, commander of the interior troops and a line of generals. They took the salute before an array of hardware: tanks and howitzers, armoured jeeps and air-defence missile systems, as fighter jets and helicopters conducted a fly-past over the square. Cadets from the Heydar Aliyev Azerbaijan Military High School marched before the podium, singing the national anthem adopted by the new Azeri state in the midst of the Nagorno-Karabakh war:

> *Azerbaijan! Azerbaijan!*
> *You are a country of heroes!*
> *We will die that you might live!*
> *We will shed our blood to defend you!*
> *Long live your tricolour banner!*
> *Thousands of people have sacrificed their lives*
> *You have become a battlefield*
> *Every soldier fighting for you*
> *Has become a hero.*[13]

The state news agency enthused in advance of the parade about 'the Smerch missile reactive volley systems – only Azerbaijan owns these systems among the South Caucasian countries. And for the first time in Azerbaijan's history, unmanned spy jets will be demonstrated . . . Also armed soldiers in the Mercedes UNIMOG and Land Rover military vehicles.' Intriguingly, they also noted that 'The most interesting part of the training-parade was a march of the three special units of the Ministry of Defense equipped with the NATO modern small arms, uniforms and masks.'[14]

This display of prowess is a direct outcome of the conflict with Armenia and of the oil revenues passing through SOFAZ into the government's budget. Military spending increased by 51 per cent in 2005, and then by another 82 per cent in 2006.[15] By October 2010, Ilham was celebrating the special place of the military

---

13   T. Bagiyev, T. Heydarov and J. Novruzov, *Azerbaijan: 100 Questions Answered*, Azerbaijan Boyuk Britaniya Ganjlari Jamiyyati, 2008, p. 11.

14   'General Training of Military Parade Held on the Occasion of 90th anniversary of Azerbaijani Armed Forces To Be Held on June 16', at en.apa.az, 25 June 2008.

15   S. Freizer, 'Nagorno-Karabakh: A Frozen Conflict that Could Boil Over', *European Voice*, 31 January 2008.

in the state expenditure: 'Next year, our total military spending will be more than $3 billion. If we consider that the entire state budget of Armenia, which continues to keep our lands under occupation, is slightly above $2 billion, we can see that the task we have set earlier that Azerbaijan's military expenses should exceed Armenia's total budget has already been fulfilled. It is a reality today. Over time, we, of course, will further increase our costs.'[16]

Among those on the podium was General Vagif Akhundov, head of the Special State Protection Service of Azerbaijan, an elite unit responsible for guarding the Baku–Tbilisi–Ceyhan oil pipeline and the South Caucasus gas pipeline. NATO had provided the service with several helicopters and vehicles in order to carry out this duty.[17] Despite sanctions, the US also played a key role in strengthening Aliyev's military. Secretary of State Colin Powell justified this as follows: 'The Administration believes that building up the capacity of Azerbaijan is important in order to . . . secure the oil flow that is critical to US national security interests.' To sidestep regulations prohibiting foreign troops in Azerbaijan, the US military hired Blackwater in 2004 to create a SEAL team to respond to crises 'during the wee hours of the night'. Mike Anderson, chief of Europe Plans and Policies division at EUCOM, explained in more detail: 'We've been equipping and training Azeri special forces with the ability to go out and take down one of their own gas and oil platforms if it was seized by terrorists . . . It's good old US interests, it's rather selfish. Certainly we've chosen to help two littoral states, Azerbaijan and Kazakhstan, but always underlying that is our own self-interest.'[18] This is another element of the Carbon Web of BP's operations in Azerbaijan – the role of the military. These training programmes and military arrangements would have been coordinated or discussed with BP, most likely with the company's head of security on the project, former SAS commander Tony Ling.

We talk through the background of the Ninetieth Anniversary Parade. Such events are actively used by the Azeri state to build pride in its newfound military power and develop a distinct martial identity for the nation. The Aliyev regime proclaims a narrative of 2,500 years of war, invasion and expansion to bolster its legitimacy today. According to the Heydar Aliyev Foundation, established by the first lady, Mehriban, 'The people of Azerbaijan have the most ancient traditions of state system establishment.'[19]

---

16   I. Aliyev, *Opening Speech at the Meeting of Cabinet of Ministers*, at president.az, 20 October 2010.

17   'NATO to Supply Azerbaijan and Georgia with New Technical Equipment', at today.az, 27 April 2007.

18   D. Stokes and S. Raphael, *Global Energy Security and American Hegemony*, Johns Hopkins University Press, 2010, pp. 137–8.

19   This is the official history of the Azeri nation, as told by government departments and most pro-government and opposition newspapers. Examples quoted in this

After defeating the Persian emperor, Alexander the Great appointed his commander Atropat to be king of Medea Minor, a region that covered territory including today's Azerbaijan. Atropatena, as it became known, was described two centuries later by the Greek historian Strabo as 'a great country as regards to its military power, because it can be represented by 10,000 horsemen and 40,000 infantrymen'.[20] According to the Azeri embassy in London, 'it is in Atropatena that the Azerbaijani identity began to be shaped.'[21]

The story continues that Turkic peoples who settled here became 'the strongest leading military and political power and the main carriers of traditions of state organization of Azerbaijan,' through the Seljuk, Sirvanshah and Safavid periods. It is this martial narrative that enables the likes of Azeri member of parliament Malahat Ibrahimgizi to declare proudly on National Salvation Day that 'Azerbaijan has always defended its independence throughout history and regained independence in the early 1990s.'[22]

Those who tell this story of Azerbaijan generally perceive Azeri nationalism, and that of Armenia, as the eruption of a long-repressed primordial consciousness. Slumbering for seventy years, Azeri nationality just needed the right opportunity – Gorbachev's reforms – to be fully released. When you juxtapose Azeris and Armenians, it seems only natural that the 'old enmity' between the two peoples will flare up again.

But this telling of the Azeri story is itself a dangerous political act. Nations – whether Germany or Croatia, Turkey or Azerbaijan – are actively constructed by individuals and parties, using historical narrative, language, rituals and territory. When the Azerbaijan Democratic Republic declared independence in May 1918, national identity was largely absent among the wider public. The ADR leadership and associated intellectuals had come to identify as Azerbaijanis, after previously subscribing to pan-Islamism and Turkism. People generally saw themselves as Muslim or Tartar subjects of the Russian Tsar.[23] Historians have argued that the majority identified primarily with 'umma consciousness',[24] and the idea of an Azerbaijani nation-state did not take root among the masses – possibly explaining

---

section include Heydar Aliyev Foundation, 'Azerbaijan from Ancient Times to the Acceptance of Islam', at azerbaijan.az; Azeri Embassy in UK, 'History of Azerbaijan', at azembassy.org.uk; 'Roots Deeper than Oil', at divainternational.ch.

20   Azeri Embassy in Sweden, 'Emergence of Early States', at azembassy.se.

21   Azeri Embassy in UK, 'History of Azerbaijan'.

22   'Azerbaijani MP: Day of National Salvation Is of Great Importance for Azerbaijani People', at today.az, 15 June 2010.

23   Suny, *Revenge of the Past*, p. 42.

24   'Umma consciousness' describes the identification of an individual with the Islamic community over and above some other grouping, such as that of nationality.

the surprising ease with which the republic was overthrown by the Red Army.[25]

Mainstream Azeri history describes Soviet power as an enemy of national identity, although ironically this period was in fact key to the formation of Azerbaijan as a nation. Across the USSR, the policy of *korenizatsiia* – 'nativisation' – used affirmative action to create national intelligentsias. Soviet ideology promoted 'national self-determination', although it opposed nationalism in politics. Being an 'Azerbaijani' within the territory of 'Azerbaijan' became an important fact of life, as the bureaucracy tried to achieve stability and to integrate this crucial oil province into the Soviet state. Cultural infrastructure like the Azeri national opera, academies of science and film studios were introduced, in parallel with the construction of new industrial cities like Sumqayit. The Oil Academy in Baku was renamed the Azerbaijani Industrial Institute in the 1930s, shortly before young Heydar Aliyev enrolled.

Although the pressure to Russify was real and the Russian language was associated with modernity, migration continued to make the Soviet Republic of Azerbaijan ever more homogeneous in character, consolidating the alignment of ethnicity with territory. Having been a multicultural city during the early years of the Oil Road, Baku was transformed by seventy years of Soviet rule into a predominantly Azerbaijani city. In parallel, because in the Soviet Union the state constantly talked about matters in terms of class, this meant that class ceased to be an issue around which dissent could be organised. Instead, ethnicity became the most effective tool for mobilising opposition – with tragic consequences for Azeris and Armenians alike.

Eighteen years before the military parade, the square we are standing in was packed day after day with hundreds of thousands of demonstrators. Still called Lenin Square, in January 1990 it was the focal point for mass rallies. The Dom Soviet building that loomed over the crowd no longer deterred anybody. These were heady days in the Soviet Union, soon after Ceauşescu was chased from power in Romania. The week before, Popular Front organisers had led crowds in dismantling frontier fences with Iran and burning border watchtowers, 'reuniting' northern and southern Azerbaijan: 'Thousands raced across the border, and there were ecstatic scenes as Azerbaijanis met their ethnic cousins from Iran for the first time in years.'[26]

As the citizens in Baku protested, the Popular Front had already split apart. Social Democrats, including Zardusht Alizade, left in protest at the nationalist direction of the dominant faction. Before another vast crowd on 13 January,

---

25   T. Swietochowski, *Russian Azerbaijan, 1905–1920: The Shaping of National Identity in a Muslim Community*, CUP, 1985, p. 193.

26   de Waal, *Black Garden*, pp. 88–9.

Popular Front leaders directed their anger towards Armenian residents. Zardusht remembered that at the rally 'there were constant anti-Armenian calls and the last call was "Long live Baku without Armenians!"' After dark, lists of addresses were distributed. Groups including refugees from Nagorno-Karabakh broke off to attack Armenians. Arzu Abdullayeva is quoted as pleading with a policeman to go to the aid of an Armenian being attacked, and being told, 'We have orders not to intervene.'[27]

Assaults continued in the following days, as did a blockade of Soviet barracks. One week on from the pogrom, Gorbachev sent in the army. A state of emergency was declared and military armour rolled out of barracks into the heart of the city. Soldiers fired on fleeing civilians; tanks crushed cars, and even ambulances; 135 citizens were killed and hundreds injured during 'Black January'. It was one of the worst scenes of repressive violence in the USSR, and effectively ended Moscow's hold over Azerbaijan. The following day almost the whole population of Baku turned out for the funerals of the victims, while thousands burned their Communist Party membership cards. In Moscow, Heydar Aliyev made his famous pronouncement to the press: 'The absolute majority of the population is behind the Popular Front.' However, as Zardusht asserted in his BBC interview in 2009, Aliyev's role in 'Black January' is still highly contentious.

By the 1990s, Azeri nationalism was able to mobilise hundreds of thousands. Yet with a limited history of true self-rule, maintaining allegiance to the new body politic required a constant remaking of identity. This endeavour intensified with Heydar Aliyev's return to power, as he began building an Azeri state in his image. Today, his portrait stares out from billboards across the country, alongside quotes promising security, freedom and wealth. Government websites show the 'Father of the Nation' looking upwards, to the future, while streets, museums and factories have all been named after him. His personality cult emphasises past support for Azeri poets, musicians and writers, while his KGB role in repressing dissident artists is conveniently forgotten.

The social vision Aliyev promoted presented him as the saviour of independence, who resurrected Azeri culture and used the oil weapon to stand up to Armenia. Like any powerful national mythology, it weaves together contested realities into simple symbols that resonate with past experience. The shared trauma of losing the cultural heartland of Nagorno-Karabakh is emphasised, basing national identity on 'misery, sorrow and perceived persecution'.[28] Meanwhile the vision offers a grand future to make up for this suffering: oil revenues will transform Baku into Dubai.

---

27   Ibid., pp. 90–1.
28   T. Goltz, 'How the Other Half Lives in Oil-Rich Azerbaijan', *Los Angeles Times*, 23 November 1997.

Since soon after its arrival in Baku, BP has reinforced the role of both the Aliyevs and oil at the centre of this national story. Through its publications and statements, its telling of the past and promises for the future, this British company has played a significant role in shaping contemporary Azeri nationalism. The terminals that mark the beginning and end of the BTC pipeline in Azerbaijan and Turkey are *both* named after the elder Aliyev. European Union officials have also contributed to this narrative: even as dictatorships were being toppled across North Africa in early 2011 and calls emerged for an 'Azeri Spring', the EU Commission president, José Manuel Barroso, paid tribute to 'Father of the Nation, Heydar Aliyev'.[29]

And this support has its rewards. BP's oil operations – the offshore rigs, and especially the BTC pipeline – have been publicly identified by the Aliyevs as 'national projects'. Those who raise concerns have been attacked as enemies of the nation, and associated with 'foreign enemies of Azerbaijan', particularly Armenia. At Baku conferences in 2002 and 2003, groups from a pro-BTC coalition claimed that 'those who are against BTC are spies of Armenia' – Armenians having acquired a noxious stereotype as manipulative and scheming. Echoing the use of anti-Jewish prejudices to undermine progressive causes elsewhere, the pro-BTC activists made allusions to Armenians to spread conspiracy theories that silenced dissent.

These virulent attacks, combined with media censorship, serve to undermine the possibility for any real debate over BP's projects. While purporting to support free discussion and public engagement, the company sat back and allowed critics to be silenced. With BP's social licence to operate in Azerbaijan intertwined with Aliyev's nationalist social vision, press officers such as Tamam Bayatly have not publicly distanced the company from the anti-Armenian conspiracy theories.

CASPIAN PLAZA, CƏFƏR CABBARLI KUÇ, BAKU, AZERBAIJAN

These days, Baku is full of GoNGOs, CoNGOs and MaNGOs – local terms for the strange progeny of the growing Azeri civil society. A GoNGO is a government-supporting NGO, while a CoNGO is a computer with one person sitting behind it promoting their name but doing little else. A MaNGO, meanwhile, is a mafia NGO, often established by relatives of those in authority, which is used primarily to launder cash.

When Heydar Aliyev returned to power in the early 1990s, he was highly suspicious of NGOs. They had not existed in Soviet Azerbaijan, and seemed to be opposed to his rule. In due course, though, he came to understand that NGOs carried recognition in the West, and that they could help his international reputation. In subsequent years the Aliyev government created hundreds

---

29   J. Barroso, 'Speech: The EU and Azerbaijan: A Shared Vision for a Strong Partnership', at europa.eu, 14 January 2011.

of imitation organisations that did little except support the internal and international standing of Heydar and Ilham Aliyev. When, in 2009, the government opposed Turkey's rapprochement with Armenia, Azeri youth charities fired off supportive letters in all directions. Previously, when the regime needed to show the international finance institutions that there was public support in Azerbaijan for the BTC pipeline, an 'Azerbaijan NGO Coalition for Supporting BTC' was created. Sabit Bagirov, who as head of SOCAR had signed an agreement with BP in front of Margaret Thatcher, was appointed to lead it.

Arzu Abdullayeva had explained to us that the government had created a 'public council to fund civil society'. She saw organisations that took this money as allied to the powerful. 'Real NGOs never take these bribes, but GoNGOs do so with great pleasure. It means that real civil society is weak, weak, weak.'

We return to the Caspian Plaza tower, where we had previously visited Emil Omarov at the National Budget Group. Taking the elevator up to the ninth floor, we find a cluster of NGOs sharing airy and intersecting rooms. The offices of each organisation are light, with pale pine furniture, white walls and numerous computer terminals. Most people here speak fluent English, and many have a Masters degree from Stanford or Harvard Business School. The unifying factor between these groups is that all are funded by the Open Society Institute – the OSI, a division of George Soros's Soros Foundation. A friendly young receptionist introduces us to staff from the Public Association for Assistance to Free Economy and Caspian Revenue Watch. The latter group is the regional coordinator for the Extractive Industries Transparency Initiative – EITI.

The EITI was launched by British Prime Minister Tony Blair in 2002. The initiative promotes disclosure of payments by multinational corporations to developing countries with natural resources, the rationale being that civil society will then be able to see how much money their governments are taking in. Driven by the UK's Department for International Development and Norway's equivalent, Norad, with backing from major oil companies, the initiative was supported by international NGOs.

Galib Efendiev, the director of Caspian Revenue Watch, tells us that 'the local EITI NGO coalition has been in our trusted hands since 2006. EITI has been a very sexy topic for at least four years. And two months ago, at the world forum in Doha, Azerbaijan was announced as the first country to fully implement the initiative.'

When we ask whether EITI has made much difference in Azerbaijan, Galib twiddles his pen and assures us of its importance. 'Sure, some people call EITI a toothless initiative, that we only get figures for income from extractives. But the issue of spending that income is outside the scope of EITI. It's intended to be kept simple, to be a universal tool that can be employed in any country regardless of the local style of government.'

'After three years of this process, we now have regular reports on payments. That's why Azerbaijan was announced as a champion of EITI.' Galib's enthusiasm is echoed by other NGOs. 'Since implementing EITI in 2003', says a Global Witness report, 'Azerbaijan has also experienced good progress in both development and poverty reduction.' The report continues by quoting Ilham Aliyev: 'We are very determined to use oil wealth to develop a strong economy, and not to depend on oil and oil prices in the future. To achieve that, we need to have a high degree of transparency in accumulating and spending oil wealth.'[30]

As we listen to Galib, it is clear that the Aliyev government has reaped recognition as a 'pioneer' for making Azerbaijan 'a champion of EITI', and indeed the Intiative's first champion. [31] But it seems to us that, while politicians and NGOs celebrated Azerbaijan's recognition at Doha in Spring 2009, they unwittingly bolstered this regime by taking its claims to transparency and diversification at face value. Ilham Aliyev presents himself as a reformer; meanwhile corruption and repression continue more or less unchecked.

Time is running on, and we do not have a chance to express our concerns. In presenting EITI as the solution to skewed development – the curse of the Billion Dollar Bridge – the initiative seems to miss the point that transparency is only one part of a far bigger set of issues. OSI and Revenue Watch have recognised that human rights abuses and corruption continue, but argue that nevertheless the Azeri EITI experience was successful because it enabled the local growth of civil society.

From Galib we shuttle over to the next meeting with Zohrab Ismayilov of the Public Association for Assistance to Free Economy. Once we have exchanged

---

30   *Oil Revenue Transparency: A Strategic Component of US Energy Security*, Global Witness, March 2007. The Global Witness report goes on to explain: 'Statistics bear out Aliyev's comments in large degree. GDP growth per capita increased from 10.4% in 1999–2000 to 25% in 2004–2005', and that, 'furthermore, foreign direct investment in Azerbaijan increased by 160% from 2002 to 2005'. Constructing and operating seven offshore oil rigs and an export pipeline will no doubt lead to soaring FDI and GDP per capita, especially in a poor and small country. But the translation of FDI and GDP growth into 'development and poverty reduction' cannot be taken for granted. Unless 'development' can include an unsustainable construction boom of hotels, the odds and historical evidence are, sadly, weighted against Azerbaijan's poor. A useful perspective on FDI is given by Bayulgen, 'Foreign Investment', which argues that oil-rich states in the developing world with authoritarian regimes tend to fare better in attracting FDI than states with democratising or hybrid regimes, and that the FDI inflow perpetuates such regimes by external legitimisation. Bayulgen probably did not expect 'external legitimisation' to include praise from anti-corruption campaign groups.
31   C. Eads and A. Tunold, *Progress Report 2007–2009: Establishing Resource Transparency*, EITI Secretariat, 2009.

business cards and settled down, he explains that corruption in the state oil company SOCAR is a big problem: 'Expenditure has increased, but the company doesn't use tenders. Sometimes SOCAR pays thirty manat for a product that should cost one manat.'

Many of those working on the ninth floor do important work in trying to prevent the Aliyev regime from totally capturing the Azeri economy. Yet we are struck that Zohrab and others are outspoken about the Aliyevs' corruption, but reticent to discuss the oil corporations' role in enabling it. Zohrab explains, 'If the companies have any impacts in Azerbaijan, it is positive. While there are problems with some oil companies in Nigeria and Angola, these factors don't exist here.'

Reflecting later on our whistle-stop tour of the Caspian Plaza, we cannot doubt that support for independent voices facing repression in Azerbaijan, as elsewhere, is extremely important. But so central is OSI's role in Baku that it has acquired disproportionate power in moulding the 'local growth of civil society'.[32] Much of its funding is provided in parallel with another US-based funder, the Eurasia Foundation, which supports 'programs that build democratic and free market institutions' in the former Soviet Union.[33] These two foundations play a significant role in fostering a partially critical sphere that stands outside the regime, but also ensure that the voices of supported NGOs are subtly directed. They loudly criticise local corruption and revenue mismanagement, but not the bigger question about the transformation of Azerbaijan into a resource colony. The role the country should play in the world economy is taken as read, and Ilham Aliyev is inadvertently portrayed as an acceptable autocrat. We are reminded of what Arzu said to us: 'When you ask "Democracy or oil?", oil comes top. So, we demand, "Don't sell our democracy for oil".'

MATBUAT AVENUE, BAKU, AZERBAIJAN

Walking in Baku is challenging. The construction boom means that buildings, roads and overpasses have sprung up everywhere, and street maps have not kept pace. Sometimes road names have changed only on our map, at other times only on the street sign.

Heading to a meeting with Zardusht Alizade, we are confronted with an urban military base straddling the route we had planned to take. The road is where the map says it should be, but lying across it is a metal barrier: the road then runs past a guard post and in between rows of parked tanks. Civilians are nowhere in sight

---

32 Despite OSI's annual budget in Azerbaijan consisting of only around $3 million, its impact is significant because it focuses on supporting oppositional groups that receive no government funding.

33 'Resource Links', at soros.org.

– only officers in pristine uniforms chatting as they stroll by. We are nervous that we have already put ourselves at risk by talking to government critics. Walking through a military base is probably not the smartest plan.

But we are late, having already got lost once, and we do not want to keep Zardusht waiting. So we take a deep breath and plunge on, studiously ignoring the sentry guarding the barrier. Once through it, it dawns on us that this is a military training college. The security, at least for two lost foreigners, is comparatively lax.

On this quiet, dusty Baku street, flanked by large trees blooming with plastic bags snagged on their branches, stands the building we are heading for. Finding the way in is less easy. Two entrances give onto a car workshop and a general store respectively. Finally, we discover a third door down a side alley, with a handwritten sign in English announcing that a committee meeting has been moved. This bodes well.

Inside lies Baku's only independent journalism school. Zardusht welcomes us into his little corner office. Tight and compact, the room barely accomodates its two paper-strewn desks and a cabinet of books. With a broad smile on his tanned face and bright eyes, Zardusht offers us a choice of Rafaello or Russian chocolates. He is delighted to see us, reminiscing about his stay in London with us seven years ago.

Zardusht seems to take after his namesake Zarathustra, the founder of Zoroastrianism who opposed the existing caste and class structures in Persia 3,000 years ago. As a founder of the original Popular Front opposition in the 1980s, Zardusht had promoted democracy and improvement of the social situation in Azerbaijan. But as the nationalist wing of the Front began to dominate and push for conflict with Armenia, Zardusht and his allies quit and founded the Social Democrat Party instead.

'When we were starting the Azeri democracy movement', Zardusht remembers, 'I was afraid that the country would go the same way as Egypt.' He had spent time there between 1969 and 1971, on secondment from the Soviet Army, and saw the impact that oil had on the powerful. 'And now we have gone the same way. We have a corrupt anti-national elite which controls information, oil and gas in order to enrich itself. Our ruling class is immoral.'

In recent years he has distanced himself from party politics in favour of this journalism school he has founded. But he also volunteers as chairman of the Open Society Institute, Azerbaijan. The presence of Zardusht in this position further illustrates the complexities and contradictions in OSI's role in Baku. Warm and effusive, he speaks highly of others and is humble about his own role. He confirms much of what we have heard elsewhere.

'BP has never supported independent civil society. You should ask Mayis about this. He was in the OSI monitoring group, and criticised the pipeline. So BP said to OSI, "We will support your programme, but only if Mayis is not part of the coalition." This is one of the conditions they put on participating in our programmes. Of course, they pursue their interests as a corporation – they support only those who support them, who say BP is soft, very good, very clean – GoNGOs. There are many GoNGOs in this city. Many are former real activists, who then became hunters of grants. I never respect such GoNGOs. I recognise their right to live and my right to not respect them.'

Young women and men periodically pop their heads in to ask questions, and Zardusht patiently deals with each of them. We can see how he built up a movement of dedicated and loyal activists against Soviet oppression in the late 1980s. Respect and affection beam from the eyes of his students.

This is not the only journalism school in Baku; BP itself has run joint courses with the British Council. Zardusht admits that this programme is a good thing because it teaches the basics of journalism. But the benefits are limited. If a journalist tries to use this method to investigate BP, he says, 'they will become an enemy like Mayis. Both the government and BP try to stop Mayis speaking. They try to close his mouth, to keep him silent.' As he describes BP's attempts to silence criticism, Zardusht imitates a fist crushing somebody.

Warming to his theme, Zardusht argues that the Aliyev dynasty and BP are winning at Azerbaijan's expense. He feels that the oil revenues could be used to develop, to build other works, to create a future without oil, without gas. But instead, 'our very clever English-speaking president has learned how to run a dictatorship and manipulate civil society for his own benefit'. The restrictions on speech and strong control of media are such that allowing limited civil society is profitable for the government. Zardusht points out that Soros's programmes, including OSI, have been closed by the Russian government but allowed to operate in Azerbaijan. 'The government here even collaborates with our OSI health programmes. Does this mean that we live in a democracy? No! But this all works well for BP.'

After two hours, Zardusht apologises profusely that he needs to leave. 'I need to go to an OSI board meeting – it's time to disburse George's money again.' He gives us a lift back into the centre of Baku, and as we drive through the city he says,

'When colleagues from America visit, they ask me: "Why don't you recognise the beautiful buildings, the nice cars, the expensive shops? People must enjoy this. Surely this is a good transformation of society?" I answer, "No – this is not my society. That is part of the corrupt state apparatus. The oil will end, BP will leave, the elite will move to their fancy houses in London and Paris. And what will be left behind?" Lots of empty skyscrapers that we can't keep clean.'

Part II THE ROAD

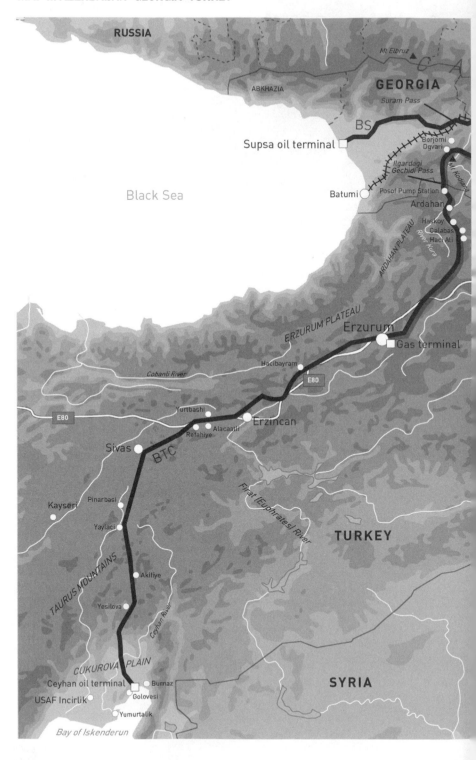

MAP III AZERBAIJAN–GEORGIA–TURKEY

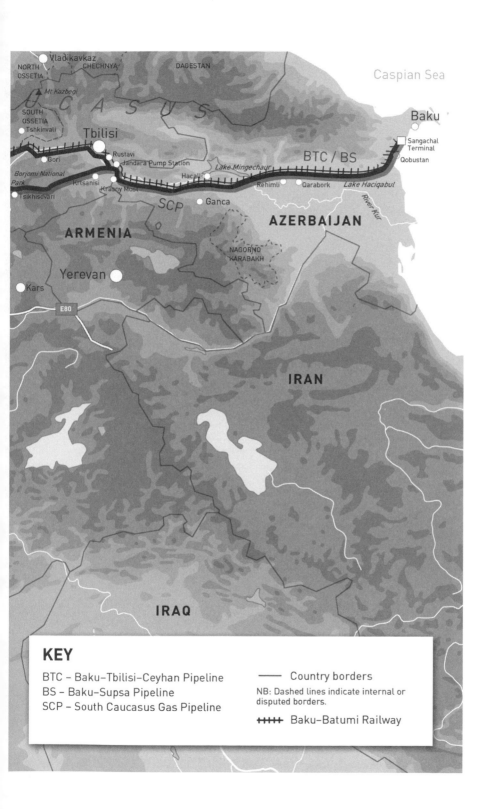

KEY

BTC – Baku–Tbilisi–Ceyhan Pipeline
BS – Baku–Supsa Pipeline
SCP – South Caucasus Gas Pipeline

—— Country borders

NB: Dashed lines indicate internal or disputed borders.

+++++ Baku–Batumi Railway

5 THE WIDE STREAM OF OIL GUSHED OVER THE GREASY EARTH

BIBI HEYBAT, BAKU, AZERBAIJAN

The highway is a hectic turmoil of trucks and cars, dust and potholes, as it takes us away from the city. We are leaving Baku behind, to follow the Baku–Tbilisi–Ceyhan pipeline westwards and investigate the situation in the villages on the Azeri plains, in the Georgian mountains and on the Turkish plateau. To track the oil, we had planned to travel with a hired driver, but none would accompany us in Azerbaijan. All those whom Mayis approached turned down the job as soon as they learned that we would be following the pipeline. Eventually Mehdi, Mayis's brother from far out of town, agreed to come to Baku and take us.

Cramming into Mehdi's dirty white Lada, we followed the coast road south. Through the rear window we see the distant Absheron Peninsula and the tower blocks of Baku begin to drop away from view. We reach the suburb of Bibi Heybat, where Taghiyev and the Soviet generations that followed him turned a village into a maelstrom of drilling rigs, pipelines and crude-soaked soil.

Like Balakhani further north, this industrial devastation attracts its photojournalists and voyeurs of decay. The stretch of rusted derricks and nodding donkeys was immortalised in *The World is Not Enough*, the James Bond film that John Browne referred to in his autobiography. In travel guides today the area is known as the 'James Bond Oilfield'.

Almost a hundred years previously Ali, a character in Kurban Said's novel, described the scene: 'Soon we saw the oil derricks of Bibi-Eibat. The black scaffolding looked like an evil dark wood. The smell of oil filled the air. Workers, oil dripping from their hands, stood near drill holes, where the wide stream of oil gushed over the greasy earth.'[1]

We are following one of the ancient trading routes from Baku. After its conquest by the Persians in 530 BCE, this region was a province of the empire to the south. The states of Atropatena and Albania, whose independence was eventually carved out of the Persian Empire, continued to trade with the cities to the south. After the

---

1   Said, *Ali and Nino*, p. 94.

Arabs conquered the region in the seventh century CE, long camel trains travelled along this coast heading for Tabriz, Baghdad, Esfahan and Basra carrying 'bales' of crude oil. This was oil for heating and light, warfare and medicine.

Arab writers such as Abu Ishaq Istahri described the process of digging up and trading the strange substance in this distant city of the Abbasid Caliphate. Marco Polo told his Venetian readers of 'a fountain of oil, which discharges so great a quantity as to furnish loading for many camels . . . It is also good for burning. In the neighbouring country no other is used in their lamps and the people come from distant parts to procure it.'[2]

Eventually, in the nineteenth century, control from the Muslim south was replaced by the expanding imperial Russian power from across the Caucasus Mountains to the north. Baku became a border town of the Tsarist Empire, and the trade routes switched to tankers on the Volga and wagons on the rail line to the west.

BTC KP 0 – 187 KM – ŞIXOV BEACH, AZERBAIJAN

As we round the headland at Bibi Heybat, the wide Caspian spreads out before us, blue-grey and littered with the structures of the oil industry. We pass a strip of resort hotels. Outside each stand lines of palm trees, imported, Mayis tells us, from Dubai or Brazil at great expense – like the shrubs and water brought to the park at Villa Petrolea by Ludvig Nobel.

The Caspian, not so much a sea as the world's largest salt lake, is filled from the north by the rivers Volga and Ural, draining the steppe and the taiga, washing down from the heartland of Russia. Marco Polo said that the Caspian in the 1280s 'partakes of the nature of a lake not communicating with any other sea . . . The sea produces an abundance of fish, particularly sturgeon and salmon at the mouth of the rivers.'

The immense body of water before us is heavily affected by the flow rate of the two rivers. In the summer of 2009 there was a prolonged drought in western Russia. There were fears that the level of the Caspian would drop as much as three metres, and the nutrient load become so heavy that the algae would bloom and the fish population collapse – fish like the Caspian sturgeon, which is the source of caviar. The historic emblem of this sea, and the livelihoods of those who fish in it, is in serious danger. The sturgeon is threatened by the pollutants down the Volga, and a film of crude, in some places half a centimetre thick, has formed on parts of the Caspian as a result of oil-drilling.[3]

---

2   M. Polo, transl. William Marsden, *The Travels of Marco Polo*, Wordsworth Classics of World Literature, 1997, pp. 16–17.

3   M. Javadi and N. Sagheb, 'Caspian Caviar in Peril', *Azerbaijan International* 2: 3 (1994), pp. 50–2.

The road runs close to the shore, and we can see the hulks of jack-up drilling rigs, while far off in the haze are spindly silhouettes of jetties and shallow water platforms, steel centipedes crawling along the surface of the sea. The jack-ups, great pylons at each corner, look like upturned tables, their legs rising in the air. Belonging to oil service companies such as Transocean and Schlumberger, these workhorses of the offshore industry form another segment of the Carbon Web. Rented out to the oil corporations, they are pulled by tugs on to prospective fields to drill wells through the seabed below.

For the Azeri territory we see before us, the sea, is quartered out in fourteen irregularly shaped concession blocks. On the oil maps that indicate them, each block is marked with a name, such as ACG or Lerik, and the titles of the new owners: AIOC, ExxonMobil, BP, Total, Agip, and so on. It is to and from these blocks that the drilling rigs are dragged.

We leave the headland and begin to traverse the flat lands along the shoreline of Şixov Beach. This is a desert not of sand but of mud, made from the ancient bed of the Caspian when the lake was swollen by meltwaters after the last Ice Age. On our left is the grey-green sea, on our right the grey-brown mud desert. To an eye used to the verdant greens of Western Europe or nurtured on images of Arabian sand dunes, this landscape, glimpsed through the windows among the passing trucks, is hard to love. We think of lines in *Ali and Nino*: 'I loved the flat sea, the flat desert and the old town between them. The noisy crowd who come looking for oil, find it, get rich and leave again . . . don't love the desert.'[4]

On either side of the road lie indeterminate industrial buildings, a cement works, and beyond it a SOCAR terminal with quotations from Heydar Aliyev painted on its walls:

Azerbaijan will remain independent!

A State with a strong economy is capable of everything!

Just across the road a large signpost reads: 'Deepwater Jacket Factory named after Heydar Aliyev'. It was in this former Soviet rig yard that six of ACG's mammoth platforms were assembled. The great majority of the 15,000 Azeri workers employed during the construction of the platforms were engaged here. These temporary workers were employed not by Azeri companies, but by a battalion of foreign corporations, including McDermott of the US, Bouygues Offshore of France, Emtunga International of Sweden, and Saipem of Italy. Despite Heyder Aliyev's slogan about the building of a strong economy, the 'Contract of the Century' was biased against Azeri firms doing this work, and in favour of the

---

4   Said, *Ali and Nino*, p. 17.

international companies that BP contracts around the world. This is the engineering part of BP's Carbon Web, which, like the foreign policy, finance and the military elements, was also crucial in the conquest of the Caspian.

BP's biggest contractor in Azerbaijan, McDermott, was subject in 2005 to the only successful labour strike in recent Azeri history. Arzu had told us how, despite significant corporate pressure, the walkouts by local workers continued for some time and succeeded in raising their salary. But later on Zardusht had suggested that the strike's success was partly a ploy by the state, who chose not to block it but instead used it to pressure the foreign companies in their own interests.

To our left, a strip of empty beach is neatly fenced off. A line of orange-and-yellow markers protrude from the water and continue up the beach. This is the finishing point of the 187-kilometre pipeline that runs across the bed of the Caspian from the ACG field. These banal posts on this scrap of beach mark the spot where 80 per cent of Azerbaijan's oil, and most of its gas, comes ashore. This is the physical reality of all those conversations and negotiations, struggles and deals, which took place in meeting rooms and hotels, government buildings and corporate offices beyond the rocky headland to the north. Here, out of view, the oil is pumped under the busy highway and the Aztrans railway line, into the Sangachal Terminal.

We turn off the main road and head towards the sentry cabin at the gates of the terminal. Saplings, neatly planted, fringe the roadside, thin bare whips rising from desert mud. Above us a triple billboard points in three directions, displaying a map of the BTC pipeline, Heydar Aliyev's face with a thin smile, and the legend:

Heydar Aliyev Adina Baki–Tbilisi–Ceyhan Boru Kemeri 2005[5]

BTC KP 1 – 188 KM – SANGACHAL, AZERBAIJAN

Sangachal is a gathering point for oil and gas from all over the Caspian, both pumped from BP's offshore wells in Azeri waters and shipped in from Kazakhstan and Turkmenistan, beyond the horizon to the east and the north. Crude is brought across the sea on tankers, then siphoned onto railcars. An engine shunts the load slowly up the line to the Sangachal Terminal, where the oil is moved into storage tanks to await passage to the BTC pipeline. It is a slow, cumbersome and costly process of transhipment, so there have been various proposals to build a pipeline under the Caspian – effectively an extension of the BTC pipeline to the east.

Fifty kilometres to the south is the sister of the Azeri–Chirag–Gunashli oilfield, the Shah Deniz gas field. In 1992 BP began negotiating for a contract to explore the seabed off the southern coast of Azerbaijan. Four years later, in June 1996, the Shah Deniz production-sharing agreement was signed. It gave a consortium of companies led by BP access to a sea area of 860 square kilometres – two and a half times the area of the

---

5   Heydar Aliyev Baku–Tbilisi–Ceyhan pipeline 2005.

ACG licence. Three years on the drilling rigs discovered a massive gas field. The consortium, uninterested in the sale of the gas to the domestic markets of the Caucasus states, began to plan the construction of an export pipeline, a twin to BTC, which was by then inching towards legal reality. Eventually, in May 2006, gas was pumped from the Shah Deniz platform, to Sangachal, and then on through the South Caucasus Pipeline, across Azerbaijan and Georgia, to Erzurum in eastern Turkey.

By the time of this first delivery, the Shah Deniz field was a significant pawn in the political game of Western European energy supplies. And Sangachal had become the largest oil and gas terminal in the world outside the Middle East, a place of immense strategic importance.

We wait in the wind while we are checked and the guards make tea in their gatehouse. Inside the high security fence lie stocky flare towers, processing compounds and fat yellow storage tanks like upside-down buckets. Everything here is either yellow or white. Low-rise Sangachal stretches out in all directions across the desert. More construction is planned to process the growing output of Shah Deniz. Soon the terminal will cover 800 hectares.

After a brief exploratory detour around the site, we pull up at the visitor centre – the Caspian Energy Centre – for our appointment. Under a sign announcing that 'Pipelines awaken ancient history', we are welcomed by Ismayil Miriyev, the centre's manager. On our way to the kitchen in search of tea, we pass photographs of past visitors to Sangachal: President Erdogan of Turkey, President Toomas Ilves of Estonia, Swiss President Pascal Couchepin and Senator (as of 2005) Barack Obama. 'He was friendly', says Ismayil. 'He came with a group of senators visiting Central Asia and Azerbaijan. It was a geopolitical thing. Politicians like this frequently visit us. If they're in Baku, they'll probably visit our centre. We don't display photographs of all of them. But when Obama became president, we remembered that he had visited and we dug the photograph out of our archives.'

Next we are shown the handprints in clay of John Browne, Prince Andrew, US Secretary of Energy Samuel Bodman, Turkish President Sezer, Georgian President Saakashvili, and of course Ilham Aliyev himself. 'They were all here for the big launch event.' This was the official opening ceremony of the BTC pipeline on 25 May 2005. As we look at the accompanying images we think of the demonstration that had taken place outside the Oil Academy four days before, brutally put down by the police because it 'would interfere with preparations for the official opening'.[6]

Clearly proud of the centre, Ismayil explains its genesis. 'We wanted to have a special place for visitors. That way they wouldn't interrupt normal work, but we could still explain how everything functions.' The Caspian Energy Centre is a perfect emblem for a particular phase in the life of BP. Nine months after the signing of the 'Contract of the Century', Browne advanced to the pinnacle of his career,

---

6   Abdullayeva et al., *Report on Monitoring*.

the post of chief executive of BP. He approached his new role with whirlwind energy, determined – as the youngest ever CEO of BP – to leave his mark. Within a year and a half two events had modified the tone of his tenure.

On 10 November 1995 the writer and activist Ken Saro-Wiwa and eight of his Ogoni comrades were hanged by the Nigerian government. Saro-Wiwa had been a figurehead of a movement demanding justice for the suffering and exploitation caused by Shell and other oil companies during their half-century in the region. The impact on Shell – which was partly responsible for Saro-Wiwa's judicial murder – was dramatic. Its petrol stations and offices were blockaded, there was widespread public scrutiny, and staff morale was badly affected. Although not in the firing line at the time, BP looked on anxiously. As a staff member based in Nigeria in 1995 later said, 'Corporate social responsibility in BP was born the morning after Ken Saro-Wiwa was hanged.'[7]

In October 1996, the BBC's investigative programme, *Panorama*, broadcast stories on BP's role in assisting and financing paramilitary 'death squads' in Colombia. It looked as though the company was about to suffer its own Ken Saro-Wiwa moment. But the BP management acted fast. Political staff were rushed from BP's offices in Washington to Bogotá. The head of BP Colombia appeared on UK TV to defend the company's practices, and mainstream NGOs were quickly drawn into a 'stakeholder dialogue'. The tactics worked, the storm passed: the value of aggressive corporate social responsibility was proved, and the tone of the Browne era set.

BP then announced that its BTC pipeline, planned to run between the Caspian and the Mediterranean, would meet the highest standards of corporate social responsibility. The promise was that this project would be different, would show that the oil industry could act with social and environmental sensitivity, and would herald a new era. The promise was central to the selling of the project in distant cities such as London, Washington and Brussels, and to groups such as BP staff, investors and the media. As we shall see, this promise had multiple impacts along the 1,750-kilometre route. Here in Sangachal it manifested itself in the saplings that line the entrance road of the terminal, in the Caspian Energy Centre, and in the tale of the 'tortoises of Sangachal'.

Spur-thighed tortoises are one of Azerbaijan's endangered species, vulnerable because they hibernate underground in winter and can be injured during earthworks. A BP survey revealed that the tortoises were to be found on this stretch of the Caspian coast and that care would be needed to ensure their breeding grounds were not disturbed during the construction of the terminal, this 'new town' in the desert.

BP's efforts for the tortoises received considerable publicity. Photos of the creatures sheltering in the gloved hand of a BP community liaison officer were to be seen in numerous internal and external company publications. The eight tortoises found

---

7   Authors' interview with Irene Gerlach.

during construction work were moved to a special enclosure. To be sure, the tortoises benefited – in that they survived; but so too did the company's reputation, staff morale, and ultimately BP's ability to do business in Azerbaijan. It was a perfect illustration of the corporate mantra about the 'Triple Bottom Line – People, Planet, Profit'.

Key to corporate social responsibility is the corporation's presentation of itself as open and transparent – hence the Caspian Energy Centre. As Ismayil explains, 'We realised that we could bring children here to educate them about the role of oil and BP in Azerbaijan.'

In the presentation room, we are introduced to our presenter, Orxan Abasov, an Azeri in his mid-twenties. He had been sent to train at the Natural History Museum in London, and is keen to return for further studies. There are seats for more than thirty, but there are only the two of us. Orxan, though, happily runs through his PowerPoint presentation, picking out the issues he finds most interesting with a laser pointer.

The construction of Sangachal began in 1996: land was levelled, ditches dug, walls built and fences erected. At its opening in 1997 it was already a large terminal, receiving 150,000 barrels every day. When the new ACG platforms were built offshore, there was a parallel expansion on shore: more processing compounds, more and larger storage tanks. Stage by stage, Sangachal spread across the desert until it was capable of processing 1.2 million barrels a day.

The quantity of oil arriving from the subsea pipeline running under the muddy beach varies heavily from day to day, depending on the geological pressure in the oil reservoirs deep under the sea. One day it can fall as low as 500,000 barrels, on another it might be as high as 900,000. By the summer of 2008, it hit record production of 1 million barrels a day on five consecutive days.

The crude that Chevron sends from Kazakhstan, Orxan explains, is of significantly lower quality and has higher sulphur levels than 'Azeri Light' – the oil extracted by BP. When the two are blended together in the BTC pipeline, Chevron covers the value lost to the other BTC Co. shareholders – as the eleven partners in the pipeline are known – according to a complex algorithm. Orxan is happy to tell this tale. He is visibly proud of 'our Azeri Light'. Interestingly, despite his clear loyalty to BP, another identity creeps into Orxan's speech. At various points during the presentation he uses 'we' to refer to BP, or Azeris, or even SOCAR. So when he describes the shareholding of the contracts for the Inam and Alov fields, Orxan explains that, as a result of its later negotiations, 'we managed to get a larger stake'. The 'we' here is SOCAR, the Azeri state company, which took a 50 per cent holding in the licence, compared to only 10 per cent in ACG.

Despite its great yellow storage tanks, Sangachal can only hold two and a half days' worth of maximum production: 2.5 million barrels. 'If we can't export for longer than this, we have to shut down the offshore platforms. This means losing a lot of money. Furthermore, when we shut down production, the wells can't always be restarted identically, so we can lose pressure. So platform shutdown is our absolute last option.'

This last option was taken during summer 2008, when the Russia–Georgia war led to a shut-in of BP's major fields after pipelines were bombed and threatened. Unlike his more senior colleague Aydin Gasimov in Villa Petrolea, Orxan is more forthcoming, explaining that eventually they were forced to use trains to carry crude over the Caucasus to the Black Sea, until the railway was blown up by a mine. The last remaining export route to the West was the Baku–Novorrosisk pipeline through Russia, which BP does not generally use. But oil prices were still at near-record highs, so BP used its pre-emptive rights to prioritise its exports over SOCAR's.

Orxan seems pleased with the changes the revenues have brought to his city. 'We've built six new bridges. Lots of roads and tower blocks. If the oil prices stay low like now, then the construction projects slow down, waiting until it rises again before resuming.' Apparently the ACG platforms are not profitable if the global price of oil drops to below $40 or $45 per barrel – a figure that is significantly higher than the point at which fields in the Middle East cease to make a profit. This high cost is partly due to the expense of piping the oil to Ceyhan. 'If the price falls below this for a period of time, production isn't worthwhile, so the platforms might shut down.'

Among Orxan's slides there is one particularly striking image: a graph of the history of oil production in Azerbaijan. It shows four peaks: in 1904, 1941, 1968 and 2010. The history of Azerbaijan is generally described as having two or three 'Oil Booms': the first in the 'Age of the Oil Barons', the second in the build-up to the 'Great Patriotic War', and the third in the 'Post-Soviet Renaissance'.[8] The successes of the post-war Soviet oil industry in the 1960s do not quite fit this narrative, and are rarely described as a boom.

The slide also shows that after the peak of 2010 comes a predicted rapid decline. This graph, in fact, illustrates exactly what we have heard many times in Baku from concerned critics: that despite government and corporate claims, Azerbaijan is reaching 'peak production'. Emil Omarov of the National Budget Group had told us, 'But now, when people hear that the oil production will peak next year, they ask where the benefits have gone.'

The prospect of rapidly declining revenues is not new in Azerbaijan. There were 'Oil Slumps' in the 1910s, the 1940s and then in the 1970s. Each time, these have been accompanied by moves to diversify the economy away from the simple extraction and export of crude. The oil baron Taghiyev sold out his holdings to the British financier James Viashnau at the turn of the century, and invested in cotton mills, a caviar farm, and agricultural projects. Sumqayit represents Orjonikizde's 1930s drive to create petrochemicals and industrial products from the raw materials that flowed from the

---

8   The second – during the 1930s and early 1940s – is also often omitted by Western commentators.

Absheron Peninsula. Soviet Azerbaijan in the 1970s and 1980s under Heydar Aliyev increased investment in the production of vegetables and cotton.

The question arising from Orxan's data is: How will Azerbaijan navigate the coming 'Oil Slump'? This is precisely the challenge that SOFAZ is supposed to address, but the 'six new bridges, lots of roads and tower blocks' that Orxan celebrates cannot solve this problem. As Zardusht asked, 'What will be left behind? Lots of empty skyscrapers that we can't keep clean.'

We would like to quiz Orxan, but the presentation is over and it is time to leave Sangachal, and we do so having been unable to see the place we would dearly love to visit. The control room is far beyond the reach of the visitors invited to the Centre; it lies in the 'forbidden zone' of Sangachal. We have seen a photograph of it in a BP report: two men in black overalls stare intently at a computer screen; one points at line of data while the other works a mouse. The caption reads: 'Firdovsi Isayev, control room technician and Ibragim Teregulov, production superintendent at combined control room at Sangachal terminal.'[9] Somewhere further in, beyond the wire fences that mark the sections of this installation not open to the public, must be the room in which BP staff monitor the pumping of oil and gas from the offshore rigs into the terminal, and out into the BTC pipeline, through Georgia and Turkey, to the depot at Ceyhan. Orxan had explained that the flow rate from ACG varies by the day, even by the hour, and that the value of the crude also fluctuates in accordance with the global oil price.

In July 2008, BP was extracting close to 1 million barrels of crude most days. On the eleventh day of that month the oil price hit a historic $147 a barrel, giving the throughput a potential value of around $147 million a day. Two months later the gas blowout on Central Azeri forced the company to shut down its wells, reducing extraction by two-thirds. A combination of the Credit Crunch and a rapid decline in petrol demand due to record prices had already brought the oil price down to $60 a barrel. This meant that, by September 2008, the output of the fields was generating a potential value of only $21 million a day. In seventy days the value of the output of oil from ACG had fallen by over 85 per cent.

On the face of it, production superintendents in the monitoring room simply watch the movement of raw geology through the system. But they are in effect working in an almighty counting-house in the desert.

BTC KP 25 – 212 KM – QOBUSTAN, AZERBAIJAN

Leaving Sangachal behind, we continue south on the coastal highway, the grey expanse of the Caspian a constant on our left; to our right, the land rises into the desert hills of Qobustan. Seated in the front are Mayis and Mehdi, ubiquitous Azeri black flat caps on their heads.

---

9   'BP in Azerbaijan: Sustainability Report 2007', BP, 2008, p. 6.

Just four generations of a family might have lived through the maelstrom of the 140 years since the industrial exploitation of oil began. Most industry and government literature describes a first oil boom in the late nineteenth century, and the period after the mid-1990s as the second oil boom. Each time, however, the boom has given rise to radical social upheavals – or perhaps the other way round. Calling these periods of concentrated change 'oil booms' focuses attention on the geology, technology and capital, as though the changes were almost inevitable and inherently positive.

According to this story, the Tsar removed the dead hand of state ownership from the land in 1872 – and the oil-driven world blossomed. The collapse of the Soviet Union removed the nonsense of a corrupt and backward nationalised industry – and the oil-driven world blossomed again.

But, in reality, the transformation of Baku from a walled city with Zoroastrian temples, Shia mosques and camel trains to a city of grid streets and mansions, the squalor of Balakhani and Bibi Heybat – this transformation was a social upheaval, guided largely from St Petersburg, Paris and London. It gave birth not only to the oil barons, but also to the ecological and social hell of the oilfields and the pogroms of 1905 and 1918.

The next transition – omitted from the more neoliberal accounts – from a Baku dominated by oil barons and foreign corporations like Royal Dutch Shell into the socialist city of Avraamov's *Symphony of Factory Sirens*, the Oil Academy, and the technological brilliance of Neft Dashlari – this too was a social upheaval, directed from Moscow. And it too was accompanied by the Stalinist incarcerations at Bayil, and the hell of Sumqayit.

Finally, Baku's metamorphosis from a dusty Soviet metropolis dominated by the Aliyev clan to a city of glass-and-steel tower blocks, fashion stores and the 'Billion Dollar Bridge' dominated by the Aliyev clan – this too is a social upheaval, influenced from offices in London, Washington and Brussels. It was also accompanied by the poverty of Binəgədi and more prisoners in Bayil.

The constant drilling of holes in the desert and the seabed was celebrated by those who directed it, both capitalist and state socialist. And all – Ludvig Nobel, Stalin, John Browne, Ilham Aliyev – all have sung of these wells as engines of human advancement, and wrapped the gigantic enterprise in a heavy cloak of positivity, with no space for doubt. In just this manner the company celebrates the care lavished on the eight Sangachal tortoises while remaining silent over the imprisonment of journalists and the slums of Binəgədi.

A policeman flags down our car, and we stop on the hard shoulder as Mehdi accompanies the officer back down the road to pay the statutory bribe for a 'speeding offence'. While we wait, we consult our map and trace the route of the pipeline that we will be following – west across the open desert, before it rises to climb into the far Caucasus mountains.

6 IF THE PIPELINE BURNS, I'LL BURN WITH IT

BTC KP 55 – 242 KM – LAKE HACIQABUL, AZERBAIJAN

A large Steppe Eagle circles leisurely overhead. Wings spread, it glides over us, passing above the road faster than Mehdi's Lada. We are an hour west of Sangachal now, following the oil as it leaves the Caspian behind and crosses the Azeri desert. Lake Hacıqabul stretches out on our left, blue and still, unexpected in the dry ground around us. On the steppe to our right, between us and the hills rising to the north, a train thunders west, a caravan of fat black tankers strung out in a line. Loaded with Exxon's oil, this train is destined for Batumi, on the Georgian Black Sea coast.

Closer yet, metal stakes with yellow hats with numbers stencilled in black paint appear every kilometre, marking the pipeline route:

61   62   63   64   65

Below the soil, the BTC pipeline runs parallel with the train tracks, along with its twin sisters, the South Caucasus gas pipeline and the older Baku–Supsa line. From Sangachal, it takes ten days to pump Caspian crude, unrefined, through the steel pipe of BTC, 1,768 kilometres to the Turkish Mediterranean coast. We can track its markers, following the oil as it is pushed across deserts and mountains, fields and forests.

Oil trains were first dragged west along this route 125 years ago, fuelled by *ostatki* or 'leftovers', the liquid fuel remaining after the refineries in Baku's Black Town had extracted lighting kerosene from crude. When this railway line was built across the Caucasus in 1883, locomotives and steamers in Europe and the US were still predominantly coal-powered. The notion of liquid petroleum fuel was widely ridiculed in Berlin, London and New York, but in the Caspian region it was already taken for granted.[1]

Until this train track brought access to the seaports in the West, the steamers sailing from Baku could only export to Persian and Russian markets around the

---

1   See C. Marvin, *The Region of the Eternal Fire*, W. H. Allen & Co., 1884.

Caspian, and to the Volga and Ural river-basins. The Nobels quickly saturated the Russian market, increasing kerosene consumption many times over. But the real prize lay beyond the Tsar's empire: the potential consumers in Western Europe and the Far East, which were monopolised by Rockefeller's Standard Oil. Several oil barons, finding it difficult to break into the Russian market in which the Nobels held a dominant position, explored the idea of constructing a railway from Baku to the Black Sea port of Batumi. The coastal town had just been seized from the Ottoman Sultan Abdulhamid II by the Tsarist armies in the Russo-Turkish War of 1877–78, and Tsar Alexander II was keen to consolidate his new military base and develop the city as a port.

When Alphonse Rothschild, director of the French branch of the Rothschild Bank, arrived in Baku in 1883, he brought the capital to make this mountain-crossing plan a reality. Initially barred from direct investment in oilfields by anti-Jewish legislation brought in by the new Tsar Alexander III, the Rothschilds concentrated instead on oil distribution. With previous experience of financing railway construction in Europe, the Rothschilds approached the Tsar with a proposal to complete a project previously proposed by two Russian-Armenian oil magnates, A. A. Bunge and S. S. Palashkovski, who had gone bankrupt. With Alexander III's approval, construction of the line began. From Baku, it crossed the desert, followed the valley of the River Kura up to Tbilisi, went over the high Suram Pass, and down the River Rioni to Batumi. Baku kerosene could now be shipped from the Black Sea coast, through the Bosphorus, to markets all over the world. Deliveries were soon being made to Fiume, Trieste, Marseilles, Barcelona, Antwerp and London. Railway tonnage soared, and between 1884 and 1887 the number of tank cars went from a few hundred to several thousand.

The construction, with its gangs of labourers, embankments, cuttings, tunnels and bridges, spearheaded the transformation of the Caucasus from a mountain region to an industrial heartland of the Russian Empire. The railway was completed within two years, and soon the continued dominance of the Nobels, and now the Rothschilds, over the Azeri oil barons became clear. Of the oil cars that travelled the line, 450 were owned by the Nobels and a hundred by the Rothschilds. Soon the 'proverbially cautious Rothschilds' had 'thrown themselves with vigour' into Baku's oil scene, purchasing the Batumi Oil Refining and Trading Company (usually known by its Russian acronym BNITO) and founding a second entity, the Caspian–Black Sea Oil Company.[2] Between 1884 and 1887, they invested nearly £2,000,000 – equivalent to £2.2 billion today.[3] This was an enormous sum at a time when a rail oil tanker cost a mere £75. As

---

2   N. Ferguson, *The World's Banker: A History of the House of Rothschild,* Weidenfeld & Nicholson, 1998, p. 880.

3   Marvin, *Region of the Eternal Fire*, p. 332.

the heavy engines pulled the crude westwards, the trains rumbled onwards past the hut in Gori where Joseph Djugashvili was growing up.

As extraction increased, the railway developed bottlenecks at the steep Suram Pass in Georgia, where two engines were needed to push and pull just eight tankers over the summit. The lowest point in the mountain range dividing lush western Georgia from the drier east, the Pass is over 1,000 metres above sea level. By 1886, increasing drilling in Baku showed that expanding the capacity of this Oil Road could be profitable – the oil baron and philanthropist Zeynalabin Taghiyev had just hit his gusher in Bibi Heybat. With additional financing from Taghiyev as well as Ludvig Nobel, the Rothschilds began to construct a kerosene pipeline running alongside the railway, together with a telephone connection.

But work was slow, and St Petersburg initially only approved construction of the line across the sixty steepest kilometres in central Georgia. It took nearly two decades and a new Tsar before permission was granted to construct the full pipeline to Batumi on the Black Sea, where it arrived in 1906.

The railway and the pipeline reconfigured the geopolitics of the lands between Baku and Batumi, between the Caspian and the Black Sea. For a century and a half it had been the fault-line between two empires, Russia and Persia. Now its orientation was towards Western Europe. New economic and political forces were created as Russia, France, Britain, Austro-Hungary and a number of companies redefined the region as an 'export corridor' in which they held substantial economic interests – eventually leading to the British occupation of the Caucasus with 40,000 troops in 1918. The train network and oil port created a growing working class in Tbilisi and Batumi, both of which later became centres of Bolshevik activity.

In 1929, after the Soviet conquest of the region, kerosene exports were dwindling in an age of electric light and petrol-fuelled transport, so a parallel pipeline for crude was opened from Baku to Batumi. This new construction supplied the refinery of Batumi, where petrol was produced and sold into European markets by the Soviet Union. However, barely more than a decade later the pipeline was dismantled again. Retreating rapidly in the face of the invading Nazi army, Soviet forces took the pipeline sections with them to Western Siberia, where they rebuilt it to fuel the Red Army's counter-attack.

In the post-war period more pipelines were laid through the Caucasus, providing various pathways along which to transport Azeri crude to distant Soviet consumption centres. By the late 1980s most of these were disused, with the likes of Sumqayit making the region primarily a refining and petrochemical hub. So in the mid-1990s, when BP began to plan expansion and extraction from the ACG field, it had a variety of potential oil export routes. From the earliest negotiations between the Western companies and the Azeris, the promise to construct a route was included in the contracts – such as that signed by Browne and Sabit Bagirov in front of Thatcher in September 1992. The most obvious and cheapest route to use appeared to be Baku–Novorossiysk, a pipeline that runs north along the Caspian coast into Russia, before bending west through Chechnya towards the northern Black Sea port of Novorossiysk. The pipeline already existed and would only need upgrading, and Novorossiysk was well appointed, having been the export terminal for oil produced in the Maikop and Grozny fields, on the northern side of the Caucasus, since the 1880s.

But BP's interests did not coincide with those of US policymakers. In a post-Soviet world, the United States could take advantage of Russia's vulnerability. From 1993 onwards, national security officials in President Bill Clinton's administration were staking out a strategic interest in the region, claiming 'legitimate political reasons for an aggressive US presence in the Caspian'.[4] The idea of a new east–west 'energy corridor' that avoided Russian territory was being promoted in conference rooms in Washington, DC.[5] The deputy national security advisor to the president, Sandy Berger, pulled together a group of high-level government officials and began to issue policy guidance on the importance of Caspian oil reserves to the US, and the need for defence cooperation with Azerbaijan.[6] In mid-1995, when it became clear that BP and the Azerbaijan International Operating Company intended to use the line from Baku to Novorossiysk to export initial 'Early Oil' crude across Russian territory, Berger sprang into action. Twice that summer Berger met Terry Adams, the BP executive then running AIOC, and laid down the law: the game must be played according to US rules. Rather than spend $50 million fixing up the existing pipeline, BP should construct a new $250 million line from Sangachal to Georgia's Black Sea port of Supsa, thus bypassing Russia. Berger was persuasive, especially since he was backed up by the subsidised loans offered by the World Bank and other international finance institutions.

Furthermore, the Baku–Novorossiysk pipeline was looking problematic. In September 1991 the Chechens declared independence from Russia, and over the following six years a brutal war took place. During the fighting the prospect of Caspian oil using the Baku–Novorossiysk pipeline was a significant factor, as the route of the pipeline passed through the Chechen capital of Grozny. The British journalist Sebastian Smith wrote:

> In the North Caucasus you only have to say 'neftprovod', or 'the oil pipeline', and everyone knows what you mean. Not many people have ever seen it or really know exactly where it is, but there's no mistaking what pipeline you are talking about.

---

4   J. Joseph, *Pipeline Diplomacy: The Clinton Administration's Fight for Baku–Ceyhan*, Woodrow Wilson School of Public and International Affairs, 1999.

5   S. Cornell, *The Guns of August 2008: Russia's War in Georgia*, M. E. Sharpe, 2009, p. 38.

6   Joseph, *Pipeline Diplomacy*, 1999.

The Baku–Novorossisysk pipeline has its own presence, like the mountains, and when people talk about the war in Chechnya, they think of the pipeline.[7]

Eventually, in November 1996, Russian forces withdrew, and the Chechens now had de facto independence. Running through their territory was the pipeline – although its opening was delayed, partly due to a complex set of negotiations with the new Chechen government demanding a share of the transit fees along their section of the pipe. The Russian government was obviously deeply opposed to such a strategic oil route passing across the land of a hostile state, and in 1999 fighting broke out again as the Russian army invaded. Pumping through the pipeline soon stopped, and the oil from AIOC was now transported by rail to Novorossiysk, so as to avoid the Chechen war zone. Over the following months a new pipeline, known as the Chechen Bypass, was constructed by the Russian company Transneft to carry the crude to the Black Sea port via a route that avoided Chechnya.

By this time Baku–Novorossiysk had ceased to be such a vital artery for the oil companies. In September 1995, BP and AIOC had agreed to build what became known as the Baku–Supsa pipeline. The Clinton administration, meanwhile, had developed an innocuous-sounding phrase in which to frame its foreign energy policy towards the Caspian: they called for 'multiple pipelines'.[8] In this formulation, Baku–Novorossiysk was titled the Northern Route Export Pipeline (NREP), and Baku–Supsa formally termed the Western Route Export Pipeline (WREP).

Built to pump 115,000 barrels of oil per day, Baku–Supsa could only carry a fraction of the 1 million barrels that AIOC planned to extract daily from its offshore fields. With the pipeline to Novorossisyk looking undependable, how would the remaining 885,000 barrels of oil a day be transported to global markets?

BP, it seems, was keen to link Sangachal to the Iranian pipeline system in order to transport Azeri crude to the terminals of the Persian Gulf; but US policy was strongly opposed to this. However simple and financially viable a short pipeline to Northern Iran appeared, reliance on Tehran was not an option. Nor was another idea then being floated: a pipeline across Central Asia to China.

Pressure for multiple westbound pipelines continued to be exerted by Washington and London throughout the 1990s. Berger was promoted to national security advisor and worked closely with Richard Morningstar, who was appointed ambassador for Caspian Basin energy diplomacy. Together they lobbied for construction of the Baku–Tbilisi–Ceyhan pipeline through countries sympathetic to US policy. Berger and Morningstar achieved their goal in 1999 when the intergovernmental agreement – a treaty – was signed between Azerbaijan, Georgia

---

7   S. Smith, *In Allah's Mountains*, I. B.Tauris, 1998, p. 73.

8   D. Morgan and D. Ottaway, 'Azerbaijan's Riches Alter the Chessboard', *Washington Post*, 4 October 1998, p. 3.

and Turkey. Three years later BP formed the Baku–Tbilisi–Ceyhan Pipeline Company (BTC Co.), together with Statoil, Total, Chevron and other oil companies, in order to construct and operate the pipeline.

In the 1880s the Rothschilds' railway and pipeline, driven by financial imperatives, caused major political transformations. Now, with BP's pipelines through the Caucasus, the geopolitics came first. Morningstar himself stated how the fundamental objective of US policy in the Caspian was 'not simply to build oil and gas pipelines. Rather, it is to use those pipelines, which must be commercially viable, as tools for establishing a political and economic framework.'[9]

In the heat, we can hear through the open car windows the rhythm of the wagons on the rails laid down at the end of the nineteenth century. Alongside them run three new pipelines built as the twenty-first century was starting. The oldest, Baku–Supsa, constructed in the late 1990s, was later joined by younger but larger twin sisters: the oil-carrying Baku–Tbilisi–Ceyhan and the gas-pumping South Caucasus Pipeline, buried together in one trench.

KP 187 – 374 KM – QARABORK, AZERBAIJAN

'They came yesterday. They were here yesterday. Men in red suits.' 'How many?'

'Eight. We tried to talk with them, but they wouldn't talk. They just stayed outside the fence and looked. We tried to wave down their cars, but they wouldn't stop.'

Visiting the village of Qarabork in May 2003, we had an uncanny sense that we, people from distant cities, were following on the heels of another group from the same cities. These eight men in red boiler suits were surely the team of engineers who were staying in the same hotel as us in Gənca in Central Azerbaijan. We had seen them in their BTC overalls climbing the stairs with heavy holdalls as we sat talking on the landing. At least four of the group were from England, guys in their forties and fifties. We overheard them say that they needed to visit four more sites.

The small village of Qarabork, 187 kilometres along the pipeline from the Sangachal Terminal, lies west of the desert, where the River Kura waters the lush green fields. We had come to this village six years previously, as it was the site of a piece of complex engineering. Along the pipeline's route through Azerbaijan and Georgia, there were only two places where its construction would involve destroying houses; Qarabork was one of them. BP was keen to avoid knocking down homes and thus forcing resettlement, as this might have made it more difficult to source public funds to finance the construction. Certainly it would have altered the profile of an already controversial project with the public in cities such as London. So in Qarabork the engineers explored the option of running the pipeline underneath the home of Mansura Ibishova.

---

9 R. Morningstar, 'Testimony: Commercial Viability of a Caspian Sea Main Export Energy Pipeline', Senate Subcommittee on East Asian and Pacific Affairs, 3 March 1999.

Mansura's house was a fine structure of two storeys. Built of wood and raised off the ground on stilts, it had a front veranda and a garden dotted with fruit trees, neatly bounded by plank fencing. At the back there was a large vegetable patch, a clump of bamboo, and the fields watered by the Kura.

The elderly Mansura was tiny and could not have been much over five foot. Her small, deeply lined face was tightly hemmed by an orange headscarf, and her eyes were almost frantic as she explained: 'They are going to tunnel under the house, but they won't give us any compensation.'

They came in early 2002. They were foreigners. They brought a document in Azeri, which she signed, but could not read. It was in the Latin alphabet, and like most of her generation she only reads Cyrillic, the standard script until President Heydar Aliyev decreed that it change. They left a brochure entitled *Caspian Sea Oil and Gas Export Project*. The men said she would have to move and would get compensation. She stopped growing her tomatoes and potatoes. Then she heard nothing.

A hoopoe flapped across the yard and landed briefly in one of the fruit trees. The sun was bright, but in the shade of the house it was cool. We stood talking with Mansura and her daughter as friends and children gathered around us, including a tiny baby girl in a fluorescent top and a boy of six or seven with a shaved head. He looked thin, his scalp bald in patches.

The municipality had told her the company would build a tunnel under the house, so they would not have to move – so they would receive no compensation. Under the terms of the pipeline agreement, any farmer whose land was disrupted by the construction work was entitled to compensation equivalent to the value of their lost crops.

She wanted compensation. She would rather they knocked down her house. She did not want to live over the pipeline. She said her neighbour had declared: 'If the pipeline burns, I'll burn with it.' But her neighbour was mad. Mansura said: 'If I don't get compensation, I'll write to President Aliyev'.

We paced out the width of the construction corridor: forty-four metres in total.[10] The entire garden was only thirty-eight metres across. In the still air we could almost sense the future pipeline coming from the east, passing beneath the house and hurrying away towards Georgia. The thought of that oil, a million barrels a day, moving at two metres per second, flowing under the kitchen at night, the baby girl in her cot, Mansura asleep, her headscarf on the dresser beside her.

We had visited Qarabork as part of a fact-finding mission carried out by the network of organisations raising concerns over the impacts of the pipeline's construction. This coalition included both the Azeri Centre for Civic Initiatives, for which Mayis worked, and the Committee of Oil Industry Workers' Rights Protection led by Mirvary Gahramanli, the Georgian group Green Alternative,

---

10   'Resettlement Action Plan: Azerbaijan', BTC Co., November 2002.

the CEE Bankwatch Network in Central and Eastern Europe and Rome's Campagna per la Riforma della Banca Mondiale. In England, Friends of the Earth, the Corner House, the Kurdish Human Rights Project, Rising Tide and Platform were heavily involved, with many more in other countries.[11]

Much of the coalition's campaign focused on the 'Lender Group' – the gathering of international finance institutions, export credit agencies and high street banks who were planning to provide $1.6 billion of loans towards the BTC pipeline. The public officials at the European Bank for Reconstruction and Development and the International Finance Corporation – part of the World Bank group – as well as the various European, US and Japanese export credit agencies, had received strong steers from their respective governments to support BTC during the early 2000s. Both the US and EU had stated their geopolitical interests in ensuring that Caspian crude was pumped westwards.

The remit of these international finance institutions is to use public money for the development of poorer countries. Consequently they regularly offer loans to multinationals to construct fossil-fuel projects that export natural resources. These loans are explicitly directed towards promoting liberalised economic structures in which foreign corporations can make substantial profits.

From BP's point of view, public finance provided not only capital, but, crucially, political support. The contribution of funds from Western export credit agencies indicated that the states to which they belonged would ally themselves with BP in any future arguments over BTC with the governments of Azerbaijan, Georgia and Turkey. As John Browne later explained, 'We also needed the [international finance institutions] to underpin our property rights . . . That would reduce the risk for the companies involved.'[12]

Because these public institutions use taxpayers' money, and because of sustained campaigning by civil society groups, most of them are subject to some level of public oversight. Publicly funded projects need to meet basic standards on issues such as forced resettlement – the concern at Qarabork. Hence the local, national and international campaigns highlighted the threatened impacts of the pipeline's construction in meetings and protests addressed to those public officials.

BISHOPSGATE, LONDON

Five weeks after our visit to Mansura in May 2003, we met with Jeff Jeter, senior environmental advisor of the European Bank for Reconstruction and

---

11   At times Amnesty International and WWF were also drawn in. Other groups that were involved included Urgewald in Berlin, Friends of the Earth Netherlands (Milieudefensie), Friends of the Earth USA, Friends of the Earth France (Amis de la Terre), Friends of the Earth International, and the Bank Information Center in Washington, DC.

12   Browne, *Beyond Business*, p. 170.

Development, at Bishopsgate in the City of London. We had seen him the previous week and he had asked for a further meeting, as he was keen to know the details of 'the place where the pipeline runs under a house'.

His interest put us in a morally difficult position. Jeff had mentioned that 'if the pipeline goes under a house we can't fund the project'. However, if we told Jeff about this house, would he tell the company, and would the company in turn tell the state authorities in Azerbaijan? Would our actions lead to the family of Mansura coming under threat?

We had warmed to Jeff in that first meeting. He was friendly, looked concerned, and was tentative in his assertions. On the phone he had been chatty, filled with an American camaraderie. He was a civil servant of the financial realm: surely he would stand neutral between us and BP, listen, and take careful action?

As we had remembered it, Jeff had also agreed to confidentiality, meaning that he would not talk to the company before checking with us, for fear of setting off a chain of repercussions leading back to Mansura. But when we met him he started off by explaining how he had already talked to BTC Co.,[13] and how they had clarified their position to him.

Across the lined paper of his notebook his black biro drew the ground-plan of Mansura's house, and then a second, with an orchard between them. 'BP says they can pass between these two houses and underneath the orchard. They didn't want to dig a trench and lay a pipe because of the disruption it would cause to the two households, so they've decided to do HDD – horizontal directional drilling. At two points on the route they are doing HDD, at point 169 km and . . . I can't remember the other one.'

We switch tack, talking about international standards on the proximity of pipelines to occupied buildings: BS 8010 Code of Practice for Pipelines on Land – subsection 2.4.2.1 for oil and subsection 2.4.2.2 for gas, amended in 1993, setting out the British standard for such matters.

He asks for the printout we have brought along, so that it can be photocopied. A young woman returns shortly with the A4 sheets, and Jeff deals with our concerns one by one: 'It's clear that if the thickness of the pipe wall is sufficient then the regulations for line J in the diagram 2.1 apply . . . that means the minimum distance is 3 meters. I don't think your assertion about the danger deriving from the distance between the gas pipeline and a dwelling can be correct'. He rounds up by saying: 'BTC just wouldn't put a pipeline in an unsafe setting, let me tell you. I've worked on this project for two years, and the care they give to safety...' There is a powerful sense of the presences beyond the room, with its wall of glass looking out over the

13   BTC Co. was the company formed to construct and operate the pipeline. As BP was the lead partner in BTC Co., however, their names were often interchangeable when discussing the project.

Square Mile – of the meeting that Jeff must have had with the BP officials and engineers, of our time in Mansura's garden with the hoopoe flying about.

We should have resisted arguing it on technical grounds, where the masterly self-assurance of numbers renders everything solvable. We allowed ourselves to defer to the absent engineers. We failed to make Jeff defer to the absent Mansura. And did this mean that we might have put her in a difficult position for nothing?

We said that the woman had told us the pipeline would pass under her house. Jeff said the engineers had told him that things were following standard procedures. We should have said: 'But if BTC are so sure it is safe, why haven't they properly informed the householders? Why are they terrified? Why does she *want* to be moved?'

In the months following this meeting, the cavalcade of machines and men involved in laying the BTC pipeline approached Qarabork from the east. First the land was staked out, then a section of topsoil twenty-eight metres across was removed, and mounded carefully along one side of the bare strip stretching far off into the distance. Then the lorries came, each carrying three massive sections of black pipe. A Caterpillar truck with a magnetic grabbing arm lifted each length through the air and lowered it onto a cushion of white plastic sandbags. The pipes were laid out in a line, stretching kilometre after kilometre across the fields and streams.

Each section was guided into its place in the strip, and the welders set to work inside their silver steel huts, lifted into place over each joint. Next the diggers came, cutting a deep trench through the landscape, the raw earth heaped to one side. The pipes, now welded together, were lifted by a team of machines and laid in the trench. In due course the earth was backfilled and the topsoil replaced. Then the army of labourers in yellow hard hats, dark glasses and orange flurescent jackets moved on, heading west towards Georgia.

But near this village the standard method of laying the pipe halted, and both BTC and SCP plunged deeper underground, under the road and under the gap between the houses.

BTC KP 187 – 374 KM – QARABORK, AZERBAIJAN

Six years later, we return to Qarabork with Mayis. The fig trees are in full leaf and the land along the stream is thick with undergrowth. Mansura and her daughter appear to have aged a great deal. Mansura's hair is still covered in a bright headscarf, but we notice that her shoes are torn and that she is wearing multiple layers of socks. The house feels cold, heated only by a small wood stove, despite the vast quantities of gas being pumped past so close by.

The marker posts delineating the pipe's route run just beyond the garden fence. Neither she nor her daughter feel any safer now that construction is over. Ultimately it matters little to them whether the pipeline passes under their house or their orchard.

Both are part of their home, and were there an explosion, the slight difference in route would be academic – their wooden fence will not protect them. A couple of times a week they feel a vibration that shakes the house, which did not happen before the pipeline was built. Cracks have started to appear in the walls.

Why did we tell Jeff Jeter that compliance with British standards was all that was required for a pipeline in Azerbaijan? Why did we get sucked into the language of the regulatory detail? After all, the pipeline runs near numerous ongoing conflict zones, has been targeted by both Russian and Kurdish bombs and is patrolled by both local military forces and BP's own security guards. Qarabork lies only 40 kilometres from the frontline of the 'frozen conflict' of Nagorno-Karabakh.

'Nobody comes to check on us, to see that we are still alive', Mansura says.

BTC KP 264 – 451 KM – RƏHIMLI, AZERBAIJAN

We were sitting on the grass, in the shade of a few trees, with two women who were refugees from Nagorno-Karabakh. They pointed to the village where they lived – a purple silhouette on the far side of the field. They had no land there. There was running water in the village, but no gas supply. They lived on food parcels delivered every month: one kilo of sugar, one litre of oil, one kilo of rice per person.

One of the two women said that she wished she had been killed by Armenians rather than have to live like this. She and the other woman had put down their loads at the edge of the field. We had seen them bent low under heavy bundles of firewood, trudging across the plough, their brightly coloured clothing – oranges and reds – against the brown earth.

They told us that they had spent two and a half hours gathering wood beyond the main road. The bundles were enough for one day – wood for cooking and boiling water. They gathered wood every day. The first woman had six in her family, the second had five. There were children with them, playing among the trees. One of them, a boy of perhaps ten years, had also been carrying a bundle of firewood.

A metre beneath us, 140,000 barrels of oil a day passed from the Chirag field to the Supsa terminal. It was one o'clock on 9 May 2003 in the field at Rəhimli, near Yevlax in central Azerbaijan. BP's main pipeline had not yet been built, but its smaller Baku–Supsa route to the Black Sea was already pumping. It was 9 a.m. in London, and the International Petroleum Exchange was just opening, a barrel of crude trading at $30.20. That meant that beneath the bundles of firewood was fuel worth roughly $4,200,000. No wonder the oil companies devoted so many years to negotiating the deal they achieved. No wonder they call the agreement the 'Contract of the Century'. No wonder BP reports to its shareholders that Azerbaijan is a profit centre.

Together with Mayis we had driven twenty kilometres west of Qarabork, along the main highway still heading away from Sangachal. We were searching for the field near the village of Rəhimli where we had sat and talked with the women six years previously, the marker posts of the pipelines acting as our guides. Quite suddenly we spot the trees and then the marker for SCP, the South Caucasus gas pipeline. Mehdi stops the car and we clamber out.

The Azeri economy was once heavily based on gas. Major grid expansion projects in the 1960s and 1970s led to widespread gas use for heating homes, with 80 per cent of Azerbaijan's 1.8 million households hooked up by 1990. The main power plants also ran off natural gas, so the fuel had a far higher level of penetration than in Western European economies, well before the 'dash for gas' in Britain and elsewhere. After the Soviet Union fell apart the grid deteriorated, and soon less than half of all households could receive gas, especially those outside Baku.[14]

Today, BP, the public banks and the Azeri government have rebuilt elements of Azerbaijan's gas infrastructure. But rather than heating homes in the villages and cities, much of the fuel is pumped from the Shah Deniz field to Sangachal, into the South Caucasus pipeline, and then westwards out of the country.

The SCP was completed in 2007 to force an annual 8.8 billion cubic metres of Caspian gas across the Caucasus mountains to the city of Erzurum on the Anatolian plateau, where it enters the existing Turkish gas network and is sent onwards to Ankara and İstanbul. The companies and the European Union intend that a new 4,000-kilometre pipeline should extend beyond the SCP across Bulgaria, Romania and Hungary into Central Europe, locking Azerbaijan into the expanding European gas grid. Representatives of the five partner countries in the project all attended the Vienna State Opera and saw a production of Verdi's *Nabucco*, about a Persian emperor, and named the pipeline after it.[15] If built, it would fuel power stations and domestic cookers in Austria, Germany and across Europe. Ultimately, if all goes according to plan, a vast cobweb of pipelines will extend outwards in all directions from Europe, reaching into the Arctic, Central Asia and the Niger Delta.

The EU is promoting increased gas consumption at a time when the extraction of gas from within the member states is set to decline. This will create a major shortfall in coming years. By 2020, the EU expects to consume 650 billion cubic metres of gas annually, compared to 530 billion in 2010. For this to happen while domestic extraction falls, imports of gas will need to rise by 50 per cent over the same ten-year period.[16] The European Commission has devised a two-pronged strategy to address the shortfall. Internally, the twenty-seven member countries have been liberalising and integrating the pan-EU gas market, while separating energy supply companies from transportation companies.

---

14   J. Bowden, 'Azerbaijan: From Gas Importer to Gas Exporter', in S Pirani, ed., *Russian and CIS Gas Markets and Their Impact on Europe*, OUP, 2009.
15   T. de Waal, *The Caucasus: An Introduction*, OUP, 2010, p. 185.
16   R. ten Hoedt and K. Beckman, 'For Nabucco It Is Now or Never', *European Energy Review*, 4 November 2010.

In parallel, a concerted drive to build infrastructure to transfer fuel resources to Europe is led by European Commission civil servants working on energy and external relations, backed by financial support from the European Investment Bank and the European Bank for Reconstruction and Development. New pipelines are to be laid across thousands of kilometres of mountains, sea, desert and tundra. Running north, east and south, these will remove natural resources from 'producer countries' and transfer them to EU consumers in the dominant economy.

The EU describes its plans as assuring 'security of supply' for the future. Working closely with European energy companies, its aim is to guarantee the increased provision of gas to European markets over coming decades. The argument runs that

> Europe is one of the world's largest demand centres for gas. The Caspian and the Middle East make up the largest gas reserve region in the world. Today, there is no direct link between these two important demand and supply markets. To link those two markets through the Southern Corridor, i.e. Turkey and the south of Europe, is the logical thing to do.[17]

It is perhaps unsurprising that the EU should find it 'logical' to transfer the gas resources of the Middle East, the Caspian, Siberia, the Russian and Scandinavian Arctic, North Africa and the Gulf of Guinea to the EU. Except, of course, that these resources do not flow of their own accord. This is not a rain catchment area in which mountain streams head downhill, joining tributaries and rivers to provide water to the city in the valley. Gas is lighter than crude, but it still requires pressure to force it down a pipeline, while political and financial forces determine the route along which it is transported.

This web of gas pipelines, then, is centred on Brussels. Presentations by Commission officials and gas company executives show these threads fanning out in all directions – images that make the web appear natural, geographically determined. The reality is that the web is the outcome of intense lobbying, billions of dollars of loans, and the balance of political and economic power.

Jean-Arnold Vinois of the European Commission's Energy Directorate General and Marco Alvera, senior vice-president for the Italian oil company ENI, gave parallel dinner presentations on gas pipelines and security of supply to the European Energy Forum in Brussels in October 2008 – only weeks after the gas leak at Central Azeri, and with much of BP's Caspian extraction shut down. These two government and corporate leaders celebrated 'Europe's unique position in respect of gas', comparing the EU's advantageous location to that of East Asia and

---

17   Ibid.

North America.[18] While these other dominant economies and sites of global gas consumption also expect to rely heavily on imports in the future, Europe is surrounded by potential sources that are all accessible by pipelines.[19]

Very long pipelines. If Azeri gas from the Caspian does reach Austria, it will have travelled over 5,000 kilometres. This is the 'Southern Corridor', and the Nabucco pipeline is also intended to suck gas from Iraq, Egypt and possibly Iran into Central Europe. Meanwhile, the proposed Trans-Sahara Gas Pipeline would run for 4,300 kilometres northwards, from the coastal Niger Delta across the entire Sahara to Hassi R'Mel in Algeria, where it would connect with existing lines that cross the Mediterranean to Spain and Italy. European companies, such as Shell, have been eager to support the plans, and EU Energy Commissioner Andris Piebalgs has offered to help finance the $21 billion project through the European Investment Bank.[20]

When Vinois presented to the assembled diners from European corporations and governments in 2008, he referred to these schemes as 'European priority projects' that 'must be included in national strategic plans'.[21] The EU's 'four corridors' strategy aims to tap into Central Asian and Middle Eastern, Russian, Scandinavian, and North and West African reserves, by extending, broadening and strengthening these import 'corridors' to ship more gas from greater and greater distances.

The term 'energy corridor', used in policy documents and speeches, disguises the fact that these are pieces of one-way infrastructure that enable a long-term resource grab, locking extracted fuel into the European gas grid. The Shah Deniz field off Baku, Turkmeni reserves yet to be discovered, this ploughed field at Rəhimli we are standing in – they all play a role in a particular vision of Europe's energy future.

The trees at the edge of the field where we had sat with the women six years ago are now joined by more familiar marker posts. We turn from them, clamber into Mehdi's mud-spattered Lada, and continue west.

---

18   J. Vinois, *Security of Gas Supply in the EU*, European Energy Forum, 6 October 2008; M. Alvera, *Security of Supply: Does the Future Lay on Gas Pipelines / Infrastructure?*, European Energy Forum, 6 October 2008.

19   The recent rapid expansion in the US of shale gas extraction – known as 'fracking' – has led to a drop in demand for imports.

20   'EU Offers $21 Billion for Trans-Saharan Pipeline', afrol.com, 18 September 2008.

21   J. Vinois, *Security of Gas Supply in the EU*.

7 SCHRADER'S INSTRUCTION IS PAPER FOR THE TOILET

BTC KP 320 – 507 KM – HACALLI, AZERBAIJAN

The Easter sky is overcast on this bitingly cold morning. Light rain falls on the windscreen as we pass flat and fertile land. There are fields full of short wheat and clover, and shepherds herding small flocks of long-eared sheep. The land tilts away to the River Kura in the north.

We are headed for the village of Hacalli, which Mayis has visited many times over the past five years. The pipelines cross its land and there has been a long-running dispute over compensation – as there has in a number of villages along the route in Azerbaijan.

But today Mayis is tired and the roads are confusing, so it is taking us a while to find Hacalli. Outside the nearby village of Lǝk, we spot the marker posts running at right-angles to us, heading west. By the roadside stands one of BTC's block valves: positioned every few kilometres along the pipelines, these valves can shut off the flow of oil in an emergency. The small, square compounds are surrounded by high steel fencing and a concrete blast wall covered with smooth, pale grey cement. An outer fence is surmounted by CCTV cameras at each corner.

Mayis's brother Mehdi pulls over to ask for directions from a man in a bright orange BTC jumpsuit, standing next to the compound entrance. Not having taken photographs, we think little of the encounter as we follow his instructions to take the first left in Lǝk.

Two ponds mark the beginning of Hacalli. Black-winged stilts feed in the shallows, while swallows flit across the water's surface in pursuit of insects. A combine harvester rusts nearby. Mayis explains that in Soviet times land like this was either in a *kolkhoz*, a production cooperative, or a *sovkhoz*, a state farm. Three years after Heydar Aliyev returned to power, a Land Commission was set up in each village to divide up the farmland. The process, overseen by local Aliyev appointees, was notoriously corrupt. Large machines such as this combine were 'privatised', and in many cases left to rot.

We stop in the village. Each house is surrounded by a high wall, made either of large round river boulders or creamy grey cement blocks. Our host Mehman welcomes us into his compound. He is probably five foot six, strongly built, with another black flat cap, an eagle nose and a neatly clipped moustache.

Walking through a muddy yard containing an elm tree and piles of straw bales, we take off our shoes at the door and enter a long, thin room. With large wooden-framed windows on three sides, this room is very cold – we are glad to have been offered slippers. The walls are sparsely decorated: just a large poster of the Masjid al-Haram in Mecca and some prints of black-and-gold Arabic calligraphy.

Mehman's diminutive mother comes out from behind a curtain and greets us. His three children hang around, including a six-year-old bundled up in a furry jacket, hat and striped gloves.

Mehman and Mayis converse intently in Azeri; Mayis translates. Many families in the village, he says, have been affected by the forty-four-metre-wide pipeline corridor. During the construction period, when the topsoil was removed, deep trenches dug across the land, and the army of machines came to weld the pipes and crane them into the ground, these smallholders who live mostly off their farms were unable to use their fields. Once the project was complete and the topsoil reinstated, the land was returned to the farmers. Every landowner was supposed to receive compensation for not being able to grow their crops for several years, equivalent to their lost income; but fourteen families in the village did not receive any compensation at all. It seems that BP made some payments, but to the wrong people.

Mayis draws a diagram in his notebook to demonstrate the issue. 'BP claimed Mehman's land was over there – far away from the route. But it is not there, it is right here on the route.' The sums at stake are substantial for the families of Hacalli. According to BP's compensation guidelines, most of them should have been paid around $4,000, equivalent to over a year's salary. Such sums are insignificant to a company of BP's size; but, like any corporation, it seeks to maximise profits, and in this instance saved money by not making additional payments.

BP has repeatedly refused to deal with the issue, insisting that Mehman and the others' claims are groundless. They say that the issue is one of local corruption, and so not their responsibility. While the company clearly faced a challenge in arranging payments to villagers, Mayis believes they are acting arrogantly. 'BP took their land. It must make sure it compensates the right people. They can't just say "We gave somebody the money, now they can sort it out between themselves".'

The fourteen families took their complaint to both the local court and the Azeri supreme court, but both rejected their cases. The judicial system is widely recognised to be both corrupt and politicised. The families wanted to push the issue into the international legal arena. So Mayis, together with the Corner House and Kurdish Human Rights Project, is trying to take their cases to the European

Court of Human Rights. Mehman explains, 'We've been to court several times already. And Dawson came here, he sat on that sofa too.'

The name 'Dawson' can be heard throughout the small villages on the Azeri plains, Georgian mountains and Turkish plateau, where opinions differ over his identity: sometimes he is a British minister, sometimes a European diplomat, sometimes a lawyer. 'Dawson', in fact, is Duncan Lawson, a British civil servant then in the Department of Trade and Industry (DTI). His visit along the route resulted from years of pressure by Nick Hildyard of the Corner House.

The Organisation for Economic Cooperation and Development (OECD), has adopted guidelines on responsible business practices for multinational enterprises (MNEs). Complaints about a breach in guidelines can be made to the OECD's National Contact Point, the NCP, in the country where the multinational company is headquartered. For BP this is of course Britain. This NCP is a civil servant based in an industry-related department. In the UK's case, this was Duncan Lawson, working out of the DTI. Thus, during the public campaign challenging BTC, Hildyard had raised Hacalli's problems with the NCP at the DTI , invoking the OECD's MNE guidelines. The acronym-heavy structure gives an insight into the inaccessibility of this complaints process.

Together with allies in the region and across Europe, Hildyard has been driving a complaint against BP for violations across Azerbaijan, Georgia and Turkey since 2003. For years the British government dragged its feet, hoping the complaint would go away. After challenging repeated attempts to dismiss the issues, Hildyard pushed 'Dawson' at least to visit the pipeline. Eager to please a British government department, BP promised to cover costs and drive the civil servant to all relevant locations, but Hildyard insisted on a strict equity protocol. So 'Dawson' spent half his time with BP, and half hosted by local campaigners.

We have with us a thick document – BP's official response to Lawson's report, a heap of A4 photocopies in its see-through plastic sleeve.

One of these is a copy of a handwritten note in Azeri, signed on 10 November 2005 by various BP officials and the village's Executive Power – a state representative appointed in every community by the president to oversee the village. The letter states that the land complaint issue is groundless, and has been thrown out of court. This sheet of paper was carried back to BP Azerbaijan's offices at Villa Petrolea, where it was translated and typed up. Gathered together with other Azeri paperwork, it was sent to BP's head office in London to be collated with similar documents from Georgia and Turkey. Packaged neatly, the final response was handed to the DTI in December 2005.

Bizarrely, BP then refused permission for this response to be shared with the complainants: Corner House, Mayis and the others who had raised the original concerns. Only in February 2009, after three years and threats of legal action, was the document released – with strict guidelines that it must not be digitised or shared with others, including community partners in Turkey. In March 2009, Hildyard gave us hard copies, with which we have returned to Hacalli.

A man runs across the yard outside and enters the house out of breath, introducing himself, between gasps, as the village mayor. He has received a call from the BTC worker who gave us directions to Hacalli, and who claimed he had seen two foreigners in a car with a map, who had come to plant mines along the pipeline. The mayor tells us that the local police force, the Ministry of National Security, and the Executive Power are all on their way to interrogate us.

Unsure what to do, we turn to Mayis, who sits up sternly, straightening his back and his tie. Presenting a confident façade, he announces to us, rather cryptically, 'We will explain in cold blood'.

A police major enters the house, ruddy-cheeked, in a uniform bedecked with insignias, and a large fur hat. We remain sitting, but shake his hand. He sits across the coffee table from us, and tells us to accompany him to the police station. Mayis refuses, stating that we have done nothing wrong, and that we would only go if the officer produced a written warrant for our arrest.

Outside, three squad cars block the entrance to Mehman's compound, and several police guard the gate. Two more men enter the house. One is a quiet man with a mouth full of gold teeth: the village's Executive Power. The other, evidently the more senior, wears a pinstripe suit and black overcoat, and exudes anger. Sitting down opposite Mayis, he announces that he is from the MTN, the feared Ministry of National Security, successor to the KGB in Azerbaijan.

Apparently, we have been near strategic infrastructure, and our presence is highly problematic. He is here to investigate and needs our documents. Now!

Mayis: Why should I show you my passport? Show me your documentation that you can demand it first.

MTN: No! You need to show me your documentation first. We already took your brother's ID when we saw him waiting in the car outside.

Mayis: Why should I? And you need to give my brother's ID back.

MTN: Bill Schrader of BP signed an order that everybody must be stopped and checked who asks questions, takes pictures or is looking around near the pipeline.

Mayis: I'm sorry to be rude, but this instruction signed by Schrader is paper for the toilet. For me, the important document is the constitution of Azerbaijan. As citizens, we have a right to move in the country freely. Who is Schrader? We have our own president, Ilham Aliyev – not Schrader.

MTN: Please don't use rude words like that. Do you not know what BTC is? This is very strategic territory; you cannot be here. There are pipelines going to Supsa, Erzurum and Ceyhan. You don't have any right to visit the strategic villages without permission from relevant bodies.

Mayis: You can't teach me about BTC. I have spoken about it to members of the

German Bundestag, the European and the Italian parliament. Who are these 'relevant bodies'? If people know that Schrader has to give permission for going places, this will cause problems for Azerbaijan in Europe. Why are you creating a bad reputation for Azerbaijan by acting like this?

Throughout this fierce exchange between Mayis and the secret policeman across the small coffee table with its white lace tablecloth, everybody else – Mehman, and his wife, mother and three children – stand stock still around the room. The major, still wearing his furry hat, pours himself tea.

Mayis explains that his name is Mayis Gulaliyev, but refuses to show his ID and demands to see their documents. We hand our passports to the MTN official, who scribbles our names down into his notebook with a blue biro. To our amazement, his notebook is a 2007 BP pocket diary – a diary two years out of date. Here is a senior state security policeman using cast-off stationery. Perhaps it tells us something about the proximity of company and state. We ask the official's name.

MTN: I am Nazim Babayev, deputy head in the Gəncə branch of the Milli Təhlukəsizlik Nazirliyi security police – the second office in the country. You are not allowed to stop near the pipeline.

Mayis: Where are the signs? Do you have signs saying 'Drive quickly' or 'Don't stop'? Are there signs saying 'This is territory of national security – you cannot be here'? Is there a sign above the village warning 'Closed area – village of strategic importance'. No, there isn't. So I have the right to come here, to travel under the constitution.

During these exchanges, Mayis takes a position of moral authority, facing down the police by explaining that they are denigrating the constitution while he is defending it. Fighting abuse by invoking the constitution echoes the struggles of Soviet and Eastern European dissidents such as Sakarov and Havel.

Mayis argues it out, until after a long time Nazim and the police major back down, realising that they are not going to succeed in intimidating him. They try to laugh it off. 'I already know who you are, Mayis, I have seen you in the newspapers.'

It is made clear that we are to be detained inside the house while BTC security officers decide whether or not to take the issue to the State Special Protection Service of Azerbaijan. This is the elite military unit, directly under the command of President Aliyev, whose responsibilities include guarding the BTC and SCP pipelines.[1] With that the officials leave, and a ripple of relief spreads across the room. Mayis's body relaxes, and he slumps back into his armchair. Mehman's family, silent during the questioning, erupt: 'We have never seen this many police

---

1   Republic of Azerbaijan Special State Protection Service, 'Another World-Scale Confidence', at dmx.gov.az.

here before. If somebody dies and we call 1,000 times for them to come, these people will not come. And now they send three cars and fifteen police!'

Two police cars remain parked outside, blocking the gateway. With the smell of something delicious wafting in from the kitchen and hungry bellies as the adrenaline subsides, Mayis gleefully translates that, since we are under house arrest, we will have to have lunch here.

Over vegetable fritters and stewed apricots, Mayis explains that he is very conscious of his body language during interactions like this, that every move helps prevent him from being cowed. He wears a tie, so that it is clear he is from Baku, and did not rise when the policemen came in; nor did he shake their hands. 'Because otherwise they take your hand behind your back and handcuff you, just to show their power. And then you've lost.'

Mehman, smiling and ebullient when we arrived, is now quiet and anxious, afraid of repercussions. He farms his land, but also works part-time as a maintenance man in the village school, and his wife is the school cleaner. They are worried that the Executive Power will make them lose their jobs.

This man – the quiet man with the gold teeth – is Mubariz Mammador. In November 2005, he had countersigned BP's letter to 'Dawson' stating that the villagers had no grounds for compensation. Significantly, while village mayors are elected by their communities, the Executive Power in every village is appointed through the presidential apparatus. This system created by the Aliyevs gives the regime control over what is effectively a parallel power structure throughout society, with authority over local issues including schools, elections and land. The local Executive Power is involved in policing the pipeline, including suppressing dissent, and has authority over these people's livelihoods.

Apparently, after each of Mayis's previous visits, the Executive Power put pressure on Mehman and his friends to drop their complaints. 'If they are angry because of our complaints, they can take our jobs. Also, they can easily claim that we have narcotics, and then arrest us.' Mehman's neighbour Zahed, who also received no compensation for his land, adds that the police have come to his home at night several times to harass him. 'Very few of us have telephones of any sort, so it is hard to communicate – to tell Mayis what happens here.'

Finally Mehdi, stuck outside with the police throughout the detention, enters and announces that the last squad cars have now left. It seems they were called away, and left no indication as to what would now happen – so we presume that we are free to go. 'I told the police, "Please don't wait here for me – you should be out there making money for your families by the roadside!"' Everybody bursts out laughing, understanding his reference to the police's habit of randomly stopping motorists and demanding bribes.

He continues, to more laughter, 'When they arrived and said they were looking for foreigners who were planting mines, I told them, "You have reported Feyzalla's bombs"!' A policeman working in nineteenth-century Tsarist Russia, Feyzalla was the hero of a popular Azeri novel. When ordered by his superiors to find bombs, he reports a whole delivery of spherical explosives that turn out to be watermelons.

We make our way out to the disputed fields, with both of us and Mehman and Zahed crammed into the back of Mehdi's Lada, bumping down the street past the old combine and the village pond, out onto the wide flatness of the wheat and clover fields. The land stretches away to purple hills in the distance.

A track of pale brown earth takes us through the crops. Startled by us, a flock of larks scatters. There, to our left and right, are the yellow markers of both BTC and SCP in close parallel, running across the land. The 300-kilometre post stands nearby. The crude being pumped under us left Sangachal almost two days ago, and was drilled from beneath the deep Caspian waters within the last week.

With Mehman's instructions we pace out his land: 100 metres in one direction, 30 metres in the other. The pipeline corridor runs right through his field. 'This is my land, and the pipeline clearly runs through it. If this is not my land, someone should show me where mine is.'

The wind blows cold from the east, as the larks call out to each other. We walk back towards the white Lada, following the three men in their flat black caps.

The events in Hacalli on that Easter weekend in April 2009 expose the nature of 'security' imposed by this industrial infrastructure, and the restrictions placed on local villagers in standing up for their rights. No one was tortured, and the overall dynamic might not appear traumatic; but Mayis is correct when he argues that the MTN and BTC guards along the route increase 'fear in our society – you can see it in their faces. How can you fight against corruption when you are intimidated like this?'

In effect, the land and villages alongside the pipeline have been turned into a security zone. Just as Mehman had feared, months later the Executive Power caused him to lose his job, having him fired as the maintenance man in the village school. Feeling a level of responsibility due to our presence, we try to support him from afar through these harsh times. We know that we responded to a request to visit Hacalli, to hear their complaints, but remain troubled over our role in Mehman's life.

BP's interconnectedness with the Aliyev regime goes beyond underwriting it with revenues. The company's cooperation with the repressive system operates on multiple levels: local Executive Powers in villages, the Azeri secret service, and the troops of the Special State Protection Service of Azerbaijan. Nazim Babayev threatened Mayis by citing a document apparently signed by the president of BP

Azerbaijan and the state security police.[2] The close collaboration is evident from the speedy phone calls and responses between the orange-jumpsuited BTC man and the MTN headquarters in Gəncə after we asked for directions. In the case of Hacalli, these institutions have enabled BP to avoid settling the issue of whether the correct families have been compensated.

In the face of this pressure, it is not surprising to hear the despair in Mayis's voice when he asks, 'How many years can a man fight, without achievements? I am very tired – psychologically, not physically. Of course, we have some small victories – some people were compensated because of our demands. But we are pushing for something bigger. Our essential aims are to provide justice – but they give this money to avoid providing justice.'

---

2 BP denied the existence of this document in a phone call with Platform in June 2009. However, a Bilateral Security Protocol for BP facilities was signed in 2007, covering the use of force and cooperation between BP and Azerbaijan. More detailed procedures for the Azeri Export Pipelines Protection Department were agreed with BP in 2009. *BP in Azerbaijan: Sustainability Report 2010*, BP, 2011, p. 19.

8 DO YOU HAVE ANY BOOKS?

Pulling into the city of Gəncə after dark, following an hour's slow drive from Hacallı, we find what was once the Soviet Intourist building still open, newly renovated and renamed the Gəncə Hotel. Azerbaijan's second city, pronounced 'Ganja', has been a place of trade for millennia. Following the Seljuk conquest in the eleventh century, the importance of the town on the main route west from Baku grew. Camel trains, some loaded with bales of crude oil, passed through here headed for Tbilisi, Erzerum and İstanbul. Centuries later the Baku–Batumi Railway was built through the town. More recently, the city witnessed repeated battles and insurrection. After a battle at Gəncə the armies of Tsar Nicholas I marched into Persia and won the decisive victory that led to the Treaty of Turkmenchay and the annexation of Transcaucasia into the Russian Empire. It was in Gəncə that the troops of the Azerbaijani Democratic Republic fought their last battle against the Red Army in 1920, and here that Heydar Aliyev faced down a rebellion in June 1993, beginning his return to power.

Despite Gəncə's continued role as a regional transport hub, late-night food offerings are meagre. The kebab stalls are closed, and all we can find is a *piti* tavern about to shut. *Piti* is a soup of mutton, chickpeas, tomatoes and potatoes baked in individual crocks, but we are too late for something like this. There is only one potato left, the meat is finished, and the heat has been turned off. We settle for mugs of cold broth with large globs of mutton fat.

As we make slow progress through our dinner, Mayis tells us the story of the official BTC pipeline-monitoring process back in 2004 and 2005. 'The Open Society Institute, OSI, had agreed to run a monitoring programme of the pipeline together with BP.' At this time, Sabit Bagirov was still chair of OSI, and an advisor to the process. He arranged a roundtable, where he announced a competition to choose NGOs for four monitoring teams. 'Our organisation, Centre for Civic Intiatives, was selected to be in the human rights team.'

Each team was given explanations of the BTC construction process, as well as certain problems to look for and procedures to document. Mayis continues: 'Then a "monitoring maestro" was brought in, to teach us – Clive Morgan, an auditor from Wales who has done much work for oil companies.' Meanwhile, Galib Efendiev, of Revenue Watch, who we had met in the Caspian Plaza in Baku, repeatedly encouraged Mayis to be critical of BP, but not too critical: 'We want to organise another monitoring next year. So please do good reports so we can continue this project.'

By the beginning of 2005, Mayis had conducted his research in a number of villages along the pipeline, including Hacalli, and circulated his findings to the rest of the human rights team, asking to see what the other members had discovered. It turned out that nobody else had travelled to the affected areas. The others emailed back that Mayis's report was great, and apologised for being lazy. But after fifteen days all the monitors received a letter from Sabit as OSI coordinator. It contained a loaded question: Which of them, asked Sabit, was prepared to put their signature under Mayis's report?

Mayis was away in Prague for training. In his absence, his fellow monitors discussed his report with Sabit. They then wrote him a joint letter that told him he had no right to include their names, and that he should not include the villagers' complaints. 'I was furious', says Mayis. Two days before they had been in favour of the report; now they had all, unaccountably, reversed their opinions.

When Mayis returned from Prague, the group of monitors met again. Sabit was irate from the start, demanding that all quotes and names needed to be excluded. The others concurred, and tried to cajole and intimidate Mayis into agreement. Their main argument was about safety for the landowners, which Mayis considered 'ridiculous' as the landowners had wanted their names listed in the hope that their specific complaints would be addressed.

Mayis explains that the general political climate in Azerbaijan is clearly repressive, but points out that, if the monitoring teams considered complaining about BP to be too dangerous, 'this means that there was collusion between the company and the new KGB. And this was a major denial of freedom of speech by BTC – an issue which I felt we had to raise loudly.' The meeting had continued until 10 p.m., with Mayis's head ringing from everybody's comments and Sabit's anger. In the end, he agreed to exclude individuals' names on the condition that specific villages were identified and that he could speak at the final press conference.

After they had printed an Azeri edition of the report, the 'monitoring expert' Clive Morgan edited the English version. Mayis felt that Morgan's changes toned down the villagers' concerns over human rights violations and made the conclusions less assertive. For Morgan, the 'professionalisation' of the report apparently meant making it less critical.

Before the press conference, Morgan announced that they needed to rehearse. He set up a video-camera and acted as a journalist asking questions. Mayis remembers how each time he said something critical, he was instructed how to change it. In the end, he explained that the whole process made a mockery of genuine monitoring. He said to camera: 'The Open Society Institute is trying to have close relations with BP, to work together with them. It is covering up the real impacts.' Morgan turned off the video in alarm: 'No, no, no, no! You can't say this.'

The day before the conference, a press release was prepared. Mayis fought to include the line: 'We found many human rights violations.' But when he arrived at the OSI office the next morning, the sentence was gone. 'I was angry. I took the paper and ripped it up. Then I went directly to the International Press Centre for the press conference.' But Sabit, Galib, Morgan and the other team coordinators arrived before him. The room was full of journalists, but the others had taken all the places on the podium. Mayis did not want to add a chair and sit at the edge, thinking that they would cut him out from the camera view. So he told the coordinator of the social group, 'Get up, this is my place.' He asked 'Why?' and Mayis responded, 'Because you are a slave of BP.' 'So they let me sit there, to prevent a scandal in front of the journalists.'

'I demanded to speak at the end. I explained that there were many human rights violations, and that BP wanted to hide them.' The press conference was supposed to be strictly one hour, but it was extended so the others could speak again, to attack and criticise Mayis personally, saying: 'He is alone, he is wrong, he doesn't know what he is saying.'

The next day, not one newspaper raised the issue of human rights violations; even the photo captions did not mention Mayis's name, only the names of those sitting on either side of him. 'They called it a monitoring process. But what is the result of their watching? Has it changed anything?'

We had had Mayis in mind when, at our meeting at Villa Petrolea, we asked Aydin Gasimov of BP what had changed as a result of the monitoring programme. He had replied that it had 'taught Azeri NGOs to monitor and audit big projects like pipelines'. In this view, the purpose of 'monitoring' is not neccessarily to improve the infrastructure being monitored, but appears instead to mean teaching monitors that a human rights violation is not really a human rights violation.

As we toy with our *piti* and listen to Mayis, we are struck by how the attempts of villagers to have their voices heard is smothered at all levels, and by how courageous and determined Mayis is. For over four years he has kept faith with the likes of Mehman and his family as they struggle to gain some kind of justice, while others in the Baku NGO world have long since moved on.

Walking back to the old Intourist hotel, we pass through Gəncə's great main square, at its centre a cluster of plane trees full of rooks cawing in the darkness. Dominating one side of the square is the grand, colonnaded city hall, a Stalinist relic. But Gəncə's most colossal architecture is to be found in the suburbs. Sergo Orjonikidze, fellow Bolshevik activist and Stalin's Bailov prison-mate, played a key role in the transformation of Gəncə as head of the Soviet Higher Economic Council from 1928, and was heavily involved in developing the Soviet Union's first two Five-Year Plans of 1928 and 1933. Under his direction, the city underwent rapid industrialisation, with many new factories and metalworks built. From some distance away we can see a towering red-brick chimney with the date '1932' painted high up in four white numerals.

Despite the pre-World War I growth of Baku, Tbilisi and Batumi, and the building of the railway connecting them, the Caucasus, like the rest of the USSR, had remained a largely agrarian society. All this was to change in a single decade: the 1930s. In ten years, the Soviet Union's economy was industrialised – a process that had taken England over a century. 'Soviet urbanisation, in tempo and scale, is without parallel in history', wrote Isaac Deutscher.[1] The collectivisation of land, the mechanisation of agriculture and the development of cities such as Gəncə and Sumqayit transformed the region.

In 1932 Hubert Knickerbocker, a journalist with the *New York Evening Post*, wrote of a visit to Azerbaijan in terms that, viewed from Depression-era America, must have seemed utopian: 'I drove over twenty miles of perfect asphalt pavement through mile after mile of new settlements, snowy white, the architecture neo-oriental . . . The street system that replaced horse-cars four years ago is the best in Russia. The new electric inter-urban line connecting the "Black City" where the wells are thickest has the most artistic station.' Walking around, Knickerbocker heard a shot ring out, and traced it to a shooting range with a political theme: 'Hit a Capitalist and up rises a Social Democrat. Hit a hog and his head changes to that of a fat-jowled banker . . . Baku, though rich, is still Red.'[2]

Rapid industrialisation, of course, needed massive quantities of fuel. But much of the oil from the Caspian oilfields was exported in order to keep foreign currency flooding into the USSR. Knickerbocker described how the oil workers had an immense 'determination to get out every barrel with the utmost speed and convert it as quickly as possible into dollars so desperately needed for the Five-Year Plan'. With the Soviet oil industry under the remit of the Higher Economic Council, Orjonikidze was effectively the chairman of one of the world's major oil corporations, a rival to Shell and the Anglo-Persian Oil Company. When the first Five-Year Plan started, in 1928, oil production stood at 11.7 million tonnes; by the end of the five years, it had almost doubled.[3]

---

1   R. Suny, *The Soviet Experiment: Russia, The USSR, and the Successor States*, OUP, 1998, p. 249.
2   H. R. Knickerbocker, 'The Soviet Five-Year Plan', *International Affairs* 10: 4 (July 1931).
3   A. Nove, *Economic History of the USSR*, Penguin, 1991, p. 192.

From 1928 to 1940, industrial output in the USSR grew by 17 per cent each year – a growth rate unparalleled before or since, including in China. The new steel and stone buildings, mechanised mass transport and grand palaces of culture, in Gəncə and elsewhere, 'were a promise of the coming rewards for the sacrifices and pain that they had endured during the "Great Stalinist Breakthrough".[4] Orjonikidze himself did not live to see this new world, probably committing suicide due to Stalin's Great Purge.[5]

By the start of the fifth Five-Year Plan, in 1951, Gəncə had become one of the industrial cities of the Soviet Union. But the sacrifices required were immense. Without the capital resources or colonies that the Western economies had, Soviet industry was built on the backs and the bodies of its workers and peasants. Millions toiled in the Gulags, constructing canals and roads. Even in those factories which did not depend on penal labour, workers were tied to their jobs through restrictive 'Labour Books'.

The following day, after dusk, we explore the suburbs of the city, walking to the rusted gates of a metallurgy plant famed in the Soviet Union, now a great hulk dominating acres of grassy wasteland, concrete and brick rubble. Train tracks run into the bushes and past the ruined walls of derelict warehouses. Redundant cranes rise above the collapsed roofs, giants looming in the dark. A couple on an evening stroll nearby explain that, only two days previously, Gəncə's aluminium factory had announced its closure. With the loss of 800 jobs, it symbolises the end of an eighty-year vision for the city.

As with Sumqayit, decades of heavy industry have left their legacy in the earth, water and air. A 1993 study found dangerous levels of polychlorinated biphenyls in the soils around Gəncə's manufacturing sites. Near the industrial zone once stood the medieval mausoleum of Nizami Gencevi – Azerbaijan's national poet, who in the twelfth century wrote and retold Persian and Arabic love stories such as *Layli and Majnoon* and *Khosrow and Shirin*. By the 1970s, airborne pollution from the aluminium plant was eroding the limestone mausoleum. It collapsed entirely in 1988.

When the numbers '1932' were painted on the factory chimney, it was seen as a monument to the vision of the Soviet state, a new economic power. Seventy-five years later we can read it as a relic from an era of brutal forced industrialisation. How much harder it is to read the industrial infrastructure of the pipeline. It seems innocent and mundane, silent beneath fields dotted with flowers or great expanses of plough-land. Yet BTC is also a monument – both to a vision of Western power

---

4   Suny, *Soviet Experiment*, p. 250.
5   Orjonikidze was registered as dying from a heart attack, but Khrushchev made the suicide claim in his famous Secret Speech in 1956.

projected across the Caucasus, and to a vision of the new Azeri state and its reasserted independence. Outside the ruined metallurgy plant we find ourselves asking: How will people look at the pipeline seventy-five years hence?

The new infrastructure of the BTC pipeline does not bring with it the labour camps and purges of the 1930s and 1940s, yet this steel pipe also causes death and destruction. Each year, the pipeline can pump 365 million barrels of crude onto the world market. These can then be converted into more carbon dioxide emissions than Belgium and Denmark produce together – over 150 million tonnes of CO_2 a year. These emissions are changing the Earth's climate, and it is estimated that over 300,000 people die from climate change every year.[6] The exact figures can be disputed, but ultimately the logic is simple: pumping crude through the pipeline leads to more climate change and to many more associated deaths.

The connection between carbon dioxide emissions and the altering of the Earth's atmosphere acquired scientific currrency during the 1970s. By 1992 it was of such concern that the United Nations Framework on Climate Change Convention was signed – the ultimate foundation for the Kyoto Protocol. In the same years that John Browne and his team were fighting to gain access to the reserves of hydrocarbons beneath the Caspian, this international treaty-based process of addressing climate change had started. The ACG rigs, Shah Deniz and the BTC pipeline were all built when there was general public recognition of the dangers of transferring carbon from beneath the ground into the atmosphere.

The oil industry, financial institutions and governments obfuscate, disclaim responsibility, and insist that they are answering the higher priority of meeting the needs of modern society. But one day, will those who have consciously chosen to profit from continued fossil-fuel extraction, despite prior knowledge that this will lead to more deaths, be held to account? Some judges have already begun to engage with questions of responsibility for climate change.

But court cases are unlikely to be successful without a political shift that makes this catastrophe, and the fossil-fuel structures that help drive it, as unacceptable as Stalin's industrialism. It is a transition that will not happen without conflict. For both forms of industrial endeavour – the factory of 1932 and BTC – have delivered prosperity, wealth and modernity to some parts of society, and death and destruction to others: those without power.

BTC KP 442 – 629 KM – KRAZNY MOST, AZERBAIJAN

The *marshrutka* pulls up at its final destination three hours north-west of Gəncə, the end of the road in Azerbaijan. Mayis has brought us to the border with Georgia, so we bid him farewell.

---

6 L. Gray, 'Climate Change 'Kills 300,000 Every Year', *Daily Telegraph*, 29 May 2009.

We clamber out of the shared taxi, grab our bags, and are faced with some low grey buildings, a maze of barbed-wire fencing, and tired border guards lounging in the shade. The sun glares down as we weave our way to the right entrance. An upturned bucket and a couple of packets of cigarettes lie unattended on the ground; the seller must have wandered off – there are not many customers around.

Three uniformed, fur-hatted border guards ask to see our papers. 'What were you doing in Azerbaijan? Where have you been? What have you done? Did you take any photos? Let us look at your camera.'

We should have expected this. Our camera has photographs from the pipeline route on it: images of marker posts in Qarabork and Rəhimli, of the field at Hacallı. We procrastinate, while Mika takes the battery out and fiddles with the lens in the hope of getting a chance to wipe the memory; but the guards watch closely. They take the camera, and our hearts sink. As Mayis had pointed out, there were no signs in Hacallı warning that taking photographs was forbidden, but we know that our having pictures of the pipeline will alarm the border guards. Our British–Kurdish friend Kerim Yildiz of the Kurdish Human Rights Project was deported from Azerbaijan in February 2005 purely for asking questions about BTC in Baku.

An English-speaking soldier examines the camera and flicks through the photographs. Within seconds he has returned it. Apparently he has not accessed the photos correctly. 'Only three photographs! From your entire time in Azerbaijan? Do you not find our country beautiful?' Thanking our lucky stars, we explain that we emailed our favourite pictures back to England.

The Xram River gurgles in a small valley to our right. An enormous flock of sheep stretches up the hillside beyond, obscuring all but the border watchtowers at the top. The three soldiers wave us through, but we are stopped a few metres later by two prosperous-looking customs officials. They glare at our rucksacks: clearly they are not keen to dig through all our belongings. But their next question puts us on edge again. 'Do you have any books?'

Not hash or heroin. Nor weapons or explosives. Nor even large quantities of currency. Books.

We had been warned that carrying printed matter in Azerbaijan could land us in trouble. Mayis had told us the saga of publishing Platform's book about the planned BTC pipeline, entitled *Some Common Concerns*. In 2003 he had translated it into both Russian and Azeri. First he published the Russian version, inviting BP, opposition MPs and NGOs to the release. The response was fierce. Sabit Bagirov, coordinator of the pro-BTC coalition, threw a copy of the book across the table, shouting: 'It is very dangerous to publish such books in Azerbaijan. You are supporting the Armenian occupation. You should be careful!' Several newspapers ran articles attacking Mayis. A long piece in the Popular Front's *Azadlıq* newspaper attacked the book as dangerous, asking why the National Security Ministry had not stopped it from being released. The article was signed 'Saadet Jahangirqizi'. Mayis believes the author was a BP staff member.

Nor was the MTN, the secret police, slow to act. The original publisher was intimidated to try and prevent the distribution of the printed Russian books. When Mayis tried to have the Azeri translation printed, he discovered that publishers had been warned not to do so. 'I couldn't find anybody in Baku to print it – it seemed like the MTN had spoken to everybody!' Many had received a call making clear that this book had been deemed 'enemy propaganda'. 'Clearly, the government was trying to ban a version of *Some Common Concerns* that most Azeris could read. So I announced publicly that I would print it across the border, in Dagestan. A couple of months later, when attention was elsewhere, we had it printed by a large company that belongs to an ally of the regime. Because the company is so close to power, they don't check what they're printing as carefully. And the MTN probably didn't even think to warn them!'

Within days there was another storm of criticism and attacks on the book, but it was too late. Mayis and the Centre for Civic Initiatives had the books, and had begun distributing them.

'Books?' repeats the border official. Opening one of our rucksacks, Mika hands over the large volume of photographs of BTC, prepared for the 2005 Presidential launch of the pipeline and given to us by Orxan Abassov at Sangachal. Unable to read the English text, the customs official turns the pages, until he hits on one with curvy non-Latin script. 'Aaaah – Armenian!' he says, clearly happy to have caught us with something controversial. 'No, Georgian', James responds. 'A present from BP.'

The book seems to have generated enough excitement for the day, and we are waved on through a tightly fenced corridor, checked by three more soldiers, and then we have our exit visas.

We make our way towards no man's land. Then behind us there is a noise, and a soldier is running alongside the fence, sprinting after us. We speed up, hoping to cross the line before he reaches us, but it looks unlikely. 'What's your name?' he shouts. And then: 'American tourists?' We smile, and we're through.

To our left is an old, disused bridge built of red brick: Krasny Most. Once the main crossing between the two countries, Krasny Most was the scene of the Red Army invasion of Menshevik Georgia in 1921. Following the collapse of Tsarist Russia, the Democratic Republic of Georgia declared itself an independent state on 26 May 1918, two days before the new government of the Azeri Republic also made its proclamation of independence, while in exile in Tbilisi. Ruled by the Menshevik Socialist party, Georgia requested aid and protection from the Western Allies, and therefore welcomed in British troops six months later – those battalions that included James's grandfather and General Thompson of Baku. But the withdrawal of British forces in 1919 left Georgia vulnerable to the advance of the Red Army into the Caucasus. By November 1920 both independent Azerbaijan and Armenia had fallen, and Georgia stood alone.

In the early hours of 16 February 1921, 17,000 troops, 3,000 horses, 400 machine guns and four armoured cars poured over Krasny Most under the command of Sergo Orjonikidze. Using the engines that pulled the oil wagons along the railway 4 Baku, the Bolsheviks intended to move five powerful armoured trains and eight tanks across the border. But further down the line the Georgian Army blew up the Poylu Railway Bridge.

Despite strong Georgian resistance, the overwhelming number of troops helped the Red Army reach the outskirts of Tbilisi quickly.[7] Once the bridge was repaired, the armoured trains tore through the Georgian defences and the government withdrew its last forces west towards Batumi. Nine days after the crossing of Krasny Most, Orjonikidze, riding a white horse, triumphantly led his soldiers into Tbilisi.

After the new Soviet Socialist Republic of Georgia was established and absorbed into the USSR, the Baku–Batumi Railway ran again through a single political unit, carrying oil to the Black Sea port. Lenin launched the Soviet Union's New Economic Plan; production in Baku slowly began to mount, following the disruption of war and revolution. The Soviets engaged American, British, German and Norwegian companies to upgrade refineries and drilling technology in the oilfields of Bibi Heybat and Balakhani. The kerosene pipeline that ran parallel to the railway was repaired and augmented: the Oil Road had been re-established.

A lone moneychanger stands in no man's land on the new bridge, built parallel with the red brick arch. Beyond him is the Georgian border post in a smart new building with white walls, CCTV, an X-ray machine, and a digital camera to photograph us as we enter. A sign announces that this is an EU-sponsored checkpoint.

BTC KP 446 – 633 KM – ჯანდარა (JANDARA), GEORGIA

The *marshrutka* minibus to Rustavi, the first big city in Georgia, takes us near the massive Jandara Pumping Station. The size of five football pitches, this looks like a refinery humming in the morning air. Pipes, cylindrical oil-storage tanks and metal towers dominate the surrounding fields. We had passed it before on a train bound for Baku, and seen its yellow and red lights rear out of the surrounding

---

7 'Georgians also had several modern airplanes that were of much better quality than those in possession of the Red Army. However, due to the absence of proper oil and spare parts that the government refused to purchase, Georgian pilots were incapable of taking full advantage of their technical superiority.' A. Andersen and G. Partskhaladze, 'Soviet–Georgian War and Sovietization of Georgia 1921', *Revue historique des Armées* 254 (2009).

darkness. A flare lit up the night and the white smoke rose from chimneys into the sky. It is daytime now, and the smell of sulphur fills our nostrils.

This is one of eight pumping stations built along the BTC pipeline, two of which are in Georgia. Together, they can force the weight of a million barrels of oil a day over the Caucasus mountains. In Azerbaijan the 440 kilometres of pipe run relatively flat, rising gradually from sea level. In Georgia, a length of just over half that distance becomes increasingly difficult, as BTC traverses the 2,500-metre-high Kodiana Pass. To shift this much liquid geology over such a distance requires immense energy. The pumps at Jandara, working constantly, are driven by five turbines fuelled by gas from the parallel SCP pipeline. These are effectively power stations, providing electricity not to the villages nearby, but power to the pumps that force the crude onwards and upwards, towards the tankers waiting on the Mediterranean.

Our *marshrutka* passes through a string of villages. In truth it is more like one long ribbon village. On either side of the road is a continuous line of houses, one deep, with a break of a few yards between the exit sign of one village and the welcome sign of the next. The indicators of spring are all around: cherry blossom in the yards, the land fresh brown and recently tilled. Five water buffalo chew on reeds. A man digs with a long-handled spade. Great egrets and hooded crows pick for grubs in the fields. Turkeys and pigs huddle by the sides of the road, near tiny churches, newly built and in good repair.

White steel 'grapevine crosses' stand ten feet tall by the roadside. With curiously drooping arms, these symbols are said to have been spread in the fourth century by Saint Nino. To avoid Roman repression, she escaped beyond the borders of the empire and evangelised in what is now Georgia, carrying a crucifix made from a grapevine entwined with her own hair. It remains unique to the Georgian Orthodox Church, – a distinct branch of Christianity that has been central to Georgia's identity over the centuries. Since the disintegration of the Soviet Union, the Georgian Church has grown in strength and is courted by politicians.

Sheep graze the short grass and the remains of last year's crops. Lines of poplars and willows criss-cross the landscape. The fields are dusty brown, quite distinct from those of western Georgia, where in the Black Sea watershed the woods are verdant and wet. This difference in climate is ancient, but modern shifts are making themselves felt. Days later, we visit Marina Shvangiradze of Georgia's Department of Environment, who explains to us that eastern Georgia is already experiencing major impacts of climate change. Local agriculture is especially hard-hit, with longer periods of drought and higher temperatures. Combined with strong spring winds, these meteorological changes have had adverse effects on agriculture: wheat production has halved, while sunflower crops have failed entirely. Georgia's central cities of Tbilisi and Rustavi are already struggling with falling water supply.

* * *

Far to the north we catch a glimpse of the Greater Caucasus. Among those peaks is Mount Kazbegi, one of the national emblems of Georgia, and the crag to which Prometheus was bound. This vast mountain range has historically sheltered Georgia and Azerbaijan from invasions from the north. Twenty years after the Red Army swept along the Caspian coast into Baku, and then Yerevan and Tbilisi, Soviet forces looked to the Caucasus as a defensive wall against another invader – the German Army.

In 1941, the forces of Nazi Germany launched a three-pronged, lightning attack across the Reich's eastern border. Punching through Soviet defences, they occupied wide swathes of territory. With 3.6 million soldiers, backed by 50,000 pieces of artillery and thousands of aircraft and tanks, this was the largest land invasion in history. Hitler had announced: 'This war will be a battle of annihilation . . . It will be very different from the war in the West.'[8] The Nazi plan was that the western parts of the USSR should be permanently annexed, in a model copied from the French and British empires. The war aim was partly to acquire resource colonies for the Reich – grain from the Ukraine and oil from the Caucasus; a redirecting of the Oil Road.

Moscow held out during the brutal winter battle of 1941. Then, in Operation Blau, over a million German soldiers advanced south and east, aiming for the oilfields of Maikop, Grozny and Baku. A swift pincer movement at Kharkov captured 250,000 Red Army soldiers. The Soviets retreated, destroying oilfields north of the Greater Caucasus to prevent them falling in German hands. Within weeks the fascists had reached Orjonikidze, the main town on the northern side of the mountains, now known as Vladikavkaz.[9]

The German Sixth Army was now in the shadow of Mount Kazbegi, on the border with Soviet Socialist Republic of Georgia and within reach of Baku. Anticipating its capture, Hitler's generals presented him with a cake decorated with a Baku oil rig. The Führer had earlier declared: 'unless we get Baku's oil, the war is lost'. Indeed in 1942, over 70 per cent of all Soviet tanks, aeroplanes and armoured vehicles were fuelled by oil from just two fields – Bibi Heybat and Balakhani. Without this crude, the Soviet mechanised forces would have ground to a halt. Since the Red Army's 1921 cavalry-led invasion of Georgia, the Soviet military had become mechanised and oil-fuelled, able to field 30,000 tanks, more than the rest of the world combined.

In the build-up to the war, oil extraction had been steadily growing. The day the Germans invaded, men and women were drafted into the oilfields as into the

---

8 Fifty-seven per cent of Soviet prisoners of war died after capture, while only 3.5 per cent of British and US prisoners met the same fate. Suny, *Soviet Experiment*.

9 The town was named after Sergo Orjonikidze, and remained so despite his suicide and fall from favour four years previously.

army. A week later, workers moved onto twelve-hour shifts, with no holidays. A year later, shifts ran for eighteen hours, seven days a week, with no rest days. As the last years of World War I had illustrated, oil was now the cornerstone of all modern warfare.

Once the German Army was within striking distance of Azerbaijan, Stalin ordered Baku's oil industry to be evacuated beyond the Urals. Ten thousand workers and all the drilling rigs from Baku were redeployed to the Volga, Tatarstan and Kazakhstan regions. Sections of the Baku–Batumi pipeline were disassembled and shipped east, and 764 wells were capped with concrete.

Azeri oil experts soon made Tatarstan 'the second Baku'. Within a year, Soviet oil extraction had returned to pre-war levels and the Nazis had failed to take Baku. The entire German Sixth Army was lost in the freezing ruins of Stalingrad; the Germans lost more men in one month than during the entire war on the western fronts. With enough oil to fuel its tanks, the Red Army slowly drove the Germans backwards. By March 1945, fascist casualties on Soviet territory had passed 6 million – 80 per cent of total German losses during the war.

But Baku oil production had crashed. With the imminent arrival of the fascist army, the oil engineers had aimed to destroy the wells rather than seal them temporarily. Even though the Germans never crossed the Caucasus mountains, their presence ended Baku's supremacy as the oil-producing centre of the Soviet Union. Its position was now shared with Tatarstan and Siberia. When work began on the next phase of development in Baku, offshore at Neft Dashlari, the new Cold War had halted the oil trade with the West. Until the 1930s the Oil Road had run north to Russia as well as west through Azerbaijan and Georgia by railway and pipeline. Now it ran overwhelmingly to the north.

BTC KP 475 – 662 KM – რუსთავი (RUSTAVI), GEORGIA

Lines of *Khrushchevki* stretch across the Gabardan steppe. The hazy silhouettes of these housing tower blocks are interspersed by steel mill chimneys with white and red stripes. The fifth Five-Year Plan, launched in 1951, doubled investment in housing construction. The next Plan, in 1956, doubled that sum again – although, as Khrushchev had declared in Baku, 'these are only temporary homes'. The quality of materials, the methods of construction and the aesthetics of these blocks were sacrificed to speed and quantity.

While such buildings are common throughout the suburbs of Azerbaijan and Georgia's ancient cities, Rustavi is almost totally composed of them. In a region where most communities have centuries if not millennia of history, modern Rustavi is just sixty years old. The life of this new Soviet city started with a vast metallurgical plant built on the banks of the River Mtkvari, the Georgian name for the Kura, whose course we have been following since Qarabork. Founded in 1941, the factory was built by German prisoners of war captured as the Red Army pushed back the

Nazi invasion. Stalin's 'war economy' brought steelworks, chemical plants, pharma-ceuticals factories and a new rail hub: a station on the Baku–Batumi line. The Rustavi metallurgical plant became Georgia's largest employer. The immense factory administration building was more imposing than the seat of Georgia's parliament in Tbilisi. Throughout the 1950s the *Khrushchevki* spread across the nearby steppe, housing thousands of workers. Barely a decade after it was founded, the city had around ninety massive plants, making it a vital cog in the Soviet machine.

Rustavi's success relied on the Soviet Union's integrated industrial strategy to source materials and market products. Baku, Sumqayit, Gəncə, Rustavi – all were closely connected within one system. The rapid collapse of the USSR after 1990 saw its separation into new nation-states, each with distinct tax systems and currencies, and the destruction of the formal structures of organisation between resource base, factories and markets.

Rustavi is now left with poverty, crime, locally produced vodka and Georgia's first intensive security prison. Sixty-five per cent of the workforce is unem-ployed, despite the city's population shrinking by over a quarter in twenty years. The metallurgical plant itself was privatised and, in 2005, sold off to Sheerness-based Thames Steel. Various dealings, involving accusations of corruption, led to the steelworks being taken from the UK investor again and handed over to Kolkhi, a British-run shell company. Today its future is unclear. Although the plant still manufactures steel pipes for the oil industry, there are reports that parts of the factory are being sold off as scrap metal.[10]

In the first days of January 2004, Merabi Vacheishvili and Eleonora Digmelashvili, two friends from Rustavi's *Khrushchevki*, in the eighteenth and nineteenth sub-districts of the town, saw heavy trucks and tractors clearing land nearby. Puzzled – not having been told about any planned construction work near their homes – they asked the orange-jumpsuited workers what was happening. They soon discovered that these were preparations for the construction of the BTC pipeline. While both knew of the pipeline and had heard of its importance, neither had been told that it would come so close to their homes. Four multi-storey apartment blocks, housing 700 families, were all within 250 metres of the planned works.

Concern quickly spread among the community. The buildings, low quality to start with, were dilapidated, and the pipeline construction risked fundamental structural damage. Later that month, the mayor of Rustavi admitted that he 'had no clue that the pipeline would go so close to the buildings'.[11] It is not surprising

---

10   'British Investor Wants Rustavi Plant Back', *Georgian Times*, 26 October 2009, at geotimes.ge.

11   M. Vacheishvili and E. Digmelashvili, 'Complaint to the IFC Compliance Advisor/Ombudsman', 16 March 2004, at bankwatch.org.

that neither Eleonora nor Merabi, nor other residents, nor even the mayor, were expecting the pipeline in their neighbourhood. The maps distributed by BTC Co. two years previously had indicated that the pipeline would run ten to twenty kilometres away from the edge of Rustavi. The inhabitants of the eighteenth and nineteenth sub-districts became even more worried once they realised that BTC Co. had declared a permanent 'security zone' of 500 metres around the pipeline, in which the construction of schools and hospitals was prohibited, apparently for safety reasons.[12] But the security zone now incorporated the eighteenth and nineteenth sub-districts. It seemed that BTC Co. could lay its pipes as close to Georgian homes as it liked, but once the pipeline was buried, nothing could be built within 250 metres of it.

Frustrated that BP was failing to take their concerns seriously, the residents decided to take action. On 7 February 2004, around 400 people living in the *Khrushchevki* organised a protest strike, demanding that the local council, national government and BP listen to them. During the strike they blockaded construction sites and stopped work on the pipeline. Then the police arrived and attacked the residents. 'We were beaten cruelly, despite the fact that the majority were women and children', reported Eleonora and Merabi. The police leaders claimed that 'they had orders from government to devastate elements that will create any problems to BTC pipeline construction'.[13]

Later that month, the Rustavi residents called BTC Co.'s community liaison officer, Ana Petriashvili, to ask for a meeting. As part of John Browne's promise to make BTC a model of corporate social responsibility, BP had hired community liaison officers to emphasise their commitment to transparency and engagement, creating a team dedicated to communicating with those living along the pipeline. This promise did not quite match Eleonora and Merabi's experience of Ana Petriashvili, who was rude, used abusive language, and told them she was 'spending too much time with people like us, and she knows that people are trying to solve their social problems at the expense of BTC Co. She tried to assure us that the pipeline is safe.' When they demanded documentation on safety standards, Petriashvili apparently replied airily that BP had promised the Georgian government that it would comply with the highest Western standards.[14]

* * *

12   The agreements upon which BTC and SCP were built delineated a forty-four-metre-wide construction corridor in which both pipelines would be buried – as we witnessed at Qarabork and Hacalli; but this corridor sat within a 500-metre-wide corridor in which no buildings were to be constructed. However, the pipeline could pass within 250 metres of existing buildings. *Resettlement Action Plan: Georgia*, BP, December 2002.

13   Vacheishvili and Digmelashvili, 'Complaint'.

14   Ibid.

Walking the streets between the *Khrushchevki*, we come across a yard used for storing oil pipes near the railway line. There are no familiar BP logos, only Maersk-branded shipping containers and carefully stacked piles of black pipes – spare sections of BTC, in case a length of the line needs replacing. But despite the nearby metallurgical plant making oil pipes, this pile and those already laid in the ground across Azerbaijan and Georgia were not manufactured in Rustavi. BP found the most cost-effective deal in Japan. Between sixty and seventy shiploads travelled through the East China Sea, the Indian Ocean, the Suez Canal, the Bosphorus and the Black Sea, carrying the 150,000 pipe segments from the other side of the world.[15] Those before us travelled up the railway from Batumi, and were stacked here before being taken, three at a time, to the construction sites by truck.

In the distant metropolis of Moscow, Rustavi – like Gəncə and Sumqayit – was planned out as a 'centre of production' to which iron ore and coal were transported. Now the city has been left to rot, and, according to plans made in other distant capitals, it has been redefined as a 'corridor'. Natural resources of the highest value are pumped through the fringes of the city, to be processed and consumed elsewhere.

---

15   'BTC Section – Pipeline Construction Begins', *Azerbaijan International* 11: 1 (Spring 2003), pp. 74–9.

9 WITHOUT HAVING TO AMEND LOCAL LAWS, WE WENT ABOVE OR AROUND THEM BY USING A TREATY

თბილისი **(TBILISI), GEORGIA**

Tbilisi, Georgia's capital, is built along the steep-sided Mtkvari Gorge. Having drained two-thirds of the country and north-eastern Turkey, the Mtkvari river is now a *café au lait*–coloured swirl passing through a deep concrete channel, rushing east towards the Caspian. Men stand on both banks, fishing in small groups. The city stretches up the steep hillsides above them. On the ridge of Mount Mtatsminda, which looms over the city, a radio mast flickers with a set of coloured fairy lights, looking like Blackpool Tower. Further east stands a huge aluminium statue of 'Mother Georgia', holding a sword and a cup of wine. At her feet, the oak trees in the Botanical Garden are coming into bright yellow-green leaf.

The BTC pipeline runs south of the city. As the line passes through neither Baku nor Ceyhan, a more accurate but less useful name for it would be the Sangachal–Rustavi–Gölovesı pipeline. Tbilisi is less of an 'oil city' than Baku – a transit point rather than a beginning or an end. Nevertheless, the pipeline has burrowed its way deep into the city's body politic, economy and environment.

We are standing by the Church of St George of Kashveti on the central Rustavelis Gamziri – Rustaveli Avenue – waiting to meet Manana Kochladze, an old friend who has spent much of her last eight years challenging BP and the Georgian government over the pipeline. She will be our companion on the Georgian stretch of our journey. Rustavelis Gamziri is wide and dusty. It is spring, the wettest time of the year. The rain last night was heavy enough to wake us. Yet despite this, everything is covered with dust. The pavement, the road, the cars, the window-panes: a thin grey gauze that bleaches the colours of signs or stone, tree bark or paintwork.

Named after the twelfth-century national poet Shota Rustaveli, this avenue is the spine of Tbilisi, lined with the city's landmarks: parliament, opera house, national theatre, major churches and large hotels. At the far end of the street is Tavisuplebis Moedani – Freedom Square. This open space has been renamed several times over the past two centuries, according to who has been in power.

When Georgia was under Tsarist rule it was Yerevan Square, but when the country was absorbed into the Soviet Union it became Beria Square, and then Lenin Square. Visiting businessmen meet in the sparkling Courtyard Marriott across from the Museum of Fine Art, once the imperial Russian theological seminary, renowned as a boarding school for revolutionaries in the late nineteenth century. In 1907, its most famous alumnus, Stalin, returned from Baku, and with forty brigands led a dramatic stagecoach robbery in broad daylight in this square. This spectacular direct action caused an international media frenzy, with London's *Daily Mirror* announcing: 'Rain of Bombs: Revolutionaries Hurl Destruction'.[1]

The European flag, a circle of twelve stars on a blue ground, can be seen hanging from every vaguely official-looking building. Georgia is not a member of the EU – despite the government's ardent desire to join. Visibly, however, there seems more enthusiasm for the EU in Tbilisi than in most member states. Georgia does belong to the Council of Europe – the international organisation focused on legal standards and human rights, comprising forty-seven European states including Russia – which uses the same flag as the EU.[2] No other country invests more significance in its membership of the Council. In Georgia, the flag is clearly used as a symbol of its allegiance to the West, and hostility to its northern neighbour, Russia. This allegiance and hostility is particularly acute in this spring of 2009, for only eight months ago years of tensions between Georgia and Russia resulted in open warfare over the region of South Ossetia.

It is midday on Sunday, and the streets are bustling. There is no restriction on opening hours: food stores are busy, as are internet cafés, restaurants and 'slot clubs' – the local name for slot-machine joints. The crowds are thickest around the metro entrance, McDonalds and the Church of St George of Kashveti, where we stand. People streaming through its wrought-iron gates are greeted by priests in brown, pink, blue and red vestments – the bright colours contrasting with everybody else's black clothing. Black is *the* colour of Georgia. Young and old, male and female, wear black trousers, black jackets, black skirts, black shirts, setting off pale skin and black hair.

Manana arrives at the church and we head off to find a restaurant in the Old City. We settle down to a meal including cheese *khachapuri* and wine from Kakheti. Georgia is inseparable from wine: there are more than 400 varieties, and drinking it at the table is part of the nation's identity. The rituals of the *tamada*, the toastmaster, may have evolved partly as a way for the Georgians to distinguish themselves from the vodka-drinking Russians. Manana's life is divided between her organisation, Green Alternative, and her four-year-old

1   Montefiore, *Young Stalin*, p. 154 – picture plate.
2   Other non-EU members of the Council of Europe include Russia, Turkey, Norway, Azerbaijan, Switzerland and Armenia.

son. With wavy red hair below her shoulders, a grey woollen cardigan and no make-up apart from red nail varnish, Manana defies the Georgian stereotype.

As part of the Central and Eastern Europe Bankwatch network, Green Alternative campaigns on public lending to energy infrastructure projects. Focusing on the European Bank for Reconstruction and Development and the European Investment Bank, Green Alternative plays a crucial role in the coalition of NGOs that raise concerns about the BTC pipeline. Manana and her colleagues deal with the environmental and social inheritance of the Soviet Union and oppose the negative effects of twenty-first-century energy projects. While using the political levers of EU legislation, they remain wary of Brussels's geopolitical and energy-dominance intentions. Manana raises concerns about the loans from the public banks for infrastructure projects across Eastern Europe and Central Asia, but Georgian issues clearly remain at the front of her mind.

As we finish our meal Manana explains: 'Georgia needs to think of its own future. But the economists and the politicians are obsessed with transit, to the exclusion of everything else.' She says that being a transit country does not really bring any benefits. 'The oil enters in a pipe, and leaves in a pipe. A handful of people get work and the government gets some loose change – and that's it. The banks say it will make us independent. But in reality, it just shifts dependence on to other actors, such as the maintenance of the EU–Azeri relationship.' She believes that the only body that cannot lose out in this situation is BP, for the profit made on the sale of crude from the offshore oilfields means that it has already recouped its investment on the ACG and Shah Deniz platforms, and on the Baku–Supsa, BTC and SCP pipelines.

Leaving the restaurant, we walk west along Rustavelis Gamziri until it becomes Chavchavadze Avenue, named after the poet and lawyer who led Georgia's National Revival in the late nineteenth century. Prince Ilia Chavchavadze promoted a liberal nationalism that opposed both the Tsarist Empire and the growing Marxist movements. Chavchavadze exalted the paternalistic relationship between local nobles and peasants as a counterpoint to socialism.[3] He was assassinated with his wife in 1907, the same year as the stagecoach robbery in Yerevan Square. Those behind the murder were never identified. Some blamed Tsar Nicholas I's secret police, but his most obvious rivals in Georgia were the socialist Mensheviks. More recently, it has been claimed the twenty-two-year-old Sergo Orjonikidze was responsible, with Stalin's knowledge.[4] The mantle of Chavchavadze's original political party has now been claimed by current President Mikheil Saakashvili's conservative nationalist United National Movement.

---

3   Suny, *Revenge of the Past*, p. 121.
4   Montefiore, *Young Stalin*, p. 187n.

The streets become more thickly lined with trees as we enter the neighbourhood of Vake. Small street stalls mix with luxury stores, embassies with old high-rise blocks. One of the latter houses Green Alternative. Manana guides us to the entrance, where dogs sleep in the shade and faded 'Stop Russia' stickers adorn the wall. The ancient elevator creaks as it ascends. It is a long way up.

Inside the office, the sun-filled space feels like many campaign headquarters throughout Europe. Computers on desks, leaflets from old and new campaigns, posters on the walls, and coffee. Piles of reports are stacked up for distribution.

Manana and her colleague Keti Gujaraidze have visited all the villages along the route of the pipeline in Georgia many times, spending days with local residents, helping them file complaints and bringing journalists to hear their stories. In 2003 they discovered that an entire village had been omitted from BTC's supposedly comprehensive Impact Assessment Study. The 600 residents of the village of Dgvari lived less than a kilometre downhill from the pipeline, and were threatened by severe landslides exacerbated by construction. During our own visits to Dgvari in previous years we had witnessed collapsing homes and a community pleading to be resettled.

In their journeys along the pipeline, Green Alternative have often found the security forces very assertive. Manana describes how armed BTC guards prevented Keti from filming the Jandara Pumping Station from a good distance away, and detained her for two hours. 'She was stuck in the snow and couldn't leave as they were pointing guns at her.' She explained to them that she was not inside the designated security area of the pumping station, but they made her wait for a long time in sub-zero temperatures. 'It was extremely cold, in the middle of winter.'

Manana and Keti believe that the benefits that BTC was supposed to bring to Georgia are looking thinner and thinner. At pre-construction press conferences and town hall meetings across Georgia, BP staff repeatedly promised the project would employ 5,000 people in the pipe-laying work. But there was a pattern that each time, only minutes later, Georgian government representatives would refer to far higher figures, such as 100,000 jobs – a huge number for a country of less than 5 million. BP did not challenge this disinformation. Now that the pipeline construction period is over, it is clear to all that the number of permanent jobs provided to BTC is small. The high figures appear to have originated from then President Eduard Shevardnadze's attempts to present the project as the panacea for most of Georgia's social problems.

The primary longer-term economic benefits publicised by the Georgian government were the revenues from transit fees. Effectively a tax on the movement of oil across a state's territory, such revenues are standard for countries hosting pipelines, although Azerbaijan waived them from Baku–Supsa, BTC and SCP. In Georgia's case, the state is due to receive around $50 million a year, if the pipeline is pumping at full capacity – a sum that comprises around 1 per cent of

Georgia's $4 billion annual budget. But this income needs to be balanced against the costs Georgia expends in meeting its own obligations towards the pipeline, primarily security. Under the Host Government Agreement, the legal treaty underpinning the pipeline's status and outlining Georgia's commitments, protecting the pipeline is the responsibility of the host country. Georgia has never released figures for the cost of permanently deploying several hundred Ministry of Interior soldiers along the pipeline's route.

In the spring of 2009, most of Green Alternative's fury is directed at the current president, Mikheil Saakashvili. As Manana explains, 'Taking Georgia to war, his economic policies, the aggressive privatisation, the environmental impacts – none of his decisions make sense. And he's so unpredictable. The only thing you can expect is that he will build more fountains next year!' She had not expected much from him, as he had been the justice minister in Shevardnadze's government before 2003. Even so, she had not thought Saakashvili would be more authoritarian than his predecessor. She explains that this began in 2004, when, soon after becoming president, he changed the constitution and removed powers from parliament. 'For a long time, foreign agencies didn't recognise this or weren't interested, as they liked Saakashvili. The EU wouldn't listen when we raised these concerns.'

Unhappiness with the Columbia University–educated Saakashvili seems widespread in Tbilisi. Walls, underpasses and billboards are graffitied with a single word scrawled across them: 'Ratom?' – meaning 'Why?' Everywhere there are stickers with an image of Saakashvili's smiling face in the crosshairs of a target, with a question mark superimposed. At first nobody claimed responsibility for these slogans and images, helping to build up the hype around them. But after a while the movement behind the posters – calling itself 'Ratom?' – went public, releasing several videos on to the oppositional TV channel Kavkasia, asking the question: 'Mikheil Saakashvili is still President! Why?'

Ratom? has joined together with a plethora of existing opposition groups – both long-term critics and recent ministerial defectors from Saakashvili's cabinet – calling on the president to resign. Despite strong divergences and confusion over their politics, most of the opposition is united in calling for mass protests on 9 April 2009, the anniversary of Georgia's post-Soviet declaration of independence in 1991. A major rally outside parliament has been announced. Leaders insist that they will remain on the streets until Saakashvili resigns.

What everybody agrees on is that Saakashvili made a huge mistake in attacking South Ossetia in August 2008. The decision resulted in war with Russia and a devastating defeat for Georgia. The tiny republic of South Ossetia was trying to break away from the main state of Georgia, and its fighters were backed by the Russians. There is a widely held view on the Georgian streets that the presence of the BTC pipeline passing through the country had made President Saakashvili overconfident of US, EU and NATO support for Georgia against Russian military force. It was a catastrophic miscalculation: Western interests focus primarily on the pipeline's security, not on South Ossetia. The inaction of the Western powers led to bitter disappointment and a slow recognition of the real intentions of European and American politicians.[5]

On the day of the demonstration itself, the main Rustavelis Gamziri between the parliament building and the Kashveti Church has been transformed from a busy thoroughfare into a rally. Barricades stop the traffic and thousands fill the street, chanting or listening to speeches. Many are carrying flags, most with Georgian national symbols or crosses, and several people hold up placards mocking Saakashvili's penchant for building fountains and sports stadia.

For Georgians, the large parliament building is not only the seat of power, but carries memories of uprisings and conflicts that ended regimes and brought down presidents. Today, its walls are daubed with recent graffiti – 'Fuck NATO' and 'Fuck USA'. 'People used to be pro-American, but Bush's support for Saakashvili has turned this around', comments a photographer next to us in the crowd. 'There were protests at the US embassy after the 2007 and 2008 elections. The frustration with the US is not about the lack of support during the war – everybody knows that was unrealistic. The anger is because the US, and the EU, are happy with Saakashvili's pro-Western position and looked the other way when elections were falsified and he tried to crush the opposition.'

Studies by US policy analysts concur with this view, observing that strong personalised ties 'between Washington and Tbilisi prevented the US from using its power and influence to credibly restrain the Saakashvili government'.[6]

Another protestor chimes in, 'Nobody is interested in Georgia as a nation, they all just want access to our territory – whether for a pipeline, or our ports, or an airbase for transit to Afghanistan. Everybody is trying to pull Georgia onto its side, pulling in different directions, north or west. But Georgia has its own culture, ancient church and script. Why do we need to be under US or Russian control?'

We watch opposition leaders take turns to climb the stage on the parliament steps, face the crowd and denounce Saakashvili. Many hope for a repeat of the Rose Revolution's mass street protests that deposed the previous president, Eduard Shevardnadze, in 2003. There is tension in the air; the crowd is both angry and anxious. The last big protests were met with a police crackdown. *Spetznaz* riot forces chased people from central Tbilisi into outlying areas, where they set upon small groups of them. Everybody wonders whether the *spetznaz* will be deployed

---

5   P. Jawad, *Europe's New Neighborhood on the Verge of War: What Role for the EU in Georgia?*, Peace Research Institute (Frankfurt), 2006.

6   Quoted in S. Blank, 'From Neglect to Duress', in S. Cornell, *The Guns of August 2008: Russia's War in Georgia*, M. E. Sharpe, 2009.

again, and how much violence the government is prepared to use to clear Rustavelis Gamziri.

The police presence seems surprisingly light. A few heavily armed guards watch from the top steps of the parliament, in front of its firmly closed front gates. Apart from that, there is barely a police officer in sight. 'That doesn't mean they're not nearby,' comments a friend. 'Saakashvili will have hundreds of them on standby, waiting.'

Sure enough, exploring around the back of the parliament building, we find an unguarded gap in the wall. Peering through it, we can see scores of police in body armour crouching behind shields. Some practise swinging their heavy wooden batons. Those that have lifted their helmet visors reveal balaclavas masking their faces. Tanks and water cannons are lined up in rows, ready to go.

The riot equipment is an indicator of how Saakashvili has built up certain key support communities since coming to power, especially among the security forces, whose agencies' budgets have increased tenfold in recent years. Everywhere there are new police stations with enormous glass windows. The running joke is that these buildings are the major achievement of the Rose Revolution, and that the large glass walls represent Saakashvili's understanding of increased transparency.

Although almost everybody we meet wants to see Saakashvili gone, nobody wants the previous president, Eduard Shevardnadze, to return. Like Heydar Aliyev in Azerbaijan, Shevardnadze dominated the Georgian political scene throughout the 1970s and 1980s. The two Caucasus leaders had parallel careers – usually as rivals, on rare occasions cooperating. Shevardnadze headed the Georgian Communist Party from the early 1970s, before being promoted to the politburo of the USSR in 1978, four years ahead of his Azeri contemporary. Shevardnadze, a legendary master of intrigue, acquired the soubriquet 'the White Fox'. But he was also seen as ruthless in cracking down on both corruption and dissidents.

As Brezhnev succeeded Khrushchev as general secretary of the USSR, Soviet institutions became increasingly ossified: corruption and disillusionment were pervasive. But Shevardnadze, along with his politburo colleague Mikhail Gorbachev, recognised the need for change, stating, 'We can't go on living like this.' During long walks on the Black Sea coast, the two planned a new movement, centred around *perestroika* – meaning 'restructuring' – and *glasnost* – meaning 'openness'. Together they built a political project based on the vision of a democratised socialist republic, which aimed to roll back the power of Party bureaucrats, bring a halt to repression and introduce greater freedoms and rights. The transition proposed was deep, yet the pair remained inspired by the pre-Stalinist possibilities of Soviet socialism, which they believed could still present an alternative to capitalism.

In 1985 Gorbachev was appointed general secretary of the Soviet Union, and quickly moved to secure Shevardnadze's promotion to foreign minister. Their gain was Aliyev's loss, for he too had hoped to take the controlling position in the USSR. So while Shevardnadze was implementing *perestroika*, facilitating German reunification and the Soviet withdrawal from Eastern Europe, Aliyev was part of the authoritarian 'old guard' that resisted any change, and was ultimately ejected from the politburo over corruption.

Shevardnadze's 'Sinatra Doctrine' – that Eastern European countries should 'do it their way' – led eventually to Georgia declaring independence in April 1991. But the new leader, Zviad Gamsakhurdia, soon alienated his own supporters with an aggressive 'Georgia for the Georgians' agenda. Within a year, he was forced to take shelter inside the parliament building as an uprising swept the city. The 'Hundred Metres War' shut down the heart of Tbilisi, with heavy firing across the street we are standing on, until Gamsakhurdia eventually escaped during a lull in the shooting.

Having resigned as foreign minister of the fast-collapsing Soviet Union in December 1991, Shevardnadze was invited back to Tbilisi by an interim Military Council established after the fighting. In March 1992, he was appointed president. Over the next twelve years, there were two conflicts in regions trying to break away from the main state of Georgia: the first war in South Ossetia, then the war in Abkhazia. Ironically, given his anti-bribery drives during the Soviet period, Georgia became increasingly corrupt during Shevardnadze's rule. Allies and members of his family were seen to be enriching themselves at the country's expense, controlling much of the national economy. Falsification and vote-rigging during the November 2003 elections added to the growing popular anger. These trends echoed what was happening in Baku, but Shevardnadze's rule was weaker than Aliyev's – in part because the latter had so carefully courted Western governments and companies.

Protestors from across the country came to Tbilisi and surrounded parliament for twenty days. When Shevardnadze attempted to open the new parliamentary session, on 22 November 2003, oppositionists led by Saakashvili burst into the hall with roses and stopped proceedings. Shevardnadze resigned the next day, ending his long hold over Georgian politics, and the Rose Revolution was hailed as a victory.

US enthusiasm for the toppling of Shevardnadze was built on the recognition that his position in Georgia had become untenable. But the Western powers had long been supportive of Shevardnadze, especially because of his role in bringing the BTC pipeline through Georgia. He described it himself as the 'crowning glory' of his presidency.

Shevardnadze had been an eager ally to the US deputy national security advisor, Sandy Berger. Together they persuaded BP to build the initial Baku–Supsa pipeline in 1995. Over the following four years Shevardnadze supported the Clinton administration's demands for the BTC and SCP pipelines, arguing that these would deliver not only economic benefits for Georgia, but also NATO membership. Just as Aliyev laid the political and cultural foundations in Azerbaijan for Western control of the new pipelines running from the Caspian, so Shevardnadze ensured acceptance in Georgia – the two fierce rivals collaborating together.

In November 1999, the Çıragan Palace, a residence of the Ottoman sultan on the Bosphorus in İstanbul, was buzzing with dignitaries and political leaders. Fifty-five heads of state had gathered for a summit of the Organisation for Security and Cooperation in Europe. BP and its allies chose this occasion to sign publicly the legal treaty underpinning the BTC pipeline. Shevardnadze and Aliyev sat either side of Bill Clinton and President Süleyman Demirel of Turkey, as they put their signatures to the Inter-Governmental Agreement. US Energy Secretary Bill Richardson stressed, 'This is not just another oil and gas deal and this is not just another pipeline. It has the potential to change the whole geopolitics in the region.'[7]

He was right. Like the 'Contract of the Centurys' impact on the Azeri economy, these documents reshaped the future of Azerbaijan, Georgia and Turkey by entrenching the position of the oil corporations in the region. The drafting of the various agreements was carried out by Baker Botts, the firm of lawyers contracted in by BP – an element in that part of the Carbon Web related to law. At Baker Botts's headquarters in Houston, George Goolsby oversaw the work on the pipeline.

By the time he became engaged in the BTC, Goolsby had already been involved in Caspian oil for nearly a decade, constructing the contracts that had created the Azerbaijan International Oil Consortium and the Baku–Supsa pipeline.[8] On the thirty-sixth floor of One Shell Plaza in central Houston, his office looked out over raised freeways and skyscrapers, and, in the distance, refineries and petrochemical plants stretching along Galveston Bay towards Texas City. Renowned for his perfectly coiffed hair and declamatory Texan voice, Goolsby worked for a company that had been promoting oil interests from the industry's earliest days. Baker Botts was founded in Houston in 1840, before the oil rush, by an ardent defender of the interests of slave-owners.[9]

---

7   T. Babali, 'Implications of the Baku–Tbilisi–Ceyhan Main Oil Pipeline Project', *Perceptions*, Winter 2005.

8   Much of the research for this section was conducted by Greg Muttitt of Platform and Nick Hildyard at the Corner House in producing their paper, 'Turbo-Charging Investor Sovereignty: Investor Agreements and Corporate Colonialism', Platform/Corner House, 2006.

9   For the history of Peter Gray, Baker Botts and slavery, see the online summaries

The İstanbul Summit came after two years of drafting the Inter-Governmental Agreement and Host Government Agreements, with Goolsby constantly shuttling between London, Baku, Tbilisi, Ankara, Washington and Houston. Creating the legal framework to maximise profits and defend BP's interests for the coming forty years across three countries was a complex task. To make things more straightforward, the Baker Botts legal team drafted the Host Government Agreements to sidestep existing legislation in all three countries. In Goolsby's words, 'Without having to amend local laws, we went above or around them by using a treaty.' [10]

The Agreements – which stand both as international treaties and private contracts with sovereign states – do this by overriding all existing and future domestic law apart from the constitutions of the states in question. The Agreements cover 'everything from land acquisition and tax codes to environmental regulations and indemnification against liability for military security actions'.[11] A new tax structure was created to override existing rates and to exempt all contractors working on the pipeline from domestic taxes. Any disputes between a host government and the oil companies were removed from the jurisdiction of Azeri, Georgian or Turkish courts. Disagreements would be settled in the international tribunals, in Stockholm, Geneva or London. 'The foreign companies want confidence', explained Goolsby.

The Agreements specifically guaranteed the 'freedom of petroleum transit', effectively claiming a right of freedom of movement for oil itself.[12] By contrast, and as a consequence of the Agreements, the three host governments – of Azerbaijan, Georgia and Turkey – all but surrendered sovereignty over the corridor of the pipeline route. In doing so, they abrogated their power to protect their own citizens from environmental damage or health hazards, and surrendered the possibility of improving regulations on the pipeline for the next four decades. Instead they locked themselves into a 'frozen', and drastically weakened, regulatory environment.[13]

Security was a key issue, for the planned pipeline would run around and through various conflict zones. For example, at Qarabork, in Azerbaijan, it lies forty

---

of documents held by the University of Texas Library: 'Guide to the Judge Peter W. Gray Papers 1841–1870, at www.lib.utexas.edu.

10   D. Eviatar, 'Wildcat Lawyering', *American Lawyer*, November 2002.

11   Ibid.

12   A. S. Reyes, 'Protecting the 'Freedom of Transit of Petroleum: Transnational Lawyers Making (Up) International Law in the Caspian', *Berkeley Journal of International Law* 24: 3 (2006).

13   Muttitt and Hildyard, 'Turbo-Charging Investor Sovereignty'. See also Center for International Environmental Law, 'The Baku–Tbilisi–Ceyhan Pipeline Project Compromises the Rule of Law', 2003.

kilometres from the ceasefire line of the unresolved Nagorno-Karabakh war. The Agreements stipulated that each host government must take responsibility for defending the pipeline with its own military forces. This was the legal requirement that led, among other things, to the creation of the Special State Protection Service of Azerbaijan – whom we had nearly met in Hacalli. Careful examination of the documents by Amnesty International revealed that certain clauses risked encouraging severe human rights abuses, particularly in their call for a militarised response to 'civil disturbances'.[14] But, knowing of BP's experiences in Colombia, Goolsby ensured that the corporation was exempt from any legal responsibility for human rights abuses committed by soldiers or police defending the pipeline.

Some politicians in the three states were unhappy with certain clauses, but Goolsby pushed back hard, taking advantage wherever the governments had weak negotiating positions. As he explained, 'We had to say to the government a lot, "If you don't create a usable legal structure, no one will invest in this".'[15] But the building of these legal structures took a tremendous amount of labour. As well as his colleagues in Houston, Goolsby had access to the services of four young Azeri lawyers based in Baku working for Baker Botts, overseen by British expatriate Christine Ferguson and a pipeline expert, Anthony Higginson. Between them, Goolsby's team put in 40,000 hours of work in the two years leading up to the signing of the Agreements in İstanbul.

Of course, Baker Botts was merely representing its clients' interests. But as we stand among the crowd outside the Georgian parliament on Rustavelis Gamziri, it is abundantly clear how powerless the Georgian governments have been. Unlike the Azeris, they did not possess the resources – oil and gas – for which the different corporations were competing so fiercely. Their sole asset was that of being a transit country wedged between a place of drilling and a place of consumption – an 'energy corridor' as delineated largely by Washington and Brussels, whose governments Georgia saw as vital allies.

Furthermore, as Goolsby strove to create 'a corridor of stability' for his clients, the key state through which it passed – Georgia – was undergoing two decades of intense upheaval. In the period between John Browne's first visit to Baku in July 1990 and this street protest demanding the resignation of the president in the spring of 2009, Georgia achieved independence from the Soviet Union, underwent two 'revolutions', lost a large portion of its territory in the course of three wars, and saw its industrial economy collapse. No surprise, then, that its bargaining position in relation to BP was incredibly weak.

---

14   Amnesty International, *Human Rights on the Line: The Baku–Tbilisi–Ceyhan (BTC) Pipeline Project*, May 2003, p. 5.

15   Eviatar, 'Wildcat Lawyering'.

10 WE CLOSED IT DOWN TO THE MEDIA

BTC KP 467 – 654 KM – ახალი სამგორი **(AKHALI-SAMGORI), GEORGIA**

'I saw it on TV first of all . . . yes, they bombed everywhere, right across Georgia, from Mount Kazbegi to Borjomi – they were trying to create a corridor to connect up with Armenia.' The man we are talking to has the broadest, warmest smile, revealing a gold front tooth. His jeans are faded and dirty and his brown shoes are crusted with mud. A flat black cap hides grey hair.

We have come looking for a line of bomb craters – possibly caused by Russian jets during the August 2008 South Ossetia war. Manana has brought us to a cluster of shacks and rusty wire fences in search of someone who might have actually seen the planes. As we near the first shed, we realise it is a sty. A piglet roams about outside a pen within which lies an enormous sow. Five dogs come running towards us, fast, barking. They look alarmingly keen to bite. Thankfully, seconds later, the man in the black cap appears and whistles to his hounds.

This little cluster of farmed plots is on disused land. The pipelines run at right-angles to the valley, down one side and then up the far slope. We have been following the oil and gas corridor for the last two or three hours, via the marker. Post numbers 26 and 27 lie on the eastern and western lips of this valley. It must be over three years since they buried the pipeline and finished the works here, and everything looks remarkably discreet. We are surprised at how quickly it has been swallowed up by the landscape. Only by looking carefully can one follow the route across the grazing land – a slight dip, a discolouration in the grass, a greater density of stones.

Eight months ago, on 8 August 2008, the Russian Army advanced into South Ossetia, eighty kilometres north-west of our current location, and routed the Georgian Army. There was much speculation as to whether they would capture, bomb or destroy the BTC pipeline, so carefully created to be outside the Russian sphere of influence. Any Russian attack on the pipeline itself would have undermined Georgia's reputation as a reliable and secure 'transit corridor'; on the other hand, it might have brought immediate military intervention from the US or NATO, in order to back up the fast-collapsing Georgian forces.

Various Georgian ministers did in fact claim that the BTC pipeline route was bombed by Russian aircraft, but that there had been no direct hits. A British journalist filed a report describing a neat line of bomb craters crossing the BTC route. The Georgian state hailed this as evidence, while the Russians continued to deny it, Putin snidely asserting: 'We are treating *our* energy facilities carefully and we do not intend to cause damage to anything.'[1] BP sided with Russia. 'These reports are groundless', stated Tamam Bayatly, the company spokesperson in Villa Petrolea. 'No explosion occurred in Georgian sector of BTC.'[2] A BP briefing to the pipeline investors claimed that media coverage referring to bombings was 'fanciful'.[3]

So what really happened? The journalist who filed the report was the *Wall Street Journal*'s Guy Chazan, based in London. Before setting off on our journey we met him in a pizza restaurant near St Paul's. Showing us sketches he had made at the time of the line of craters, Guy explained how there were two attacks on BTC. The first was in the early morning of 9 August, around the 25 km marker. The second was on 12 August, by the 27 km marker. Guy, an experienced journalist and a Russophile, had been visiting the Caucasus since the early 1990s – almost two decades. He undoubtedly knew what he was looking at.

Who, then, dropped the bombs? And why did BP issue such a strong denial that there had been any attack? It is just possible that the Georgians dropped the bombs themselves, to leverage greater Western support. A Russian attack, however, seemed far more likely. But this gives rise to another question: were the bombs meant to blow up the pipeline, or merely intended to demonstrate that Russia had the power to do whatever it wanted?

We had come to Georgia expecting to see a line of craters – to take photos, to try to work out whether or not the Russians had aimed directly at the pipelines, and to ask local villagers what they remembered. But things are not that simple.

We had left the Green Alternative offices in Tbilisi earlier that day with Manana and Keti. Their driver, Ramazi, is a neat, short man in a striped French-style black-and-white jersey. His grip on the wheel is loose and the car swings in erratic directions. This is extreme driving. We try to focus on other things. But with the vehicle jerking from side to side and bouncing over potholes, it is a hair-raising ride.

Our first sighting of the pipeline is by the main road just outside Rustavi, whose tower blocks rise like a wall from the flat, dusty steppe. We are about to pull in off

---

1   M. Kochladze, 'Pipe Dreams Shattered in Georgia', 26 September 2008, at brettonwoodsproject.org.

2   N. Mustafayez, 'BP-Azerbaijan Refutes Reports that Russian Planes Bombed BTC', 12 August 2008, at en.apa.az.

3   'The Baku–Tbilisi–Ceyhan Pipeline Project – DSU Update', BTC, October 2008, p. 36 (released under FOIA by ECGD on 26 March 2010).

the highway to take a look at a pipeline block valve behind its wire fence when we spot two vehicles beside it. One is a military jeep, the other a white BTC four-by-four. The people in them are staring at us: time to drive on rapidly. As in Azerbaijan, there is no formal law, nor any signs saying that a citizen cannot approach or photograph the pipeline, but we know from experience to avoid state and corporate pipeline patrols. After all, the pipeline corridor defined by the Host Government Agreement is effectively an autonomous space set apart within Georgian national territory – a semi-forbidden zone.

Some kilometres on, we spot a marker at the top of a rise: number '24 km', meaning 24 kilometers from the Azeri–Georgian border. We pull off and follow a bumping track till we hit the next marker: 25 km. There are strange mounds of earth everywhere here. Trying to make out a line of craters is going to be near-impossible. The route of the pipeline is clear, though, because the topsoil has not been properly replaced after it was laid.

This is puzzling, because Guy referred explicitly to bombs having been dropped around marker 25 km. We have another piece of evidence. Manana had contacted the Georgian Oil and Gas Corporation for information about the bombing, and they had sent over a DVD with video clips and stills of officials visiting crater sites, taken on 10 and 12 August 2008 – the days following the bombing raids. We have the DVD with us, and use a laptop to scrutinise it again. It only confuses us more. The landscape is all wrong. In the videos, the grass is much higher, the land lower and marshier, with the craters in a valley between hillsides. Even the design of the posts seems different.

We drive on, to the valley between 26 km and 27 km, thinking this must be the place in the video. But still no sign. We climb a nearby hillock: perhaps a view will help us. But nothing – just the valley with a stream running gently through it, and a flock of goldfinches that twitter past. Nearby are the shacks and sties that lead us to the farmer in the flat black cap. We had expected him to recollect the bombing and the craters, to tell us that people had come and filled them in. But no, his first line is: 'I saw it on TV'. His house is only half a kilometre from the pipeline.

This is getting more and more confusing. We approach another farming family, who are living in the ruins of a former Soviet collective farm. There is an old woman and two middle-aged men, one of whom speaks fluent English. 'No, we weren't here last August. We take the cattle to the mountains.' We show him the video. 'That's not here', he says. 'In the summer the grass is all gone round here. That's why we move elsewhere.'

It's dawning on us that the markers shown in the video are not those of BTC. The giveaway is the design – the BTC marker posts are taller, and the black kilometre numbers are smaller than in the video.

We begin to think the videos might be fake: an attempt by the Georgian government to use the country's position as an 'energy corridor', and BTC's high profile, to bring the Western powers it serves into the conflict on its side. Manana, initially sceptical of this idea, starts to think the same. The regime, she tells us, has repeatedly released fake videos to promote its own interests. Three films were recently produced purporting to show one of the opposition parties buying weapons. The police claim the videos resulted from a sting operation, but few believe they are real. During the suppression of popular protests in November 2007, the regime also released videos that tried to compromise the oppositionists. These were widely believed to be fake. Perhaps this DVD of Russian bomb craters falls into the same pattern?

Finally we decide to risk approaching the pipeline guards. A couple of these distant green figures have been watching us from the block valve compound at 28 km. Manana advises us to avoid alarming them, so we leave the car some way off and set out on foot. As we approach, we can see that the guards are wearing Georgian Army fatigues and combat gear, with semi-automatics slung over their shoulders. Later, reading documents released to Platform, we realise that they must be part of the State Pipeline Security Force, made up of 500 troops provided by the Ministry of Interior. Their role is the same as the Special State Protection Service troops in Azerbaijan.

The four soldiers we approach are friendly and relaxed, apparently unbothered that we have been roaming around this stretch of pipeline for the last few hours. We ask them the same questions: No, they weren't here at the time, but over in South Ossetia. Also, the pipeline wasn't bombed here, but at BP's parallel Baku–Supsa pipeline, several kilometres away.

Ah. It seems we have been hunting not just in the wrong place, but along the wrong pipeline. This would explain why the marker post in the video did not look right. But the light is fading fast, and Manana needs to return to her four-year-old boy in Tbilisi. We will have to pick up the trail tomorrow.

Here we are, scrabbling around at the fringes of BP, trying to understand and describe. Far off in the heart of its empire, in the offices of investors in London, it is supposedly a world of hard facts, lists of figures, statistics, solid data. At least here we know that we are in a maze of unknowns, of slipping and sliding possibilities.

Setting out early the following morning, we reach the village of Akhali-Samgori, outside which the three pipelines – BTC, SCP and Baku–Supsa – in a rare moment, come close together. By comparing the post designs, we prove that the video shows markers along Baku–Supsa, not BTC, despite Guy's report and Georgian government claims otherwise.

In Akhali-Samgori we talk to a group of villagers gathered round a standpipe. An elderly woman is filling plastic containers with water and preparing to carry them to her house. Those we speak to complain that the pipelines run within metres of their homes. If the gas pipe explodes, they say, the whole village could be wiped out. Precisely this happened to the residents of Machuca in Colombia in 1998, when BP's pipeline there was blown up by guerrillas: sixty-six villagers died and hundreds more were wounded.[4] 'We were afraid even before the recent war, but more so now', one of the villagers tells us. 'We feel like the village is occupied by the pipelines. Many of us weren't even properly compensated, and none of us have gas. The gas could kill us – but we can't cook with it.'

We ask about the bombing. To our delight, one of the men says he knows where the craters are. At last. He hops into the front seat and gives directions to Ramazi. We retrace our route back to BTC 24 km marker, where yesterday we turned off the road, but now we carry on, into a wide valley. How could we not have noticed this valley before? The hills begin to assume a familiar shape – we have seen them before, in the video. The valley is lush and verdant, as it should be. We turn off the road, bumping and lurching along a track. And there, clear as day, is a line of gaping craters running down the hillside and along the valley floor. Between them, the Baku–Supsa markers. A herd of cows grazes nearby.

The car pulls up. Camera in hand, we head for the post 25 km post. Around it are great mounds of earth and holes in the ground, several metres deep. When we climb down into them, we can only just see out. The route of the pipeline is obvious – the grass paler – so we pace out distances. The bombs fell about thirty metres apart. The two lines – one picked out by the marker posts, the other by craters – cross each other at right-angles. The bombs only just missed the pipeline: there are deep craters just fifteen metres either side of the route. Uncannily, we can hear distant explosions, but these are from training exercises at the Vaziani military base to our north.

There is another line of craters, at a more acute angle, higher up the hillside. We count at least forty-five bombs dropped on this field. There must have been two bombing runs, with one pilot starting too early and either running out of bombs – or pulling out – before reaching the pipe.

Back in the car, we go in search of Baku–Supsa 27 km, following the pipeline markers north-west. Suddenly there is a horseman up ahead, a young man on a mangy steed. There is a hint of red draped over his saddle – could he be a BTC guard? From our studious reading of *Horizon*, BP's in-house magazine, we have an image of well-equipped 'civilian security' riders patrolling the route. Yet with his uniform half-off, a peaked cap rather than the regulation white safety helmet, and a sad-looking nag, he is a forlorn figure. Manana chats with him a little, he makes no attempt to stop us, and we part ways.

---

4   G. Muttitt and J. Marriott, *Some Common Concerns: Imagining BP's Azerbaijan–Georgia–Turkey Pipelines System*, CRBM/CEE Bankwatch Network/Corner House/FoEI/Kurdish Human Rights Project/Platform, 2002.

Ten minutes' drive further on, the 27 km marker stands in tall grass. The ground ten metres from the pipeline has been torn up by an enormous crater: it is deep, with a large pool of water in the bottom, and at least four metres across. This must have been a mighty bomb. On the hillside overlooking the site is an abandoned Soviet airbase, with great hangars and bunkers built into the ground. The Russian Army occupied this site until a few years back, when they agreed to leave their Georgian bases. This was a targeted bombing run aimed at the pipeline – surely not an attack on the Georgian Vaziani base gone wrong.

We try to work out the sequence of events. On 5 August 2008, just days before the start of the Georgia–Russia conflict, hundreds of miles west, near the town of Refahiye in Turkey, Kurdish PKK fighters blew up a section of the BTC. BP shut down the pipeline and immediately switched export to the recently refurbished Baku–Supsa. Although pumping at only a fraction of the capacity of BTC –150,000 barrrels per day, rather than 1 million – Baku–Supsa allowed at least some Caspian crude to be exported. Within days of the switch, Russian bombers dropped forty-five explosive devices by the 25 km marker on the Baku–Supsa route. Despite the near miss, BP continued to ship its highly valuable cargo through the pipeline until Russian forces advanced across it near Gori, on 11 August.

On 12 August, BP announced it was suspending export through both Baku–Supsa and SCP, in addition to BTC. That night, another Russian plane dropped a series of bombs next to Baku–Supsa's 27 km marker. Meanwhile, the Russian military continued to station its tanks on top of Baku–Supsa near Gori for another two weeks.

So why did the press release of the Georgian Oil and Gas Corporation – the GOGC – inform the world that BTC was bombed when in fact it was Baku–Supsa? And why did BP deny that anything at all had happened, to journalists and British civil servants? Time to go and find out.

Two days after seeing the craters, we went to visit first Matthew Taylor, head of BP Georgia External Affairs, and then GOGC. BP Georgia is headquartered in a discreet building next door to a university faculty, in the quiet Saburtalo district of Tbilisi. We go through a security check, past a roadblock, around the back to where the entrance is hidden; we hand in our passports, get security passes, go through a turnstile: security here is tight. We are met in the lobby by Tamila Chantladze, BP's senior PR advisor in the country. Smiling and friendly, Tamila has worked for BP Georgia for nine years. She gives the impression of being the backbone of the company's public image here, watching expat heads of external affairs come and go.

We go upstairs into an open-plan office, where Matthew Taylor, tall and suave, offers us coffee and ushers us into his room. As we talk he is relaxed almost to the point of indifference, swinging back and forth on the back legs of his chair, occasionally checking the mobile that lies on the desk in front of him.

We skirt round a number of topics before coming to the point. Did the Russians bomb the pipeline? 'Who knows?' Matthew responds nonchalantly. 'You should ask the Russians.' But then he grows serious.

'Our public position to the media is that we were aware of no direct hit on our pipelines. There were marks within metres of Baku–Supsa, near where the pipelines separate. There's also the Vaziani airbase nearby; maybe they were aiming for that. But it's quite a few kilometres away. We had no interest in perpetuating the story, so we closed it down to the media.' Then he adds, 'The Georgian government tried to pull us in over the bombing, crying foul to the West. We didn't feel it was substantiated enough. But we wouldn't have done it anyway. We have to be extremely neutral in these situations. There was possibly some intimidation of Georgia by Russia, raising questions for Europe and the West whether Kazakh oil and Turkmen gas should come this way. But if they had bombed BTC, that would have been global; after all, we're about 1 per cent of global oil consumption.'

This might seem like a small percentage, but on a global level a loss of this crude into the international markets would have had a dramatic impact on the world oil price, especially during the summer of 2008 when oil was trading at a historic high. 'As it was, we shut down Baku–Supsa when the Russians reached Gori, as we couldn't guarantee the security of our staff. It had only reopened in July anyway, following years of repairs.'

We emerge back into the street after forty-five minutes, and the public relations magic dust is wearing thin. BP had 'closed down the story' that the Georgians were trying to make public, and had done so by downplaying the incident. The deep craters that we had stood in had been reduced, in Matthew's phrase, to 'marks'.

A taxi takes us to the offices of the Georgian Oil and Gas Corporation, out on the Kakheti Highway. The office block is visible from a distance, bold as brass with flags outside and a large sign on the main road to the airport. But for all its pomp, you can tell immediately on entering the lobby that power lies elsewhere. It is the exact opposite of BP Georgia's offices. There is a sense of listlessness inside the building. The massive lobby is bare, with a wilting houseplant in a corner. A woman behind a small serving hatch in a kiosk sleepily gives us passes.

We are met by Tamuna Shoshiashvili, PR manager for GOGC. She and her assistant Sofia guide us upstairs, past a score of aerial photos of the construction of BTC and SCP. But the Georgian company's role in the pipelines is purely regulatory; it does not own a stake in either of them. Tamuna's office feels far removed from Matthew's. Filled with dark-brown rather than light furniture, it lacks his functional whiteboard and flipcharts. Plain light bulbs hang through crude holes drilled in the ceiling. On one wall she displays a 'Certificate of Achievement: Workshop for Energy PR Workers and Energy Journalists'.

We raise the issue of the bombing, and Tamuna puts forward her version of the events of 9 and 12 August. The bombs, she says, were dropped on BTC. When we query this, she changes her story: it was Baku–Supsa, she means. She remembers bringing a white-haired journalist – Guy Chazan – when they first visited the site. Looking over the video and stills together, we recognise Tamuna picking her way over the bombed earth in heels and a skirt. She explains how she came in on 9 August dressed for a normal day in the office, and was whisked away without time to change. Then they rushed out a press release and the images.

Was she surprised at how little international coverage the bombing got? She is not sure it was so small. Was she surprised at how BP refused to engage with the story? She says we should ask them. We explain that Matthew Taylor told us they 'closed down the story'. Tamuna pauses slightly, then says, deliberately, 'It's very interesting what you are asking.' Does she think the presence of the pipelines makes Georgia a target? 'Oh, I couldn't answer that.'

As we discuss events, it becomes apparent that, if there was a battle between BP and the Georgian state over the public presentation of the events, it took place higher up the ladder than Tamuna's office, at ministerial or at least GOGC board level.

Before we leave, Tamuna has Sofia stand on a chair and stretch to the top of a cupboard in her office. She grabs a precariously balanced lump of steel and drops it into our hands. 'One of our souvenirs from the pipeline last August', she says. Twisted and deformed, with no readable inscription, the reddish-brown lump of shrapnel from the site of the craters on Baku–Supsa offers no clue to its secrets.

* Conflicting first hand & media reports from Georgia of Russian troops within Georgia, occupying territory (rapidly changing picture but includes Poti, c. 20km from Supsa, Senaki, Gori, c. 40km from Tbilisi) making risk to operating personnel uncertain and increasing.
* BTC sites have not reported any bombs in the vicinity of our assets.
* Non-essential foreign staff & contractors continue to be relocated to Turkey & Azerbaijan by road.[5]
12 August 2008 – Memo from BP to banks in BTC Lender Group, 12 August 2008

It was his assessment that the BTC had NOT been targetted in recent actions. I pointed out that the bombs fell very close to the pipeline but he said they were sure

5   Email from BP to Société Générale, subject: 'RE: BTC: Fightings in Georgia', 12 August 2008, p. 28 (released under FOIA by ECGD on 26 March 2010).

this was simply related to its proximity to the base not a specific targeting.[6]
Memo from British embassy in Tbilisi reporting on a meeting with BP, 19
September 2008

*There was no indication that either BTC or the Western Route were targeted or bombed
by the Russians. We were aware of these highly misleading news reports at the time and
are more than happy to refute these claims. Moreover, both pipelines were extensively
surveyed before re-starting.*[7]
Email from BP to UK Export Guarantee Credit Group, 17 November 2008

Digging into the memos and emails we obtained through freedom of information requests, we can construct a likely sequence of events. At perhaps 4 a.m.
Georgian time on 9 August 2008, data from US spy satellites observing the
Caucasus conflict was being processed by several analysts at the National
Geospatial-Intelligence Agency (NGA) located at Fort Hood in Texas – the largest military base in the USA. It would have been 5 p.m. in Texas, the end of a
regular working day for the members of the geospatial intelligence cell. Their
imagery-extraction and models had picked up the bomb craters crossing Baku–
Supsa. The team's analysis was passed up the ladder to the NGA headquarters in
the wealthy Bethesda district of Washington, DC. Here, beside the Potomac
River, a GEOINT staff officer wrote up the analysis into a brief presentation, and
circulated it to the Pentagon, the undersecretary of defence (intelligence) and
the CIA's South Caucasus Desk. The brief would have been read carefully, for the
pipeline system is both the USA's and Britain's primary political and economic
interest in Georgia.

The staff officer's job description also covers liaison with private industry, so
his next call was most likely to BP America. How did the conversation go? 'Sir,
your pipeline in the Caucasus has just been bombed. You might want to check it.
No, not BTC – that was shut down a few days ago. The small one, Baku–Supsa.' BP
head office in London will have quickly passed the message on to Bill Schrader in
Baku and Neil Dunn, Matthew's superior in Tbilisi. Schrader and Dunn probably
decided, as Taylor told us, that BP 'had no interest in perpetuating the story' and
came up with a response plan.

Meanwhile, the staff officer in Bethesda continued sharing the satellite data.
With whom? He probably informed the British Ministry of Defence, one of the
USA's only three geospatial intelligence partners. Yet the emails obtained by

---

6   Digest of email from British Embassy Tbilisi meeting with BP, subject: 'Meeting
with BP', 19 September 2008, p. 26 (released under FOIA by FCO on 12 April 2010).
7   Email from BP to ECGD, subject: 'RE: News 141108', ECGD, 17 November
2008, p. 37 (released under FOIA by ECGD on 26 March 2010).

Platform show that, despite repeated queries by British government departments, BP continued to describe reports of the Russians targeting its pipelines as 'fanciful', 'erroneous' and 'incorrect', claiming that 'there was no indication that either BTC or the Western Route were targeted or bombed by the Russians'.[8] No indication, that is, apart from the forty-five bomb craters.

And did the Americans inform the Georgian military, the liaison officers trained by US Marines at Krtsanisi Training Base outside Tbilisi? Maybe the Georgian oil officials at GOGC first learned about the attack from Washington, rather than from local farmers or government officials.

That same night, Russian military command reviewed the events that had taken place along Baku–Supsa. Russian spy satellites orbiting near their US twins will have trained their cameras onto the route, to assess the level of damage. By 1.30 a.m. Georgia time, the pilots of the TU-22M3 bombers would have returned to Mozdok airbase in Russia's North Ossetian Republic and been debriefed. Were they reprimanded for missing the pipeline? Or congratulated for the carefully placed near-miss? Once the outcomes of the bombing flight were clear, military planners probably sat down and decided whether or not to make more attempts.

Irrespective of the exact sequencing, military, civilian and corporate personnel in Washington, London and Moscow all discussed the field of craters near Akhali-Samgori in south-eastern Georgia during those August days. The Georgians themselves were almost certainly the last to find out about the bombing. And when they tried to make a fuss about it by sending out a press release – in the words of Matthew, 'trying to drag BP in' – the issue barely registered with the international media, despite Tamuna's assertions to the contrary. With both BP and Putin saying that nothing had happened, the news outlets were not interested.

Why did BP keep Baku–Supsa running for so long – nearly five full days – after the bombing? It would seem highly irresponsible to keep open a pipeline pumping 150,000 barrels of oil per day following bombing raids that might have ruptured or weakened it. One would also expect BP to have rushed out to marker 25 km on the morning of 9 August, cordoned off the area and verified that the pipeline had not been damaged. But the GOGC videos indicate no BP presence at all.

What, then, were the Russians trying to do? It looks as if they did not want to bomb BTC itself. Had they wanted to do so, the planes could easily have struck slightly to the east of Akhali-Samgori, where all three pipelines run in a tight corridor for the first twenty kilometres from the Azeri border. Or they could have targeted the BTC and SCP pumping station at Jandara, easily visible from the air.

---

8   Email from BP to Société Générale, subject: 'RE: BTC Shutdown Lender Update 15th August, 2008', 15 August 2008, p. 25 (released under FOIA by ECGD on 26 March 2010); 'Baku–Tbilisi–Ceyhan Pipeline Project – DSU Update', p. 36. 'RE: News 141108', p. 37.

The Russian military knew that BTC was already out of action following the PKK attack in Turkey. They also knew that striking the flagship pipeline might trigger direct US support for Georgia.

By bombing Baku–Supsa, Russia demonstrated its ability to take out the country's oil infrastructure at will, while maintaining deniability and avoiding responsibility for the outcomes – such as cleaning up an oil spill. It could impress on the Georgian population that acting as a 'transit corridor' to the West made it a greater target without securing the country additional protection. Whether intended or not, BP's international cover-up helped Russia's portrayal of the Georgians as hysterically crying wolf. Like the negotiations over the Host Government Agreements, these events once again show the weakness of Georgia in relation to the company.

On close inspection, cracks appear in BP's public downplaying of the events of August 2008. A quote in *Horizon* contradicts this portrayal. A production technician on Baku–Supsa, Archil Monaselidze, was on duty at pump station number 13 during the conflict, and commented: 'These were very difficult times. During the conflict, we kept the station lights off so as not to attract attention. I saw military jets fly over, and there were tanks stationed in my village for some time.'[9]

So many questions arise from these craters. We are reminded of the remark by Rory Sullivan of Insight Investment that the pipeline was a 'done deal'. Despite BP's labours to present BTC as a successfully closed project, it remains a live creature, playing a role in a war of tanks, bombs and perceptions.

---

9 M. Naughton, 'Teams Unite to Manage Tough Times', *Horizon: The Global Publication for BP People* 7 (December 2008), p. 36.

11 WE LIVE IN A CORRIDOR OF VIOLENCE

გორი (GORI), GEORGIA

Since achieving independence in 1989, Georgia has undergone a series of often chaotic transformations. The transition from one ideology to another – communism to nationalism – and the near-total collapse of its industrial economy was accompanied by a coup and intense internal conflict. Demands for autonomy in the regions of South Ossetia and Abkhazia were met by a rigid insistence on national unity from Tbilisi. Tensions spiralled, leading to war in both regions, each one breaking away and declaring itself an independent republic. A ragtag and newly assembled Georgian National Guard fought against Ossetian and Abkhaz militias, who were backed by Russian soldiers and fighters from the Confederation of Mountain Peoples of the Caucasus. Atrocities were committed on both sides, with many thousands dead and missing.

The conflicts ground to an uneasy ceasefire, but were followed by the targeting of ethnic Georgians by others in the breakaway republics. When the fighting halted, a mass exodus from the war-torn regions brought several hundred thousand refugees to Tbilisi, where they were crammed into government buildings, hospitals and schools. Hotels in the city centre became vertical refugee camps for over a decade. When we visited the capital in 1998, we saw scores of families living in the dark, cavernous underpasses of Tbilisi's main train station.

In the world of international diplomacy, these conflicts of the early 1990s came to be referred to as 'frozen'. Although there was no resolution, and there remained the constant fear that fighting could erupt again, the ongoing tension did not stop the development of the Oil Road. President Shevardnadze, a determined supporter of the project, was committed to the pipelines passing through Georgia. In 1996, a mere three years after the temporary halt to fighting in South Ossetia, agreement was reached to pass the Baku–Supsa pipeline close to Gori, just twenty kilometres from the ceasefire line. The 'energy corridor' passed by, just as it had snaked through Qarabork, only forty kilometres from the frontline of the Nagorno-Karabakh war.

Negotiations and conflict-resolution processes were supposed to resolve the issues, but those in power on both sides were unwilling to make any concessions. Over time, the possibility of a settlement looked ever more remote, as the construction of the energy pipelines, the possibility of Georgia joining NATO, and a wider deterioration of relations between the West and Russia pulled Georgia increasingly towards the West.[1] The issues of the oil wealth in the Caspian Sea and the routing of pipelines exacerbated destabilisation by generating fierce international competition between those attempting to gain a foothold in the region.[2] The war of August 2008, and the bomb craters on the pipeline near Akhali-Samgori, took place in the context of this destabilisation.

Ramazi drives us along Highway 1, west from Tbilisi and up the valley of the Mtkvari River, following the route of the Baku–Batumi Railway as it climbs towards the Suram Pass. The road, set high in the foothills of the Caucasus, gives us a view over the wide dun-coloured vale. Beyond Gori, we take the exit for Tskhinvali, the capital of South Ossetia. This narrow route – one lane in each direction – runs north to the South Ossetian heartland, through the Liakhvi Gorge and on to the Roki Tunnel, the sole road connection to North Ossetia and Russia.

This was the route that Georgian troops took before attacking Ossetian militias in Tskhinvali on the night of 7 August 2008. It is the same stretch of tarmac that they retreated down two days later, abandoning their bombed-out trucks and sustaining many casualties. Shortly afterwards, the road shuddered under the tracks of a column of 1,200 Russian tanks advancing south and threatening to split the territory of Georgia in half. Many of the fleeing civilians walked through the forests to avoid the troops on the road.

Seventy-one-year-old Gusein Melanashvili is one of these refugees. Digging the soil outside a tiny white blockhouse just east of the same road, Gusein remembers the last night he saw his village. As the Russian planes began bombing raids on 8 August on Kekhvi, up in the Liakhvi Gorge, he says, 'We fled with whatever we were holding – nobody had time to pack.' As he and his family drove down a dirt track, a bomb exploded ahead of them. 'It shattered the windscreen onto me. My head was bleeding. We abandoned the car. As we ran, we could see the Russian tanks. There were so many, they jammed up the road, all the way from the Roki Tunnel to Tskhinvali.'

Gusein made it to Tbilisi, where he camped for five months in a makeshift refugee centre at the Institute for the Protection of Flora. Now, having returned to western Georgia, he shares this small cement cube with his wife and two little grandsons. Surrounding us are 500 identical new-built structures in a neat grid.

---

1   S. Blank, 'From Neglect to Duress', in Cornell, *Guns of August 2008*, p. 106.
2   B. Coppieters, ed., *Contested Borders in the Caucasus*, VUB Press, 1996, p. 9.

Resting his shovel against the wall, Gusein sits down on his doorstep with his back against the thin plastic door. He teases his three-year-old grandson, pinching his shoulder and making him giggle. Born in Kekhvi in the Liakhvi Gorge, Gusein left briefly to study, then returned to the village to work as a teacher for twenty-six years, and as school principal for another twenty-five – a public servant throughout the Khrushchev, Brezhnev and Gorbachev years. Now he survives off a handout of 25 lari a month – about £20 – from UNICEF. This financial support is about to end, and he has been promised a one-off payment of 200 lari by the Georgian government.

But Gusein says that he does not want aid from the US or Europe, and that he does not need this refugee house. He just wants to return to his land, and then will manage on his own. Despite his intense desire to return, Gusein is trying to make the temporary building and plot allotted to his family in this bleak camp more homely. A pickaxe that he was using to split the hard earth lies by his feet. While we speak, Gusein's friend, also in his seventies, is working the soil with a shovel, clearing stones. Most of the other householders nearby have also begun turning the earth, as spring is arriving fast. Gusein hopes to grow tomatoes, and his friend inspects six *smorodina* stakes that should become redcurrant bushes.

They all seem unconcerned by the chill wind that cancels out the heat of the April sun. The sound of the strong blast is exaggerated by vehicles speeding by on the road to Tshkinvali: the monitoring jeeps of the Organisation for Security and Cooperation in Europe (OSCE) heading south to Tbilisi for a Saturday in the city, and the armoured cars of the EU driving north to the ceasefire line.

As he speaks, Gusein emphasises his points, gesturing with his left hand, holding up either one or two of his enormous fingers. His right hand remains clenched in a fist, resting on his thigh.

Gusein says that he used to teach Georgians, Ossetians and Armenians in his school. Historically, he feels that Georgians and Ossetians did not have a bad relationship. He accuses Russia of laying the foundations for the conflict by encouraging separatists after the collapse of the Soviet Union, but he blames the Saakashvili government for the loss of his home. 'Even I know that nobody can start a war with Russia and win. The state should not have started the war. Now we have lost everything. Now we are beggars, depending on external help.' He begins wiping his eyes as he talks about his home, unembarrassed to cry in front of his friend. 'My home was heaven compared to here. When I was living there, I had everything I needed, I was happy. Now I've lost everything.'

We clamber back into the car and head north towards the frontline. Two kilometres along the road, a large OSCE base looms up. Its international flags and white peacekeeping jeeps symbolically proclaim, 'There shall be no fighting here' – or at least that somebody in a flak jacket and an armoured vehicle will monitor any fighting that does happen.

Fifty metres beyond the entrance to the base, the familiar marker posts indicate that the Baku–Supsa pipeline is passing under the road. Running from east to west, the line funnels 150,000 barrels of crude under this tarmac every day.

This is where the Russian tanks rumbled over the pipeline on 11 August 2008. We have already seen the bomb craters at Akhali-Samgori that indicated a near collision between Russian explosives and BP's infrastructure. Here on the road to Tskhinvali, the tanks passed over the pipeline. They stayed for a fortnight, before withdrawing to where they are now: only a few kilometres further north from here.

Two men have parked a battered blue Ford in a deep puddle by the side of the road, where a stream has overflown its banks next to the pipeline marker. They use the water as a makeshift car wash, scrubbing their vehicle clean, as $5 million worth of crude passes beneath their feet.

There are many obstacles between Gusein's refugee house and his home in Liakhvi Gorge: military checkpoints run by Russians, Georgians and Ossetians; the OSCE and EU monitors; and running beneath them, BP's pipeline.

BTC KP 484– 671 KM – კრწანისი (KRTSANISI), GEORGIA

The following day Manana takes us to meet another family displaced by war: ethnic Georgians who had fled from the fighting in Abkhazia in 1993. Driving over the steep ridge separating Tbilisi from the south, we leave the apartment blocks of the city behind us. The landscape turns to pasture and gentle hills. We are heading to Krtsanisi, whose villagers repeatedly made headline news when they opposed the building of BTC by blocking roads and construction sites.

Approaching the village, we pass through a small pine forest in which low buildings are laid out, connected by gravel paths. It looks like a quiet university campus in the woods, with students strolling between departments. Yet these students are wearing camouflage, and the proliferation of semi-automatic rifles disturbs the image of academic seclusion. This is the Georgian National Military Academy.

It is also the primary US military installation in the Caucasus. The presence of Western soldiers here was the outcome of presidents Shevardnadze and Saakashvili's efforts to move Georgia into the US geostrategic orbit. Alongside lobbying to join NATO, both men supported the wars on Afghanistan and Iraq, opening up Georgian airspace and bases to assist the US missions. Georgian forces were sent to Kabul and to Baghdad. In return, the US European Command embarked on an ambitious support programme for its new ally in the region. They constructed a training base, a weapons range and an ammunition depot here at Krtsanisi, as well as radar bases near the oil ports of Batumi and Supsa on the Black Sea. The US secretary of state, Colin Powell, visited this base in the woods in 2003 to inspect Special Forces training Georgian soldiers in counter-insurgency combat.

The previous year, the first contingent of US troops had arrived in Tbilisi. According to the US Army, the 'Georgia Train and Equip Program' was a 150-strong troop force which would assist the Georgian Army in 'ground combat skills, marksmanship and urban operations related to service in Iraq'[3] – skills that would presumably also be useful in fighting Abkhaz and Ossetian militias. Asked about the deployment, a BP spokeswoman replied that 'the pipelines will of course benefit from the military presence'.[4] Three months after the troops arrived, the BTC company, responsible for the pipeline's construction, was formally established. When Saakashvili came to power following the Rose Revolution, the engagement with US forces only increased. Soon this was one of the USA's largest in-country training programmes in the world. Meanwhile, in an echo of developments in Baku, the Georgian military budget grew more than a hundredfold between 2001 and 2008, reaching levels of 25 per cent of the national budget.[5]

Despite this military buildup, the Georgian Army was routed in the five-day South Ossetian War of August 2008. The army's fortunes were not helped by the fact that 2,000 of the nation's finest troops were out of the country, stationed in Baghdad. The US Air Force dutifully air-dropped them back to their barracks in Georgia, but not before the fighting around Gori had stopped.

Leaving the US base behind, we drive through a dusty valley strewn with plastic bags. As Krtsanisi village appears in front of us, we spot the markers of BTC and SCP on our left. For the past twenty kilometres these two pipelines have run on a path quite separate from Baku–Supsa, which swings north of Tbilisi. From now on our journey will follow BTC as it heads for the Turkish coast at Ceyhan. At Krtsanisi the marker posts show the two lines climbing up the hill, heading straight for the village. As we approach, we see marker 484 km within twenty-five metres of the buildings. The pipes run under the land between the houses and the local school.

This four-street village has only about a hundred homes. Each is set in its own fenced-in plot of land, used for cattle-grazing or dotted with fruit bushes. The paths between the houses are unpaved. Today they are dry and dusty, but when it rains they must turn to mud. There are few people outside.

A man in his fifties, wearing slippers, joins us on the path in front of his house. He explains that the pipelines are bad for Krtsanisi: 'How can they not be? They run though the village.' Petitions had been made before the construction period, demanding resettlement for the whole community. BP refused, saying the

---

3   J. Moore, 'Republic of Georgia Puts Her Best into Iraq Fight', United States European Command, 1 September 2005, at eucom.mil.

4   N. P. Walsh, 'Oil Fuels US Army Role in Georgia', *Observer*, 12 May 2002.

5   'Press Release: 2009 Budget Adopted', Government of Georgia, Ministry of Finance, 12 January 2009.

villagers would be safe, but the man questions whether this is possible when the pipelines run so close to people's homes. Although willing to share these thoughts, he is not particularly forthcoming. His neighbours are even less open to speaking. Whether this reflects a suspicion of outsiders or a fear of the consequences of talking to them is unclear.

After walking through the village, Manana brings us to the home of the Pangani family. A woman in her thirties, talkative and extrovert, invites us into her front yard. Bright quilts hang from the second-floor veranda, airing in the sunlight. Her husband, a large man in a pale tracksuit, is casting seed to a flock of grey and speckled hens with thick feathery legs. Introducing herself as Pikria, she seats us on a bench in a strip of shade, and starts talking. Manana translates for us.

'We have a small plot', Pikria says, 'but we don't know if we are still allowed to access it because it's close to the pipeline.' She explains that when the contractors were digging the trenches, they ruined the irrigation channel that brings water to the fields. 'So now everything is very dry. The land is not much use without water. BP used to send the police force instead of coming to speak to us themselves.'

We are joined by Pikria's mother, Vardo. When she talks, Vardo's fingers are more expressive than her words, moving in time with her argument and emphasising her statements. 'In the beginning we wrote letters and made petitions, asking to be resettled somewhere else. They didn't listen to us, so the people of the village made many protests. We went to Tbilisi and demonstrated outside government offices. We also blocked the highway leading to Rustavi. But the government wasn't listening – they sent the *spetznaz*. It was a very bad situation; they even beat the children. The people tried to block the pipe-laying in the trench, and so the *spetznaz* attacked us again. It was so bad that it was on the international TV. Relatives in Greece and other countries were phoning to check up on us.'

The sun beats down. The narrow line of shade covering our bench gets thinner and thinner. The Panganis insist that we come inside and drink something. An old episode of *The Bold and the Beautiful* is showing on TV, dubbed into Georgian. One wall is covered with an array of icons – images and newspaper cuttings of Jesus, St George and the Dragon, and Saint Nino.

Vardo explains that differing compensation payments to the village's 115 families caused division, tension and 'great tragedy in relationships in the village'. She feels this partly explains why people in the village would not speak to us. 'Some people in the village are afraid of others – that's why they won't speak. But I think Saakashvili is enough to be afraid of.'

Vardo is not sure how long the village has been here, but it is a settlement made up entirely of refugees. Most of the other families are from the mountain region Svaneti, displaced by landslides, but the Panganis are from Abkhazia. 'We came sixteen years ago, after my husband was killed during the war. First we lived in a cramped school in Tbilisi.' Like Gusein, near Gori, they must have come to

Krtsanisi when they knew that their return to their home would not be swift; they have remained here since. Perhaps Gusein, too, will still be living in his cube of a house in fifteen years' time.

A bowl of yellow apples from the garden is already on the table, alongside a plate of fig rolls broken into pieces. While her mother makes coffee, Pikria holds forth, balancing on the end of the sofa. 'I think the pipelines bring a great threat to our village. Our home has become a very dangerous place. We are surrounded on three sides, by the pipeline and several military sites. There is much shooting – we live in a corridor of violence.' She explains how both Georgian and US soldiers often train in the village, running down the paths between the houses. 'Sometimes I walk out of my gate and find men in camouflage with guns crouching behind my fence – I've screamed several times. I don't understand, why do they do this in our village? I think maybe it's because the pipeline is so close. Many of us experienced the war in Abkhazia, so it's easy to make people panic.'

It seems this is how the US Special Forces teach their Georgian students 'ground combat skills' and 'urban operations'. Nearby villages simulate Iraqi or Afghan communities, and the Pangani family have become unwitting bystanders in military training exercises.

Pikria feels the village's position is especially dangerous, given the new tension with Russia. She explains that, during the recent war of August 2008, they could hear distant bombs falling and were frightened. 'The easiest way to impact the military base would be to bomb the pipeline; then the village would be gone.' She says that during the pipeline construction the villagers forced BP into meetings over safety, but felt they received no answers. The issue even went to the local court: 'I'm a lawyer, so I observed the court hearings over our disputes. But it was always delayed. In the end it came to nothing.' We think of the craters near Akhali-Samgori, only a few kilometres to the east.

While Pikria's speaking, her husband turns the TV volume up to watch the news. It briefly shows an opposition rally and then we spot Saakashvili outside the Ministry of Interior. Seeing him, Pikria curses. 'Satan. The war with Russia was his fault. Always emphasising how strong the Georgian Army is and trying to provoke. All he is good for is designing pretty and pointless fountains.'

Pikria is smart: she knows who is responsible. Soon after we arrived, she had mentioned the name Ed Johnson. General Manager of BP Georgia until 2005, Johnson oversaw the company's lobbying of Shevardnadze and the relationship-building with Saakashvili after the Rose Revolution; he was in post during the pipeline construction period, when the riot police battered the Krtsanisi villagers.[6]

---

6   'BP's $3.6 Bln Pipeline Runs Into Georgian Strikes, Revolution', 2 January 2004, at bloomberg.com.

It is rare to hear people along the pipeline name names – usually it is just 'the company' or 'BP' or 'BTC Co'. One of Pikria's first lines to Manana was: 'How do we sue Ed Johnson? Can we do this in England or America?' Here is someone who has identified an individual who she believes is responsible for her predicament, and wants to hold him judicially accountable. She knows it will be impossible to hold him to account in Georgia, but hopes that the British or American judicial system might be fairer. The sad reality is that getting Johnson into court would be challenging. Persuading a UK or US judge to hear cases on a company's practices abroad is difficult – achieving a guilty verdict harder still. So, for the time being, the Texan Ed Johnson need not worry about being called before a jury, and can focus on his job expanding BP's offshore platforms in Norwegian waters.

This large living room, with its sofas covered in drapes, reminds us of the hours we spent in the house of Mehmen in Hacalli. How different the response in Azerbaijan is to the impacts of the pipeline from that in Georgia. Mansura Ibishova in Qarabork seemed powerless even though BTC and SCP effectively passed through her home. She placed faith in the idea of writing to President Aliyev. Mehmen and his neighbours were intimidated by the Executive Power in their village, who was effectively protecting BP's assets. Here in Krtsanisi, as at Rustavi, residents had blockaded the construction sites, and thereby succeeded in bringing the issue to the attention of national and international media. Pikria knows perfectly well that President Saakashvili will not defend her from the actions of Ed Johnson's company. It seems to us that the determination of these Georgian citizens to defend their rights has been greatly strengthened by the work of Manana, Keti and their colleagues, whose position is so much less beleaguered than that of Mayis.

Eventually, Vardo announces that they need to tend their cattle; it is time for them to be taken to their pastures. Bidding farewell, we see the six family cows already gathered by the gate, waiting patiently to amble out to their grazing.

12 IT IS ASH TO THE EYES

ზორჯომი (BORJOMI), GEORGIA

The Debate

Onward crawls the mighty army,
Like a cloud released;
Dark, enveloping, alarming,
Heading for the East.
[...]
And the great Caucasian mountain,
Gloomy and morose,
Tried but could not finish counting
The advancing rows.

Mikhail Lermontov, 1841[1]

A Georgian myth tells that when God was dividing up the world between the different peoples, the Georgians missed their chance to choose a homeland because they were sleeping off a festive drinking spree. When they awoke, everything was gone, with the exception of that part of the world that the Almighty had been reserving for himself, which was heaven on earth. 'Where can we go?' pleaded the Georgians. 'We were only late because we were toasting you and celebrating your glory!' A flattered God responded, 'Well, I guess I'll have to give you a piece of paradise.'

It is not hard to see why the Georgian creation legend describes these mountains as a paradise. Steep hillsides are covered with a green blanket of oak, maple

---

1   See M. Lermontov, transl. A. Liberman, 'The Debate', *Major Poetical Works*, University of Minnesota Press, 1983, pp. 255–9.

and beech. The forests on the slopes hide wolf packs, wild boar and the last remaining Caucasus leopards. In the company of Manana and Keti, with Ramazi at the wheel, we wind back and forth along a canyon. Below us the Mtkvari River forces its way through the mountains as it heads towards Tbilisi and Azerbaijan, changing its name to the Kura before it spills into the Caspian. The roar of the spring meltwater echoes across the gorge as it throws itself against the rocks. Wooden rope bridges, painted blue, span the wide torrent and sway in the cool breeze. Each walkway leads to a small village surrounded by yellow and red fences.

The local springs, sulphurous and mineral-rich, are credited with relieving a host of ailments, from digestive disorders and menstrual irregularities to nervousness and incontinence. The viceroy of the Russian province of Transcaucasus, Grand Duke Mikhail Romanov, celebrated the area's natural beauty and curative powers, banned excessive hunting and encouraged aristocrats to build luxurious country houses here. Borjomi was transformed into a resort, 'the pearl of the Caucasus', known for its Tsarist summer palaces and sanatoria, and later frequented by Soviet Communist Party apparatchiks. But this imperial development was part of an expansion that was not all so picturesque.

In his poem 'The Debate', the Russian poet Mikhail Lermontov imagined the Caucasus mountains Elbrus and Kazbegi in conversation, bearing witness to an unending Tsarist frontier war. Mount Kazbegi believes that nothing will change in the East in 1,000 years. The slow-flowing Egyptian Nile, the argila-smokers of Tehran and the sleepy Georgians are all as they were. Elbrus, the taller of the two, can see further to the north, where the thundering ranks of Russians are sweeping down, 'battalions on the march, drummers flailing, cannons creaking forward, their wicks already lit'.[2] Unlike Pushkin, who had romanticised the Caucasus wars, Lermontov denounced the brutal Russian anti-insurgency campaign, picturing the Tsarist Army's actions as imperial occupation and enslavement.

The southward expansion of the Orthodox Russian Empire involved the mass expulsion of hundreds of thousands of Muslim Circassians or Cherkez. The Tsar's defeat at the hands of the Ottoman Empire in the Crimean War led Russia to identify many of its Muslim subjects as potential sympathisers with the Ottomans. Between 1860 and 1864, the populations of mountain villages were targeted for 'resettlement' into Ottoman lands, causing a traumatic exodus across the Black Sea and creating the proud Circassian diaspora in Jordan, Syria and Turkey's Taurus mountains.[3] The removal of peoples and cultures from the Caucasus would be echoed by Stalin's deportations of Pontic Greeks, Meshkheti Turks and Chechens eighty years later.

2   Ibid.
3   Cornell, *Guns of August*, p. 21.

This conquest and expulsion laid the basis for a transformation of the Caucasus. While soldiers were emptying the mountains of their inhabitants, Grand Duke Mikhail Romanov was promoting the therapeutic benefits of Borjomi to his fellow aristocrats. This transformation of the mountains into a place of relaxation and recreation was the counterpoint to that of Baku and Batumi into places of resource extraction and exportation.

In the middle of the region of Borjomi lies the town of that name. We arrive at 8 a.m. on a chill weekday, but the place is crowded with visitors. They have not stopped for the themed playgrounds or the landscaped gardens. Instead, the passengers that spill out of the coaches hurry towards a glass pavilion, lining up to fill containers with the fresh mineral water that has an unusual taste: sour and salty, with a hint of sulphur. The mountain springs and the region itself, the Borjomi-Kharagauli National Park, are beloved by all Georgians.

Bottled mineral water from these springs was famed across the Soviet Union, and remains popular throughout Russia. Indeed, with the collapse of Georgia's industrial centres, such as Rustavi, Borjomi water had come to constitute as much as 10 per cent of Georgia's export trade.[4] So when it was announced that the BTC pipeline would skirt the edge of the national park and pass through the catchment area in which the springs were located, residents, businesspeople and environmentalists alike were up in arms.

On a previous visit to the town, in 2003, we had met Jacques Fleury, CEO of the Georgian Glass and Mineral Water Co. This company had obtained the rights to bottle and sell the water at the time of the demise of the Georgian socialist economy. He had explained the problem posed by the plans for BTC. 'If you are a consumer of, let's say, Evian, and you learn that a major export pipeline is going to cross its water reserve, what will be your reaction? You will switch the brand. Even if no leak occurs, exports of Borjomi will dramatically fall.'[5]

It was hardly surprising that Fleury and his colleagues, in alliance with the Worldwide Fund for Nature in Georgia and the UK, took their complaint to the European Bank for Reconstruction and Development (EBRD) in the City of London. Indeed the international coalition of NGOs that challenged BTC campaigned heavily on the threats to Borjomi.

Manana travelled several times to Washington, DC, trying to raise these issues with the International Finance Corporation – an arm of the World Bank, and one of the group of institutions intending to provide a loan to BTC. Protests over Borjomi spread to many countries in Europe and the US, with demonstrations

---

4 'Extreme Oil: BTC Pipeline Georgia – Technology and Environment', at pbs. org.

5 M. Katik and G. Kandelaki, *Environmental Activists Not Reassured by Baku–Tbilisi–Ceyhan Pipeline Hearings*, 16 September 2003, at eurasianet.org.

outside the offices of BP, pipeline construction companies such as AMEC, and government ministries such as the UK Department for International Development. The latter provides an executive director who formally represents the UK at the World Bank. At the time this was the minister, Hilary Benn MP, and he was vigorously lobbied. Friends of the Earth mobilised hundreds of people to build a cloth pipeline from the EBRD, down Bishopsgate, past RBS, to the headquarters of BP in Finsbury Circus: a pipeline to illustrate the flow of public money into a private corporation that was threatening Borjomi.

In the midst of this we had been in Georgia, and Manana and Keti had arranged for us to meet Professor Mirian Gviritshvili and three other scientists at the offices of Green Alternative.

Mirian, the principal scientist at the Tbilisi Botanic Gardens, had a profusion of bushy white hair. The District of Borjomi, and in particular the Tskhratskaro Pass through which BP planned to lay the pipeline, were of particular importance, he explained – one of the twenty-five most biodiverse places on Earth. 'This is an ecological crime, not only in my opinion, but also in the opinion of the most famous Georgian hydrologist.'

In its initial plans, BP had proposed three possible BTC routes through Georgia: the Eastern Corridor, the Central Corridor, and the Western Corridor. Only in 2002 had it become clear that the Central Corridor had been chosen, and consequently that Borjomi was under threat.

The scientists had suggested modifications of the proposed route. They had made studies and drawn up plans for the line to run via Karakaja, further south. In October 2002, they had a meeting scheduled with BP, including the company's Georgian head, Ed Johnson. They had been hopeful that the company would switch routes by announcing an addendum to the Environmental Impact Assessment scheduled for later that month. It seemed there was an opportunity for change, but the meeting was abruptly called off, and the addendum delivered nothing.

The pressure built up through November 2002, with the Georgian environment minister, Nino Chkhobadze, refusing to sign off on the projected pipeline route. With the deadline for a final decision looming, she was subjected to intensive lobbying from BP and US officials, but on 30 November she announced on live TV that she would not allow the route that threatened Borjomi. Late that Sunday night she was escorted from her home to the president's office. After intensive discussions with President Shevardnadze, she re-emerged bleary-eyed at 3 a.m., announcing that she had, after all, signed off on the route. Later, she explained: 'The pressure came above all from the company, and it was pressure not only directed toward me, but also toward the president.'[6]

6   R. Khatchadourian, 'The Price of Progress: Oil Execs Muscle US-Backed

BP said at the time that it would undertake work to meet the environment minister's 'conditions of permit'. But five months after that November night when we had our meeting with Mirian, according to the professor, BP had done nothing. 'Yes, BP have talked of doing studies, just like they talked about the viability of alternative routes to avoid Borjomi. But I don't believe them; it's just for show. It's all ash to the eyes.'

BTC KP 643 – 830 KM – დგვარი (DGVARI), GEORGIA

From the centre of Borjomi, Ramazi drives us up through the pines along a steep road that becomes a track. Our white car crawls through the dense forest towards the village of Dgvari, which lives under the threat of landslides from the mountains above. We are returning to the place of a vivid meeting in the spring of 2003.

Then we had come to hear what villagers expected from BTC. A middle-aged man had invited us in, leading us through the main house, a garden and an orchard to a kind of private summer house. Several people were seated inside, among them a woman who was neatly smoothing out pastry with a thin rolling-pin and dropping parcels filled with meat into a cauldron, her daughter watching quietly. After a short while, the daughter fished out the *khinkali* dumplings with a ladle and brought them to the table. From a sound system in the main house came tracks by Bob Marley, Leonard Cohen and Queen.

The man playing host plied us liberally with lethally strong homemade vodka, *cha cha*. The first shots came from a reused Borjomi Mineral Water bottle, later glasses from an old vodka container made in Glasgow. There was much laughter as we spluttered. Our eyes watered under alcoholic blows.

Our host beamed as he told us his opinion of the pipeline. The others also chimed in – six men and five women, all gathered in this summer house. Everybody was smiling and laughing: we should stay longer, they said, and then they would take us into the forest.

In the conversation that passed around it became clear that they believed the pipeline would increase the landslides and destroy the villagers' homes. They declared they would not allow the pipeline to be built nearby – the residents of Dgvari would stand there and stop it being built if necessary. In four days' time a man from the World Bank was apparently coming to see the problems of the village. If matters deteriorated, they declared they wanted the whole village resettled. The host joked, 'Perhaps to Washington, where there's less snow.'

For a period of nearly twelve months a constellation of forces seemed to operate in harmony: the international NGO coalition, the Georgian environment minister, the outraged Tbilisi professionals such as Mirian, the businesses who bottled

Pipeline through Environmental Treasure', 22 April 2003, at villagevoice.com.

Borjomi water, the villagers along the pipeline route, and the wider public who was angry with President Shevardnadze. This combined opposition came close to preventing public funds being provided from the World Bank, the EBRD, and possibly the export credit agencies.

Without public finance, which brought with it the political backing of states such as Germany, France, Italy, the UK, the US and Japan, the loans from private banks would have been far less likely – at least not with the interest rates BP desired. The company and governments of Britain, the US and the EU were concerned by the threat that these forces of civil society posed to the project and to this particular vision of the Oil Road.

John Browne, then CEO of BP, recalled the NGO campaign in his autobiography: 'So began a battle. Jim Wolfensohn, President of the World Bank, and the executive directors of the Bank came under enormous pressure not to finance the pipeline.' Browne described his conversations with Wolfensohn.

> He called me one evening at my London apartment. He was very agitated: 'We cannot get this through'. He was worried that he could not carry his board because of the intense lobbying by various NGOs. My response was predictable: 'We need to get this done. In the end we need to say what we are doing is right. We should not be scared off by people, some of whom are making things up.' What else could I say? . . . Jim Wolfensohn and I were long-standing friends but the intensity of the negotiations nearly made us fall out.[7]

At the time those of us in the NGO coalition had no idea of the personal closeness of Browne and Wolfensohn; nor did we understand quite how hard the company was fighting back against us. Browne later wrote: 'As I had learned, from bitter experience, we could not ignore any of them [the NGOs]. We had to take all their concerns seriously, engage in discussion and attempt to resolve differences.'[8]

Browne's references to 'engagement' are given a different twist by a BP-produced document obtained by Nick Hildyard of the Corner House and Doug Norlen of Pacific Environment. The document includes a slide from a presentation given by an unnamed member of BP staff to civil servants and representatives of institutions who planned to lend funds to the pipeline. It illustrates the company's real 'engagement' plan. Published in the illustrations of this book, the slide shows a page divided into four quarters with different civil society organisations mapped across them. Each NGO is placed in a quadrant according to how the company felt it should address its concerns. In the top right-hand square are the logos of large bodies considered to be most

---

7   Browne, *Beyond Business*, pp. 170–1.
8   Ibid.

sympathetic to BP, such as Amnesty International, the Open Society Institute and WWF. The names of the Corner House, the Kurdish Human Rights Project, CEE Bankwatch, Georgia Greens (referring almost certainly to Green Alternative) and Friends of the Earth are situated in the bottom left-hand square, as they are considered to be the least sympathetic. A note in the margin indicates that there is 'no need to engage [them] actively'. Instead, BP's advice was to only 'engage opportunistically'. The document reveals that the company was briefing the banks and export credit agencies on a strategy to neutralise opposition by co-opting large NGOs and marginalising others.

This strategy employed in London and Washington has remarkable echoes of the processes in Baku, where the government nurtured the 'pro-BTC coalition' while denouncing activists like Mayis.

By the spring of 2009, the area around Dgvari had undergone three years of construction work and three years of the pipeline pumping oil. As had been feared, during the building of the line, landslides had become worse and cracks had appeared in the walls of the houses. Roman Gogoladze, a farmer, was quoted at the time: 'Big powers – the oil companies and the government – are destroying our homes and our land. They are playing their money games and ignore people like us.'⁹ The village had not been resettled. There had been talk of a $1 million offer of aid from BP, negotiated by the World Bank, but it had never materialised. As we drive back down the mountain track, Manana explains that the villagers' hospitality has evaporated, as they feel bitter towards strangers bearing promises.

We make our way to Atskuri and spend an afternoon talking with Zuzunna, a secondary school teacher. After the political battle over BTC in 2002 came those struggles over the construction of the pipeline. She talks of how the company used heavy lorries to bring materials and equipment into the mountain villages. In Atskuri the trucks had passed just below an ancient hilltop fortress. The vibrations caused regular landslides and rock-falls onto the homes below. Following Zuzunna's leadership, residents blocked the road. Once again, complaints were raised with the European Bank for Reconstruction and Development and the World Bank. The villagers demanded that BP reroute its vehicles and take responsibility for repairs. They were partially successful: the company put up signs saying: 'Trucks, don't go this way, take the other road', but the instruction was not enforced, and many of the drivers ignore the signs.

As trenches were dug across the Borjomi region and pipes laid, there were repeated blockades of roads and construction sites as villagers challenged the prioritisation of a company and its investors over their own livelihoods. As at

---

9   K. Cooke, 'Power Games in the Caucasus', BBC News, 7 May 2006.

Krtsanisi and Rustavi, resistance was met with a harsh response from the police. 'When we protested against the pipeline, the police came and beat people up', proclaimed the villagers of Dgvari.[10] There were reports of intimidation towards those who raised concerns, with BTC employees allegedly threatening physical violence or a reduction in the compensation that landholders were due.[11] Ed Johnson, the head of BP Georgia, complained in 2004: 'Every single day there is a disruption that has something to do with getting more from the government or from us.'[12] In all, more than 300 direct action protests took place in Georgia alone between 2003 and 2005.[13]

As we talk, the TV is on in the background, showing Russian news. At around 6 p.m. Georgian time – 3 p.m. in the UK – reports start coming through of the G20 protests in the City of London. 'Why are people in London protesting?' Zuzunna asks. At that point, the Camp for Climate Action had set up its tents on Bishopsgate, metres from the EBRD and RBS. Criticised for giving loan finance to BTC, as well as other fossil fuel projects, an RBS branch had already had its windows smashed, and the riot police were forcing protestors back with their batons. We talk about the connection to Atskuri and the anger of people towards the banks.

ბორჯომი (BORJOMI), GEORGIA

In a basement bar in Borjomi, we share homemade red wine and cheese *kachapuri* with Manana and Keti. It is a local dive with fairy lights and a soundtrack we recognise from *Mimino*, a Soviet hit comedy about a Georgian helicopter pilot who leaves his mountain village for adventures on international planes. Keti begins to tell us 'the story of Green Alternative and the drunk BTC workers'.

In 2004, a local Green Alternative volunteer was having a drink in a nearby bar when she overheard a group of BTC foreign workers talking about their jobs. She brought them a round of drinks, whereupon they announced that they would be in the area longer than expected, because they had received orders to dig the pipeline up again – something needed fixing. Then they went tight-lipped. Even when plied with more vodka shots, they refused to talk. The emails flew back and forth between Manana in Georgia and campaigners in England, but no one knew what the cause was.

Manana, Keti and their colleague Nino decided to dig deeper. They drove into

---

10   Ibid.

11   K. Macdonald, *The Reality of Rights: Barriers to Accessing Remedies when Business Operates Beyond Borders*, Corporate Responsibility Coalition and London School of Economics, 2009.

12   'BP's $3.6 Bln Pipeline Runs Into Georgian Strikes, Revolution', bloomberg.com.

13   Macdonald, *Reality of Rights*, p. 33.

the Borjomi mountains, looking for workers excavating pipes. Following close by the line, they came across sections that, previously buried in the ground, were now exposed and surrounded by freshly dug earth. As they passed one of these sites with labourers at work, the car 'broke down'. Their driver Ramazi got to work under the bonnet, while Manana and the others acted like lost tourists, taking photographs of the forested slopes and the construction site. 'The workers thought it was so strange – three girls lost in the mountains. But they were not suspicious at all, because Ramazi played his part so well, and we took lots of photos. But then, when we returned to the car – it was actually broken!'

The full story of what was happening only emerged after investigative journalist Michael Gillard, working for the *Sunday Times* Insight team, tracked down Derek Mortimore, a leading pipeline corrosion engineer hired by BP. Mortimore is one of a handful of world experts called on when pipelines fail: 'We are the real environmentalists', he states. 'We try to stop pipelines from rupturing.' The most frequent cause he cites is external corrosion, mostly on account of the coating that seals the pipeline.[14]

According to Gillard's investigation, in the early summer of 2002 a two-page memo from BP's London headquarters was sent to Paul Stretch, then BP's technical manager at Villa Petrolea in Baku. The memo compared anti-corrosion coatings supplied by four companies. At stake was a multimillion-dollar contract to coat the 'field joints' on the BTC pipeline. Each section of the pipeline, each length of steel pipe, comes wrapped in plastic to protect it from external corrosion. After the steel ends of two sections are welded together, this so-called field joint – the most vulnerable place on any pipeline – is coated to seal the weld itself from corrosion. 'To ensure full protection, the field joint coating must adhere to both the steel and its plastic jacket for the entire design life. In this case, forty years underground.'[15]

Both Paul Stretch and Rod Hensman, BP's senior project engineer in Azerbaijan, were alarmed that the memo seemed to be pushing hard for a liquid epoxy paint called SPC 2888, named after its Canadian manufacturing company, Speciality Polymer Coatings. It was a coating whose effectiveness on a plastic-wrapped pipeline like BTC was unknown. The two managers contacted Mortimore, who was already advising BP on its Caspian offshore operations, for a second opinion.

Mortimore quickly pointed out that the proposed SPC 2888 coating was entirely unsuitable: 'Liquid epoxy paints have very limited flexibility and adhesion when applied to plastic-coated pipelines and would not protect the field joint from rapid corrosion. I felt BP would be burying thousands of environmental time bombs.' Comparative laboratory tests, he said, had deemed SPC

---

14   M. Gillard, *The Contract of the Century: A Special Investigation*, 29 November 2004, at spinwatch.org.uk.
15   Ibid.

2888 'poor' on key issues, and raised serious questions over its ability to stick: the liquid epoxy coating came off the pipe in large pieces. The bond would be 'particularly reduced' in cold weather, according to Mortimore, who predicted that the sealant would crack during the winter months – clearly a problem in the mountains around Borjomi.

Yet when the BP project team in London produced its assessment of the comparative tests, they omitted from the ranking table any results where SPC 2888 had failed or performed badly, thereby allowing it to come first out of all the competing coatings. The UK parliament Select Committee on Trade and Industry would later hear how BP ignored the concerns raised, and chose this coating as the only sealant to be used on the 60,000 field joints in Azerbaijan and Georgia.[16] Alarmed about the decision, Mortimore wrote to John Browne to warn of disaster, but was told there was 'no value in a meeting'.[17] Precisely why the company stuck so closely to the Canadian company has never been clarified.

The first field joint was coated in August 2003. By mid-November that year, Mortimore's predictions were coming true. Routine pipeline patrols discovered that sections of the pipe, welded together but not yet buried below ground, showed cracked field joints, with rust seeping through the coating. SPC 2888 was peeling off.[18] With the pipeline already mired in controversy, BP tried to keep this failure a secret – especially from the World Bank, the EBRD and export credit agencies. For despite the company's success in the battle over Borjomi, and construction of the pipeline being well underway, the financing deal with the Lenders Group was still not completed.

In February 2004, as pipeline workers were dispatched to construction sites to excavate trenches and reapply the coating, BP finally signed the formal package for a $2.6 billion loan at a ceremony in Baku. Representatives of all the lenders were there, and it took two full days to sign the documents with the 17,000 signatures required. The pipeline's financing had finally been concluded after a two-year battle, and the objections raised from so many quarters had contributed to the delaying of BTC by about a year.

Only twelve days after the ceremony, Gillard's exposé ran in the *Sunday Times*, featuring the testimony of Mortimore, now a public whistleblower. In response, BP mobilised its supporters. The UK's then trade minister, Mike O'Brien, insisted that the pipeline was still safe, while the British Export Credit Guarantee

---

16   M. Gillard, 'Second Memorandum by Michael Gillard', in *Implementation of ECGD's Business Principles – Ninth Report of Session 2004–5, Vol. 2*, UK Parliament Select Committee on Trade and Industry, 8 March 2005.

17   Gillard, 'Contract of the Century'.

18   WorleyParsons Energy Services, *Appendix 2: Desktop Study Final Report Field Joint Coating Review*, UK Parliament Select Committee on Trade and Industry, March 2005.

Department argued that the flaws were merely an 'application problem' caused by workers not warming up the coating properly. The experts critical of BP's decision countered that this would not solve the problem of liquid epoxy ultimately not sticking well to plastic: 'The chemistry', they said, 'is totally wrong.' With delays mounting, BP developed a novel approach to resolving the remaining problems. Inspectors assessing the pipe joints were given clear guidelines: even if the coating 'peeled in large pieces' from the pipe, it should be designated 'a pass'.[19]

Back in the Borjomi bar, Manana and Keti have little faith in BP's promises that the issue has been dealt with. 'Now that the pipeline's buried and invisible, everything is supposed to be fine. But we know that the coating is flaking off and that there could be a leak at any point.'

BTC KP 625 – 812 KM – ციხისჯვარი (TSIKHISDVARI), GEORGIA

Early the next morning we head into the mountains along a potholed road in the lee of snow-capped Mount Karakaja, brilliant white against the blue sky. The road winds up and up, passing beyond the forested Mtkvari River valley into steep pine-clad hills. The depth of the snow increases steadily.

Onwards across a high alpine pasture, we reach an upland plateau where modern hotels sit cheek-by-jowl with fields ploughed by oxen. Spring is strengthening its hold as we watch: rivulets of fresh meltwater run through small coppices, and yellow and purple flowers emerge from the snow. Ramazi turns a sharp corner at the last minute, and we are faced with the unlikely sight of two brand new concrete silos and a bright yellow JCB excavator beside them.

Ten minutes further, things became clearer: there is a substantial building site with heavy trucks and diggers, thick-set guys in dark glasses, orange jumpsuits and white helmets with BTC logos. But the pipeline has been pumping for three years, so what is this construction work, we ask Manana.

She explains that BP is building six enormous dams to hold back oil in case of a leak. This mitigation system is not a direct response to the concerns about the pipeline coating failing, but rather an answer to the protests about the threats to the Borjomi catchment. Here, in smooth grey concrete painted with black bituminous sealant, with rusting reinforcing bars and thick-walled pipes, is BP's solution. Each dam is built across an existing stream, and the structure has sluice gates that are left open. If the pipeline cracks higher up the mountainside and thousands of barrels of crude spills into one of these streams, the sluice gates are to be shut and the oil prevented from running down the mountain. The works seem incongruous here. We look at them with a feeling of ambivalence, for they represent the product of the campaigning of which we were a part.

---

19   D. Mortimore, *Appendix 4: Response from Derek Mortimore to ECGD Submission*, UK Parliament Select Committee on Trade and Industry, March 2005.

We drive past the construction site and stop at the edge of the next settlement. There is a weathered bust of Stalin balanced on a fence post overlooking the track. A group of villagers nearby complain about the trucks clogging up their roads, and cracking the walls and foundations of their homes.

Further up the mountain Ramazi guides the car through the mud and into a wide valley of pasture, with the snow having only recently melted and the grass dun green, criss-crossed with fences of pale, sun-bleached pine. All around us, a great ring of mountains with bald peaks rises above the pine forests. Between the meadows and the forest lies the Greek village of Tsikhisdvari. These are descendants of Pontic Greeks, who first settled on the Black Sea coast nearly 3,000 years ago. In the turbulence created by the Tsarist conquest, they moved up into these high mountains. Decades later many were deported under Stalin, but those families that remained or returned built colourful houses with pyramidal roofs of corrugated iron. Some are painted a shade of bright blue, reminiscent of homes in the Cyclades.

Walking along the muddy village street, we come upon a large house full of people, its doors wide open. A crowd is gathered outside. Manana discovers that this is a wake – a young relative of the household has died in Greece. She explains that in the post-Soviet years many of the Tsikhisdvari residents have returned to Greece, if 'returning' can be used to describe a migration somewhat similar to the idea of Anglo-Saxon Londoners relocating to Germany. As the crowd begins to thin, we start talking to a woman with wispy red hair. She invites us to her house for coffee. A doorway in the fence on the main street takes us into her yard, where several neat piles of fresh logs, an axe and a black woolly dog share the shade. Inside the house we are joined by her daughter-in-law.

The room is spotless, with wide wooden floorboards painted brown. There is a divan with covers on it, a wood-burning stove, a sideboard with six carefully tended cactuses. The radiant woman with the red hair becomes a whirl of activity, hurrying back and forth, bringing food to the table – much more than a cup of coffee. Keti, Manana and Ramazi join us at the table, laden with sweet pickled walnuts, piles of chocolate sponge, glasses of deep red grape juice and shots of grape liqueur. It turns out that she is originally from Borjomi town. She had followed her son up the mountain when he moved here for work and then settled down with his village sweetheart.

Her criticisms of BP are many, so we are surprised to discover that it was the pipeline that brought her here – her son got work as a horseback security guard for BTC. She hurries off to bring his contract, a sheet of white A4 with an official stamp and signatures, crumpled into a see-through sleeve – a precious document in a house with few books. It transpires that he has to provide his own horse and cover all its costs, which absorbs much of his meagre pay packet. A horse, she explains, eats twice what a cow needs, while producing no milk. When the horse becomes sick, her son has to pay for the vet. One of his fellow guards lost his job when his mount died. Now we understand better the indifference shown to us by the scrawny horse and rider at the bomb craters near Akhali-Samgori.

The sunlight floods into this airy wooden room. Looking out across the rooftops, a compact stone church on a rocky hillock marks the centre of the extensive village. Georgia is dotted with post-Soviet churches built in the past ten years, but this one is different, with its weathered stone and Greek inscription above the western door. It must date from when the villagers settled here in the nineteenth century – a rare survivor of the Soviet period. Beyond it lies the dark green of the forest and the sharp white of the mountains.

After saying goodbye, we have one further place to visit. We want to verify the existence of a military checkpoint that is said to hinder the villagers from walking up the hill to the higher pastures and the hot-sulphur springs, as they have done for generations. The passage up this track is now described by BTC Co. as 'crossing the pipeline corridor', and therefore apparently requires an ID card and checks by troops from the Ministry of Interior. Bumping along the dirt road, we soon see the concrete wall of another oil spill catchment dam. Further up the hillside, we can see the familiar pipeline markers. Absorbed in trying to read the route of BTC across the bright green of the distant pasture, we fail to notice a sandbagged wooden hut just on our right. Suddenly we are surrounded by several angry soldiers levelling their guns at us and shouting that we must turn back. Ramazi spins the car around, and we are heading fast downhill again. Clearly the pipeline corridor is militarised here, as at other places, but these soldiers are not as relaxed as those near Akhali-Samgori. The government troops working to protect BP's infrastructure have control over access not just to the route itself, but also to the meadows, forests and mountains above it. This is the outcome of the work of George Goolsby, the lawyer at Baker Botts who oversaw the writing of Host Government Agreements concerning the state's obligations on security.

John Willet, *The New Sobriety: Art and Politics in the Weimar Period 1917–33*, Thames & Hudson, 1978

Conducting Arseny Avraamov's the *Symphony of Factory Sirens* in Baku in 1922 for the fifth anniversary of the October Revolution. The orchestra consisted of foghorns of the Caspian Fleet, factory sirens, bus horns and a huge cast of choirs.

The Baku–Batumi oil train, stationary behind two Georgian men. Photo taken by Alfred Lyttelton Marriott in 1901.

Andrea Scaringella

The scar caused by the construction corridor of BP's Baku–Tbilisi–Ceyhan pipeline in Georgia, August 2005.

A meeting between British civil servant Duncan Lawson (left), Mayis Gulaliyev (right) and villagers affected by the BTC pipeline in Azerbaijan, August 2005.

Andrea Scaringella

Ferhat Kaya standing in the snow on the BTC pipeline route near Ardahan in north-eastern Turkey, winter 2005.

Global NGO Framework

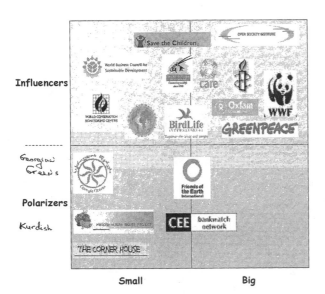

Influencers

Polarizers

Georgian & Greek's

Kurdish

Small   Big

Engage in logical manner as part of Licence to Operate at BU level (e.g. Public Consultation and Disclosure) and continue routine Reputation Process at Corporate Level.

Programme is **'Project Driven'** by us

Engage on key issues;

Social – Oxfam etc
Revenue management – Soros etc
Environmental – WWF, Birdlife etc
Human rights – Amnesty
Shock tactics – Greenpeace

No need to engage actively; this would only legitimize their case. But by all means engage oportunistically.

Recognise their targets are the IFIs

Balance their arguments with lobby campaign to politicians and IFI boards

Operate as 'cells' with small representation in each country.

Programme is **'Event Driven'** by them i.e. meetings like; J'berg, WTO, IMF etc

A table from a BP-produced briefing revealing 'divide and conquer' tactics to undermine NGO opposition to the pipeline in 2003. It shows the logos of organisations such as Kurdish Human Rights Project, the Corner House, CARE International, the Open Society Institute and Amnesty International. (See Chapter 12.)

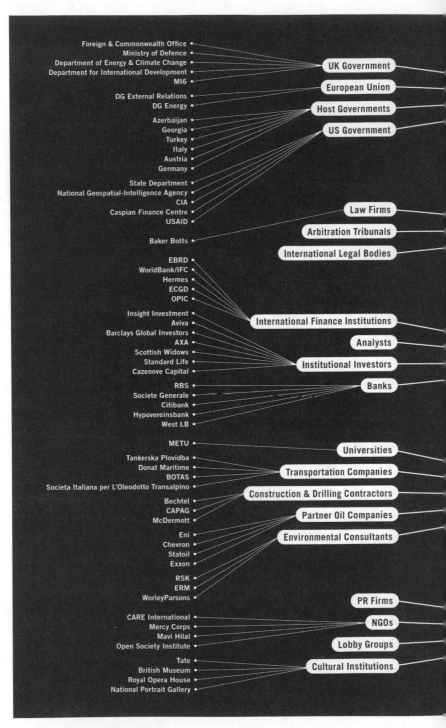

Part of the Carbon Web that surrounds BP, and has participated in the creation and maintenance of the Oil Road.

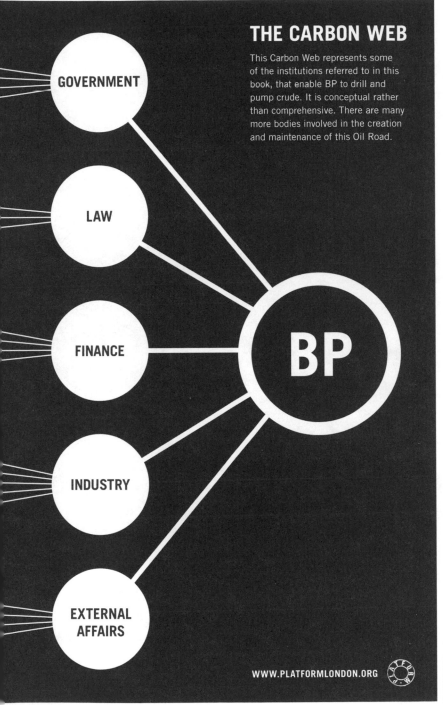

THE CARBON WEB

This Carbon Web represents some of the institutions referred to in this book, that enable BP to drill and pump crude. It is conceptual rather than comprehensive. There are many more bodies involved in the creation and maintenance of this Oil Road.

GOVERNMENT

LAW

FINANCE

BP

INDUSTRY

EXTERNAL AFFAIRS

WWW.PLATFORMLONDON.ORG

The SIOT Oil Terminal in Muggia, after the 1972 attack. The Palestinian Black September claimed responsibility, explaining that they targeted the TAL pipeline terminal because it supplied Germany, which armed both Israel and Jordan.

13 I WILL STOP YOU, I'LL SMASH YOUR CAMERA!

Crossing the Georgian–Turkish border at Türgözü is slow, but the weather in these high mountains is blissful: bright sun and barely a breath of wind. Having left Manana, Keti and Ramazi, we are travelling south by bus; in the opposite direction rolls a stream of articulated trucks with Iranian registration plates, heading towards Russia. Georgian border guards in an EU-funded office check our passports, keying in data and taking digital photographs. Once each individual is approved, an electronic gate opens. Fortress Europe is in operation, ensuring that the supposed 'undesirables' are prevented from entering. The Georgian officials give a hard time to three Russian women in bright clothing. Two are allowed to cross, but the third is turned back. The border guards in Azerbaijan were keen to block unwanted books; here, people are denied entry.

Travellers gather on the grassy verge in the middle of the Turkish border compound, between the police office and the customs shed. A man prays. Another shares his lunch with us. A British-Czech family are taking a week's holiday from Tbilisi in their little green Niva. They have no map, but know the names of nearby cities. He works for the British Council, running an English teacher-training programme for the Georgian military.

Twenty years ago, the scene here was rather different. Türkgözü was the only direct border between the Soviet Union and NATO – a frontline across which soldiers from opposing blocs faced each other directly. As a crossing, Türkgözü was only opened in 1994, but today the frontier is largely inconsequential in the wider geopolitical context. US power is projected further east and north. Unless Russia can break Georgia's NATO alliances, this border has little strategic importance to the West, except to enforce migration restrictions.

In the two hours we wait, 50,000 barrels of crude are pumped under the scrubland nearby. It flows without a pause, for the Host Government Agreements enshrined the priority of 'freedom of movement' for the oil. Nevertheless, this border represents an important marker for the pipeline. Up until this point, through Azerbaijan and Georgia, the pipeline was constructed, and is operated by, the BTC Co. consortium, led by BP. But for the remaining 1,076 kilometres to the Mediterranean, the consortium only has supervisory control. Now, the pipeline belongs to BOTAŞ, the Turkish state oil company. BTC Co. paid it $1.4 billion under the Turnkey Agreement to construct this section of the route by 26 May 2005. Since completion, BOTAŞ has overseen this pipeline's operation. BOTAŞ also took on the construction of the SCP gas pipeline, running largely in parallel with BTC until it comes to its finishing point at the eastern Turkish city of Erzurum, where it delivers its load into the Turkish national gas grid.

Across the border, the road continues to rise. The rugged landscape becomes hidden beneath a smooth white blanket of snow, even now, in April. The scar left by the buried pipeline is invisible at this time of year on this high plateau. Even the orange marker posts are barely discernible.

The crude is pumped up and up, into the Yanlizçam mountains. Our bus slows as the road twists and turns in sharp hairpin bends. We climb the Ilgardağı Geçidi Pass – at 2,540 metres one of the highest passes in Europe. A wall of compacted snow, three metres high, lines our route.

Emerging out of the glaring whiteness is Turkey's first pump station, at Posof, sister to the one we saw in Jandara, Georgia. A three-metre-high chain-link fence, topped with barbed wire, surrounds a dense industrial plant, which comprises three large storage tanks, a row of five steel chimneys and a jungle of pipes. Fifty workers keep the station running, supervising the pumps that push the oil west. They work two weeks on site before catching the company shuttle back to Ardahan for a short leave and being replaced by another shift. Next to the oil installation, also surrounded by deep snowdrifts, stands a brand new three-storey military base, complete with helipad, staffed by members of the Jandarma, the Turkish militarised police force.

BTC and SCP are now running across a historic political fault-line. They pass through what was once the frontier of the Roman Empire, the eastern *limes*. For over 2,000 years these mountains of the Lower Caucasus have been disputed borderlands between rival empires, imperial troops fighting back and forth through the thin air of the high plateau.

The towns and villages of this region have changed hands repeatedly. Today we are travelling deep inside Turkey, but this land was once part of Russia and, before that, Georgia. It was even briefly under British control. A hundred kilometres to the west, where these mountains drop down to the Black Sea, lies the city of Batumi, back across the current border in Georgia. In the eighth century BCE, Greek merchants founded a trading colony here, naming it Bathys, or 'Deep' for its harbour. Six hundred years on, the town was overshadowed by a nearby Roman fort. As that empire's successor, Byzantium, waned, the region was conquered by the kingdom of

Georgia. The rise of the Ottomans meant that, by the sixteenth century, the Turks had captured the city and this plateau from the kingdom of Georgia. However, following the Tsarist expansion into the Caucasus and the defeat of Sultan Abdulhamid II in 1878, these borderlands became part of the Russian Empire.

Batumi was a pivotal Tsarist port and, along with Tbilisi and Baku, a building block in the industrialisation of the Transcaucasian Province and the new Kars Province, established over the region through which we are now travelling. Only six years after the city and borderlands were absorbed into the empire, the railway from Baku arrived, turning Batumi into an oil-export route between the Caspian and the world market. A harbour was built for the transhipment of kerosene. Soon Ludvig Nobel established a refinery and the Rothschilds purchased the Batumi Oil Refining and Trading Company. Of the 16,000 workers who migrated into the growing city, many were Georgians, Turks, Greeks and Armenians from these high borderlands. Almost a thousand were employed in the Rothschilds' refinery and kerosene-canning works.

In November 1901, Stalin, newly arrived from Tbilisi as an organiser for the Russian Social Democratic Workers Party, gleefully announced: 'I'm working for the Rothschilds!' as he obtained employment at their plant. Conditions were appalling for the labourers from the mountains, and agitation began. There was arson at the refinery, an assassination attempt on the Rothschilds' manager, and, on 9 March 1902, a massive strike. The company called in the army, who fired on the strikers – thirteen workers were shot dead. As he was arrested and deported to Siberia, Stalin proclaimed: 'We're going to overthrow the Tsar, the Rothschilds and the Nobels.'[1] Fifteen years later, his prediction would come true.

Much of the oil produced by this troubled plant was carried away on British tankers owned by Shell. When the Rothschilds sold all their Russian assets to Shell in 1911, the centrepiece of Batumi's economy was now in British hands. However, all oil exports from the harbour came to a halt at the outbreak of World War I, as Batumi focused instead on supplying Russian troops fighting high up on this plateau. The landscape through which our bus takes us was one of the most brutal battlegrounds in World War I. For four years, men from the villages and the cities were slaughtered up here, until the Revolution caused the Russian Front to collapse. At the Treaty of Brest-Litovsk in March 1918, the borderlands were handed to the Ottomans, but by the following November, Batumi was occupied by the British. For eighteen months the oil port and this hinterland were under the control of a military governor, just like Baku.

In June 1920 the British evacuated the region. Nine months later, Batumi was the last redoubt of the government of independent Menshevik Georgia. It fell to the Red Army and was absorbed into the Soviet Union. During the first

---

1   Montefiore, *Young Stalin*, pp. 91–8.

forty-three years of the Oil Road, Batumi changed hands six times. But the plateau finally became separated from the city on the coast; the land and villages we are now passing through became part of the territory of the new Turkish Republic.

BTC KP 759 – 946 KM – ARDAHAN, TURKEY

At last Ardahan appears on the horizon – unsheltered in the openness, like a settlement on the tundra. We descend from the distant ring of snow-covered peaks, straight into town. Maybe this lack of natural defences explains why the city castle established by the Ottoman Sultan Selim the Grim fell to one army after another. Rebuilt as a Tsarist barracks, the fortress stands on an outcrop guarding the river.

This is the invisible corner of modern Turkey. Ardahan barely registers in the national consciousness, let alone beyond the nation's borders. Tourism is nonexistent, infrastructure minimal. Few Turkish citizens outside the region have any reason to come here – unless they are posted here by the army.

A cold wind blows across the vast plain, 1,800 metres above sea level. We pass wastelands of rubbish heaps. Plastic bags lie everywhere – white, blue, pink, black – in the spaces between and behind buildings. Jackdaws and the occasional stray dog pick through the garbage.

Ardahan has the atmosphere of a garrison town. Soldiers guard entrances to religious and government buildings; tanks are parked down side streets, and infantry conduct exercises in surrounding fields. Plainclothes policemen shadow outsiders.

We make our way to a small hotel and a joyous meeting with Mehmet Ali Uslu, an old friend from Ankara with whom we have travelled in Turkey before. He will accompany us again on this journey along the pipeline. We tease him over his new closely cropped haircut that seems to make his face beam even more than usual. After the long journey we need to go and find something to eat.

By the time we head back to the hotel it is nightfall, and the streets are empty apart from a small pack of dogs. A roving squad car pulls up beside the three of us, suspicious of our intentions. Looking through our bags, the policeman barks, 'What's in that bottle?' 'Water', we answer. He remains unconvinced until we glug it down exaggeratedly.

Formerly, Ardahan's importance derived from its proximity to the Soviet border. Now, with limited external danger to Turkey's territory, the reason for the city's continued militarisation is an internal enemy: the Kurds. Since Turkey was established as a nation-state in 1923, the existence of the Kurds as a separate people has been perceived as a threat to its sovereignty. Under Atatürk's leadership, official decrees banned Kurdish schools, organisations and publications as part of the forced assimilation of minorities into Turkish culture. The Kurdish language was forbidden, villages were renamed to sound Turkish, and parents could not give their children Kurdish names. In 2002, the head of the Registry Department in Ardahan faced criminal charges after issuing identity papers for children named 'Berivan', 'Rojhat' and 'Rojin'. Use of the letters 'x', 'w' and 'q' was made illegal, as they do not exist in the Turkish alphabet. Kurdish music, clothes, festivals, and the combining of the symbolic colours red, yellow and green – all have been banned at various times.

During the 1990s, in the face of widespread rebellion, the Turkish Army's activities in the region led to the destruction of 4,000 villages and the displacement of 3 million people. Since that time, bombing raids on the Kurdistan Workers' Party (PKK) and attacks on communities in south-eastern Turkey have continued. Policing in Kurdish areas is largely in the hands of the Jandarma, a militarised police force reviled by many across Turkey. Although the recent government of the conservative Justice and Development Party (AKP) has introduced some reforms and eased certain language restrictions, Turkey's 15 million Kurds still face constant abuse, repression and attempts to assimilate and erase their culture.

Initially, the BTC pipeline was due to run south from the Georgian border, turning west through the Kurdish heartland of south-eastern Turkey. But the active presence of Kurdish resistance movements in the region pushed the oil companies to rethink their plans – especially given the PKK's repeated bombing of the Kirkuk–Ceyhan pipeline over the years. BTC's route now bypasses the region to the north. It runs along the Euphrates and the main west–east highway through Central Anatolia. Yet it was impossible for the oil companies to bypass Turkey's Kurdish population entirely. The provinces of Ardahan, Kars and Erzurum are all home to sizable Kurdish minorities that, in places, comprise up to 40 per cent of the population. State discrimination and repression is the norm here, but uprisings are rare.

In the autumn of 2001, news of BP's plans to build BTC across eastern Turkey came to the attention of civil society groups in London. The Kurdish Human Rights Project (KHRP) became concerned that the pipeline's route would create a 'militarised corridor', with a greater presence of Turkish Army forces and Jandarma in Kurdish villages. Kerim Yıldız, the head of KHRP, argued that the pipeline threatened to escalate state violence and further impoverish Kurdish communities. The company was quick to react, with Barry Halton, BTC regional affairs director, making strenuous efforts to befriend KHRP and pull Yıldız into supporting the pipeline. But Yıldız, working closely with Nick Hildyard of the Corner House, was wary of Halton's professional interests.

Yıldız's fears were borne out three years later, as construction of BTC began in Ardahan province. In May 2004, Ferhat Kaya, chairman of the Ardahan branch of the leftist pro-Kurdish political party DEHAP, met with villagers whose livelihoods were being affected by the laying of the route. He was picked up by the police and taken into custody, beaten and tortured. Ferhat is a Turk, but his position in DEHAP helped him build connections with Kurdish communities, though it also exposed him to state pressure.

The Turkish state repeatedly harasses and imprisons elected Kurdish politicians, and bans their party every few years. Previous incarnations of DEHAP include HADEP and DEP. Each saw its leadership arrested, its offices shut down and membership proscribed. Every time this happens, the activists regroup and reorganise, launching a similar party with a different name. By the time we arrive in town with Mehmet Ali, DEHAP has also been closed down, with the Democratic Society Party (DTP) taking its place.

We have arranged to meet Ferhat at a press conference of the DTP. Three floors up a dirty stairwell from the Turkish equivalent of a pound store, the two-room office with smoke-blackened windows is crammed with plastic chairs, the walls lined with posters. Eighty leading members of the party have just been arrested across Turkey on trumped-up terrorism charges. The state is trying to shut down the DTP, so local party offices across the country are denouncing the arrests and proclaiming their loyalty to the cause. Here, fifteen members crowd around the single brown desk to pose for a local TV camera while reading aloud a solidarity statement. They all know that this could be enough to have their names added to the blacklist. The risk is obvious, as everybody in the room has had to run the gauntlet of twenty armed policemen surrounding the entrance to the building. Three uniformed soldiers video us as we walk up the stairs. Mehmet Ali explains that they are from the Jandarma Information Terror Control unit.

But imprisonment is not the greatest risk for those active on Kurdish issues. The windows of the office do not let in much light, because they are covered in black scorch-marks – evidence of a recent attempt to firebomb the party's headquarters. The attack followed a public pro-Kurdish rally on the street outside, at which Turkish Nationalists threw stones at the speakers.

After the press conference, Ferhat takes us to his favourite café on Kongre Caddesi – Congress Street, one of the many Kurdish establishments constantly threatened with bankruptcy due to the boycotting of their premises by Turkish government employees. In a town dominated by the army and its ancillaries, this has a big impact on trade. Ferhat's age is hard to determine because of his skinniness and cheeky grin, and also because he is always moving – whether smoking, on his phone, or talking politics. He is supposed to run the family hardware store, but it appears this has to wait until he is not busy supporting villagers or babysitting his three-year-old niece.

In the 1990s Ferhat studied sociology at Eskişehir University, until obliged to drop out because his family did not have the money to support him. He was conscripted into the military and posted to Edirne in western Turkey, on the Greek border, where the military sends known leftists and Islamists. While he was there, a friend in the records office showed him his file: it dated back to primary school. There were numerous references to his being 'antisocial', which Ferhat finds ridiculous. 'Antisocial!' he snorts. 'They should just write that I was political.'

Ferhat spends his life under surveillance. When he moves around Ardahan or visits villages outside, he is usually followed by unmarked Jandarma cars. He points out of the café window to one parked nearby, whose exceptionally long antenna is a giveaway. His home was raided by the police without warning a few months before, but his mother managed to save his computer by sitting on it. He jokes about how his friends are used to being filmed, but it clearly places strains on many of his relationships.

We sit drinking coffee at the Formica tables. He expects the police to listen in to everybody's phone calls today because of the press conference, so he plans to wait until the next day before ringing people to arrange meetings: 'They'll probably be listening tomorrow as well, but maybe not.' Despite his nonchalant descriptions of police harassment, Ferhat currently faces two major prison sentences. In one case he is charged with referring to Abdullah Öcalan, the leader of the Kurdish resistance movement in solitary confinement on a prison island, as 'Mr Öcalan'.

We talk specifically about his arrest and torture in May 2004. He believes that it was the direct result of his having raised issues about the BTC pipeline. In Turkey, he explains, those opposing a 'national project' of this status are frequently denounced as enemies of the state. His words remind us of Mayis in Azerbaijan.

BTC KP 774 – 961 KM – HASKÖY HOÇVAN, TURKEY

A *dolmuş* – a shared minibus taxi seating sixteen passengers – carries Mehmet Ali and us south across the plateau and slowly up the valley. To our right the waters of the Kura meander through the grassland. This river will become the Mtkvari as it flows through Georgia, before regaining its name as the Kura in Azerbaijan. Snow falls, veiling the landscape. Clusters of low homes lie near to the road. In the early twentieth century, before the Armenian genocide, these villages were predominantly Armenian; now they are mostly Kurdish. For much of the winter, this road is closed and the snowbound communities are largely cut off from the town. To us, the high banks of snow on the verges represent midwinter; but to the locals on this bus they mark the arrival of spring.

Ferhat has spent much time supporting complaints about the pipeline raised by communities near Ardahan, and we are heading for Hasköy-Hoçvan, one of the largest villages, which gives its name to the county. When we arrive, the heart of the village is a sea of mud, churned up by cows. The herding of cattle is the core of farming in this region, with the cows driven up to the high mountain pastures, or *yayla*, in the summer and then back to the villages in winter. We pick our way across the mud to the village tearoom and wait for another lift. Twenty men sit playing cards in air thick with cigarette smoke. The room is quiet except for the slap of cards on tables.

Suddenly the tinny sound of a Tannoy outside interrupts the calm. We look around furtively, concerned that it is a message broadcast by the military police. On a visit we made four years previously, Jandarma walked into a meeting in this same room and demanded explanations. But no, this is an announcement from loudspeakers on the mosque, the public address system for the village. Mehmet Ali translates: 'The wolf has eaten a cow, number ninety-seven.' A wolf, hungry at the end of winter, must have taken a small cow. These communities are far more vulnerable to the elements than we are used to.

We leave, again in a *dolmuş*, hoping to avoid the attention of the police. As we turn a corner on the village street, we pass in front of a large concrete building, surrounded by wire-mesh fences. Several storeys high, with newly painted walls, it is a Jandarma barracks, guarded by sentry boxes and helmeted soldiers holding automatic rifles. The base dwarfs the school across the street.

BTC KP 777 – 964 KM – ÇALABAŞ, TURKEY

The minibus turns off the main road through Hasköy-Hoçvan County, and follows a winding stream towards the village of Çalabaş. The turf-roofed homes have been built into the hillside, making them nearly invisible from above; cows graze on the roofs. The sixty families in the village survive by keeping cattle and geese.

Walls of dried cow dung stand upright, solidly packed into piles, each stack some six metres long and two metres high. This is fuel for heating and cooking in the winter months. The entire plateau is largely treeless, so wood is scarce. There is no gas supply, and electricity is intermittent. Among the houses, the narrow track that is the village's main street runs up to the communal tap. Women and girls balance buckets on their heads, carrying water home.

Next to the tap stands the village store, run by Ali Kurdoğlu – Ali 'Son of a Wolf'. The small dark room feels like a cave. Neatly stacked boxes of Ülker biscuits, Signal toothpaste and Uhu glue line the shop, although most people come here to buy Viceroy or Anadolu cigarettes. The faces of film director Yılmaz Güney and Ahmet Kaya, a famous Kurdish singer and poet, stare down from the walls. Handwritten sayings and short poems have been taped to the low beams, although the lack of light makes them hard to read. Benches run along the edge of the room, making this the village's social space. 'There is no internet in Çalabaş. That's why my small shop is more than a shop – it's a cultural centre.'

Ali is slightly hunchbacked, with a small twisted frame. He moves with a limp. He is a local champion of Kurdish rights and a vocal opponent of the pipeline. A close friend of Ferhat's, he also faces a potential three-year imprisonment for his activism.

Ali says that Çalabaş has been hit particularly hard by the pipeline because of the village's Kurdish identity. He has heard that Turkish Nationalist villages received better compensation for land expropriated by BTC and SCP, as well as larger community investment projects, including mosques and morgues. Expressing dissent is far more dangerous for a Kurd from Çalabaş than for a Turk from nearby Kurtulpınar, he says. Despite the dangers, the villagers from Çalabaş had attempted to protest against the construction, blocking bulldozers and stopping work.

As he serves the occasional customer, Ali explains how the two pipelines, BTC and SCP, run either side of Çalabaş, cutting through the fields where wheat and barley grow in the summer. 'We are truly living in an energy corridor – the alley between the energy flows. This is a strategic area.' Having an invisible 'strategic area' imposed on your community is a sad fate. We understand his point, having recently witnessed the Executive Power at Hacallı in Azerbaijan, and the troops of the Ministry of Interior at Tsikhisdvari in Georgia.

The present is already difficult, with Jandarma forces repeatedly harassing him for speaking out. He receives threatening phone calls and is often taken into custody, usually after visits by international delegations. His phone is tapped – the police want to be clear that 'they know what's going on'. In 2005, Ali was interviewed by the British civil servant 'Dawson', or rather Duncan Lawson, during the same journey that took him to Azerbaijan. Days before the visit, Ali was phoned by the provincial governor's office and ordered not to say anything critical. He expects that he will receive more hassle tomorrow, following our visit. But, he shrugs, 'they don't scare me. They want to dissuade others from coming forward.'

A set of weighing scales sits on Ali's counter, alongside a small black-and-white TV and, on top of it, three publications: a Kurdish literary magazine published by a friend in İstanbul, the DTP party manifesto, and the Turkish Republic's constitution. Ali explains that he refers to this last document regularly when defending himself against police harassment. It brings to mind Mayis's staunch use of the Azeri constitution against the secret policeman in Hacallı.

Ali believes that if the war between the government and the PKK escalates, life in Çalabaş will become more dangerous. Many homes are close to the pipeline route, and the military would use Çalabaş's location and the conflict as an excuse to increase pressure and control.

As we talk, the door is flung open and a man in uniform stands silhouetted in the entrance. We are suddenly on tenterhooks. 'Police? Jandarma?' But the man in the blue jacket with yellow trim smiles broadly. He is from Pall Mall cigarettes, here on a stock-take. He punches a few details into his handheld digital recorder, turns down the offer of tea, and heads on.

Mehmet Ali says that he is surprised to find a man with Ali's articulate political views in a tiny village like this. It turns out that Ali is a returnee, having lived for thirteen years in İstanbul – where he worked in a print shop, wrote poetry and was actively involved in Kurdish politics – before coming back to Çalabaş (a rarity in itself) in 2004, and opening his shop. He still writes – Kurdoğlu is his pen name – publishing poetry and articles on his walls, in local newspapers and online.

Despite feeling a deep affinity with Çalabaş, he is torn between staying and leaving again for the big city.

A combination of poverty and state harassment has driven many villagers away. Some 550 families from Çalabaş now live in İstanbul – almost ten times the number remaining in the village. Others have moved to İzmir and Ankara, while the more mobile have made it to Berlin and London. Most of those in İstanbul have ended up in the vast, sprawling Kurdish suburbs, including the *gecekondus* – shacks built on squatted land, often adjacent to landfill sites. Ali describes how Çalabaş is considered *varoş* – a disadvantaged and poor area – but he feels that most of those who leave end up merely in another, more distant *varoş*.

HARINGEY, NORTH LONDON

Haringey's Green Lanes is hectic. Kurdish and Turkish corner stores with boxes of oranges and tomatoes piled high on the pavement outside stand next to packed cafés and restaurants serving freshly baked *lahmacuns*, *pides* and lentil soup. Off the busy road, a side street ends below a railway embankment. Tucked between the last house and the grey palisade fencing is a squat two-storey building that houses the Kurdish Community Centre. A mural of the smiling face of the imprisoned leader of the PKK, Abdullah Öcalan, welcomes visitors. Inside, the centre is dominated by a large hall. A small café booth serves piping-hot sweet tea for 20p. Kurdish flags and framed photographs of fallen resistance fighters – many from London – adorn the walls. A large poster demands 'Freedom for Öcalan – Peace in Kurdistan'.

The hall often contains just a handful of men chatting, or kids participating in after-school Kurdish-language classes. But today the room is heaving. It is February, and the month of celebrations marking Newroz – Kurdish New Year – has just begun. In Turkey, Newroz parties are frequently banned and shut down. Here in exile, the Kurdish community can welcome in the New Year at will, so the hall is filled with families enjoying themselves. Songs are sung about lost lovers and hopes for freedom. Speeches remember those who cannot be here, sitting in prisons far away. Several youth groups perform traditional dances at the front, but each dance ends with most of the room joining in.

A Platform-organised exhibition of photographs and poetry from along the route of the pipeline stands upright on white display boards. The faces of Ali in Çalabaş, the *muhtar* (mayor) of Hasköy-Hoçvan, and Mayis in Baku, stare out at the festivities. Adults guess where the photographs were taken by the landscape. Three nine-year-old boys choose their own interaction with the exhibition by taking biros to the prints and crossing out all Turkish flags in the background. Other frenzied children chase around the room, playing tag and dodging the dancers. The old sit on plastic chairs clapping to the music.

All the while, we are watched over by images on the walls of the young Kurdish women and men of Haringey who chose to return to their homelands and go up into the mountains, never to return.

BTC KP 780 – 967 KM – HACI ALI, TURKEY

Poor farmers always make room for a calf in their home, close by the fire, next to where they lay their own beds. They bed the calf in fresh grass mixed with flowers. The hut then smells of spring flowers, of grass, of calf-dung and of the young animal. The smell of a calf is like the smell of milk. If anyone opened his hand wide to caress an ear with the palm, he would feel a pleasant thrill, it was so soft and cool.[2]
Yaşar Kemal, *İnce Memed*, 1955

The River Kura winds between these isolated Kurdish villages, twisting into loops and meanders, leaving oxbow lakes to serve as memorials to its past course. Jackdaws probe the fields in search of seeds and larvae as herds of cattle wander the plain. We cross the pipeline again, spotting the marker posts – punctuation points in the vastness. The wind blows light snow across the road.

There is a strange mist rising from the land. We peer at it though the bus windows and realise it is steam rising from the newly ploughed fields of black earth – both near to the road and far away at the base of the mountains. The landscape has three strata: black earth, grey steam, white mountains.

Half an hour's journey from Çalabaş, our *dolmuş* turns off the road and pulls into another village, stopping on the muddy street between more turf-roofed houses. In the distance boys in blue-and-black uniforms are returning from school. A pair of women in their bright headscarves stand out against the low grey sky.

The people we are visiting are in close contact with Ferhat, but travelling out of Ardahan with him would have drawn too much attention from the Jandarma, so we have arrived in the village of Hacı Ali with Mehmet Ali. We meet with two farmers who guide us to some rough grazing land about 200 metres from the houses. Under it flows one of the pipelines. Unlike in Azerbaijan and Georgia, its course across the land is dramatically obvious. The pipe has just been covered in a mound of rocks and earth some two metres high – an earth barrier stretching away in both directions. Crossing this mound involves clambering up on all fours and carefully sliding down the other side; our arms and clothes are soon brown with mud.

For a short while we stand on the other side of the mound, staring at it. The boulders make it look like a construction site where work is still taking place. In Azerbaijan and Georgia, once the pipeline was buried, the topsoil of the fields was carefully reinstated in order that the route should be barely noticeable. Why the

---

2   Y. Kemal, *Memed, My Hawk*, Panther Press, 1998 (1955 in Turkish).

difference here? The answer lies in the fact that this is not, we realise, the route of BTC – which runs nearby – but that of its younger twin sister, the SCP. The pile of boulders reflects a difference in the financial and legal structures around the two pipelines. For the first 692 kilometres from Baku, the two siblings lie parallel in one ditch. At the Turkish border, however, SCP separates from BTC. The state oil company BOTAŞ has responsibility for the construction of BTC, and after that its operation – but it does so under the Turnkey agreement, the contract from the pipelines' owner, BTC Co. In contrast, BOTAŞ not only constructed and operates the SCP, but also owns the pipeline in Turkey. The land that covers BTC and SCP might have been reinstated with the same care, but the two different owners have enforced different standards. The two pipes continue to run near one another until they reach Erzurum, but often on different sides of hills and villages. Now we realise that distinguishing the two is going to be easy, as the scar left above the gas line is so much clearer. The pipe has been 'buried', but that is the extent of the reinstatement works. This explains why everywhere along the route villages are full of complaints about the *doğal gaz boru hattı* – 'natural gas pipeline'.

The group has now grown to six farmers. One bends down to pick up a large bone – what appears to be a cow's jaw. He explains that two cows from Hacı Ali died because of the lack of proper reinstatement. They got stuck in the mud and broke their legs on rocks: a disaster in villages as poor as this.

We head back to the house of one of the farmers, having been invited to tea. Another turf-roofed home with white-washed boulder walls. Inside we find a rich smell of warmth and damp earth. When we ask how many cows the family has, the farmer gestures for us to follow him, pushing open a wooden door leading straight off the main room into the byre. There is an overpowering smell of dung. Light falls through a gap in the roof, and we can see the cattle tethered to the walls, roped to a wooden rail. There are five cows, a fine two-year-old bull, and, curled up on the ground, three calves not more than a few weeks old. Their coats are the softest strawberry-rowan colour. Our host beams proudly.

Back in the main room, chickens hide under our bench. Tea is served – brewed on the dung-fuelled heater. The farmer, who lives with his wife and four young children, explains how permanently losing the strip of land to the continuous mound of the pipeline route has affected the family's livelihood. Apart from having a section of grazing destroyed, it has become difficult for his cattle to get to his field on the far side of the mound. One of the lost cows belonged to him.

Questions about compensation are met with a snort of derision. We have heard elsewhere in Turkey that compensation paid to villagers who lost land to SCP was even lower than that paid for losses to BTC. The farmer says that cash payments from the companies were so measly that it was barely worth applying. There were no jobs to be gained from the pipeline, while the community investment projects that came with BTC have proved to be worse than useless. An artificial insemination programme for the cattle, run on behalf of BTC Co. by an organisation called Mavi Hilal (Blue Crescent), resulted in fewer pregnancies than usual. The project workers claimed the programme would lead to higher milk yields but, as in the nearby villages of Hasköy-Hoçvan and Çalabaş, here in Hacı Ali the scheme apparently led to a significant loss of income.

As we drive away in the *dolmuş*, we discuss with Mehmet Ali the difficulty of explaining to these villagers how the difference between the two pipelines came about. The international NGO campaign complained to the oil companies, banks and export credit agencies that the Turkish section of the gas pipeline was being built to lower standards than the sections in Azerbaijan and Georgia. But the institutions behind the project answered that SCP in Turkey was not their responsibility.

It is obvious that, without the preceding 692 kilometres of pipe across Azerbaijan and Georgia, there would be no gas to fill the section of SCP running from the Turkish border to Erzurum; and that, without the pipeline that now runs under the land of Hacı Ali and connects with the Turkish grid at Erzurum, the gas pumped from the Caspian Sea would never reach its desired market. While responsibility for operating different sections may change along the route, the pipeline remains one integrated project, constructed at the same time, with each section relying on the other. However, the companies and those financing the project chose to define the Turkish section of SCP as another pipeline, and therefore not their responsibility.

Not all Western government institutions agreed with this line. USAID, the American aid department that studied BTC, recognised that the total project was 'not economically viable without the Turkish section. Consequently [the] projects and the Turkish section are mutually dependent and [therefore] USAID considered them as one project for environmental assessment purposes.'[3] Indeed BP, although it disclaims responsibility for SCP in Turkey, ironically prides itself on having built the Baku–Tbilisi–Erzurum gas pipeline. It draws the entire pipeline route onto maps used in its own presentations, and does not exclude the Turkish section.

HARBOUR EXCHANGE SQUARE, CANARY WHARF, LONDON

Located in a sixteen-floor glass-plated tower at Canary Wharf, the UK Export Credit Guarantee Department (ECGD) provides state-subsidised credit and insurance to British exports, which in cases like this include overseas

---

3 *Multilateral Development Bank Assistance Proposals Likely to Have Adverse Impacts on the Environment, Natural Resources, Public Health and Indigenous Peoples: September 2002–October 2004*, USAID, 2004.

construction projects. The ECGD guarantees that companies will not lose out if an overseas buyer fails to meet its payment obligations: any loss will be covered by the taxpayer. The British state provides this support for 'strategic sectors' of the British economy that help further foreign policy aims – industries such as arms manufacturing and fossil-fuel extraction.

As head of the ECGD's Business Principles Unit, David Allwood is responsible for 'project impact screening and analysis'. His office is on one of the top four floors of the Exchange Tower in Harbour Exchange Square. Finance and PR companies fill the lower levels; Barclays Bank rents seven floors for itself. It was Allwood who assessed the probable impacts of BTC's construction and operation and, having done so, gave his public approval to over £80 million of ECGD support to the pipeline; the final total amount is not public, and it is possible that the sum could be double that figure.[4] The guarantee thus covers between 2 and 4 per cent of the pipeline's total costs. This may appear a small proportion, but combined with the support of export credit agencies from Germany, France, the USA, Italy and Japan, it is not insignificant. Crucially, the export credit agencies provide a level of political guarantee and insurance to the oil companies, thereby reducing their risk exposure. Funding from the EBRD and the World Bank performs the same function.

Financing is theoretically supposed to go only to those projects that meet defined standards, and it is Allwood's job to ensure these standards are met. He has two other staff members working on his team, but the ECGD finances many projects simultaneously, so in reality there was less than one full-time person assigned to making an informed recommendation on the credit line of between £80 million and £160 million for BTC.

Furthermore, Allwood's report on BTC's impacts was somehow deemed 'confidential'. It took a protracted legal battle by Nick Hildyard of the Corner House to force the ECGD to disclose it. The department's lawyers fought hard, combining personal attacks on Hildyard with legal argument.[5] In the process, however, Hildyard also forced the ECGD to release the list of local environmental laws in Georgia, Azerbaijan and Turkey from which the oil companies had exempted themselves through the Host Government Agreements drawn up by George Goolsby. This was an important revelation: BP and the institutions lending public funds to the pipeline had always claimed that no local laws were bypassed.

---

4   Documents released under FOIA indicate that an additional $150 million to $250 million in overseas investment insurance could have been provided by the ECGD, as well as the public credit line of $150 million. N. Hildyard, K. Yildiz, M. Minio-Paluello, N. Rau and M. Kochladze, 'Regional Conflict and BTC Pipeline: Concerns over ECGD's Due Diligence', Corner House, 26 August 2008, at baku.org.uk.

5   Private communication between authors and Nick Hildyard.

Looking back on the years of meetings and letters between Hildyard and the ECGD, it seems that Allwood's job was structured to present the department's support for BTC as principled, rather than to ensure that the project it financed actually followed sound human rights and environmental principles.

BTC KP 759 – 946 KM – ARDAHAN, TURKEY

Every village we visited in the area repeated the same complaint that we had heard in Hacı Ali: that the scheme set up to compensate villagers for the pipeline's construction through their fields – the artificial insemination programme for their livestock – was fundamentally flawed. This was part of the BTC Community Investment Programme (CIP), run out of BP's offices in Ankara – a sister to the CIP programmes in Georgia and Azerbaijan that we had been told about by Irina and Aydin at the Villa Petrolea in Baku. With the complaints of villagers echoing in our ears, we wanted to visit the NGO administering the programme, Mavi Hilal.

Across a small park from the firebombed pro-Kurdish DTP office, we climb the stairs to the Mavi Hilal headquarters in central Ardahan, on the third floor of a nondescript block. BTC magazines and paraphernalia dot the desks. The walls are covered with small photos of people standing in fields or constructing wells. Handwritten captions explain the scenes.

The director is not in, but the project workers are happy to talk. Anıl Çoban, the health coordinator, explains that Mavi Hilal works in thirty-seven communities along BTC's Turkish route, mostly focusing on agricultural services such as water, cattle and bees. Over 1,000 hives have been distributed. The quiet 'bee man' standing next to Anıl trains people to maintain them. Mostly, Mavi Hilal provides equipment and materials, expecting villagers to contribute in cash or in kind. In Hasköy-Hoçvan the organization provided pipes for a new water network, which the villagers then had to lay themselves. We have seen a sign in Hasköy, outside the hall where the men played cards, informing residents how BTC brought piped water to the village. Anıl was not here when this project began, but is palpably proud that it is complete.

We ask whether they ever receive complaints from disgruntled villagers. Apparently not: everybody is happy, especially with the new milk cooperatives that have been set up. There have been a few grumbles from some villages about not having received beehives, but then Mavi Hilal does not have the money to cover everybody. Anıl adds, 'People should be happy if something good is done. Sometimes, they might not be, as BTC and the government tell them dreams. But that's what those promises are – things just in dreams.'

Clearly, NGOs such as Mavi Hilal have a challenge navigating between villagers' expectations of what the BTC pipeline can do for them and the reality of their budgets. Despite this, the description of events we are given is not reassuring. Something Anıl does not mention – but which we know from our own observation – is that the new water supply in Hasköy does not work. The pump for the water should run off electricity, but the villagers are too poor to pay for it. The pipes lie unused.

BTC KP 729 – 916 KM – DEREKÖY, TURKEY

Two years previously, the same quiet 'bee man' played a very different part in demonstrating Mavi Hilal's role in the villages to us. In June 2007, together with Ferhat and our translator Ülkü, Mika interviewed and filmed some farmers, including Cümü and Binali in Dereköy, a community of Alevi Muslims north of Ardahan. Villagers were laying out their concerns when a white Mavi Hilal jeep drove past four times, with the passengers staring out.

> Cümü: They always think we're stupid, because we wear these peasant caps. They gave us a bag of chalk – to show that they were helping us.
> [*The Mavi Hilal jeep pulls up and the project worker jumps out and runs over, wearing his full-body white bee suit.*]
> Bee Man: What are you doing here? Put that camera away!
> Ülkü: Why are you being so aggressive?
> Bee Man: I will stop you, I'll smash your camera!
> Ülkü: What are you scared of?
> Bee Man: I'm not scared of anything – they should stop filming!
> Cümü: They are filming me, and they can film you, there are no problems. You are distributing the bees as you want. Unfairly.
> Bee Man: Shhh, don't dig into that issue, I'm here privately.
> Cümü: But you can't be private while you're in this car – this is an official car.
> Bee Man: We are not official, this is civil society. [*To us*] What is your name?
> Ülkü: I'm not saying.
> Bee Man: [*Very threatening*] What does this mean, 'I'm not saying'?
> Binali: Are these people or stones? You drove past and ignored us, and now you come shouting?
> Cümü: The pipeline came through my field, but I didn't get any bees – they only gave help to those with an uncle in Ankara. Why don't you help the poorest – are you helping poor people?
> Bee Man: No, we're not. They shouldn't film.
> Binali: Well, why don't you leave, then they won't be filming you.
> Bee Man: Did they get permission to film? They must have permission from the Vali [provincial governor].
> Binali: Are you an authority here? Why is this up to you?
> Bee Man: Give me the *muhtar's* [village mayor's] phone number.
> Binali: Just go to his house, it's over there. I lost my field and I'm talking about the problems with the stones. I don't have anything to do with the bees, so why are you bothering us?

Bee Man: They shouldn't film me.

Binali: They weren't filming you, they were filming me. Is my freedom in your pocket?

Mika: I can explain…

Bee Man: [*To Mika*] No! No! [*To villagers*] You are not supposed to talk.

Cümü: Why shouldn't we speak? We are citizens. We are trying to solve our problems.

The Mavi Hilal workers left as abruptly as they had arrived, speeding down the narrow dirt road. Five minutes of conversation later, a Jandarma vehicle showed up. It had clearly been summoned by the 'bee man'. Mika had just enough time to switch the tapes in the video camera, hiding the original in a sock and inserting a blank cassette, before police piled out of the van, shouting for us to come with them. Ferhat had managed to slip away, but Ülkü and Mika were loaded into the covered back of the green armoured truck and driven off to the regional Jandarma headquarters.

There, Mika's detention involved being yelled at by the commanding officer while an orderly knelt at his feet shining his boots. Other officers demanded to watch the videotape, but were disappointed when it showed them a mere thirty seconds of footage of Dereköy's main road. Mustafa Gündoğdu, from the Kurdish Human Rights Project in London, phoned to check that Mika and Ülkü were okay, not revealing his Kurdish identity or exile in Britain. This was followed by a call from a less friendly UK official: Dan Wilson, second secretary for energy and environment at the British embassy in Ankara. Wilson insisted that it was not acceptable to visit villages affected by the pipeline without permission, whether or not Mika was near the pipeline itself. Nowhere, however, is there any official statement of such a prohibition in Turkish law. Rather, as in Azerbaijan and Georgia, the arbitrary power of the state was being utilised to prevent BP's pipeline being scrutinised.

Mika and Ülkü were held for several hours. They passed some of the time exchanging Skype IDs with conscripts from İstanbul who wished they were studying sociology. Eventually, after background checks, a brief interrogation and receipt of a signed 'protocol', they were released and told to stay away from Dereköy.

BTC KP 759 – 946 KM – ARDAHAN, TURKEY

In Ardahan, the chill wind rips advertising banners off the walls as we take a last walk around town with Ferhat and Mehmet Ali. Torn election flags hang across the streets – the banners of the ultranationalist MHP party, the religious-nationalist AKP, the secular-nationalist CHP, and the pro-Kurdish DTP. A young soldier stands straight in the sentry post next to the mosque. In the poor eastern part of town, Kurdish men load a stubborn cow onto a pickup, and women in headscarves feed geese.

Everywhere there are dark birds sifting through the rubbish for morsels. We have noticed them around the town, out on the fields and in the villages. All members of the crow family: jackdaws, rooks, magpies and hooded crows. There is the occasional rough-legged buzzard and some house sparrows, but overwhelmingly, this is crowland.

The town consists of three types of building: low-rise 1960s concrete blocks several storeys high, flat turf-roofed homes with five-foot doorways like those in the nearby villages, and a third type of dwelling: single-storey, built from well-hewn granite. These are neat reddish-grey houses, with solid window sills and door frames. We notice an inscription on the keystone of a doorway – '1910', followed by a different script: Armenian. These homes were once Armenian. Some are occupied, others ruined. Ferhat explains that, at one time, most residents of Ardahan were Armenian. Now there are none. Only ghosts. We peer behind shop signs or at house fronts looking for the telltale inscriptions. Many more are dated 1910 and 1911.

One hundred years ago, eight out of ten of the city's 10,000 inhabitants were Armenian, living on the fault-line between empires. Tsarist Russia had long desired this eastern territory of the Ottomans. After defeating the sultan in 1878, the Tsar annexed Ardahan and the surrounding region, and established Kars Province. Russian control lasted only forty years, until Leon Trotsky's signature at Brest-Litovsk in 1918 formally returned this territory to the Ottomans.

But the order from the Ottoman government to expel Armenians from the empire had already been given, in April 1915, while World War I raged in this border country. Those living here may have survived longer than their cousins further west; but by the time Ardahan had been returned to Turkey and Atatürk had established the Turkish Republic, in 1923, the Armenian community of this town was no more. The inhabitants of these homes had joined over 1 million others, force-marched south to the Syrian desert, killed in their thousands by Lake Van, or escaping into exile.

Dusk falls. The jackdaws leave their daily labour of picking the fields and rubbish heaps. Wheeling in great flocks above the town, they come to roost in the trees of the Atatürk Park, between the Mavi Hilal and DTP offices, amid the empty Armenian homes. We watch in amazement as thousands upon thousands pour out of the sky. They cram the branches of this tight little wood, filling every tree – black rags falling from the dark sky, their voices chattering, chattering, filling the air. Bodies huddled tight, lit by the sodium glare of a streetlight also illuminating a golden statue of Atatürk. Crowlands. Ghostlands.

14 NO-ONE WANTS THIS PIPELINE ON THEIR CV: IT'S AN EMBARRASSMENT

EUPHRATES VALLEY, CENTRAL ANATOLIA

İstanbul House of Detention
I love my country:
I have swung on its plane trees
I have slept in its prisons.
Nothing lifts my spirits like its songs and tobacco.

My country:
so big
It seems endless.
it seems that it is endless to go around.
Edirné, Izmir, Ulukıshla, Marash, Trabzon, Erzurum.
All I know of the Erzurum plateau are its songs

and I'm ashamed to say
I never crossed the Taurus
to visit the cotton pickers
in the south.

Nazım Hikmet, 1939[1]

Our carriage trundles slowly across the plateau from Erzurum. Together with Mehmet Ali, we picked up the train just south of Ardahan, close to the border with Armenia. We are now moving due west, both following the pipeline and in

---

1 'İstanbul House of Detention', 1939, from N. Hikmet, transl. R. Blasing and M. Konuk, *Poems of Nazim Hikmet*, Persea Books, 1994.

the wake of a mass human migration. Many of the homes and villages we glimpse from the windows appear deserted or barely inhabited. It feels as if the train from the east has swept up those it passes, depositing them eventually in the slums of Ankara and İstanbul. Long stretches of this railway follow the ancient trade route that connected Tehran to İstanbul and Sofia, part of the Silk Road, travelled by mules, horses and camel trains. Today, the E80 highway, thundering with trucks and cars, runs in parallel with the train. The railway track from Ankara to the eastern cities of Erzurum and Kars was opened in 1939 – a symbol of the bold modernity of the Turkish Republic. The coal-driven engines thrust into a land that was then almost entirely without oil-driven vehicles.

Passing through Erzurum and Erzincan provinces, the Doğu Ekspresi (Eastern Express) stops at countless village stations with no platforms. Sometimes the train halts in open fields, where the passengers wait patiently to board. At other times we make five-minute stops, but nobody climbs on or off the train. Once, a young boy walks alongside the carriages selling quinces to passengers. Mehmet Ali reaches down from our window to buy a couple. We are already four hours late – did he see us coming, or was he waiting here the whole time?

As the train moves across the Erzurum plateau, we take turns reading and discussing Nazım Hikmet. Ground-breaking both within Turkish literature and internationally, Hikmet's poems evoke the romantic beauty of the villages and towns of Anatolia while explicitly confronting political oppression. Hikmet, a lifelong member of the Turkish Communist Party, was imprisoned for over a decade and stripped of his citizenship. Sent into exile, he spent long periods in the Soviet Union, travelling south to Baku and Tbilisi to be closer to his home-land. He believed that harnessing industrialisation to socialism would rescue the toiling poor from poverty. Both his aesthetic and social visions were heavily inspired by Futurism.

> I sat at his deathbed
> He said to read him a poem
> About the sun and the sea
> Nuclear reactors and satellites
> The greatness of humanity[2]

Hikmet remained persuaded of the liberating power of technology throughout his life. Fifty years later, many on both the right and the left remain convinced of this kind of modernity as a solution to social, environmental and economic prob-lems. So much of the literature around the BTC pipeline, from within the industry,

---

2 'The Optimist', 1958, from Hikmet, *Poems of Nazim Hikmet*.

in governments or the media, sees the project as essentially benefiting human development, and the problems it creates as easily solvable.

Yet Hikmet believed in the need for a change in power relations. He regarded inequality as the underlying cause of suffering, for which political shifts were the essential primary solution. Technology was merely a tool to be harnessed and put to use by social struggles. The real solution lay in people, not the machine:

> *Love clouds, machines, and books*
> *But people above all.*[3]

As we read, the railway enters a landscape of steep canyons and narrow gorges. This is the area of Lot B of BTC in Turkey, the second of the three sections of its route between the Caucasus and the Mediterranean. In the distance we catch glimpses of occasional pipeline markers. Opening the back door in the last carriage, we get a better view by hanging off the rear of the train, catching the wind and watching the river we are shadowing. The tracks share the gorge it has cut from the surrounding rock over millennia. Rope bridges span the water, reminding us of Borjomi.

This little river, jumping and foaming over rapids, is the Firat, the beginning of the Euphrates. It has yet to gather momentum from the rain falling on the mountains of the Taurus, before broadening out and feeding the fertile crescent of Syria and Iraq. We are still very close to the Black Sea, but any crude that leaks from BTC here would drain into the Euphrates, bound towards Fallujah, Basra and the Persian Gulf.

It is strange to think of these two rivers running in parallel – the first visible, accessible and composed of a substance we ingest daily, the second buried and carrying a liquid most of us have never seen, touched or smelled. Both are very present in the landscape we are travelling through; both cross multiple borders; both cause wars.

But these two rivers – of water and oil – do not flow peacefully alongside one another. One is slowly choking the other. The mighty Euphrates is drying up. In Syria families flee its drought-stricken valley. In Iraq, the shrinking of the river has decimated farms along its banks and left fishing communities ruined.

The changes to the Euphrates have many causes, among them the building of hydroelectric dams and irrigation schemes. But alterations in the climate and shifts in rainfall are central – hence the destructive relationship between these two sister rivers. Once burned, the heavy black liquid that flows towards industrial society fills the atmosphere with carbon, helps alter the temperature of the world and assists in the suffocation of the river.

---

3   'Last Letter to my Son', 1955, from Hikmet, *Poems of Nazim Hikmet*.

BTC KP 1,070 – 1,257 KM – HACIBAYRAM, TURKEY

The train passes south of Hacıbayram, between Erzurum and Erzincan. We examine a photograph of the village taken by a colleague, Greg Muttit, during a visit in the spring of 2003. It shows a man clambering about on the flat roof of a deserted building. Behind him a line of poplar trees are blurred by the breeze of a late afternoon in the uplands. The man was Fazlı Kılıç, the beekeeper. It was a village with many hives and no people.

Kılıç was born in Hacıbayram. Like those he lived alongside, he worked the fields – pasture for livestock, meadows for hay, and the flowers that feed the bees. Then the Turkish Army came, saying they were looking for Kurdish guerrillas. What followed is not clear, but every single person from the village left their homes, and the buildings were destroyed.

Those who had lived for so long in Hacıbayram were scattered, some to the *gecekondus* of Ankara and İstanbul, others to nearby villages and towns. Kılıç settled in Tercan, ten kilometres from Hacıbayram. He travelled back and forth to the deserted village to tend his hives. Sometimes he stayed overnight in the ruins.

The map we are now using on the train shows that Hacıbayram was in the path of what was then a planned industrial project. The thin black lines on the white paper were spewed out from the belly of a hard drive. This is part of the 'Social Impact Assessment for the Baku–Ceyhan Pipeline', produced by Environmental Resources Management (ERM) in London.

ERM won the contract to conduct this study in May 2000. Sometime in the following eighteen months, a team headed out to consult communities along the proposed pipeline route, to ask them their views and explain the predicted benefits of the planned project.

The study was published in June 2002. Its careful detail reassured readers in the international banks and government departments in London and Washington that time and attention had been given to the villages and fields. A little 'T' is marked by Hacıbayram on the map that we hold. It indicates that the consultation with villagers was carried out here by telephone. But when the study was in progress, the village was in ruins. There were no telephones; nor was there was anyone to answer them.

On the same afternoon that the photograph was taken, as Kılıç climbed across the roof among the hives, that 'T' lay buried in hard drives and CDs in the offices of ERM and BP. It is as though a funnel had sucked in the fields and the hay harvest, the migration and the ruins, and concentrated it into one tiny byte of information. The gentle hum of the bees, the breeze of the late afternoon, was translated into some new language, so that the eyes of those few who read it – glowing on a computer screen – could say 'yes'.

CAVENDISH SQUARE, LONDON

ERM was contracted to conduct the environmental and social impact assessment (ESIA) in Turkey, and the social impact assessment (SIA) in all three countries. These ESIAs and SIAs were both a legal requirement and a mechanism to promote the project. In their job as a consultancy, ERM were intimately involved in every twist and turn of the BTC pipeline project over the years between 2000 and 2004. The company wrote and produced BP-branded leaflets – such as the one left with Mansura Ibishova in Qarabork – and distributed them throughout Azerbaijan in 2001. They had prepared the documents that failed to inform Merabi Vacheishvili and Eleonora Digmelashvili of how close the pipeline would run to the *Khrushchevki* of Rustavi.

Months after the photo of Fazlı Kılıç was taken in Hacıbayram, the direct action group, London Rising Tide, visited ERM's offices in Cavendish Square, one block north of the Christmas bustle on Oxford Street. The campaigners had been closely engaged with the issue of the pipeline for over a year. They conducted a Monday morning surprise 'impact assessment' of ERM's office, handing out questionnaires to all employees and conducting interviews. Three activists occupied Chief Executive Robin Bidwell's office for five hours and hung banners from the windows reading: 'ERM causes climate change' and 'No public money for BP's Baku–Ceyhan pipeline'.

The leaflet they handed out to ERM staff explained: 'Your employer plays a crucial if low-key role in grooming BP's Baku–Ceyhan pipeline for public investment. We're in your office today to expose that climate change–inducing role.'

ERM was part of a cluster of environmental consultancies and public relations agencies working for the BTC project in London. These companies were part of the Carbon Web gathered around BP, like the cluster of engineering groups that built and operated the offshore oilfields in the Caspian, and the cluster of banks and export credit agencies that financed the pipelines. Recognition of how these bodies were interconnected guided direct-action protests across the UK. In February 2003 the top floor of the European Bank for Reconstruction and Development on Bishopsgate was occupied. In March the offices of RSK, another consultancy to the pipeline, were temporarily shut down. The same month the International Petroleum Exchange in the City of London was stormed, punches were thrown on the trading floor, and part of the building was closed until the Metropolitan Police arrived. In April, the BP Annual General Meeting was disrupted with stink bombs, and John Browne was heckled during his chief executive's address.[4]

ERM and other companies dismissed these protests as irrelevant. But, like the struggle over Borjomi, they contributed to the pressure on BP during the crucial months around the public banks' decision on whether to make the loan to BTC. The noise created by all these individuals and groups, from Rising Tide to Mayis's Centre for Civic Initiatives, from Amnesty International to Manana's Green

---

4 'Earth First!', *Action Update* 88 (June 2003).

Alternative, so changed public perceptions of BTC, that the *Financial Times* came to describe the project as 'the world's most controversial pipeline'.

BTC KP 1,160 – 1,347 KM – ERZINCAN, TURKEY

[There is a] city named Arzingan, where there is a manufacture of very fine cotton cloth called bombazines, as well as many other curious fabrics, which it would be tedious to enumerate. It possesses the handsomest and most excellent baths of warm water, issuing from the earth, that are anywhere to be found. Its inhabitants are for the most part native Armenians, but under the dominion of the Tartars.

The Travels of Marco Polo, 1271[5]

The train pulls into Erzincan, once one of the most beautiful cities in Anatolia – a stopping point on the trade routes east. Marco Polo told of his visit here on the journey that took him towards the Caspian and beyond. The buildings that he described – the baths of the *caravanserai* – were destroyed with the rest of the city by an earthquake in 1939, the same year that the railway was completed. Here the routes of the train and pipeline part company. So, with Mehmet Ali, we make our way on foot to the coach station. Since the 1950s and 1960s, when the Turkish Republic began to embrace the USA, a network of highways has bound the country together, supplanting the railways of the Atatürk era.

Our coach carries us through the suburbs of Erzincan and pulls into the stream of westbound traffic on the E80 highway. We gaze at the passing landscape. Along this main road, fenced-off labour camps were set up, while articulated lorries trucked thousands of tonnes of construction equipment inland from the ports. Upon these fields were stacked forty-foot sections of pipe, like those that we had seen at Rustavi, waiting to be pieced together. Bulldozers cut through forests and scooped up hillsides, waterways were diverted and explosives were used to blast the rock.

Two years after ERM's offices were occupied, in 2002, the BTC pipeline became an industrial reality along this road. The line on the map became a continuous trench running parallel with us now – it bypassed Erzurum, ran through Hacıbayram and curved around Erzincan. Digital data turned into physical fact.

However, during the construction of the project, the engineers who oversaw it found that not everything went according to plan. The design of the pipeline had been drawn up by Bechtel, working for BTC Co. But BOTAŞ, the Turkish state company responsible for laying the pipe, was slipshod in the way it implemented the scheme. Block valves, like the one we had seen outside Hacallı in Azerbaijan, are vital for the safety of the pipeline, as they shut down the onward flow of the oil in the

---

5   M. Polo, trans. William Marsden, 1818, *The Travels of Marco Polo*, Wordsworth Classics of World Literature, 1997, pp. 15–16.

event of a leak. Their position in relation to the gradient of the landscape is crucial. BOTAŞ planned to put many in completely inappropriate locations – some virtually on mountain peaks.[6] The pipeline trench was left exposed and open, allowing it to fill up with 'foreign materials' like soil and rocks that led to 'wash-outs' and the pipe shifting its position in the ground. The procedures supposed to be followed when the route crossed an earthquake fault-line were not implemented – and this in an area renowned for seismic activity, which destroyed the city of Erzincan again in 1983. 'Safety violations' occurred at all times, but when engineers on the work sites raised concerns with the BOTAŞ management, they were harassed and intimidated into keeping quiet. Several of those who spoke out were summarily sacked.[7]

In the spring of 2004, a fact-finding mission of the international NGOs concerned about the BTC pipeline travelled to this area. Among the group was Greg Muttitt of Platform. While journeying along the E80 highway, Greg realised that engineering problems were rife on the BTC route in Turkey – echoing the issue of the pipeline sealant that had been revealed in Georgia. In order to investigate the matter, he placed a low-key advert in a British expat magazine. It asked any contractors working on BTC who were concerned about the project to get in touch. The response was astounding, and comments poured in: 'No-one wants this pipeline on their cv. It's an embarrassment', read one email.[8] 'People appear to be "parked up" in jobs by their allies and friends, when they are simply not as well qualified as they should be. So-called "experts", who have just come out of university, are put on the job when they've never seen a pipeline before in their lives', said another.[9] And then: 'Early last year BP served notice on BOTAŞ because they were not performing, but it hasn't made any difference. Part of the problem is that BP has a vested financial and political interest in the project being delivered on time, which may limit how much it chooses to pressure BOTAŞ.'[10] And finally: 'I don't have much hope for the future integrity or proper maintenance and operation of [this] pipeline.'[11]

Greg spent hours in long phone conversations with oil-workers, checking the details of their accounts to ensure authenticity. To protect their identities and future job prospects, he made their statements anonymous and assigned

---

6   D. Adams, 'Memorandum Submitted by Dennis Adams', in 'Implementation of ECGD's Business Principles', House of Commons Trade and Industry Committee, 2005.
7   P. Thornton, 'Exposed: BP, Its Pipeline, and an Environmental Timebomb', *Independent*, 26 June 2004.
8   Ibid.
9   Red Baron, 'Anonymised Statement of Subcontractor Manager from 23 June 2004', in 'Submission to the House of Commons Trade & Industry Select Committee', Baku Ceyhan Campaign, 14 July 2004.
10   Ibid.
11   Adams, 'Memorandum'.

codenames to each respondent. One of the most detailed accounts came from an engineer named 'Red Baron', whose exposure of the culture of mismanagement was reported on the front page of the UK *Independent* newspaper as revealing 'an environmental timebomb'.[12] After determined pressure from Platform and the Corner House, the issue came before a parliamentary hearing in London, and a Select Committee criticised the Export Credit Guarantee Department for its conduct in financing the pipeline. Things became uncomfortable for David Allwood at his Department office in Canary Wharf.[13] But neither BOTAŞ nor BP were held to account, and the violations continued.

While the symptoms of these failings were evident in BOTAŞ's incompetence, the root cause lay in the detail of the contract determining construction – or, as the 'Red Baron' had described it: BP's 'vested financial and political interest in the project being delivered on time'.[14] Under the Turnkey Agreement with BTC Co., BOTAŞ committed to construct all 1,076 kilometres of the pipeline in Turkey by 26 May 2005 in return for a lump sum of $1.4 billion. This made BOTAŞ effectively a mega-contractor, responsible for delivering two-thirds of the entire BTC route. According to the Agreement, any overruns in the costs of construction would be covered by the Turkish national budget, as BOTAŞ is a state-owned company. At the time the Agreement was signed, industry journals described it as a 'financial coup' for BP, as analysts assessed that the real total cost of construction would probably be $2 billion. Building the pipeline at such a – realistic – cost level could have made the entire project financially unviable. By persuading BOTAŞ to construct it on the cheap, by a reduction of $600 million, BP made the project acceptable to its finance director, Byron Grote, its shareholders, and the institutions lending the money.

Rapid cost escalation during the building of infrastructure is a norm in the oil and gas industry: a BP pipeline in Alaska cost ten times its original estimate; Shell budgeted its Sakhalin II offshore project in Russia for $8 billion, but over $26 billion had been invested before it came on-stream.[15] Through the Agreement, BP insured itself against such escalation by paying for the pipeline with a lump sum. It also bound BOTAŞ to an unrealistic completion date by determining that a fine of $500,000 would have to be paid for every day the construction went over schedule.[16]

12　Thornton, 'Exposed'.
13　'Implementation of ECGD's Business Principles', House of Commons Trade and Industry Committee.
14　Red Baron, 'Anonymised Statement'.
15　M. Mansley, *Building Tomorrow's Crisis: The BTC Pipeline and BP*, Platform, 2003; W. Dam and S. Ho, 'Unusual Design Considerations Drive Selection of Sakhalin LNG Plant Facilities', *Oil and Gas*, 10 January 2001; S. Blagov, 'Russia's Sakhalin II Project Remains Under Pressure', *Eurasia Daily Monitor* 3: 232, (15 December 2006).
16　'Appendix II to Turkey HGA: Turnkey Agreement between BOTAŞ and BP etc.', BP, 19 October 2000.

These tight time constraints on BOTAŞ created a rush that led to slipshod pipe-laying by subcontractors, and to the safety of their workers being put at risk. As one of the whistleblowers explained, 'Health, safety and environmental issues were placed in succinct jeopardy in an attempt to meet time constraints.'[17] Ironically, shortcuts and engineering mistakes were major factors in BTC being completed a year late and its costs overrunning by $1,400 million.

But even before the construction was completed, BOTAŞ and BTC Co. were in dispute about who should pay for these overruns. The Turkish minister of energy was understandably unwilling to foot the bill, and arguments over the Agreement have continued down the years. The US embassy in Ankara commented in a leaked cable that 'despite record high oil prices (and profits), BP has refused to re-negotiate the terms of the contract.'[18] By April 2011, BOTAŞ had applied for international arbitration against BTC Co. due to the excessive prices the company was charging for the gas that fuels the pump stations, such as the one we had seen at Posof in the snow.[19]

The E80 highway winds up through the Kose Daghlari mountain range. Night is falling, and the swaying of the warm coach has sent Mehmet Ali to sleep. These forested peaks through the window are the northern edge of the Euphrates water-shed. For just 250 kilometres the road and the pipeline swing into the headwaters of the Çobanlı Çay, flowing red-brown towards the Black Sea. It is as though the crude takes a last glimpse backwards towards the port of Batumi and the lands of Georgia, before progressing on towards Europe.

BTC KP 1,220 – 1,407 KM – REFAHIYE, TURKEY

Eye witnesses reported that at around 23:00 local time on August 5, there was an explosion at valve number 30 in Refahiye County in Erzincan Province. The explosion was followed by a fire, sending flames up to 50 meters into the air.

Hürriyet, 6 August[20]

---

17   Red Baron, 'Anonymised Statement'.

18   US Embassy in Turkey, 'Cable 08Ankara1983: Turkey Takes BP to Court', 14 November 2008, released via cablegatesearch.net.

19   'Seeking Arbitration, BOTAS Warns BTC Pipeline Could Lose $2 Bln', 12 April 2011, at dunya.com.

20   *Hurriyet* (6 August 2008) and *Today's Zaman* (8 August 2008), quoted in G. Jenkins, 'Explosion Raises Questions About the Security of the BTC Pipeline', *Eurasia Daily Monitor* 5: 152 (8 August 2008).

BTC officials in Baku and Ceyhan control rooms recorded that the pipeline pressure was falling and closed valves 29 and 31. Additional pumping was stopped. The estimated 12,000 barrels of oil in the pipeline between valves 29 and 31 were left to burn out.

'Today's Zaman, 8 August[21]

Turkish officials have strenuously denied that the PKK was responsible for the damage and have claimed that the fire occurred due to a technical failure.[22]

Around 2 a.m., Baku time, this morning the BTC control system detected an anomaly at Block Valve 30 in Turkey and the pipeline was shut down . . . Shortly afterwards eyewitnesses alerted local authorities of a fire at that location. The fire is being contained by fire fighters. BIL, the Operator of the Turkish segment of the pipeline is leading the response . . . We have no estimate on the timing of the return of the pipeline to service.[23]

BTC letter to Société Générale, Intercreditor Agent for the pipeline, 6 August 2008

It is a moonlit night in the valley of the Çobanlı Çay as the coach pulls up. The half-light emphasises the snowy peak of Wolf Mountain, rising over the pine forests. This is Refahiye, place of another ancient *caravanserai*, stopping point on the road from İstanbul to Persia and beyond. We halt by the petrol pumps of a motel which brands itself 'SHELL – petrol turizm'. Obviously this is the one for us.

We have come to Refahiye to investigate what happened at Block Valve 30 when the pipeline exploded and caught fire, on 5 August 2008. Eyewitness photographs show vast plumes of smoke over the small square compound – like the one we had seen outside Hacallı in Azerbaijan. The pipeline was out of action for several weeks. BP was forced to export Caspian oil through the Baku–Supsa line just three days before Russian planes dropped bombs next to that pipeline system in Georgia. This is the event we asked about when we met Aydin Gasimov in Villa Petrolea and Orxan Abasov in Sangachal, from neither of whom we had learned very much. We want to discover just how critical the situation was.

We have read the letters BP sent to the banks and the export credit agencies, which we obtained after repeated Freedom of Information requests. These reveal that over 30,000 barrels of oil were spilled – almost three times as much as the

---

21   Ibid.

22   G. Winrow, 'Protection of Energy Infrastructure', in *Combating International Terrorism: Turkey's Added Value*, RUSI, October 2009.

23   'Letter from BTC Co. to Société Générale with subject "Force Majeure Event on BTC Pipeline"', 6 August 2008, p. 31 (released under FOIA by ECGD on 26 March 2010).

newspapers had reported. Four days after the explosion, on 8 August, BP sent a memo, via the French bank Société Générale, to the Lender Group of financial institutions, explaining that the site of the incident was located above an aquifer and that there was a risk of pollution reaching the nearby river.

These letters and memos were intended to reassure the lenders that BP was in control, despite the explosion and the subsequent outbreak of war in Georgia. On closer inspection, however, the letters show inconsistencies. The first report issued by the company states that the fire was *extinguished* on 11 August.[24] A later evaluation contradicts this: 'BTC adopted the strategy of allowing most of the oil to burn, rather than attempt to extinguish the fire at an early stage.'[25] But when we talked over the matter with BP staff, they admitted that the various fire brigades had indeed attempted right at the beginning to put out the fire. First they used water, then they switched to the more appropriate foam. Either way, it seems that the fire was so intense that the fleet of red trucks from Erzincan, Sivas and even Ankara was unable to put out the flames. Ultimately, the companies could not control the blaze and had to let the fire burn itself out, thereby filling the valley with smoke for nearly six days.

By picking through the paperwork, we have been trying to answer the questions that the incident throws up. Why did the fire brigade try to put the oil-driven fire out with water? Was there simply no communication between BTC Co. and the fire service? For every four barrels of crude that went up in smoke, one soaked into the nearby earth: almost 6,000 barrels of oil were spilled into the ground at Refahiye. And we read that 1,500 cubic metres of soil were contaminated and had to be excavated and stockpiled.[26]

What of the wider repercussions? What must it have felt like for men like Ibragim Teregulov in the Control Room at Sangachal when the pressure in BTC dropped? How was the news received in the top corridor at Villa Petrolea and in the pump stations at Jandara and Posof?

We have a photograph that we got from BOTAŞ in Ardahan, which shows the repair works after the fire. A white man with a square face can be seen giving orders. He is the BIL technical director, Erin Ford – the man responsible for getting the pipeline running again as soon as possible.

BIL, or BOTAŞ International Ltd, is a subsidiary of the Turkish state company that oversees the operation of the pipeline in Turkey. Once BOTAŞ had constructed BTC, they handed the running of it over to BIL. And Ford, although formally employed by BIL, was really a representative of BP, appointed by BTC Co. according to the Operating Agreement signed between the companies. Ford had started

---

24 Email from BP to Société Générale with subject, 'RE: BTC: Fightings in Georgia', 12 August 2008, p. 28 (released under FOIA by ECGD on 26 March 2010).

25 *BTC Project Environmental and Social Annual Report (Operations Phase) 2008,* BTC Co., 2009.

26 Ibid.

his career in the US oil company ARCO, in 1981. After twelve years in Alaska, BP's takeover of ARCO brought him to the deep waters of the Gulf of Mexico, before he transferred to Tbilisi and eventually Turkey.

Ford was most likely helicoptered to the explosion site at Refahiye on 6 August, along with other senior BIL staff. As manager of 600 of the company's 1,200 employees, he had ultimate responsibility for whether to put out the fire and how to build a temporary pipeline to bypass the rupture. At some point, Ford made the call to summon BP's pipeline repair team from Baku on the grounds that BIL was not up to the job. Even after the flames had died out, pipeline workers could not approach the site for forty-eight hours because of residual heat. Then it took a further twenty-four hours before workers could close surviving isolation valves and stop the crude spilling out onto the earth. Despite the chaotic decision-making we have been told about, Ford reminisced cheerfully about those summer events in BP's in-house magazine, *Horizon*: 'I was amazed at how synchronized we all worked in Turkey, Azerbaijan and Georgia . . . It made me proud of the people who work in this company; everyone went beyond their responsibilities.'[27]

Ultimately, we are most interested not in how the fire was extinguished, but what caused the explosion in the first place. Media reports quoted the Kurdish PKK as claiming responsibility, but the Turkish government claimed it was a technical fault.

The answer to this question is of great importance, because it determines who picks up the bill for repairs and losses. When the pipeline blew up, BP was left with no means of transport between its six Caspian platforms, which were extracting nearly a million barrels every day, and customers' tankers waiting in the Mediterranean. The company began to export oil through Baku–Supsa, although this pipeline can only carry a fraction of BTC's load and delivers to the eastern Black Sea, several days' journey by tanker from the Mediterranean. Unable to meet its commitments to its shipping partners, BP declared *force majeure*, claiming 'an act of terrorism'. Under the Host Government Agreements, Turkey had accepted legal responsibility for the security of the line. Should a corporate arbitration panel decide that the explosion was due to failed security, BP would be able to claim compensation for its losses from Turkey.[28]

The stakes are high. We obtained an internal update, sent by BP two days after the explosion, which showed that lost transit tariffs to BTC Co. were $5 million every day.[29] Meanwhile, far larger sums were lost by the BP division that owned the oil being pumped. In early August 2008, oil prices were hovering around $120

27   M. Naughton, 'Teams Unite to Manage Tough Times', *Horizon* 7, December 2008, p. 35.
28   I. Altunsoy, 'PKK Claims Responsibility for BTC Pipeline Explosion', 8 August 2008, at todayszaman.com.
29   Email from BP to Société Générale.

a barrel – almost a record high, from which BP could not profit.

So we try to work out which of the possible causes for the explosion is the most likely. The first possibility is that it was a technical fault. We know from the statements by the whistleblowers that construction of the pipeline in Turkey had been substandard. Infrastructure accidents had been common in the two years since oil had begun to flow along the pipeline. Only six weeks prior to the explosion, BTC's repair team completed welding work after eighteen months of problems at one point on the pipeline not far to the west.[30] In September 2008, barely a month after the fire, a faulty valve at the nearby Sivas pumping station caused a temporary shutdown.[31]

However, the second possibility – that the pipeline was blown up – appears more likely, especially given that the PKK claimed responsibility. Bahoz Erdal, second in command of the Kurdish group, explained that 'as an economic target we chose to attack the BTC pipeline because we think that attacks like these would stop Turkey from pursuing its aggression toward the Kurds'.[32] Targeting pipelines is not unusual for the PKK. In March 2008, the rebels claimed responsibility for a blast on a gas pipeline from Iran; the following November they blew up the Kirkuk–Ceyhan oil pipeline. The increased focus on pipelines coincided with a drop in hit-and-run attacks on Turkish military convoys. This shift in tactics took place at the same time that the USA started providing 'actionable real-time satellite intelligence' to the Turkish Army, gathered by the National Geospatial-Intelligence Agency at Fort Hood in Texas. This made PKK movements far harder. Blowing up BTC could have been intended partly as a message to the US military, who would have registered the explosion.

This second theory is in BP's interests, as it would mean that the damage occurred due to Turkey's failure to protect the pipeline, as required by the Host Government Agreement. In his Tbilisi office, Matthew Taylor had told us: 'Remember that security is the responsibility of government.' He added a sceptical note implying that Turkey would try to dodge any liability: 'Turkey will say it's examining the causes – investigating and investigating, for thirty years – until this is all forgotten.'

There is a further theory as to what lay behind the pipeline explosion: involvement by the 'deep state', or *derin devlet*. While, to outsiders, 'deep state' may sound overly conspiratorial, it is a very real entity to many Turks. This shadowy network – involving ultranationalist 'Grey Wolves', secular politicians, the military elite and mafia bosses – intervened regularly in Turkish politics throughout the previous three decades. It has assassinated leftist, Kurdish and Islamist activists,

---

30   'Risky Repair was Successfully Completed (KP 611)', June 2008, at botasint.com.

31   'Additional challenges for the BTC Pipeline', 18 September 2008, at bicusa.org.

32   E. Uslu, 'Is the PKK Sabotaging Strategic Energy Infrastructure in a Search for a Superpower Partner?', *Terrorism Focus (Jamestown Foundation)* 5: 42 (12 December 2008).

participated in military coups, and committed 'false flag operations' that were subsequently blamed on the PKK. Blowing up BTC would fall easily within the capabilities of this group.[33]

After settling in to our rooms at the 'SHELL – petrol turizm' motel, we discuss plans for the next day over dinner. To make better sense of the explosion, we want to hear from those living closest to it. In August 2008, Mehmet Ali was interning with Platform in London. He interviewed the *muhtar* (mayor) of Yurtbaşı by phone, who told him that the fire was close to his village. But exactly how close, we do not know. Remembering the difficulties we had finding the Russian bomb craters in Georgia, we expect a similar experience.

Before setting out the next morning, we remove anything potentially incriminating from our daypacks. Given our previous experiences of the Jandarma, we are concerned about being watched and stopped. We walk into the centre of Refahiye and find a taxi driver in a battered blue Niva who will take us to the village of Yurtbaşı.

As we drive down the E80 highway, the driver asks us why we are here, for it is pretty clear that Refahiye is not much of a tourist destination. Cautious, given the still unknown politics of our taxi driver, Mehmet Ali mumbles something about a book on the Turkish countryside. Not interested in this topic, the driver changes the subject to the major local happening of the last year – the pipeline fire: 'It burned for ten days. People were evacuated from their villages. Fire engines came from everywhere . . . Yes, it was sabotage.'

And all of a sudden, there it is. Right there, alongside the main road: a line of containers, a row of portaloos, an access road with a security guard, half a dozen men in orange BTC jumpsuits and white hard hats, and a pile of large pipes. Amazing – a mere ten minutes in the car and we have found the site of the explosion. But we want to meet the nearby residents, so the driver continues onwards for Yurtbaşı. He turns north off the road, and up a strip of asphalt towards a cluster of silver-grey corrugated iron roofs at the edge of the plain, gathered in the lee of a great cliff of sandstone. The lushness of the valley floor contrasts with the harsh greys and browns of stony dirt and scrubby plants on the mountain above.

We arrive in the heart of the village, on the mud street between the houses. Asking for the *muhtar*, we are escorted across a stream, past some willows struggling into leaf, to a pristine white mosque. The *muhtar* is away, but we are instructed to wait in a meeting room below the mosque itself: the village elders will come to talk to us. The room is painted a pale green, with posters of Mecca and the Sultanahmet Mosque on the wall. White plastic chairs surround a white plastic table on a white tiled floor. It is all spotlessly clean.

---

33   See Y. Navaro-Yashin, *Faces of the State: Secularism and Public Life in Turkey*, Princeton University Press, 2002.

In comes a man in his forties, Murat. Clean-shaven, wearing a grey striped shirt, polished black shoes and a dark suit, he looks surprisingly urban for this distant corner of Anatolia. He explains that 400 to 450 people live in Yurtbaşı, mostly subsisting on arable farming and cattle pasturing. He is intrigued by us. When we mention that James is an expert on birds, Murat wants our help in understanding why certain species are dying off. He says he suspects that it might be due to ash from the pipeline fire.

Others arrive, most prominent of whom is Ahmet. We had seen him earlier in the street, working a piece of wood with a plane. It turns out he is the stand-in imam, which fits with his priestly serenity and the way that the others defer to him.

His tone is sharp, and he starts complaining about an English MP who recently came to Turkey to make a film about orphanages. We are nonplussed, but he is clear that it represented the country in a bad way. Yet he too wants to know why bird species are declining – is it due to climate change? – and whether the pipeline fire will affect the animals, especially the bees. The ash from the fire fell all over the ground – he is worried that it could weaken the cattle, and damage their milk and meat. The companies let the fire burn for six days – would they have done the same in England?

Our conversation is interrupted by a call to prayer from the mosque Tannoy. To our surprise, nobody moves, not even the deputy imam. Far off, through the window, we can see the black marks of conifers dotted against the white peak of Wolf Mountain. The questions continue: Why do they use depleted uranium weapons in Iraq? The West is the main emitter of carbon dioxide, so what is it going to do about climate change? Mehmet Ali is getting exasperated; although he agrees with many of Ahmet's concerns, he feels that they are framed through an overly nationalist prism, obscuring Turkey's cooperation and allegiance with the 'West'.

Somehow, during the questions, the dynamic in the room shifts. The ash previously mentioned is now described as a 'fog'. Murat and the others say that the fire was not caused by sabotage, but was a technical fault: a valve cracked, then electricity sparked the conflagration. Such things happen around the world, after all. Foreign engineers worked on this pipeline, so the explosion was not BOTAŞ's fault. Suddenly it seems that the landowners were well compensated for the use of their fields by the post-fire repair equipment. The impacts of the fire were not serious, after all, and the village had substantial help from doctors, army and police.

The story has completely switched tracks. The opening concerns and questions have all evaporated, leaving a forthright assertion of the benefits of this 'Turkish pipeline', a 'national project'.

The mood alters further. The villagers want to take our photos and copy down our passport and ID card numbers. They write a statement and ask us to sign it. Mehmet Ali reads it aloud: the statement declares that the villagers spoke with us, but 'did not say anything controversial'. They are clearly trying to cover their backs, but who are they frightened of? The Jandarma? Company officials?

We ask if we can walk on the hills around the village, but that is not possible. They insist on giving us a lift back to the main highway, which amounts to escorting us off the premises. Leaving the building, we see piles of bunting with the logo of the AKP – the ruling Islamic party – left over from the recent election. 'These are nationalist and conservative villages', Mehmet Ali remarks; 'I feel uncomfortable with them'.

Murat drives us down the village road and along the E80, to a roadside *lokanta* restaurant. For a while it seems he will sit with us until we have eaten lunch and headed back to Refahiye. But as we slowly eat our kebabs and rice, he nods goodbye and leaves.

We decide to try to discover further stories of the explosion. This time we head for Alacaatlı, a village on the south side of the valley, closer still to Block Valve 30. A fresh tarmac road winds uphill towards houses clustered where green pasturelands meet a mass of conifers that stretch towards the snowy higher reaches of Wolf Mountain. As we cross the waters of the River Çobanlı and the line of BTC marker posts, we are walking through alpine flower meadows. A man passes on the road. 'Welcome', he says with a smile. Perhaps these people will be less suspicious of us.

We chat with two men from the village committee, but realise quickly that they do not want to talk. 'What about the pipeline fire?' we ask. 'We had no problem with this.' 'Can we walk through the village up onto the mountain?' 'No, there are wild bears there, and wolves; they are very wild and will harm you.' 'Can we just walk through the village?' 'No, and we're busy now.' So basically: 'go away!' Fair enough – after all, how would we respond to a group of Turkish investigators in an English village asking questions? Nevertheless, their unfriendliness is in striking contrast with the openness of Azeri, Georgian and Kurdish villagers.

Having spotted a petrol station further east, we walk towards it along the side of the E80. We pass the pipeline repair works by the ruptured valve again, the orange-jumpsuited workers now eating packed lunches in the shade of a crane. The stares of a private security guard on the access slope warn us against trying to engage the site workers in conversation.

The attendants at the petrol station are more talkative: 'The first night, I heard an explosion, like a tyre blowing out, and then the fire started. The fire was so strong that it was too hot to be here, one kilometre from the flames. It felt like everything would melt. The smoke would drift over here and everybody would start to cough. They closed part of the road because it burned for a week.'

In the car back to Refahiye, the same taxi driver tells us more: 'They evacuated everybody from Alacaatlı for seven nights. They came to Refahiye. The firemen were afraid that the forest would catch fire. Fire engines came from Erzurum,

Erzincan, Sivas, Ankara. Maybe it was sabotage, maybe not. If somebody wanted to blow it up, why not do it in the mountains far away from the road, where they won't get caught?'

We get back to the motel and try to piece together what happened. Whatever the details, there was a major international incident here: a massive fire that burned for a week, a column of smoke rising up from the valley floor, ash falling onto crops, villagers evacuated. Fire engines, helicopters, the minister of energy and natural resources, soldiers swarming over everything. Even now, nine months later, the engineers are still at work.

The reticence of villagers in relation to the incident shows how the pipeline is seen by many as a state institution that is not to be questioned. In the national debate, BTC features as a government project of strategic significance and a source of pride. Consequently, concerns about the pipeline voiced by social movements, affected communities and the media have to struggle against the dominant force of nationalism.

The pipeline's identity as the property of a foreign company is obscured. In this way it suits BP to have BOTAŞ construct and operate the Turkish section of the pipeline under the Turnkey Agreement. We had failed to appreciate this sleight of hand when lobbying the UK parliament about the poor standard of BOTAŞ's work. We wonder how planned this was. Did the BP team articulate this benefit in its strategic plans of 2000 or 2001, or was it an unforeseen but happy consequence?

It seems we will leave Refahiye without a definitive answer on the cause of the explosion that August night. But we now appreciate how Turkish nationalism provides BP with a first line of defence against criticism and investigation, just as it does in Azerbaijan. And we understand a little better what happens if the pipeline explodes and burns. It makes us think about all the places we have visited where BTC passes close to houses. Block Valve 30 was, thankfully, far from habitation. We reflect on how close the two oil and gas pipes run to Mansura Ibishova's kitchen in Qarabork, just forty kilometres from an unfinished war – and how Jeff Jeter at the EBRD had reassured us that the pipeline was safe, since the construction had conformed to British standards.

ANKARA, TURKEY

The E80 takes us west to Sivas, once the capital of the Seljuk Turks, and a halt for merchants on their journeys from Central Asia to Europe.

We leave the coach and reboard the train for Ankara, which carries us 500 kilometres away from the pipeline, to the capital of modern Turkey. In 1892, the railway from İstanbul reached what was then still a small town in the wildness of Anatolia, famous mostly for its Angora wool. Built by German engineers, the line was part of the industrialisation of the Ottoman Empire, emulating the Baku–Batumi Railway, which was built by French engineers across the Caucasus.

After a slow passage through a hot day, we eventually pull into Ankara. This is not the original nineteenth-century station, but a Bauhaus-style celebration of the Modern – again built by Germans, this time in the 1930s for Atatürk's Republic of Turkey. Mehmet Ali is delighted to be back in his home city, and hurries us towards the district of Kızılay to meet up with friends. After the great spaces of eastern Turkey, it is a shock to be shoved into the press of people in the subway. Everywhere vendors are selling fresh orange juice, pretzel-shaped *simit* snacks and a kaleidoscope of newspapers.

After the completion of the Baku–Batumi Railway in 1884, oil from the shores of the Caspian was carried to Western Europe and beyond by ship from Georgia's Black Sea port. Tankers from Batumi steamed down the narrow Bosphorus, through the centre of İstanbul, and out into the Mediterranean. In the 1990s, as the new Oil Road was being planned, this pattern could have been repeated. Crude from the Azeri–Chirag–Gunashli oilfield could be piped to Supsa and Novorossisk on the Black Sea, and there loaded on to tankers bound for the oceans and the world market. However, the speed and scale at which the companies wanted to extract the resource from the ACG field meant that tanker traffic through the Bosphorus would have grown radically. The Turkish government in Ankara was understandably opposed to increasing the risk of an oil disaster in the heart of İstanbul.

With restrictions on the volume of oil that could pass through the Bosphorus, and the US government determined that crude should not flow westwards through Russia, hammering out a deal for a pipeline across Turkey was considered an important US priority. Oil had been pumped from the Chirag offshore field down the pipeline from Baku to Supsa for almost a year when President Clinton ordered that a 'Caspian Finance Center' be established in Ankara in October 1998. This formed part of his administration's political and financial drive to make BTC a reality. By the following January, the office was up and running at the US embassy in the Turkish capital. Led by Director Peter Ballinger, the Center was staffed by officials seconded from three American trade and export credit agencies. It aimed to spearhead financing for regional energy projects.[34] According to the US Center for Strategic and International Studies, Ballinger's Center gave the United States more leverage to influence pipeline decisions in its favour 'by providing a beachhead through which American economic power can be projected into the region'.[35]

---

34 The Overseas Private Investment Corporation (OPIC), the Export–Import Bank (EXIM Bank), and the US Trade and Development Agency (USTDA). J. Joseph, *Pipeline Diplomacy: The Clinton Administration's Fight for Baku–Ceyhan*, Princeton, p. 20.

35 B. Humphrey, 'Washington Splashes Out on Caspian Dreams', 15 June 1999, at themoscowtimes.com.

Just a few months before, Clinton had appointed a special advisor for Caspian Basin energy diplomacy, Richard Morningstar, who now shuttled between the US embassies in Ankara, Tbilisi and Baku. Morningstar, who had previously been ambassador to the New Independent States of the Former Soviet Union, took up where his predecessor Sandy Berger had left off, bringing a renewed enthusiasm in Washington for westbound pipelines from the Caspian. Reviving the Coordination Group on Caspian Energy, Morningstar insisted that department representatives from State, Energy, Commerce, USAID and CIA met every three weeks to conduct the short-term strategic planning that was needed to push both the oil companies and the governments of Azerbaijan, Georgia and Turkey to build the pipeline that the US demanded.

It soon became apparent that the BTC pipeline was liable to be prohibitively expensive – and significantly less commercially viable than the alternative proposals of pumping the oil to Iran, or transporting it through Russia. Washington was explicitly opposed to these options, but the administration needed to find a way to make BTC attractive to the private oil companies. Hence Ballinger's Caspian Finance Center argued strongly that US export credit agencies should provide American taxpayers money to support BTC. To do this, both Ballinger and Morningstar had to persuade legislators to sidestep US sanctions against Azerbaijan, which remained from the war with Armenia.[36] Ballinger achieved his goal: eventually the US government provided hundreds of millions of dollars in subsidies for the construction of BTC.

Meanwhile, Morningstar's diplomacy was directed at pushing the governments of Azerbaijan, Georgia and Turkey to offer tax concessions for construction, and to agree to charge the lowest fees for the transit of oil across their countries. As he asserted, 'Turkey clearly shoulders a major responsibility for providing incentives required to make Baku–Ceyhan as commercially attractive as possible.'[37] And US government officials conveyed 'their desire that Ankara impose a cost cap on pipeline construction in order to shield the oil companies from run-away costs.'[38] It was this political pressure that lay behind BP cutting the Turnkey Agreement with BOTAŞ, thereby ensuring that two-thirds of BTC could be built $600 million cheaper than expected. Furthermore, US diplomacy ensured that the cost overruns on the pipeline were carried not by the private oil companies, but by Turkish taxpayers. Morningstar insisted:

---

36 'The US Role in the Caucasus and Central Asia: Hearing Before the Committee on International Relations', US House of Representatives, 30 April 1998.
37 H. Kazaz, 'Caspian Pipeline Conference Explores Options Besides Baku–Ceyhan', 12 October 1998, huriyetdailynews.com.
38 Joseph, *Pipeline Diplomacy*, p. 21.

The United States views its proper role with respect to Caspian pipelines as that of a facilitator. Enhancing commercial opportunities for US and other companies is one of our strategic objectives in the Caspian region. As a creature of the private sector for all but the past five and a half years, I clearly understand that pipelines will not be built if they don't make commercial sense.[39]

Ballinger stayed in Ankara as director of the Caspian Finance Center for six years, until January 2006, when the Center had 'completed its work with the commissioning of BTC'.[40] Between them, Morningstar and Ballinger helped establish the political and economic framework that enabled BTC to 'make commercial sense'. They played key roles in guaranteeing both profits for the oil companies and continued US energy dominance.

Morningstar became US ambassador to the European Union between 1999 and 2001. For the following eight years he was out of the limelight, but upon President Obama's election he was made special envoy of the secretary of state for Eurasian energy. This meant he was back on the Caucasus and Central Asian energy beat, pushing hard for the entry of Western companies into Turkmenistan's gas reserves and for the construction of the Nabucco pipeline to feed into the European grid. His labours combined with those of Jean-Arnold Vinois, at the European Commission's Energy Directorate General, to build the 'Southern Energy Corridor'. Like Sabit Bagirov in Baku – once head of SOCAR – and Byron Grote in London – BP's chief financial officer, Morningstar could be called 'an invisible father of the BTC pipeline'.

In one of the cafés of Kızılay we meet with a group of Mehmet Ali's friends. He is the joker of the pack, with his little round glasses and cheeky grin – obviously adored by his friends. They all attended Ankara's elite Middle Eastern Technical University (METU) together. In a leafy campus on the edge of this cement-grey city, METU classes are conducted entirely in English, while students discuss Žižek, Habermas and Agamben on the lawns.

Several of Mehmet Ali's friends were employed to work on BTC as engineers, or on the accompanying Community Investment Programmes. The money was comparatively good, and employment on an international project was beneficial for their CVs. Chatting about how they were initially hired, it emerges that the oil companies decided to focus their recruitment here. Not just individuals, but whole departments were drawn into the project. The university's Black Sea and Central Asia Centre was contracted by ERM in London to conduct the

---

39   R. Morningstar, 'Address to CERA Conference', Washington, DC, 7 December 1998.
40   'Peter Ballinger at Overseas Private Investment Corporation', at in.linkedin. com.

'Socio-economic Baseline Study' for the Turkish section of BTC. This was one of the set of assessments of the pipeline route that we had seen were flawed at Hacıbayram. Through this process of hiring graduates and contracting departments, academic institutions like METU became part of BTC's Carbon Web.

A handful of METU recruits remain at BP today, based in the company's Turkish head office in the Armada Tower – a blue-glass-and-granite skyscraper in the middle of Ankara to which we head for our next meeting. We bypass the first four floors of cinemas and a shopping mall – which recently won an award as 'Europe's Best Mall' – and take the elevator to the offices above.

We wait in the lobby beside TV monitors announcing that the oil tankers *Thorm Valborg* and *Thorm Marina* are currently docked at Ceyhan and loading up with oil from BTC. Hoping that this will be a more informative meeting than those in Baku and Tbilisi, we while away the time reading BP's *Horizon* magazines. The pages are filled with a sense of corporate optimism that strangely echoes the strident positivism of Soviet literature, and is apparent in some of Hikmet's poems. The features on the pipeline convey an engineering world where 'progress' is always good, every problem can be solved, and advance comes through technology. In all the words and photographs there is never a sense of loss, nor any expression of doubt.

Our host arrives. Şükran Çağlayan is corporate social responsibility manager at BP Turkey. Charming – even flirtatious – she guides us up the spiral staircase to a suite of conference rooms on the mezzanine. Taking up a mere two floors, these are the smallest BP offices we have visited, reflecting BP's overseer role in Turkey. While the pipeline operator BIL has around 1,200 employees, BP's staff in the whole country numbers only 100 people.

Şükran explains that she has worked for BP for ten years. She joined in 1999, 'before the Host Government Agreements were even signed. In a way, we were lobbying for these at first. I was involved from the design phase to implementation, through construction to operation. From the Environmental and Social Impact Assessments to the Community Investment Programmes.' Now, she explains, her job is to manage the socio-economic impacts of the pipeline.

Born in the village of Posof in Ardahan Province – near where we had seen the pump station in the snow – Şükran's family were Meshketi Turks from across the Georgian border. These are the peoples who were forcibly transported to Central Asia in 1944 by Stalin's NKVD, and who struggled to return to newly independent post-Soviet Georgia in 1991 against opposition from President Gamsakhurdia. But Şükran was fortunate, growing up across the border in eastern Turkey. She tells us that the villagers along the pipeline from the border to Sivas call her 'their local girl', something about which she is clearly proud.

Asked about managing expectations, Şükran is quick to say that this was always very difficult, and sometimes near-impossible. 'These people have nothing – you can imagine why they have these expectations. These are remote villages that nobody visits, and suddenly there's an influx of people promising change and development. And to the villagers, everybody was BOTAŞ – no distinction was drawn for BP.'

She agrees with our understanding that there was a widespread perception of BTC as a state project, rather than one created by a private company. It is clear this made her job much easier. 'We were always perceived as VIP guests wherever we went. Even when we explained that we were private sector, locals saw us as government representatives. The pipeline was perceived as a matter of honour for the country. This meant that communities thought of it as "their" pipeline. Thank god that they had this attitude all the time.'

This is a very different kind of meeting from those with Aydin Gasimov in Villa Petrolea and Matthew Taylor in Tbilisi. Şükran is plainly sincere in her dedication to improving the lives of those along the BTC route, and about using the pipeline to promote rural development. 'After our work, an oil corporation is seen as an agricultural development expert', she declares.

Şükran believes that corporate social responsibility should be focused on development, not on public relations. While this might appear an obvious point, the line between the two is often fuzzy. CSR officers are frequently trained in public relations and media management, in order to communicate brand and corporate values more effectively.[41] Şükran's take on this is forthright: 'The first thing the world should do is get rid of all these PR people in communications and external affairs. They are the ones really creating the bad image.' We wonder whether she is referring directly to Matthew Taylor and Tamam Bayatly in Baku.

BP's Community Investment Programmes in Azerbaijan and Georgia were run by large international NGOs like CARE International and Mercy Corps, as Irina and Aydin had described to us in Baku's Villa Petrolea. Şükran, who is well read on development practice, takes pride in the fact that things were different in Turkey, where BP prioritised working with local companies and organisations. 'It was a big risk in the beginning. We have spent so much money on capacity building. But it was needed. When we selected Erzurum University as a Community Investment Partner, they had no experience. Now they are trusted by the EU and donors'. We realise that Şükran must have had a part in hiring Mavi Hilal in Ardahan, and perhaps in the tie-up between British consultancy ERM and METU university.

But not everybody was happy about this policy. 'Did you know that Mercy Corps tried to sue us?' She explains that Mercy Corps, based in Washington, wanted to run the Community Investment Programme in Turkey. The NGO claimed that BP was

---

41 'How To Communicate Your Corporate Values to Consumers', *Ethical Corporation*, at ethicalcorp.com.

discriminating against them by insisting that they partner with a local organisation. Şükran continues: 'I said, "Sorry, *we* have a policy on local partners, there's nothing I can do about it." Then they tried to take us to court'.

She spells out her view that working with the right local bodies is crucial. 'In big multinationals, people have the attitude that "I know the best for everybody". We need to avoid this ethnocentric approach. The local people know best.' Şükran is also strongly critical of what she calls 'the oil men' in BP. She blames them for decisions like allowing BOTAŞ to build the SCP gas pipeline from the Georgian border to Erzurum, and avoiding responsibility for the way it was constructed. 'It's a shame, isn't it? It's awful', she says, describing the long mound of rocks and earth, like that which we had clambered over in Hacı Ali.

Şükran has a nuanced understanding of her role. 'I have maintained my funding for the work because I argue that this is not charity but a tool for risk management: to create a safe pipeline environment. I'm trying to show the oil men that it is in their interests to support my work.' She believes that the projects reduced opposition along the pipeline's route, as well as the number of court cases, and that her team provides an early-warning system of any social and political problems that might arise.

We are interrupted by a call on Şükran's mobile; a colleague from the World Bank in Washington wants to chat. Şükran says she will ring back in half an hour, and tells us we need to wrap up. What we had planned as a one-hour meeting has stretched out to three hours. She finishes off by saying: 'I'm coming from a left-wing oppositional perspective, so I can understand why people are unhappy with multinational corporations. Yashar Kemal is one of my favourite writers. We did a project in his village, a biogas project.' She walks us to the elevator, and then nips off for a quick Marlboro before her next meeting.

Outside, the traffic is heavy, and we wander down the pavement reflecting on the conversation. Şükran has such dedication to bringing 'progress' to rural Turkey. Despite the complaints about projects, such as the artificial insemination scheme near Hasköy-Hoçvan, we can see that Şükran probably improved the investment programme compared to what it would have been otherwise. And yet, this ultimately reveals what her job is intended to achieve: in softening the rough edges of this twenty-first-century Oil Road, Şükran's team legitimises the pipeline, monitors and prevents opposition.

15 THE TRENCH SIDES COULD COLLAPSE ON TOP OF CHILDREN

BTC KP 1,547 – 1,734 KM – YAYLACI, TURKEY

We travel in a hired car south-east from Ankara. It is 500 kilometres of slow driving to the point where we rejoin the pipeline, not far from where we left it at Sivas. We pass the time talking with Mehmet Ali about growing up in Turkey. He was born in the industrial city of İzmit, near İstanbul, in 1985. The state had only recently conducted elections after three years of military rule, and the army still effectively controlled the country.

Mehmet Ali explains that when Atatürk established the Turkish Republic in the ruins of the Ottoman Empire, he orientated the country away from the Middle East. He promoted a European idea of modernity, and actively suppressed any role for Islam in public life. The secular state, enforced by the army, was the supreme authority. As in the Soviet Union, industry was designated as the road of 'progress'. Indeed, under Stalin's guidance, the USSR provided the new republic with $8 million in gold roubles, and in 1933 the first Turkish Five-Year Plan was announced, drawn up along Soviet lines.[1] One result of the Plan was the building of an enormous textile factory at Kayseri in Central Anatolia, to process the raw materials from the cotton fields further south. It was a modernist town with factory, workers' housing, social club, cinema and infirmary. This icon of Nationalist industrialisation[2] was constructed in the same period as Soviet Sumqayit and Gəncə. As the economy of the country altered, consumption of oil dramatically increased, coming in rising quantities from the wells around Baku.

We drive through Kayseri, once the Roman city of Caesarea. At the crossing-point of an east–west road, and the route north from the seaports on the Mediterranean, it was visited by Venetian traders such as Marco Polo. Mehmet Ali points out that the city is now known as the heartland of the ultranationalist MHP party.

---

1   E. Zurcher, *Turkey: A Modern History*, I. B. Taurus, 2010, p. 197.
2   S. Bozdogan, *Modernism and Nation Building: Turkish Architectural Culture in the Early Republic*, University of Washington Press, 2001, p. 124.

After World War II, when Turkey's allegiance shifted towards the US, the state became a bulwark of the West against the Soviets over the border in the Caucasus. Its international role in NATO reinforced the position of the military within the country. During the Cold War, in the 1970s and 1980s, Turkish party politics was dominated by two men, Bülent Ecevit and Süleyman Demirel – the first being elected prime minister five times, and the second seven times. But the military continued to hold the strings in the background throughout these decades.

In the twenty-six years of Mehmet Ali's life, in which he attended school, studied at METU and avoided conscription in the army, the country has seen the slow growth of Islamist politics. Meanwhile, the collapse of the Soviet Union suddenly reduced the importance of Turkey's position in NATO, and the state seized upon a new geopolitical role as guardian of the future Oil Road to the West.

It was during these changes in the 1990s that Turkish governments enthusiastically supported US plans for the BTC pipeline, signed the Host Government Agreement drawn up by George Goolsby, and accepted the financial terms of the BOTAŞ Turnkey Agreement hammered out by Richard Morningstar and Peter Bellinger. Fittingly, at the key moment in November 1999 when Turkey signed its Host Government Agreement in İstanbul, Demirel was president of the Republic and Ecevit was prime minister. Both sat alongside their former Soviet enemies, Eduard Shevardnadze and Heydar Aliyev, while President Bill Clinton looked on.

We stop for the night at Pınarbaşı, ten kilometres from BTC and Block Valve 36 in LOT C, the section of the pipeline that reaches the Mediterranean. We drive south the next day. The mountains to our east are tipped with light, glowing just before sunrise. A dawn breeze is slowly dispersing the last shreds of mist on the peaks around us. Hawks soar in the moist, warm wind that has climbed from Turkey's southern coast up the slopes of the Taurus. These mountains are the last link of the great chain that stretches across Asia, spreading from the Himalayas. A blanket of Taurus Pine, cedar and oak covers the steep hillsides and deep valleys, with the occasional red-brown crags, limestone precipices and plunging waterfalls breaking the dense forests. On the flat land high between the peaks, villagers work the red earth. When it rains, this fertile soil turns to thick, sticky mud.

On a wet night in July 2004, eleven-year-old Kubilay Erekçi and Nurullah Keskin failed to return to their parents' homes in Yaylacı in the Northern Taurus. Many of the village's 150 families turned out to search for them. An eight-year-old friend of the boys said he had seen them playing near the open, flooded pipeline trench earlier in the day.[3]

---

3 These and all following details regarding this incident are sourced from the following documents obtained from the ECGD through the FOIA: J. Wingate, 'BTC Notice to Société Générale and Lenders', BTC Co., 12 July 2004; 'BTC Safety

Ray Cooper, BOTAŞ's acting site manager, was phoned about the missing children that evening at 9 p.m. He rang various officials working for BOTAŞ and another Turkish company, Limak, the construction subcontractor. Then he set up a 'crisis centre' at the distant workers' camp, near Azizli. An excavator and pumping equipment were sent to Yaylacı, and the search quickly focused on a particular ditch that was gradually drained. Once Cooper realised the children could have drowned on the construction site, he requested Jandarma protection for his workers.

Finally, just before midnight, two small bodies were pulled from the water, still clothed. Company staff had already gone, the ditch having been evacuated once it seemed likely that the boys had died. Photographs of a digger with its cab windows smashed suggest why.

How had these deaths happened? Heavy rains the week before had caused a stream diverted by construction to swell. Slipshod planning meant the water flooded the uncovered pipeline trench, which, dug a month previously, had been left unfilled. The children of Yaylacı had been playing around the construction site since work began, but this new two-metre-deep pool provided a more exciting playground. Erosion from the rain widened the trench as the sides collapsed. A photograph taken by a BTC health and safety officer on 7 July shows two boys in swimming trunks standing on the pipeline next to the flooded trench; their names are not recorded. Two days later, Nurullah and Kubilay found a wooden pallet by the pipes and dragged it to the site to use as a raft. Once on the water, their makeshift boat could not hold the two of them. The trench's steep, high sides meant that the boys were in a death-trap.

We have driven all day to return to Yaylacı, and the air of a wet evening is filled with the scent of thyme and marjoram. Near the middle of the village, a line of tall poplars provides scant cover from the downpour. Our boots are overwhelmed by the red mud flowing down the road, so we take shelter in a barn. The smell of greased farm machinery mingles with that of nearby animals. We have arranged to meet several villagers, who now join us and Mehmet Ali in the barn to escape the rain. Still angry, they explain how, once the bodies were returned to the families and the site was cleaned up, BP and Limak denied all responsibility for the boys' deaths. The two bereaved families were forced into a protracted court battle in search of some level of recognition and justice. Only in 2007 did the companies accept limited liability and settle out of court.

Yet the companies' internal investigation reports, which we have obtained through Freedom of Information requests and brought with us, show that they fully understood their responsibility. Memos describe how, a month before the accident, the site was already 'attractive to village children' who 'persistently play around the trench'. The Limak environmental officer had several times raised 'her concern that the trench sides could collapse on top of children'. Handwritten notes accompanying the photograph of the playing children read: 'I tried to scare them by telling them the police would take them to the station'; and then: 'the issue of kids swimming in open trenches had been raised continuously in meetings with the contractor ... Had action been taken this could have been [avoided].'[4]

The internal investigation made attempts to divert blame onto the villagers. They asserted that parents did not know where their children were, and that the 'children did not heed previous warnings'. But the documents reveal that the project's own safety procedures were not enforced, and that the required 'barrier' of posts and tape was not properly erected. They also raise questions over whether lessons were learned by the companies after a child was crushed by a pipe further up the line, beyond Erzurum, during the previous autumn.

BISHOPSGATE, LONDON

Five days after Kubilay and Nurullah drowned, BTC Co.'s finance manager, John Wingate, wrote a letter to the French bank Société Générale, the coordinator of the Lender Group of institutions helping to fund the pipeline, stating: 'We regret to inform you of the drowning of two children on the BTC Project in Turkey.'[5] Someone in the SocGen office then made fourteen A4 copies, and forwarded these on to the other lenders in Europe, Japan and the US. One of those copies was sent to Baba Abu at the Royal Bank of Scotland (RBS) on the top floor of 135 Bishopsgate, in the City of London.

Abu was then an associate director at RBS, which had the largest oil and gas banking division in the UK. On the day the letter arrived this division, overseen by Steve Mills, was engaged in projects across the world. Mills might have been assessing the reasonable returns for an Exxon offshore oilfield in Nigerian waters, while his deputy Colin Bousfield submitted a bid to finance the Angolan state oil company. Maybe advice specialist Michael Crosland was working on the loan agreement that made the Qatargas II project a reality. The global reach of this London office, together with its twins in Houston and Aberdeen, had led RBS to market itself as 'The Oil and Gas Bank'. The BTC pipeline loan was just a small part of its business.

In June 2003, RBS adopted the 'Equator Principles':[6] weak, self-regulatory

---

4   'BTC Pipeline Project'.
5   Wingate, 'BTC Notice'.
6   See equator-principles.com.

guidelines covering loans to infrastructure projects by private banks. These Principles, currently adopted by seventy-two bodies, were created following public campaigns over environmental and social impacts caused by bank lending. To some extent they were established in order to head off calls for a more robust set of standards and legal accountability. For the Principles focused primarily on monitoring and assessing the impacts of projects, rather than fundamentally changing the way the infrastructure was constructed.

BTC was the first major scheme to come to the private banking sector for loans after the Principles were established. Naturally, BP was determined to secure financing for the pipeline on the best terms. If the plan for BTC was shown to be compliant with the Principles, then a wider range of institutions would feel happy to finance it. However, Nick Hildyard of the Corner House, Greg Muttitt of Platform and Antonio Tricarico of the Italian group CRBM also recognised that BTC would be a test case as to whether or not the Principles had any teeth. Greg forensically scrutinised the pipeline documents, and highlighted 157 violations of the Principles.[7]

Despite an intense campaign publicising these violations, executives from RBS joined colleagues from other private banks in February 2004 at the official signing of the BTC loan agreement in Baku. This ceremony at the Gulustan Palace, overseen by President Aliyev, effectively marked the end of the long battle over Borjomi, but took place in the shadow of the scandal about the pipeline sealant. Together with the EBRD, the World Bank and the export credit agencies, fifteen major private banks combined to offer BP a $2.6 billion loan towards construction costs. BP had successfully persuaded the banks to ignore the concerns raised by campaigners and trust it that the pipeline complied with the Equator Principles.

Sheltering from the rain in Yaylacı, we look at the single sheet of A4, sent from Paris five months after the signing of the loan agreement, announcing that the eleven-year-olds Kubilay and Nurallah had drowned in the pipeline that RBS had helped to make possible. We find ourselves wondering how Abu received the news, how he relayed it to the rest of the oil and gas team, and what kind of connection was felt between the office in Bishopsgate and these muddy fields.

Viewed from a desk in London, BTC just becomes one of many industrial projects funded by RBS. Moreover, accidents are bound to happen, and BTC Co. was seemingly conducting a thorough investigation of the incident. The internal report clearly laid the blame on the subcontractor, Limak, for not filling in the ditch.

But the investigation did not ask whether this slipshod work was partly driven by the pressure on Limak from BOTAŞ to cut construction costs. That pressure was itself a direct result of the actions taken by BP, alongside Peter Bellinger and

---

7   G. Muttitt, *Evaluation of Compliance of the Baku–Tbilisi–Ceyhan (BTC) Pipeline with the Equator Principles*, Platform, 2003.

Richard Morningstar, to create the terms of the Turnkey Agreement. This agreement was crafted to ensure that the financial architecture of the pipeline would attract loans, such as that made by RBS. And it was the private banks' drive for greater profits that helped form that architecture.

This piece of paper, it seems to us, links the boys' death to BTC Co. in Baku, to Société Générale in Paris, to RBS in Bishopsgate, and beyond that to the headquarters of BP in St James's Square, and the offices of Bellinger and Morningstar in Ankara. But the reality of Kubilay and Nurallah stuck in the ditch and slowly sinking fails to break through the dry language of the incident report.

RBS itself has undergone a major convulsion since the 'credit crunch' of autumn 2008. After gambling on subprime loans, the bank was rescued from collapse by a bailout with £45 billion of British public money. But public accountability has not increased. The bank has continued to fund oil companies breaking into the Arctic, drilling along the conflict-ridden Congo–Uganda border and extracting Canadian tar sands. The bank is still receiving repayments and interest on its loan to BTC.

While the 'incident' has long since been forgotten in London, Paris, Baku and Washington, in these mountains the impact of the pipeline remains live and present. In Yaylacı, the scars are visible. The village road had coped with decades of tractors and car use, but the rumbling construction lorries left permanent, wide cracks in nearby homes, and weakened their foundations. We have seen such fissures before, in the walls of houses in Dgvari and Atskuri in Georgia, and we have heard the same stories of the companies denying responsibility. The residents of Yaylacı explain that they feel manipulated: 'They always use our weakest point, saying, "This is for the state, for the well-being of the state." They know that we don't want to undermine the Turkish state.'

BTC KP 1,654 – 1,841 KM – AKIFIYE, TURKEY

Akifiye is encircled by thick pine forest. Only one road goes in and out of it. A narrow stream flows under a tarmacked bridge just where the village begins. On one side of the road we can see the pipeline's marker posts. On the other is Gazi Temur's café, the villagers' informal meeting place. Gazi seats the three of us at one of his wooden picnic tables, while his friend Fahri explains that this is a Çerkez village. The Çerkez, or Circassians, once ruled the north-western Caucasus: present-day Kabardino-Balkaria, North Ossetia, Abkhazia and parts of Georgia. For a hundred years they held the encroaching Tsarist Russian Empire at bay, before their final defeat in 1864. Over half a million Çerkez were subsequently expelled from their native land. They resettled in the Ottoman Empire, spreading through present-day Jordan, Syria, Bulgaria and Turkey. Fahri emphasises that the Çerkez are not a Turkic people, although they speak Turkish as their primary language. Clearly the residents of Akifiye remain proud of their cultural and ethnic identity.

We are joined by two older men returning from their fields, just as Gazi brings out hot tea. He explains that when BTC staff held meetings about the pipeline here outside his café, they distributed shiny brochures. These were informative about the permanent and temporary acquisition of land, but they did not mention that the village would be turned into a construction site: 'Until the trucks arrived, we weren't expecting them. We didn't know what rights we had and what to ask for.' The heavy vehicles tore up the recently asphalted road, which had not been designed for such usage. Fahri tried to persuade his friends to block traffic and insist that BP construct a new road around the village, as nearby villages had done successfully. 'We asked them to bypass the cemetery and the stream. They agreed to the first, but not the second.' Gesturing at the water flowing under the bridge, Fahri informs us it has burst its banks every spring and autumn since the construction work artificially straightened its course, ruining the crops on the nearby fields.

All the men are worried about the risk of a spill if there is an earthquake in this tremor-prone region of Turkey. Gazi is especially worried, with his café so close to the pipeline. 'Nobody came to explain what will happen if there's a spill. Not being informed about the dangers makes me worry even more . . . We are also worried about how climate change will affect us. The last two years, there has been much less rain. We don't know if this is because of the shifting climate. If it stays dry, this will ruin our corn production. We only have two streams, and no water storage system. We are doubly threatened here, by climate change and by the pipeline.'

As the stream below us babbles, the conversation shifts to how beautiful Akifiye is. Half the village has moved away, looking for jobs in the humid coastal cities to the south of us. But every summer the population swells as the community comes back together to enjoy the cool mountain breeze and upland forests.

BTC KP 1,683 – 1,870 KM – YEŞILOVA, TURKEY

The feudal system was breaking up by itself. A class of newly enriched was coming to the fore, most of them seeking to gain possession of as much of the fertile soil as possible. They succeeded by all sorts of means in wresting the land from the poor. The landholdings of the rich steadily increased when they began to make use of the brigands as a source of pressure on the poor who were fighting to defend their rights in a life-and-death struggle for the land.[8]

Yashar Kemal, *They Burn the Thistles*, 1955

The cliffs and valleys of the Taurus Mountains have long provided refuge for populations fleeing, and then resisting, successive conquerors and oppressors. In

---

8 Y. Kemal, transl. M. Platon, *They Burn the Thistles*, William Morrow & Co., 1977.

the 1920s, as many of the Ottoman social structures dissolved and the Turkish Republic was established, outlaws roamed through the mountains, receiving support, provisions and shelter from villagers. The role these brigands played in local conflicts over land and water is evoked best in Yashar Kemal's epic tales of harsh social change and bitter battles between the peasants and the greedy *aghas*, or landlords, who covet their land.

The most famous bandit of all, İnce – or Slim – Memed, redistributed feudal land, chased *aghas* new and old out of their mansions and evaded scores of police sent to track him down. 'Every mountain villager had heard of Memed and loved him. People who knew where he was hiding would never tell.'[9]

İnce Memed was a fictional character. Yet all over the Taurus and the Çukurova – the plain that stretches from the mountains to the sea – Memed is still remembered as if he had actually stalked this land alongside his fellow villagers: Lame Ali, Big Osman, Yellow Ümmet, Mother Huru. Nor is it surprising that people dream of İnce Memed when conflicts over land continue today.

We arrive in Yeşilova, a village nestled in a deep valley between the mountains. The men are sitting at roadside tables, drinking tea as they play the card game, *pişti*. They need little prompting from us to talk about the pipeline. 'Our fields were not reinstated properly, many stones were left lying near the surface. This makes it difficult to plough . . . The compensation was terrible . . . They won't let us build on our own land.' Hasan, a thickset man with a large white moustache, starts swearing: 'They'll see. I'll fuck their pipeline. I'll fix it properly.' Hasan, we discover, only has a small plot of land, on which he had planned to build a summer cottage. 'In summer months, it becomes too hot down here in the valley, and many of us move higher up into the mountains, as it's expensive to get to the sea.' But now his land, and that of other villagers, is too close to the pipeline, and BTC Co. will not let him build there. 'The military patrol regularly. When they see us constructing, they tell us to stop. The soldiers treat us badly, even though it's our land they're walking on. They won't even let us pitch our tents.'

BTC Co. rented a forty-metre-wide 'construction corridor' from the thousands of individual farmers across whose land the pipeline was to run. Within this 'corridor' the pipe was buried, and the land was theoretically returned to its former state and handed back to the farmers, together with compensation for any crops lost during two years of building work. However, on the return of the land, the company and the farmers signed 'Reinstatement Papers', in which BTC Co. retained various rights over the 'corridor' for the full lifespan of the pipeline – forty-three years. From Sangachal in Azerbaijan to Ceyhan on the Mediterranean, villagers have been forbidden from building anything within this forty-metre strip for the next four decades. Hasan is not happy: 'They only rented this land

---

9   Ibid.

from me while they were laying the pipeline. Who are they to tell me what I can do with it now that they have finished? They can't just impose rules like that!' Sitting in the roadside café with Mehmet Ali, we have clearly found another example of the 'forbidden zone' – like the ACG oilfields off shore the coast of Baku, or the control room at the heart of Sangachal.

In Kemal's novel, *They Burn the Thistles*, İnce Memed struggles with the realisation that, having liberated his village from the oppression of Abdi Agha, Abdi's place has been taken by Bald Hamza Agha. 'Abdi went and Hamza came.'[10] Like his predecessor, Hamza proclaims that he will develop the land and improve the villages, but he turns out to be even tougher and meaner than Abdi.

It feels like the oil companies have entered folklore as the new *aghas*, using the army to patrol the land and bully the farmers. We juggle with the phrase: 'Now Hamza may have gone but BP Agha has come'. Furthermore, just like the *aghas*, the companies and their various contractors say time and again that they are trying to improve the lot of the communities along the pipeline; that many of the villagers do not know what is best for them. With the notable exception of Şükran in Ankara, all the spokespeople that we have talked to have, in all three countries, described villagers as 'self-interested', 'obsessed with the irrelevant', 'short-termist' and 'over-demanding' – and, comes the constant refrain, 'they always want more'.[11] Supposedly, the communities have not learned to appreciate 'progress', and what is needed for 'progress' to take place.

Others join in the conversation, and the game of *pişti* is put on hold. 'BOTAŞ said they would donate a library. But the 'books' they brought were just magazines.' 'When BTC came to get us to sign the Reinstatement Papers, we were so angry with them that we wanted to beat them up at the coffee house. They ran away so fast, none of us could have signed even if we'd wanted to!' Hasan jokes that he can strike back: 'They don't know who they're dealing with – I am Hasan of Mardin – I trained Apo'. He uses the Kurdish nickname, 'Apo', for Abdullah Öcalan, the head of the PKK.

---

10   Ibid.

11   Public quotes include BP Georgia Director Ed Johnson's complaint that 'Every single day there is a disruption that has something to do with getting more from the government or from us.' *BP's $3.6 Bln Pipeline Runs Into Georgian Strikes, Revolution*, 2 January 2004, at bloomberg.com.

16 DON'T SLEEP – SAVE YOUR SEA

İNCIRLIK, TURKEY

In the early morning we drive down from the Taurus into the Çukurova. Watered by the Ceyhan and Seyhan rivers, this great alluvial plain is part of what has become known as the Fertile Crescent, which stretches along the Euphrates through Syria and Mesopotamia and was one of the birthplaces of agriculture. Today it is Turkey's breadbasket – or, more accurately, its orange, wheat, tomato and corn-basket. The farms of the Çukurova export to the Middle East, Western Europe and Russia. The watermelons stacked outside Turkish and Kurdish corner stores in Haringey and Dalston originate in these fields, carried along dusty roads in tractor-drawn carts, on the first stage of their journey to north London. As we gaze at the passing fields, Yashar Kemal's description comes to mind:

> The rich earth yields a crop three times a year. Each plant is huge. It is twice, three times, five times larger than in other soils. Even the colours of the flowers, of the brilliant green grasses, of the trees are different. The greens are crystal-clear, the yellows pure yellow like amber. The reds blaze like flickering flames, and the blues are a thousand times bluer than elsewhere.[1]

Unsurprisingly, the Çukurova has long been fought over because of its potential for industrialised agriculture. In contrast to the smallholdings in the Taurus Mountains or the cattle pastures of Ardahan, the scale and fertility of this land meant that it could give a strong return on invested capital. From the early nineteenth century, Armenian landowners and Egyptian labourers transformed the plain with irrigation schemes and cotton plantations.[2] By the 1870s, much of the Çukurova was in the vast Mercimek Estate, owned by Sultan Abdulhamid II. But in 1909, pressured by spiralling debts to French investment banks, such as Société

---

1   Y. Kemal, *They Burn the Thistles.*
2   Zurcher, *Turkey: A Modern History*, p. 227.

Générale de L'Empire Ottoman,[3] the sultan ceded Mercimek to his creditors on a seventy-five-year lease. The new French landlords attempted to mechanise agricultural production in the face of stiff resistance from local peasants and the nomadic Turkomen. A decade later, in 1919, after Atatürk's declaration of Turkish independence, the French Army occupied south-eastern Anatolia. The fertile plain was one of their explicit targets for annexation, state forces being used to protect assets acquired by a private bank. They were a mirror of the British forces occupying the Caucasus to control the Baku–Batumi Railway and the oilfields on the Caspian shore.

After the withdrawal of French troops in 1922, and the reassertion of Turkish control over the area, the push to industrialise agriculture continued as part of Atatürk's drive for 'modernity'. The cotton pickers of the Çukurova fed mills across the new state, such as the *kombinat* at Kayseri, and were celebrated in Hikmet's poetry. After World War II, mechanisation accelerated using imported US equipment and migrant labour from the mountains. Production became focused on export markets. Rich landlords continued to eject peasants from the plain, and thereby expand their holdings. The decades of battles over land stretching back to the 1920s were the backdrop for Kemal's tales of İnce Memed, published in 1955. Several landowners rode the rising world price of cotton, and accumulated capital that provided the foundation of today's Çukurova Group – one of Turkey's largest conglomerates, involved in everything from construction to banking and oil drilling.[4]

Largely through Kemal's writings, the fertile plain has gained a special place in the imagination of the Turkish public. Şükran had told us in Ankara that when she first visited the village of Gölovası in 2002, then the proposed site for the new BP terminal, she had thought: 'We can't do this here, it's too beautiful. I love the Çukurova.'

As Mehmet Ali drives us across the Çukurova on the E90 highway, a massive grey military plane dips out of the sky immediately to our right. It descends sharply across the busy road, before thudding onto a runway and bouncing along the tarmac. Behind the tall barbed-wire fence of the airbase, it is just possible to make out control towers and several identical fat-bellied planes standing on the hectares of concrete.

Outside the perimeter fence, fields of green lettuce are ready to harvest. Along the verges, cows search for grass amid the rubbish. Young women with babies walk down the middle of the road with their hands outstretched, begging for

---

3   M. Sukru Hanioglu, *A Brief History of the Late Ottoman Empire*, Princeton University Press, 2008, p. 91.
4   Zurcher, *Turkey: A Modern History*, pp. 228, 307.

change. Two herds of goats pass a Shell garage, and the goatherds try to stop their animals from invading the lettuce fields. We are entering the village of İncirlik, whose name translates as 'fig orchard'.

Turkish soldiers patrolling the gates or standing in the stocky green watchtowers stare as our car loops around the airbase. Thick pine trees obscure much of the view, but the strong red of a Turkish flag is visible. A break in the conifers reveals blocks of pastel-coloured flats, alongside larger yellow detached houses with red roofs and blue benches outside. A blonde woman suns herself on a balcony.

The base's character becomes clearer after we pass the mosque of İncirlik, with its tall white minarets. The main road through the village, Atatürk Caddesi, is lined with shops targeting an obvious clientele: Freedom Furniture, Big Johnny's Barber, Alex & Joe's Hollywood Shop and Blade Tattoo Parlor.

İncirlik's primary 'base unit' is the United States Air Force 39th Air Base Wing. Five thousand US airmen and women work here, flying, refuelling and reloading the planes that feed the Western militaries in Iraq and Afghanistan. Officially, İncirlik is not a US air base, but a NATO air base. Consequently it also holds several hundred British and Turkish personnel.

By the end of World War II, the Turkish Republic – which had remained neutral for four years of conflict – felt increasingly under pressure from the Soviet Union. Stalin made it clear that he wished to regain the province of Kars. That borderland, with Ardahan at its heart, had been returned to the Ottomans under the 1918 Treaty of Brest-Litovsk. Responding to overtures from the US, Turkey joined the Marshall Plan, and US aid brought new tractors to areas such as the Çukurova.[5] In 1950, Turkish troops were sent to the Korean War; two years later, Turkey joined NATO. Soon the US Army Corps of Engineers were constructing the runways at İncirlik. It was to be a staging post for spying missions by American U2 planes into Soviet airspace over the Black Sea, the Caucasus and the Caspian. Enabling the expansion of US airpower, İncirlik changed the US Air Force's presence in Europe and Asia. Past empires, like those of the Tsars, the Ottomans and the British, were built on control and surveillance over roads, railways and shipping routes. Today the U2 planes have been replaced by satellites, like those overseen by the National Geospatial-Intelligence Agency at Fort Hood in Texas – control comes from the air and from space.

BTC KP 1,768 – 1,955 KM – GÖLOVASI, TURKEY

'We're here! We've made it!' We are filled with excitement as Mehmet Ali drives towards a range of low hills – all that remains between us and the Mediterranean. Seven large white storage tanks are visible on the hillside, marking the end of the BTC pipeline: the Ceyhan Terminal. They look out of place in the lush

---

5   N. Stone, *Turkey: A Short History*, Thames & Hudson, 2011, p. 160.

countryside, like upturned toy buckets that a giant child left behind at the seaside. They are similar to the tanks we saw 1,768 kilometres to the north-east, in Sangachal. Each barrel of crude stored here has passed through the sister tanks on the Caspian shore, and has taken ten days to cross the Caucasus mountains and the Anatolian plateau to this warm sea.

The turn-off for the Terminal is not obvious. A decaying sign standing in a field announces that we are approaching the 'eyhan Marine Terminal'. Plants obscure the 'C'; the letter 'T' has disappeared from the 'BTC' logo. A plastic bus shelter nearby is endorsed with a bold slogan: 'Given to you as a present by Isken' – Isken being the coal-fired power station whose smoke stack we can also spot over the hillside.

Turning onto the access road, we notice the difference immediately: pristine tarmac replaces the pot-holed, bumpy surface we've been driving along. As we get to the crest of the hill, a series of dirty grey tanks appear behind the sparkling white ones. The grey tanks hold Iraqi oil, pumped through the older Kirkuk–Ceyhan pipeline.

The road forks. Straight on, behind fortified fences, is the terminal itself. An armoured Jandarma jeep overtakes us, patrolling the site perimeter. A sharp right turn back onto a bumpy road takes us into the upper part of the village of Gölovası, whose residents have found themselves neighbours to an international oil terminal.

Red, green and white houses peer from behind the fig trees and cacti lining the road. Roosters crow while teenage boys and girls in blue school uniforms walk down the hill. Stopping to ask for directions, we are spotted by a stout man with a pen dangling from his shirt, hooked between the buttons. Tahsin Göregen, is chair of the local fishing cooperative. 'The pipeline is pumping now. We are still fishing. But it will all end. I will guide you to the harbour, it's only a short drive.'

As we leave the upper village, he explains that most of the 965 residents of Gölovası depend on fishing for their income. Although the traditional land of the village is very fertile, little is now owned by the farmers: their best fields were effectively purchased on a compulsory basis by BTC Co., and have become the site of the oil terminal.

'The biggest problem is that BTC is stopping us from fishing, stopping us from doing our work. The fishing area gets smaller and the forbidden area is big.' Tahsin explains that the sea off Gölovası is divided into a red zone and a green zone. The red zone is near the pier, and the fishing boats are not allowed to enter it. The green zone is larger, and surrounds the red. 'We can enter it, but must not fish in it. To reach the open sea, we must pass through the green zone. So we have lost much of our fishing area.'

'The restrictions are enforced by the BTC coastguard. But they hassle us even when we aren't in the forbidden zone. The coastguard boats are always coming to check us, and fining us for technicalities. They are driving us bankrupt and sending many people to prison.'

We emerge from the dense trees of Lower Gölovası to a small sunlit harbour filled with fishing boats. The harbour entrance faces north into a bay dominated by the BTC terminal a few hundred metres along the shoreline. Two long piers project into the Mediterranean. Further offshore, tankers lie anchored, waiting to collect their cargo. Sangachal gathered the oil from beneath the sea; at Ceyhan it is being pumped into ships that carry it across the waters.

The fishing boats putter back to the harbour in the morning sun, having hauled up nets cast the night before. Most boats are white, lined with gaudy green, red or blue stripes; on some, the decks and tiny cabins are painted brown or blue; all fly the Turkish crescent flag. At the quayside, families await each boat, passing breakfast to the fishermen and climbing on board to help with the catch. Gulls circle, waiting for scraps.

Invited on to a small blue boat, we jump from the quay and barely avoid a plunge in the water, to the amusement of those on board. Ahmet is a friend of Tahsin's, and sits together with his wife and son, working their nets, dextrously untangling pink and rainbow-coloured shrimp: the large ones end up in a bucket, the little ones go back in the sea. It looks easy, so we try our hands at it.

Most of the shrimp have caught themselves repeatedly, and are wrapped up tight. Once released from the ropes that hold them, their first reaction is to slash with claws serrated and razor sharp. Mika smiles, finally pulling a shrimp free after a ten-minute battle, but is taken by surprise when the little creature jabs a nearby thumb. Unluckily for the shrimp, it falls on the wooden deck, not in the sea.

Ahmet laughs and holds out his hands: tough, but covered in small scars. 'A shrimp fisherman's hands,' he says with a smile. 'Our shrimp are the best in the Mediterranean. This is a very fertile stretch of sea, the shallow İskenderun Bay – the marine Çukurova.'

'We take our bread from the sea. But we've had no peace since the BTC pier was built here. Now when I go out, I always have to worry if the coastguard will fine me.' New restrictions have limited the amount he can work. It used to take thirty minutes to get to the fishing grounds, but now he needs ninety minutes to get beyond the Green Zone. His boat is too small to go far offshore. 'When the pipeline was being built, they said the forbidden zone would be 400 metres. But now it's a nautical mile. How can you equate 400 metres with 1,850 metres? They never mentioned that there would be a limiting zone this size.' Ahmet is finding it impossible to fish, and friends are saying that they will leave and go elsewhere. 'Some people have already left, just in the last year. I've worked here as a fisherman since I was a child. I'm forty-two now and won't be able to do anything else.'

Like many of the fishermen, Ahmet faces fines and penalties for arbitrary violations of new regulations. He recently received an 850 lira fine and was sentenced to three months in prison for a breach he does not understand. He managed to get released on probation, but had to pay an additional fee. 'We obey the Red Zone. But even in the permitted areas, the coastguard comes and finds stupid violations, especially on our qualifications. No one else is allowed on the boats, not family members or guests. If someone is sick, he can't send his friend out instead.'

Continuing to fish here is an act of resistance in itself. The state is criminalising the Gölovası residents' very way of life, but they have refused to give up and leave. 'The company and coastguard behave in our land as if we don't exist. But even if we get sent to prison for three months, when we come out, we head straight back to the boats.'

As we talk, one of the tankers moves towards the terminal. We can make out its name, *Dugi Otok*. Some 40 metres wide and 250 long, it looms over the fishing boats, which bob in its wake. Guided to the pier by three tugs, this giant will collect 80,000 tonnes of Azeri crude. Two vans drive down the long, thin jetty. It takes them almost five minutes to reach the ship at the end.

As the families finish extracting the shrimp, the catch is carried ashore in buckets and bought by waiting traders, who will sell it on to restaurants in the nearby cities of Adana and İskenderun. The empty nets are cleaned and folded neatly, ready for the next fishing trip.

Leaving the harbour, we return to Upper Gölovası to resume our conversation with Tahsin. We find him in the middle of the village under a tree, among men playing backgammon. In a nearby shed, an older man with enormous eyebrows is making *çay*, Turkish tea.

Tahsin warns about what the coming industrialisation of the area will bring. 'The companies and government plan to make the bay into the Rotterdam of the Mediterranean. But Rotterdam cannot coexist with a fishing village like Gölovası.' In Ankara, Şükran told us that the region had been designated a 'special energy zone' in which an array of refineries and power plants would be built. Tahsin believes the fishermen are harassed this much because the authorities want to make life so hard that the villagers leave. 'We want the people who supported the pipeline, the politicians, the Scottish bank that paid for it – we want them to come and speak to us directly, to see what it is doing to our lives. They paid hundreds of millions for this, and never even came.'

Tahsin shouts across to the shed for a second round of tea, making a joke about foreigners drinking very slowly. He laughs at how one of the BP people took an hour to finish his cup.

'BTC paid so much money to send university people to do studies and to ask us questions, and then nothing happens.' His words make us think of Mehmet Ali's friends at METU and Şükran's endeavours. He says the company has never informed them about what to do if there is an oil spill in the bay. 'Anyway, in twenty years, Gölovası will be an empty village. There is barely any sea left for fishing, and the sea gives life to our village.'

* * *

Just along the coast from Gölovası harbour lies Balık Restoran – the fish restaurant at the end of the pipeline. The only structure on the beach, it has been serving visitors from Adana, Ceyhan and İskenderun for many years. The tables, in the open air, are of the ubiquitous design in white plastic, the entertainment is nonexistent and the access road is full of potholes. Balık's attraction has always been a combination of the local fish and its setting, amid palm trees, looking out onto the Mediterranean. Now, however, the scenery includes a long oil pier to the north, waiting oil tankers due east, and the German-built Isken coal-fired power station to the south. Nor is the fish catch of Gölovası any longer what it used to be.

We select our own shrimp – possibly the same ones we removed from the nets earlier – as Kemal, the young waiter in blue jeans and white shirt, talks about the further development planned for the beach. The construction of BP's terminal has already spawned a series of nearby industrial projects. Expansion plans for the short strip of coast between the BTC pier and the existing power station include five new coal-fired plants, a chemical works and a loading site for the proposed Samsun–Ceyhan oil pipeline.

As he lays out a tablecloth, Kemal remarks: 'All this industry – it destroys our health, the wheat fields, the fish. Then they give us bus shelters, and expect us to be thankful.'

Disappearing into the restaurant, he returns with shrimp sizzling in peppers and garlic, a tomato salad and toasted flatbread. While the terminal was under construction, workers, including many foreigners, came to eat here. But no longer. The fall in clientele has run in parallel with the drop in the fish catch.

'We have the best fish and shrimp, but now there are almost none left.' When we ask what Kemal thinks his village will be like in fifteen years, the answer is short: 'Dead. The whole area will be dead. For people, farming, fishing.' His words echo the fate of the Caspian fishing village of Sumqayit.

BURNAZ, TURKEY

Despite the gloom about what the future holds, not all the people of the Çukurova are sitting by and watching as their sea, beaches and fields disappear under industry and concrete.

People have learned from the nearby experiences of BTC and the Isken coal plant that battles must be fought early on. New projects need to be challenged before they are approved, financed and planned on hard drives and flipcharts in far-off capitals. Just a few kilometres north-east of the BTC terminal, local residents have been protesting since 2009, sticking up campaigning posters and disrupting corporate presentations. They are hoping to prevent the construction of five new coal-fired power plants, totalling 4,700 megawatts of output, which will be sited on a four-kilometre stretch of coast beside some of the Çukurova's finest orange groves. Fifteen such plants have been proposed for the region as a whole.

From Gölovası we drive to the beach at Burnaz to join a march. A crowd of perhaps 1,000 children and adults are gathered to oppose the complete transformation of their home. Their colourful banners proclaim: 'No industrialization of our coast', 'Protect the Çukurova' and 'Don't Sleep – Save your Sea'. Children play in the water; offshore, nine tankers lurk, waiting to grab their oil loads. With drums and *zurna* instruments playing in the background, a local resident and member of the teachers' union, Eğitim Sen, stands up to say, 'This is the result of capitalism and consumer culture. We are the people. If we don't stop our resistance, they can't build it. The company will say they are giving jobs and money, so you shouldn't go to the protests. But at the Isken coal plant, there were 300 jobs during construction. Now there are only ten for locals.'

Mehmet Ali smiles and lets the warm water roll over his toes as he translates the speech. 'This is the struggle of life. If we want to live on our bay in peace, we need to fight for it.'

1,983 KM – YUMURTALIK, TURKEY

On the sea-coast there is a city named Laiassus, a place of considerable traffic. Its port is frequented by merchants from Venice, Genoa and many other places, who trade in spiceries and drugs of different sorts, manufactures of silk and of wool, and other rich commodities. Those persons who design to travel into the interior of the Levant, usually proceed in the first instance to this port of Laiassus.

The Travels of Marco Polo, 1271[6]

Fifteen kilometres south of Gölovasi, the ruins of a sea fortress mark the former Venetian presence in Yumurtalık. Today this town lives from fishing and tourism, but 700 years ago it was the major port of Laiazzo, also known as Ayas. Here sea-based trading routes to the West met overland routes to the East, allowing goods to be shipped from what is now Beijing to Venice and back. Marco Polo disembarked here before heading inland to Kayseri, Sivas, Erzincan and then the Caspian.

In the thirteenth and fourteenth century, the Çukurova and the Taurus Mountains behind it were the territory of the small Armenian kingdom of Cilicia. Strongly allied to Western Christendom, it allowed the Venetians to establish a trading base at Laiazzo. Silk and spices from India and China crossed the Persian Gulf and the Central Asian steppes, before reaching this fortified harbour in the north-east corner of the Mediterranean.

Although the geography of the 'Silk Road' echoes that of the Oil Road, the terms of trade were utterly different. What is shipped from the BTC terminal is a raw commodity in bulk, extracted from weaker nations and transported to the

---

6   Polo, *Travels of Marco Polo*, pp. 15–16.

most powerful. By contrast the medieval ships bore small amounts of manufactured goods of the highest value, purchased by traders in the cities of the immense and powerful Mongol Empire and carried to the puny states of Western Europe. However, this highly profitable trade in luxuries was of local strategic importance, and Laiazzo became a site of struggle between Venice and its rival maritime republic of Genoa.

After the fall of Acre to the Mamluk Egyptians in 1291, and their subsequent conquest of all the Crusader ports, the Pope forbade trade with this expanding Muslim empire. The importance of Laiazzo grew, and it became the main terminus for the Venetian fleets and merchants that went to 'beyond the sea'. In 1294 a Genoese war party was dispatched to break Venice's dominance in the eastern Mediterranean. The ensuing battle saw fifty galleys clash.

Nicolò Spinola, the Genoese commander, arrived before the main Venetian fleet and captured the harbour of Laiazzo. Reading the likely wind-shifts of the day, he lashed his ships together to make a great floating fortress. Soon twenty-eight vessels from Venice, under Commodore Marco Basegio, bore down upon them. As the fleets drew nearer, a rising headwind caught the Venetian sails, turning their ships broadside to the Genoese galleys and exposing them to their guns. All but three of the Venetian ships were captured with rich cargoes. Thus the Genoese began this new war with a signal victory.

Laiazzo's fortifications are now ruins. Today's marine skirmishes are played out between the fishermen of Yumurtalık and the Turkish coastguard. There had long been a cooperative relationship between these two parties, but when a new and larger coastguard station was constructed inside the BTC complex, conflict began, with intrusive checks and a sudden increase in the scale of fines.

We make our way with Mehmet Ali to the fisherman's café a few metres from the boats in the harbour. Sinan and Mose, two of the most vocal members of the local fishing cooperative, explain that the coastguard now has four brand-new Zodiac inflatables which can easily outrun the slow fishing boats. They believe that BTC Co. supplied the Zodiacs, as well as regular petrol, food and cash payments. With thick eyebrows, a small moustache and round beard, Sinan looks the part of a jovial grandfather, and it is sad to see him so hurt.

We have come to the café beneath the fortress walls to witness a battle of words. Gathered on plastic chairs are forty-two fishermen, five coastguards in pressed white uniforms, a BOTAŞ official from the terminal, the three of us, three boys on bikes and a pet pelican making honking noises. As the head of the coastguard, in a pristine suit, begins an opening speech. Mehmet Ali whispers: 'He looks surprisingly like John Travolta, no?'

Coastguard: You must not hunt seals or turtles. This is not good, they are not to be hunted. You should stick to fish.

Mose: We don't hunt those animals – we don't even have the tools to catch them. But why do you give us such high fines for minor offences – our fines are not like traffic fines, they are much higher.

Fisherman 1: I went out fishing with three guys. They said they had papers. When the coastguard stopped us, it turned out they did have papers, but not the right ones for this type of fishing. I was fined, even though the others said it was their fault.

Pelican (*jumping on to a parked moped*): Honk, honk, honk.

Fisherman 2: You are always stopping us for silly things, and punishing us. Can the fines not be a bit flexible?

Coastguard (*impatiently tapping his shiny black shoes*): If we did that, the coastguard would become corrupt and you don't want that. I have a book in front of me, and it tells me what I need to do – that's how I do things.

Mose: Before BTC, there was nothing like this. It started with BTC.

Coastguard: Life changes.

Sinan: We need bread to feed our families.

Coastguard: This oil project is very important for our country.

Pelican (*jumping off moped, walking between chairs and sitting under table near coastguard, to watch his still tapping shoes*): Honk, honk, honk, honk.

Mose: We have many complaints against BTC and BOTAŞ.

Coastguard: We have lots of other things to do – we barely deal with you.

Fisherman 3: That's not possible – you hassle us every single day. The fines are very high and written into our criminal records. This makes it harder to get other work.

Coastguard: No they aren't.

Fisherman 3: Yes they are, and they know if you have sent us to prison.

Coastguard: Ow! (*The pelican has tried to bite the coastguard's shiny black shoes.*)

Sinan (*with a smile*): Bad pelican, come here.

BOTAŞ official: You're all so lousy – why can't you fish properly, without breaking the rules? You're just trying to have an easy ride by being corrupt.

Mose: We're fishermen, running small businesses. Operating with such high levels of punishment is very hard.

Coastguard: When we join the EU, there'll be an EU coastguard here as well, enforcing these rules even more.

Fisherman 4: Great! You're already more than enough.

After the meeting and more tea, Sinan leaves us with these parting words: 'I have been a fisherman my whole life. We lived from the sea. We used these boats to collect fish, to eat and to trade. But now we don't catch anything anymore. Oil tankers have caused much damage. The seabed is mouldy. The sea has turned its back on us, because of human behaviour.'

* * *

Our requests to visit the terminal at Ceyhan were turned down. Unlike near Baku, there is no 'Energy Visitor Centre' here, in an obscure corner of Turkey far from the capital. So we make do with the photographs in the BTC commemorative album that Orxan Abasov had given us when we met at Sangachal. There is an image of the heart of the Ceyhan complex, the Control Room. Four men stare at computer screens, and on the wall there is a line of synchronised clocks with names written beneath them – Baku, Tbilisi, Ceyhan, London – like the conference room at Villa Petrolea.

In May 2006 it was in this Control Room, and its counterpart in Sangachal, that engineers finally assessed that the pipeline was operational. Once construction was complete in all those places we have passed through – Qarabork, Tsikhisdvari, Çalabaş, Yaylacı – the steel tube was filled with Caspian crude. Michael Townshend, head of BTC Co., was in Ceyhan. With the task done, he and some colleagues dived into the warm sea – a 'cleansing moment' he had long dreamed of. Later he said, 'You actually know when it's all done when you see that physical tanker at the other end, and it's not until that moment you can say that it is all done.'[7]

We look at a second photo in the album. Two men in orange jumpsuits lean on a rail and stare out to sea at three tugs, the end of the Ceyhan oil jetty and the stern of the BP tanker *British Hawthorn*. It is Sunday, 4 June 2006. One of the men is Tony Hayward, head of BP Expro, come to witness the departure of the first tanker of Azeri crude, bound for Italy.

Forty days later BP CEO John Browne was here. He described the event in his autobiography:

13 July 2006: One of the great moments of my career was to be part of the official inauguration of the Ceyhan marine export terminal and BTC pipeline. It was a hot, sunny, clear day on the coast of the Mediterranean. You could see as far as Syria. The heads of the three 'pipeline countries' were there with me: Ahmet Necdet Sezer, President of Turkey; Ilham Aliyev, President of the Republic of Azerbaijan; and Mikheil Saakashvili, President of Georgia.

In my speech I commented not only on the heroic engineering achievements but also on the strategic significance: 'The commissioning of the Baku–Tbilisi–Ceyhan pipeline is a significant step in the long history of the oil industry. It reintegrates significant oil supplies from the Caspian into the global market for the first time in a century.'[8]

The new Oil Road was in operation.

---

7 S. Levine, *The Oil and the Glory: The Pursuit of Empire and Fortune on the Caspian Sea*, Random House, 2007, p. 380.
8 Browne, *Beyond Business*, pp. 174–5.

Part III THE SHIP

MAP IV   THE MEDITERRANEAN

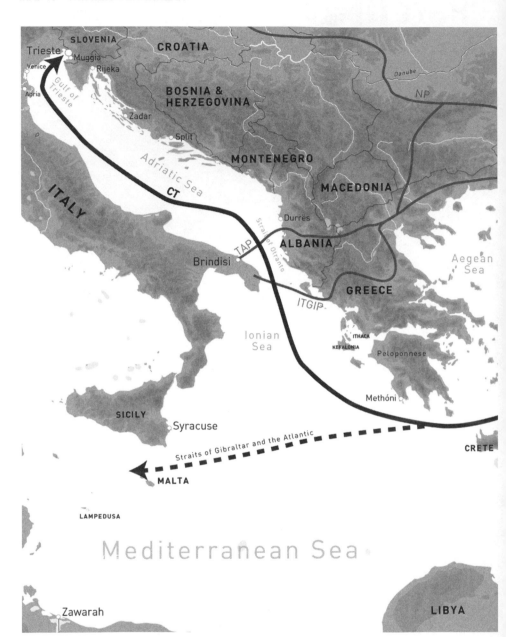

KEY

CT – Route from Ceyhan to Trieste

~~~~~~~ Ankara –Kars Railway line

Proposed Gas Pipelines
NP – Nabucco Pipeline
TAP - Trans-Adriatic Pipeline
ITGIP – Inter-connector Turkey-Greece-Italy Pipeline

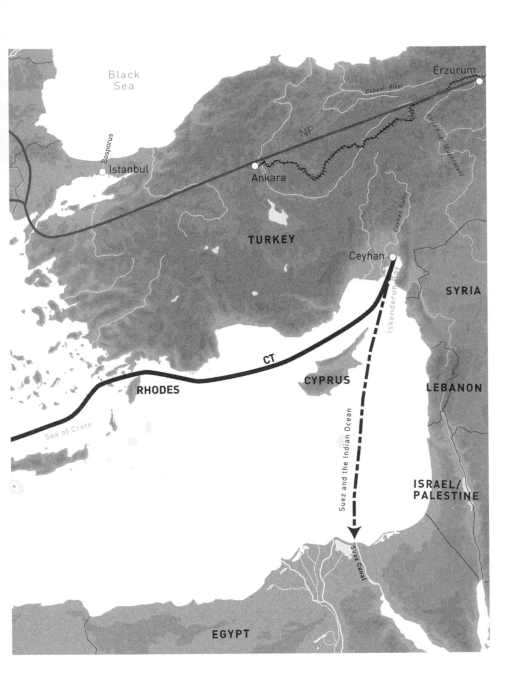

17 MILITARY FORCES SANITISE THE AREA AHEAD OF THE MERCHANT SHIPS

YUMURTALIK, TURKEY

At Yumurtalık we find our onward travel plans blocked. We have been trying to organise a journey on one of the tankers that ply the waters between the Ceyhan Terminal and Muggia, near Trieste in Italy, but it appears that for us that is impossible. Whereas some shipping lines will allow tourists on container ships – and we have crossed the Atlantic this way several times – oil tankers are another matter. It seems that, as ordinary citizens, we cannot easily travel on a ship with such a dangerous cargo, just as we would not get a cabin on a warship. Signing up as crew is also not an option: most are recruited in the Philippines, training is arduous, and the shortest contract would run for several months. Indeed, even meeting the crew of one of the tankers loading with Azeri crude is difficult, with the jetty cocooned within the perimeter fence of the terminal. Once again, we have found a 'forbidden zone', like the Control Room at Sangachal.

No passenger ferries, nor container ships with room for travellers, sail from this corner of the eastern Mediterranean to the northern reaches of the Adriatic. So, as when we sat in Bulvar Park on the harbour front in Baku and gazed in the direction of the Caspian platforms, we shall have to follow the tanker's four-day sea journey by other means.

We settle into an internet café just down the road from the Yumurtalık harbour, where the battle between the fishermen and the coastguard had taken place. Through the window we can see the beach and Yumurtalık Bay, with its Venetian ruins. Earlier this morning we stood by the fishing boats in Gölovası and watched the great bulk of the *Dugi Otok* tanker prepare to depart from the jetty of the Ceyhan Terminal. Now we log into the computer to track the ship's movement online. The website marinetraffic.com records the routes of a vast array of vessels, among them passenger ferries, yachts, container ships and tankers. A quick search brings up the details of the *Dugi Otok*, built in the Croatian city of Split and apparently launched only last year, in 2008. The website gives the exact latitude and longitude of the ship's last announced position. A Google map shows it as a red arrowhead on the blue ground of the Mediterranean Sea by the coast of Turkey, next to the tiny white line of the terminal jetty.

We will track the journey of the *Dugi Otok* to Muggia, with the use of this website and shipping forecasts, as we travel there ourselves by train via İstanbul, Bucharest and Vienna.

DAY 1, 08:43 – 0 NM – 1,955 KM – İSKENDERUN BAY, TURKEY

Deep in the belly of the tanker, the oilers and engineers are starting up the enormous diesel engine that will propel these 108,000 tonnes of steel across the water. The noise will be immense, all the crew wearing headphones. The injectors spray vaporised fuel into the six cylinders, shooting a mist of diesel molecules towards hot, densely compressed air. When the two substances collide, they ignite and combust, forcing the pistons in each cylinder up and down. The propeller shaft rotates, and with it the screw of the propeller itself, churning the water behind the ship and pushing the super-tanker forwards.

Reaching the shipping channel, the tugs release *Dugi Otok* to its own steerage. The ship's red prow smashes through the glassy Mediterranean waters, ploughing the clear blue into a mass of white. We watch from the shore as the tanker steams to the horizon, a thin plume of smoke rising from its funnel. On the ship itself, the captain and officers on the bridge will be able to see the Turkish coast dwindle to a purple line of mountains, the Taurus floating like a distant cloud.

These tankers are the emissaries of Azeri geology, camel trains of the industrial age. Picking up where the pipeline leaves off, they distribute the dark matter across the surface of the earth. Having pumped their quota of crude 1,768 kilometres down a pipe, the oil companies either sell it directly at the Ceyhan Marine Terminal or ship it onwards to refineries abroad. Tankers flagged in Liberia, the Isle of Man and Panama ply the oceans, delivering Caspian crude to import terminals in Italy, Chile, England, China and elsewhere.

This global oil trade does not just flow by itself. Every day, close to 100 million barrels of crude are collected from zones of extraction and delivered to points of consumption. Developing the Azeri–Chirag–Gunashli oilfield and constructing BTC meant more ships were built to carry the additional 1 million barrels per day. The *Dugi Otok* is one such vessel, for although she transports crude from and to a range of different terminals, the route from Ceyhan to Muggia is a key part of her itinerary.

This mass relocation of great volumes of fossil fuels requires constant coordination of logistical and financial resources. Analysts in Geneva and London assess and counter-assess the profitability of particular shipments, aiming to maximise their return. Some deliveries are based on long-term commitments, but many others are short-term contracts betting on swings in the global oil price.

Shifts in local demand redirect tankers from a short Mediterranean delivery to a major voyage across the Atlantic and through the Panama Canal.

The paths taken across the water are less predetermined than rigid pipelines, yet there is nevertheless a global network of preferred tanker routes running across seas and oceans, through straits and canals, towards the destination ports. From the Ceyhan Terminal there are two primary marine Oil Roads: one runs south along the Syrian, Lebanese and Palestinian–Israeli coast to the Suez Canal, while the other initially heads west through the Greek islands towards either the Adriatic or southern Italy, the western Mediterranean or the Straits of Gibraltar.

DAY 1, 11:09 – 48 NM – 2,044 KM – NORTH-EASTERN MEDITERRANEAN

After the *Dugi Otok* passes over the horizon, a second tanker, the *British Hawthorn*, remains moored at the terminal jetty. Both vessels are bearing Azeri crude belonging to BP, but the *British Hawthorn* is managed directly by the oil company – a rarity in the world of crude shipments. BP Shipping operates forty oil tankers itself, named mostly after trees or birds: *British Laurel*, *British Oak*, *British Eagle*. But usually the oil major contracts in shipping companies such as the Croatian firm, Tankerska Plovidba, which manages *Dugi Otok*.

The *British Hawthorn* will head for Thailand via the Suez Canal, and she is rigged to deter the threat of 'Somali Pirates'. All BP ships travelling through the Gulf of Aden are under instruction to fix double rolls of concertina razorwire around all their decks, and carry high-pressure water and foam hoses. In the past year, fast skiffs have launched from coves along Somalia's 3,000 kilometres of coast, carrying grappling hooks and rope ladders. Since the *Sirius Star*, transporting 2 million barrels of Saudi oil, was captured in November 2008 and held for $3 million in ransom, tankers have become high-profile targets.

The vessels and crew are usually released unharmed once a ransom is paid, but shipping associations nevertheless perceive themselves as a 'system under attack'. The Gulf of Aden is publicly presented as 'an important energy supply route' and a 'vital strategic artery'.[1] By late 2010, Jan Kopernicki, the president of the British Chamber of Shipping, was doing the rounds of political and military leaders, speaking of the danger to European energy supplies. 'I don't want to be alarmist, but I provide transport for essential oil and gas for this country and I want to be sure that the lights are on in Birmingham, my home city', he says. Kopernicki is also vice-president of Shell's shipping arm. In this capacity he has argued that there is a 'gaping hole in the UK's defence strategy'. He insists that British Prime Minister David

---

1   *Combating Somali Piracy: The EU's Naval Operation Atalanta*, House of Lords Select Committee on European Union, April 2010.

Cameron increase Royal Navy spending and bring forward the acquisition of a new generation of warships currently scheduled for after 2020.[2]

UK, US, EU and NATO forces – including the *HMS Portland*, a British frigate – are already prowling the waters off Somalia. Armed with Lynx helicopters, torpedos and heavy artillery, the *Portland* can easily overpower the pirate's skiffs and 'mother ships'. It forms part of the US-led Combined Task Force 151, as do Marines, SuperCobra attack helicopters and unmanned MQ-9 Reaper drones. The Task Force is just one of various naval fleets patrolling these waters. When the *British Hawthorn* passes through the Gulf of Aden, she will probably register with Operation ATALANTA. This European fleet includes warships from Germany, France, Spain and Italy empowered by the UN to use 'all necessary means' to repress piracy.[3]

ATALANTA is run from Northwood HQ, an extensive underground military complex beneath an oak wood in north-west London, just inside the M25 motorway. Many floors deep, behind steel blast-doors, Royal Navy officers coordinate the warships with nearby tanker traffic. Vessels are advised to travel in groups and at night, as 'this enables military forces to "sanitise" the area ahead of the merchant ships'.[4]

While the action takes place on the Indian Ocean, ultimate control is situated here in the bunker. Major General 'Buster' Howes is in overall command, but consults regularly with the most senior officer at sea, Rear Admiral Philippe Coindreau, a veteran of several 1980s French wars in Africa.[5] Satellite imagery is beamed in from the EU Satellite Centre in Madrid and combined with geospatial intelligence shared by US GEOINT staff at Fort Hood in Texas and Bethesda in Washington, DC. Real-time images are streamed from US drones scouring the waters off Somalia, remotely piloted from Creech Air Force Base in the Nevada Desert.[6]

The communication between Northwood and the shipping companies is conducted by Merchant Navy liaison officers such as Captain Colin Shoolbraid and Captain Michael Hawkins. Although they're based in the bunkers, and are part of the military operation, neither is actually a Royal Navy officer; both are employed by BP Shipping and seconded to the Navy.[7]

---

2   T. Jeory and M. Giannangeli, 'Piracy Will Lead to Power Cuts', 7 November 2010, at express.co.uk.

3   D. Nincic, 'Maritime Piracy: Implications for Maritime Energy Security', *Journal of Energy Security*, 19 February 2009.

4   'The Maritime Security Centre: Horn of Africa', at www.eunavfor.eu.

5   'New EU Force Commander of EUNAVFOR Somalia – Operation Atalanta', 16 August 2010, at eu-un.europa.eu; 'EU Naval Operation Against Piracy', EU Council Secretariat, November 2010, at consilium.europa.eu.

6   N. Turse, 'America's Secret Empire of Drone Bases', 17 October 2011, at huffingtonpost.com.

7   'Chamber of Shipping: Merchant Navy Seafearers Awarded Piracy Medal by Royal Navy', 4 November 2010, at politics.co.uk.

So if the drone and satellite surveillance over these distant waters shows a skiff approaching the *British Hawthorn*, it might well be BP's Captain Shoolbraid or Captain Hawkins who picks up the phone to Sunbury-on-Thames. Only a few kilometres south of Northwood, two exits down the M25, Sunbury is BP's largest global office. From here, BP Shipping monitors and manages the company's fleet.

Backed by a global military network with nodes in Texas, Madrid, Nevada, Washington, Brussels, London and the Seychelles, the *British Hawthorn* will traverse the waters near Somalia. If need be, the *HMS Portland*, Reaper drones or SuperCobra helicopters will be dispatched to ensure that this part of the Oil Road is 'sanitised'.

DAY 2, 14:17 – 428 NM – 2,748 KM – ΡΟΔΟΣ (RHODES), GREECE

We pick up the *Dugi Otok* on the marinetraffic.com website as she passes between the islands of Rhodes and Karpathos, and enters Greek territorial waters. The onscreen map shows holiday yachts, fast ferries and container ships dotted about the busy straits. The tanker is crossing the path taken by an earlier ship that carried the output of Baku oil wells in 1892, and changed the history of the global oil industry: the *Murex*. This famous ship broke John Rockefeller's monopoly of the kerosene trade in the Far East by opening the Suez Canal to oil transportation. Her voyage is celebrated as the genesis of the Royal Dutch Shell company, but is also a story of nineteenth-century businessmen weakening health and safety regulations.

By the late 1880s, the Rothschilds' Batumi Oil Refining and Trading Company was struggling to maintain its profits from Caspian oil. The challenge lay not in extracting crude, for the oilfields around Baku were proving plentiful, but in where to sell the product from the refinery. The European kerosene market was saturated with supplies from the Caspian and the US. It came not only from the Rothschilds but also from the Nobels and Rockefeller's Standard Oil. Threatened by a peak in European demand, the Rothschilds needed to expand into other markets. To do so, they had to break Standard Oil's monopoly by selling their product cheaper.

The cities of the Far East offered huge potential, but a means of transporting kerosene in bulk to these cities had to be developed. The product from the refinery at Batumi was packaged in large cans and exported. But transporting kerosene in cans across the Mediterranean and around the Cape of Good Hope made it too expensive and unable to undercut Standard Oil. A new type of ship would have to be built – an ocean-going tanker modelled on Ludvig Nobel's *Zoroaster*, which shuttled across the Caspian. Furthermore, a new shipping route to the East would need to be developed.

The Suez Canal, opened in 1869, offered a shorter journey time, which should have drastically reduced costs, but the Suez Canal Company had expressly forbidden the transit of kerosene for safety reasons. To tackle this problem, the Rothschilds went into partnership with Marcus Samuel, a merchant based in Aldgate, in the City of London. Samuel was to use his extensive network of contacts in the British trading houses that dominated European business in China, Japan and beyond. But in order to the make kerosene exports profitable, he would also need to use his political connections to dismantle the regulations governing the canal.

Samuel travelled to Batumi and then, via the railway, to Baku. On his return to London he proposed an audacious plan to lobby the British government, a major shareholder in the Suez Canal Company, to alter the restrictions set down by the company. His persuasion worked. The Conservative government of the 3rd Marquess of Salisbury supported the proposal that would enable a British company, rather than an American one, to serve the markets of the Indian Raj and imperial possessions beyond. With this achieved, Samuel set about the construction of eight tank farms across the Far East, and commissioned ten tankers to be built at shipyards in the north-east of England. The innovative design of these vessels secured insurance approval from Lloyds of London – an essential condition for passage through the canal under the now weakened regulations.

The first vessel, the *Murex*, was launched by Samuel's wife on 28 May 1892. It arrived at Batumi under the command of Captain John Coundon two months later. Within weeks, the ship had travelled back across the Black Sea, passed through the Bosphorus, and made its way through the Greek islands, bound for the Suez Canal and the East.[8]

DAY 3, 03:38 – 615 NM – 3,094 KM – NORTH OF CRETE

As our train travels westwards from İstanbul through this moonless night, we think of the tanker far to the south, in the Sea of Crete. The weather is fine – no doubt gulls swoop around the ship, riding on the *Dugi Otok*'s tailwind. The vessel will be quiet, with just one officer alone on the night watch. The pale green light from the screens of the radar tracking devices will dimly illuminate the bridge. The display panels show the presence of other craft, but the seascape beyond the windows is utter blackness. Even through his binoculars, the officer cannot see a single light in any direction, neither from a ship nor from the land. The *Dugi Otok* is invisible.

This is the usual condition for the oil tankers that constantly convey crude across the oceans. At any time of day or night, two-thirds of the world's oil supply is afloat in the holds of ships travelling far offshore.[9] These shy and awkward

---

8   See S. Howarth, *Sea Shell: Story of Shell's British Tanker Fleets 1892–1992*, Thomas Reed Publications, 1992.

9   See P. French and S. Chambers, *Oil on Water: Tankers, Pirates and the Rise of China*, Zed Books, 2010.

vessels are elusive, glimpsed only when they are docked at terminals or moored in sight of land, loaded with crude, waiting for the oil price to rise before they deliver their cargo.

But when something goes wrong, when a vessel is hijacked or runs aground, this passage of the Oil Road drops its cloak of invisibility. The *Torrey Canyon*, the *Amoco Cadiz*, the *Exxon Valdez*: the names of these tankers are iconic because oil intended to remain invisible was unleashed as a poisonous reality. Their cargoes burst like a roaring tempest into the media and our memories.

At 8 a.m. on 19 November 2002, the *Prestige* sank off Spain. It spilled 420,000 barrels of heavy fuel oil into the Atlantic, much of which washed up on the Galician coast. After the Greek captain was arrested and the clean-up began, there was an international investigation to discover whether the vessel was safe and who was responsible. The tanker was Greek-operated, owned by a Greek family using a Liberian shell company. She was officially registered in the Bahamas, and had been chartered by a Swiss-based subsidiary of a Russian conglomerate, also registered in the Bahamas. She was insured by the London Steam-Ship Owners' Mutual Insurance Association, and classed – approved as being in compliance with all rules and regulations – by the American Bureau of Shipping. For four years, the government of Spain tried to claim $700 million for damages from the American Bureau of Shipping, but got nowhere.

The *Dugi Otok* could run aground on any part of the Greek coastline. Her 790,000 barrels of Azeri Light, if spilled, would destroy the fisheries and marine life, as well as the allure of the Aegean and Ionian Islands for European holiday-makers. As tourism becomes increasingly the most lucrative industry in Greece, every passing tanker poses a disproportionate threat to the Greek economy. Yet the state gains no income, nor any transit fees, from this passage of oil through its territory. Should a disaster happen, who would carry the financial, reputational and legal consequences? Who would the Greek government try to sue? This ship, which flies a Croatian flag, is owned by Donat Maritime in Malta, managed by Tankerska Plovidba in Zadar, insured by Lloyds of London, and classed by Bureau Veritas, also in London. For this particular voyage, she has been chartered by BP Integrated Supply and Trading at Canary Wharf. On this night, the *Dugi Otok* is invisible, but her passage is watched over by the Hellenic Coast Guard, and her journey is logged by that web of companies in London.

The tanker sails on, her cargo intact, the coastal communities and the seas unscathed for now. But what remains in the hold of the *Dugi Otok* is still lethal to the environment and humanity. For the vessel is a bomb – a climatic bomb. When the crude that she carries is burned, in everything from refineries to car engines, it will release over 250,000 tonnes of carbon dioxide.[10] On average, 500 such bombs will depart from Ceyhan each year, helping to convey 125 million tonnes of carbon dioxide from the lithosphere beneath the Caspian into the global atmosphere. The pipeline system is built on the assumption that it will continue to make this delivery for forty years.

DAY 3, 12:55 – 745 NM – 3,335 KM – ΜΕΘΩΝΗ (METHONI), GREECE

The *Dugi Otok* passes around the south-western tip of the Peloponnese, just offshore from the town of Methoni and its ruined fortress. This was a Venetian trading post, guarding the route from Venice to Laiazzo and other ports and colonies in the eastern Mediterranean. We catch a glimpse of the tanker on the marinetraffic.com website – a vessel on collision course with the global climate.

The impending crash between hydrocarbons and climatic limits began to be understood in the 1970s, but was only raised seriously within government and industry in the run-up to the 1992 UN Earth Summit. Five years later, on 19 May 1997, with BP's foothold in Azerbaijan secure and the Chirag oilfield about to come on stream, BP CEO John Browne gave a pivotal speech at Stanford University in California:

> The concentration of carbon dioxide in the atmosphere is rising, and the temperature of the earth's surface is increasing. The time to consider the policy dimensions of climate change is not when the link between greenhouse gases and climate change is conclusively proven . . . but when the possibility cannot be discounted and is taken seriously by the society of which we are part.[11]

He went on to disagree with those 'who say we have to abandon the use of oil and gas', but announced that BP would control its own carbon dioxide emissions, fund scientific research into climate change, develop alternative fuels and contribute to the public policy debate.

Browne was dramatically breaking ranks with his oil industry peers, some of whom asked him if he had 'lost the plot'.[12] BP withdrew from the Global Climate Coalition, a body established by the American Petroleum Institute to lobby against any climate-related regulation. There followed a wave of apparent change within BP, including the promise to build the BTC pipeline to the highest standards of corporate social responsibility. Three years later the company was rebranded with its sunflower-like Helios logo and the strap-line 'Beyond Petroleum'. Investment in solar photovoltaics, wind-power schemes and biofuels

---

10   A conservatively low estimate, based on one barrel of crude being refined into various fuels that when burned emit 317 kg of carbon dioxide. J. Bliss, 'Carbon Dioxide Emissions Per Barrel of Crude', 20 March 2008, at numero57.net.

11   J. Browne, 'Speech: Addressing Global Climate Change', 19 May 1997, at bp.com.

12   Browne, *Beyond Business.*

increased. In 2005 a new division of the corporation was launched – BP Alternative Energy. Its head, Vivienne Cox, was given a seat at board level. Many of BP's staff were deeply committed to this shift in direction that seemed to define the 'Browne era'. Similarly, journalists and some NGOs believed that it indicated that the company was taking a new path – a belief that helped in the cooption and silencing of genuine criticism of the destructive impacts of BP's operations.

In April 2007, Browne returned to Stanford to give a tenth anniversary speech. Four days later, on 1 May 2007, he resigned from BP, ostensibly over revelations concerning his private life. However, the changes that took place in the following two years suggested that Browne's departure was partly the outcome of a power struggle within the company.

Under the new CEO, Tony Hayward, BP Alternative Energy was de-prioritised, solar facilities were cut back and Vivienne Cox left the company.[13] The company made its first significant investment into the Canadian tar sands, a highly carbon-intensive source of unconventional oil that Browne had avoided. Soon BP was supporting groups in the US that actively denied the existence of climate change.[14] It was widely understood in both BP and the wider oil industry that Hayward was not that interested in climate change. In retrospect it seems the summer of 2006 not only marked the opening of the BTC pipeline, but also the point after which BP's claim to be addressing the issue declined.

Throughout the twelve years since 1997, both Browne and Hayward's strategies had focused almost entirely on fossil fuels, and the apparent shift away from them had effectively been a fiction. Even at the high-water mark of the 'Beyond Petroleum' drive, less than 1 per cent of the company's turnover came from renewable energy. The scale at which the company extracted oil and gas from the ground continued to grow every year. It is this rate of extraction that keeps the company on collision course with the climate. Despite a decade in which BP publicly proclaimed a new path, the tankers ploughed on relentlessly, following the same routes as those of Marcus Samuel and the Rothschilds a century before them.

DAY 3, 17:55 – 815 NM – 3,464 KM – SOUTHERN IONIAN SEA

The vast engine room of the *Dugi Otok*, like a great hall several storeys high, is the realm of the chief engineer: heavy machinery, whirring shafts, grease and more grease. To walk along the multiple metal gangways is like entering a power station that burns hydrocarbon fuels in order to generate electricity, desalinate water and drive the ship onwards. Most large vessels can run on

---

13 'Vivienne Cox, Formerly of BP Alternative Energy, Joins Climate Change Capital', 24 November 2009, at greenenergyreporter.com.
14 S. Goldenberg, 'Tea Party Climate Change Deniers Funded by BP and Other Major Polluters', 24 October 2010, at guardian.co.uk.

both diesel and heavy fuel oil. The latter carries a high sulphur load, which makes the emissions from the tanker's funnel far more polluting than diesel. Under EU regulations it cannot be sold to vessels at European ports, but there is no restriction on ships burning it as they pass through European waters. Consequently, many shipping companies fill the fuel tanks of their vessels with the cheaper, heavy oil when in non-EU ports. The *Dugi Otok*'s 6S60 MC-C engine was designed by the MAN company of Augsburg in Germany to burn primarily this heavy fuel oil.

Forcing a vessel like the *Dugi Otok* through the sea requires vast quantities of energy, especially on this outward journey from Ceyhan when she is fully laden and low in the water. Very large crude tankers use sixty-two tonnes of heavy oil every day to power their engines. At $800 dollars a tonne, the daily fuel costs almost hit $50,000 just to move it forwards.[15] But as the *Dugi Otok* ploughs through the Ionian Sea, the threat to the environment comes far less from what is burned in her engine room and issues from her funnel than from what is contained in her hold.

In his Stanford, speech, Browne committed BP to 'control its own carbon dioxide emissions', and indeed the company made efforts to make its oil rigs, refineries, road tankers and offices more energy efficient – which of course also reduced costs. However, this efficiency drive did not extend to the contractors it hired or the ships that it chartered. As BP's own *Sustainability Reports* illustrated, the carbon dioxide released by the extraction processes of the company, at its oil rigs and so forth, were dwarfed by those released by the products it sold. Of the combined total of these two categories of emissions, 94 per cent came from what the company sold. The *raison d'être* of the corporation is to generate a return on capital, and this exerts a constant pressure to increase the volume of oil and gas it sells.

The sheer scale of the carbon that the company delivers to the atmosphere needs to be understood. In 2006 the UK's annual domestic emissions constituted 2.5 per cent of those of the entire world. In the same year BP's total emissions represented 5.6 per cent of the global total. This one company was responsible for over twice the combined amount of carbon dioxide produced by 62 million British citizens. These raw statistics indicate that, if the company were truly to go 'Beyond Petroleum', it would change out of all recognition. It would need rapidly to retire those assets that deliver carbon to the atmosphere, such as its tanker fleet, the BTC pipeline and the Azeri–Chirag–Gunashli oilfield. Even if Browne, Vivienne Cox and others tried to alter the path of BP with the best of intentions, the company remains fundamentally embedded in the extraction of oil and gas, and hence, like the *Dugi Otok*, very difficult to turn around.

---

15   French and Chambers, *Oil on Water*.

DAY 3, 21:51 – 870 NM – 3,566 KM – ΚΕΦΑΛΛΟΝΙΑ (KEFALONIA), IONIAN SEA

The *Dugi Otok* adjusts her course, heading north rather than west, through the Ionian Sea. This was the 'Western Ocean' across which the Greeks of the eighth century BCE journeyed with sail and oar to trade and found colonies.

Some headed to what is now Libya, others to present-day Italy and France. The new cities they established, such as Syracuse, became so powerful that, within a century, they too were creating further colonies and trading posts, such as Adria, which gave its name to the Adriatic Sea.[16] Other Greeks headed east and north, across the Black Sea, founding towns like Bathys, now Batumi. This adventuring was driven by trade, by the profit that merchants could make in supplying raw commodities of grain, fish and slaves. The demand for these resources came not only due to the rising population in the Greek city-states, but also because the fertility of the soils in those homelands was becoming depleted.

It was through these trade systems that some of the building blocks of European culture evolved: the practice whereby cities extract sustenance and wealth from distant peripheries; the idea of a 'civilised world' and of the realms of the 'barbarians'. The strangeness of those distant places and creatures is captured in the oral epic that Homer wrote down as *The Odyssey*. Perhaps this tale then acted as a form of navigational guide, or at least a source of comfort, to those Greek mariners.

The north-eastern wind has risen to Force 6, and the *Dugi Otok* pitches and rolls in the foam-topped waves off Kefalonia. To the east is the crest of Mount Neriton, the highest point on the island of Ithaca. The same winds that buffet the tanker blew Odysseus off course, and made his journey home from Troy last not a month, but twenty years.

The extraordinary story of the King of Ithaca's return remains vivid today, 2,700 years after it was transcribed. But for those Greek navigators, it was already an ancient tale. It did not portray the Mediterranean world of the eighth century BCE, but a world 500 years earlier, the Mycenaean Bronze Age. Homer's poem emphasised its antiquity by being written in a language that was archaic to its readers and listeners – as distant from them as Chaucer's English is to us.

The world that held the palaces of Odysseus at Ithaca, Nestor at Pylos, and of Agamemnon at Mycenae, famed for its golden facemask, had disappeared. The Mycenaean Age, with its network of trade routes across the Mediterranean and the Black Sea, had come to an abrupt end. The cause of its collapse is debated, but deforestation and agricultural methods had led to rapid soil erosion and a steady diminishing of productive land. Meanwhile the global climate was shifting, which produced harsh droughts in the Aegean.

---

16   B. Cunliffe, *Europe Between the Oceans: 9000 BC to AD 1000*, Yale University Press, 2008, Chapter 9.

As the archaeologist Barry Cunliffe notes, the states of the eastern Mediterranean were inherently unstable: 'They were controlled by elites who owed their power to their ability . . . to maintain a constant flow of the rare or exotic commodities used in diplomacy and trade. Failure in any part of the system would have caused the entire edifice to crumble.'[17] The landscape and history of this region provide us with a woeful lesson on the impacts of climate change and the ecological limits of society.

In late August 2007, as the *Dugi Otok* travelled along this stretch of coast on a previous journey, the breeze from the east carried a heavy smoke load from the forest fires burning uncontrollably in the northern Peloponnese. Greece has been suffering from increasing levels of drought, and the scrub and trees on the mountains have been burning with greater frequency since the 1990s.

The seaway upon which the *Dugi Otok* travels is part of the passage of oil from Azerbaijan to Western Europe, and the planned lifespan of BTC implies that tankers carrying its crude will ply this route for at least the next four decades. This relentless traffic in oil pushes up the global temperature and brings with it drought and fire. At some point the collision between the world's atmosphere and this trade will lead to the latter being constrained. But what events will force the *Dugi Otok* and her sister ships to cease their passage, and the demise of this trade route? What events will lead to the BTC pipeline being retired early, for it to become – in the language of finance – a 'stranded asset'?

DAY 4, 04:59 – 970 NM – 3,751 KM – NORTHERN IONIAN SEA

As the *Dugi Otok* leaves Corfu off her stern and enters Italian waters, she comes under the watchful gaze of the Italian Coastguard and its vessels, such as the *Bovienzo*. These boats patrol the central Mediterranean, particularly in search of migrants from North Africa heading towards the coasts of Europe. Their sea journey is notoriously dangerous. In the last week of March 2009, an estimated 1,200 passengers attempted the crossing. Of these only twenty-three survived. Hundreds of migrants went missing after two boats bound for Italy sank off Libya in separate incidents. One of the vessels was crammed with 342 people.[18]

With our UK passports in hand, we have just travelled by train effortlessly across Turkey's border with the European Union. But EU laws prevent these individuals from entering by plane or regular ferries, and they are forced to crowd into unseaworthy vessels and entrust their lives to the weather. As we had seen at Krazny Most in Georgia and at Türkgözü in Turkey, much of the EU's border control is outsourced to neighbouring countries. In the Caucasus, Brussels-funded patrols, fences and cameras hinder migrants moving west. In the central Mediterranean, control is

---

17   Ibid., p. 238.
18   'Italy-Bound Migrant Boat Sinks off Libya, 21 Dead', 30 March 2009, at reuters. com.

outsourced to Libya – then under the government of Colonel Gaddafi.[19] By 2009, Italy had supplied the Libyan Navy with six ultra-fast *Bigliani* patrol boats armed with 30mm guns, specifically to intercept Africans attempting to flee to Europe.[20] Interception is not about rescuing passengers whose boats have sunk, and there have been repeated reports of live-fire attacks by the Libyan Navy on vessels carrying migrants.[21] Military resources are expended both to obstruct the flow of people, and – in the Gulf of Aden – to enforce the flow of fossil fuels.

This effective militarisation of the Mediterranean has radically reduced the number of migrants reaching Italy. But tens of thousands are still trying to make the journey to Europe, forced into the precarious crossing in large part by the challenge of survival in the countries from which they come. One of the handful of migrants to be picked from the sea by the coastguard in March 2009 was twenty-two-year-old Moussa, whose story is typical. He had arrived in the coastal city of Zuwarah, near the Libyan–Tunisian border, from his native Niger. He joined others who came to the port asking for a boat to carry them the 300 kilometres across the sea to Malta, Sicily or the Italian island of Lampedusa.

When the appointed time arrived, Moussa was trucked west into the open Libyan Desert in the middle of the night. Several hundred others were already waiting there. Before dawn, they were guided down to a beach and told to wade out to the converted fishing boat anchored just offshore. Its small engine was running, ready to depart at the first sight of the Libyan police. They were expected to be on board, without shelter, for thirty hours.

Coming from Nigeria and Niger, Sudan and Somalia, the passengers were fleeing devastating poverty and resource wars. Drought and soil degradation have been forcing Nigerien farmers to move from village to village for decades. The dry spells are becoming longer and longer while the gaps between them shrink, making cultivation extremely challenging. Whole crops have been lost before the rainfall makes growing possible again.[22] Spreading desertification means that sometimes it is not possible simply to move to the next village. Rather than face a slow death back

---

19   Now under the National Transitional Council.
20   S. Brom and A. Kurz, eds, *Strategic Survey for Israel 2010*, Institute for National Security Studies, 2010; 'Libya: End Live Fire Against Suspected Boat Migrants, 16 December 2010, at hrw.org.
21   B. Frelick, *Pushed Back, Pushed Around: Italy's Forced Return of Boat Migrants and Asylum Seekers, Libya's Mistreatment of Migrants and Asylum Seekers*, Human Rights Watch, 2009.
22   K. Warner, C. Ehrhart and A. de Sherbinin, *In Search of Shelter: Mapping the Effects of Climate Change on Human Migration and Displacement*, United Nations University, May 2009; T. Afifi, *Niger: Case Study Report – Environmental Change and Forced Migration Scenarios*, EACH-FOR, 2009.

home, Moussa had consciously chosen to make the risky journey northwards in search of survival and a safer life.

The vessel that Moussa and his fellow voyagers took sank, hit by the fearsome *qibli*, a desiccating gale that blows from the desert and carries whirlwinds of sand. He was lucky to be picked up by the Italian Coastguard, but survival only meant internment in a camp on the island of Lampedusa, before deportation back to Libya.

This growing wave of mass migration is largely the product of shifts in the world's weather patterns. We heard stories of declining rainfall in the Caucasus and Turkey. In Central and West Africa, as more land transforms into desert, there is a more brutal illustration of how climate change impacts upon communities. All the evidence suggests that as carbon dioxide pours into the atmosphere, the cycle of droughts and migration will become more acute in the coming decades. In May 2009 the Global Humanitarian Forum, chaired by the former UN secretary general, Kofi Annan, produced a study that calculated that 600 million people will have been displaced by climate change by 2030. This is the human seascape through which oil from Azerbaijan is to be carried for the next forty years.

DAY 4, 07:29 – 1,005 NM – 3,816 KM – STRAIT OF OTRANTO, ALBANIA AND ITALY

As dawn breaks, the tanker enters the Straits of Otranto, once the busiest shipping lane of the Roman world. Wedged between Albania and the heel of Italy, this 72-kilometre liquid highway connects the Ionian Sea with the Adriatic. Across this short stretch of water, first-century sail and oar-powered triremes and liburnians hurried back and forth between the ports of Brundisium and Dyrrachium – present-day Brindisi and Durres. Senators and soldiers travelled down the Appian Way from Rome, crossed the Straits, and headed along the Via Egnatia to Byzantium. Merchants and slaves bearing silk, spices and cotton from Asia travelled in the opposite direction. This was the continuation of the trade route that ran to Sebaste (Ankara) and on to Theodosiopolis (Erzurum), and beyond the borders of the empire to the east.

This ancient artery has been identified as part of the EU's 'Southern Energy Corridor', a planned element of the European gas grid. A proposed pipeline to be built by the Norwegian company Statoil and the German E.ON would pump gas drawn from the Shah Deniz field through the Turkish network from Erzurum to Thrace, and then via the proposed Trans-Adriatic Pipeline through Albania, and under the sea to Brindisi. A parallel gas line, called the Interconnector Turkey–Greece–Italy Pipeline, is proposed to run just to the south, through Greece. Both are competing with the grander scheme of Nabucco, fighting for public funding and gas reserves. The progress of all three is high on the agenda of Richard Morningstar, special envoy of the US secretary of state for Eurasian energy, and Jean-Arnold Vinois, at the European Commission's Energy Directorate General.

We watch the *Dugi Otok* on the marinetraffic.com website, a red arrowhead navigating the straits amid the passenger ferries carrying tourists, with a sprinkling of yachts. Visibility is good, and adjusting course to avoid hazards must be easy.

DAY 5, 03:29 – 1,285 NM – 4,335 KM – DUGI OTOK, CROATIA

The Adriatic was once Venice's lake. For several hundred years, the 'Most Serene Republic' – La Serenissima – held military and economic primacy over these waters. All vessels passing through the Straits of Otranto were to offer priority to Venice's waterfront warehouses, in city districts such as the Rialto, for the purchase of their goods.

The Republic did not set out to conquer the entire coastline of the Adriatic, but all ports of significance were to operate under its direct or indirect authority. With its many natural harbours, much of today's Croatian Dalmatia was absorbed into the growing empire through adept diplomacy or military force. The administrators and lieutenants sent from the home city seldom ventured far inland. The mountains rising to the east marked the frontier, and their slopes provided Venice with a key commodity – wood. La Serenissima depended upon imported timber for its foundations (the piles driven into the lagoon upon which the city was built) and for its defence (the construction of war galleys in the Arsenale). The mountains of Dalmatia were largely deforested by Venice.

On the Croatian coast, a thin island runs parallel to the mainland. This is Dugi Otok, or 'Long Island', from which the tanker takes its name. Beyond lies the town of Zadar, home of Tankerska Plovidba, which owns and manages the vessel, contracting it out to oil-traders such as BP's Integrated Supply and Trading division.

Zadar has been a seafaring town for millennia. In 384 BCE it dispatched 300 ships to resist Greek colonisers, and the city's continuing maritime strength saw repeated conflict with the growing power of medieval Venice. Perceiving Zadar as a threat to its ambitions, La Serenissima launched assault after assault throughout the twelfth century, claiming that the town harboured pirates.

Unable to subdue this Slav rival alone, the Republic made use of superior forces. Venice was contracted to transport the Fourth Crusade to Egypt, and then Palestine. When the French knights were unable to pay their bills, the Doge Enrico Dandolo offered temporarily to ignore their debts if they helped deal with this Christian thorn in the Republic's side.[23] The Crusade was diverted, and on 10 November 1202 a fierce attack ended with the town being pillaged

---

23   A. Wiel, *Venice*, Kessinger Publishing, 1894.

and burned. To prevent Zadar's power from ever re-emerging, the Venetians tore it down brick by brick.[24]

Dandolo saw the potential for Venice to become the trading power of the eastern Mediterranean, *La Dominante*. But the strength of the Byzantine Empire and its continued control over the seaways constrained Venetian access to the Levant and the Black Sea – and thus to slaves, sugar, silks and spices. So the Doge made profitable use of the Fourth Crusade by directing it to Byzantium's capital: Constantinople.

The Byzantines had long held an important technological advantage over the West: 'Greek Fire'. This liquid was created from crude oil brought by camel train from the pits of Balakhani, near Baku. In the midst of battle the liquid was pumped through tubes and ignited, setting fire to attacking ships. But this time the Byzantines were deprived of their last line of defence: the Venetians had discovered how to treat leather with chemicals, rendering their vessels invulnerable.[25] Christendom's largest and richest city was assaulted and captured. Days of looting and plundering followed, in the most profitable of the Crusader sieges.[26]

Byzantium was divided up between the Crusader lords and Venice. Dandolo sought not vast tracts of territory, but strategic islands suitable for naval bases and harbours in which its commercial convoys might stop and resupply.[27] The Winged Lion of St Mark, the symbol of Venice, fluttered over ports and islands such as Rhodes, Methoni and Kefalonia. For five centuries, Venice's military helped secure the trading ventures in which the city's merchant families invested. The Republic's bureaucracy maintained surveillance over rival powers, subject peoples and its own citizens, to ensure stability and protect its network of interests.

With the rise of the Ottoman Turks, the Venetian galleys were pushed back. One after another, fortresses and colonies fell to the new power, whose armies marched westwards from Constantinople across the Balkans, and reached the frontier of the Republic just inland from Zadar.[28] The decline of Venice's military power went hand-in-hand with the withering of her trade routes.

Present-day Republicans in Washington, DC, seek to learn from Venice's success, perceiving in La Serenissima's domination a means of preserving US economic power without the costs of ongoing occupations.[29] Indeed, the model of Venice can help us understand how states such as Azerbaijan and Georgia lie within the imperium of the US and EU. These contemporary powers are not driven by desire for territory or tax revenues, but by desire for access to resources

24   T. Madden, *Enrico Dandolo and the Rise of Venice*, JHU Press, 2003, p. 150.

25   Stone, *Turkey: A Short History*, Thames & Hudson, 2011, p. 22.

26   J. Morris, *The Venetian Empire: A Sea Voyage*, Penguin, 1990.

27   L. Bergreen, *Marco Polo: From Venice to Xanadu*, Knopf, 2007, p. 37.

28   P. R. Magocsi, *Historical Atlas of Central Europe*, Thames & Hudson, 2002, p. 58.

29   D. Ignatius, 'From Venice, a Lesson on Empire', 20 September 2006, at washingtonpost.com.

and markets – resources such as oil, and markets such as those for oil products. But this depends upon trade routes structured in terms favourable to the West, and secured through military dominance – routes such as the 'energy corridor' along which we are travelling, which runs so close to US forces at Krtsanisi in Georgia, İncirlik in Turkey, and NATO's Aviano airbase near Venice.

DAY 5, 08:08 – 1,350 NM – 4,455 KM – NORTHERN ADRIATIC

One hundred and fifty kilometres north of Zadar lies the port city of Rijeka. Once known by its Italian name, Fiume, it was a node in the first Oil Road from the Caspian. In the early 1880s the market for kerosene in the Austro-Hungarian Empire was booming, fed mainly by the products of Rockefeller's Standard Oil, imported from the US. But the Austrian branch of the Rothschild Bank began a rival venture that would transform the Central European energy world.

Under the technical direction of Milutin Barac, a brilliant young Croatian chemist, the continent's largest refinery with the most advanced technology was built along the shore on the western edge of Fiume. By early 1884, the plant was transporting twenty train wagons a day of kerosene and other products along the Sud Bahn, north to Laibach (Ljubljana) and Vienna, Prague and Budapest – a railway majority owned by the Rothschilds. Initially the Fiume refinery processed crude from Pennsylvania, but soon the raw oil was coming from Baku. The Paris branch of the Rothschild Bank had purchased the Caucasus-based BNITO, financed the construction of the Baku–Batumi Railway, and built a fleet of tankers with Marcus Samuel to transport kerosene.

Crude was soon being transported from the shores of the Caspian on the railway across the Caucasus, and by tanker from Batumi via the Bosphorus to the northern Adriatic. It was refined into kerosene at Fiume and distributed by rail wagons as far afield as Salzburg. Each one of these stages was part-owned by either the Austrian or French House of Rothschild. This was the first incarnation of the industrial Oil Road along which we are travelling, and it lasted a mere generation.

In 1911 the Rothschilds, unsettled by the militancy of the workforce in Batumi and Baku and the destruction caused by the 1905 Revolution, sold their Caucasus assets to Royal Dutch Shell. The outbreak of World War I three years later halted all exports of oil from Batumi. The defeat of the Central Powers in 1918 saw Fiume, like her sister city Trieste, further up the Adriatic, gripped by a whirlwind of political turmoil. When the Austro-Hungarian Empire was dismantled, the oil port could no longer serve its original market. It became overwhelmed by a struggle between the Italians and their Slav neighbours.

On 12 September 1919, the Italian poet Gabriele D'Annunzio arrived triumphantly in a red sports car at the head of a column of 297 black-shirted Arditi followers, and seized the city. At first the intention was to hand the territory to Italy, but the latter refused to recognise the action, and D'Annunzio declared

Fiume the independent Regency of Carnaro, and himself as 'Duce' or 'Il Commandante'. Fiume became a crucible of political experimentation, the first self-defined fascist state. Seismic events were happening along the Oil Road – six months later the Bolsheviks seized Baku, and a year after that Ordjonikidze rode victorious into Tbilisi on a white horse.

Four days after the coup, the Futurist poet Filippo Marinetti hurried to D'Annunzio's side, filled with the excitement of what was taking place. In its fifteen-month life, the Regency was seen by many as the model of future political structures, inspiring the ambitions of Mussolini and, later, Hitler. Here the culture of dictatorship and rituals of fascism were practised and developed, including the rhetoric and the balcony address, corporatist economics, and the fascist salute. Fiume was proclaimed a purely 'Italian' city. Many Croats were expelled, including Milutin Barac, who remained responsible for the refinery's operations thirty-six years after first taking the job.[30] The plant itself, which employed 500 workers, was shut down.[31]

D'Annunzio's Regency surrendered to the troops of the kingdom of Italy in December 1920, but the fascists returned within three years. After 'The March on Rome' in 1922, one of Benito Mussolini's immediate priorities was to reduce Italy's dependence on British and American oil companies and build a state-owned industry.

Within a month of seizing power, the new regime took steps to buy the refinery from the Rothschilds, assuming full shareholder control by 1923. The Hungarian-built, Austrian-financed and Croatian-managed plant had already been selected as the 'nucleus of the Italian oil programme', and the basis for the new national oil company Agip.[32] By 1935 the refinery was among 'the most important mainstays of the country's armed forces', fuelling the invasion and occupation of Ethiopia.[33] The existing plant had been refitted to prioritise petrol production, in parallel with Italy's militarisation and colonial ambitions. Meanwhile, a new Agip refinery was constructed at Muggia, next to Trieste.

However, Mussolini's intention to be free of the foreign oil companies was far less successful than Stalin's moves in the Soviet Union, partly because Italy lacked a crude source similar to Azerbaijan's. Throughout the 1920s, the Anglo-Persian Oil Company – later BP – helped supply the fascist state with oil products, and tried, unsuccessfully, to buy a percentage of Agip. By the 1930s, Italy was Anglo-Persian's fourth largest market for gasoline.[34]

---

30   V. Dekić, *Crude Oil Processing in Rijeka: 1882–2004*, INA Industrija nafte, 2004.

31   M. A. Ledeen, *D'Annunzio: The First Duce*, Transaction Publishers, 2009, p. 109.

32   V. Dekić, 'The Oil Refinery in Rijeka: A Story of Survival' in *The Rothschild Archive: Review of the Year 2004–2005*, Rothschild Archive, 2005.

33   Dekić, *Crude Oil Processing*.

34   J. H. Bamberg, *The History of the British Petroleum Company, Vol. 2: The Anglo-Iranian Years 1928–1954*, CUP, 1994, p. 124.

After World War II, a restructured Agip grew from its fascist roots, expanding into Nigeria, Libya and ultimately the new Oil Road across the Caucasus itself. The company, now subsumed into Italy's larger oil corporation ENI, is one of the shareholders in BTC Co. Meanwhile Fiume is no longer Italian. At the end of World War II, Tito's *partizani* wrested the city from the German army, and the refinery became a key part of Yugoslav industry, eventually becoming the Croatian port of Rijeka. This city-incubator of fascism was governed by six different states in the twentieth century – echoing the upheaval in Baku and Batumi during the same period.

DAY 5, 14:00 – 1,432 NM – 4,607 KM – MUGGIA, ITALY

As the *Dugi Otok* heads north, the Adriatic is narrowing. Soon the tanker will be docking at Muggia in the Gulf of Trieste. There is a change in the rhythm of the engines as the vessel makes her final approach. The 790,000 barrels of black crude in the ship's hold are nearing the white geometry of the tank farm on the hillside overlooking the bay. The small pilot boat pulls alongside. From the bridge, the pilot instructs the vessel's officers on how to manoeuvre into port, and then to their allotted docking station at the oil terminal.

Twin tugboats move close alongside, providing a gentle nudge now and then to keep the tanker on track into the Vallone di Muggia. As the *Dugi Otok* docks at the number-one pontoon of the Societa Italiana per l'Oleodotto Transalpino, thick docking chains are run out, placed around large steel cleats, and tightened.

The arrival of a consignment of Azeri crude in Muggia has stirred activity in the office of BP Integrated Supply and Trading (IST) at Canary Wharf, in London's Docklands. From here, BP tracks its global movement of crude in pipelines, ships and storage tanks. BP IST has overseen the delivery of the crude we are following from BP Azerbaijan to BP Oil Germany through the BTC pipeline, on the *Dugi Otok*, and now through the Transalpine Pipeline.

At the point of unloading, the cargo is checked by the Camin Cargo Assurance Inspection company, working under contract for IST. The inspection team conducts the checks by using BP's Global Cargo Assurance System. This computer-based technology should issue an automatic alert if there is a variance of anything more than 0.2 per cent between what was loaded at Ceyhan and what is unloaded at Muggia. With the oil price in the spring of 2009 running at around $50 a barrel, 0.2 per cent of *Dugi Otok's* cargo could be worth $79,000.

When the crude has been pumped out of the ship's hold to the tank farm in the hills, BP's IST team will have completed their sale of Azeri oil. Soon, after the crew of the *Dugi Otok* have taken a few hours on shore, the tanker will head south again to collect another load, perhaps at Ceyhan, perhaps at another port. Her course will be determined by the oil-traders speculating on changing prices. Everything is in motion.

Part IV THE ROAD

MAP V   ITALY–AUSTRIA–GERMANY

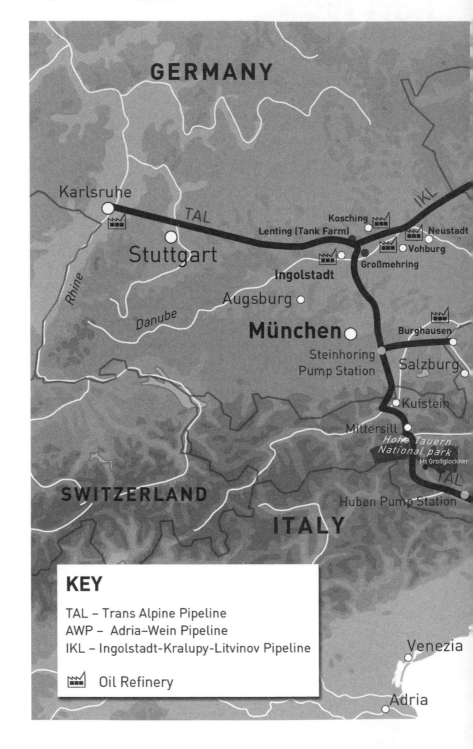

GERMANY

Karlsruhe

TAL

Kosching

Lenting (Tank Farm)

Neustadt

Vohburg

Stuttgart

Ingolstadt

Großmehring

Augsburg

IKL

Rhine

Danube

München

Burghausen

Steinhoring
Pump Station

Salzburg

Kufstein

Mittersill

Hohe Tauern
National park

Mt Großglockner

TAL

SWITZERLAND

Huben Pump Station

ITALY

Venezia

Adria

KEY

TAL – Trans Alpine Pipeline
AWP – Adria–Wein Pipeline
IKL – Ingolstadt-Kralupy-Litvinov Pipeline

Oil Refinery

18 THEY HAVE LONG ARMS . . . LIKE THE ARMS OF AN OCTOPUS

TAL KP 1 – 4,608 KM – VALLONE DI MUGGIA, ITALY

'How the pipeline works? They put the oil from these ships into tanks, at the tank farm up on the hill, then they pump it to Ingolstadt in Germany.' Our train has carried us to Trieste, and we have made our way to the town of Muggia, at the southern edge of the city. In the harbour of Muggia we meet with Marzia Piron, a marine biologist studying the Gulf of Trieste. Part of the shallow northern Adriatic, it was as rich in fish, historically, as İskenderun Bay. Marzia has brought us to Fabio, one of the local squid fishers, who is working on his boat by the quayside. Fabio talks of the Transalpine Pipeline as he picks the *seppia* from his nets, his hands and clothing covered in their black ink. His family have been fishermen in the region for over four centuries. His father moved his boat here in the 1960s from the harbour of Capodistria, which is now across the border in Slovenia and known as Koper. In referring to it by its former name, Fabio shows that his family is one of the thousands of Italians who left Yugoslavia as refugees in the two decades after World War II.

The harsh wind of the Adriatic *bora* whistles through the rigging of the yachts in the adjacent marina. Across the blue of the Vallone di Muggia, this wide inlet of the Gulf, the foot ferries track back and forth to Trieste. Fabio knows Marzia well, and quickly warms to his theme. 'There was a big oil spill in the Vallone in 1974 or '75. They swept all the oil into this harbour in order to pump it out. But the mud at the bottom of the Vallone is contaminated. The tankers churn up the mud, which gets onto the nets: it's a lot of work cleaning them.' He says there are too many 'forbidden areas' in the Gulf, because of the *zona*, the channel for the ships, which makes fishing difficult. 'Sometimes there are ten or twelve ships waiting for the oil terminal, and the Golfo is little'. We ask if he has problems with the coastguards. 'I'd better not say anything about the coastguard. They work to get money from the fishermen and not to solve our problems.' He says fishing has declined because the species of fish have changed, as the water has become warmer since the 1970s; all the phosphorous pollution means that algae have bloomed. 'The worst year was in 1987 – we had to stop the *seppia* fishing.' As we part, he concludes: 'I worked at the Esso refinery here. I was happy to work there until it closed on 22 November 1987 – I remember the date well.'

We have lunch with Marzia on the terrace of the Ristorante Marina. There is the sound of couples conversing at the other tables, the click-clack of the waitress's heels, the clatter of plates in the kitchen, and the far-off rumble of some industrial plant. Through the blurred, thick polythene windows is the Vallone; the dimpled surface of the water constantly moving, and the bulk of two tankers can be seen. We can make out the *Dugi Otok*, riding higher in the water after unloading, and the *Zarifa Aliyeva*, named after Ilham Aliyev's mother. The oil pumped from the hold of the tanker passes through a pipeline to the Valle Dolina storage tanks belonging to Societa Italiana per l'Oleodotto Transalpino – known as SIOT. From the tank farm it will be pushed through the Transalpine Pipeline over the Alps to Germany.

The restaurant, like the yachts, belongs to the sedate, leisured realm of the European middle class. It feels a long way from the near-deserted Balık Restoran in Gölovası. Muggia happily trades on its Venetian past. Scrubbed lions of San Marco are mounted above the archway in the old town walls. This was a bastion of the Republic facing the Austrians in Trieste across the Vallone. Meanwhile SIOT is tucked away up the valley beyond signs that say 'No Entrance' in three languages. Few tourists ever notice the immense hub of energy and wealth that lies in the hills.

It is only May, but the heat of the afternoon is pounding. Foolishly, we leave Marzia and walk along the main road, which is heavy with traffic, to the east of Muggia, across the weed-clogged River Ospo. We want to visit the place once occupied by the Aquilina refinery, where Fabio worked. There is nothing there, just a great expanse of gravel, broken concrete and scrub. This is the site of the Agip plant built under Mussolini in the 1930s. After the war it was brought by Exxon, who ran it until its closure in the late 1980s. But now the land has lain barren for over twenty years. Fabio said that the soil is contaminated and that they would have to remove all of it in order to reuse the place. It reminds us of staring at the factory sites in Gəncə.

The Transalpine Pipeline, known as TAL, and the SIOT terminal, are children of the Cold War. Both are products and creators of a particular set of geopolitical realities. The Soviet Union constructed the southern branch of the Druzhba, or Friendship, pipeline from Russia to Czechoslovakia and Hungary between 1960 and 1964. The Bratsvo, or Brotherhood, gas pipeline followed soon after. Flush with Khrushchev's promise of economic plenty, the USSR now provided cheap oil and gas to countries such as East Germany, whose armies, only two decades before, had invaded the Soviet Union, reaching as far as the peaks of the Caucasus. Former enemies now embraced with friendship and brotherhood.

The Transalpine Pipeline was a counterpoint to the Soviet ones. Driven by US and UK capital, it would link Italy, Austria and West Germany – all previously Axis powers, whose industrial infrastructure the Allies had bombed. Austria and West Germany were still divided into areas of military control by the victorious Allies, and the pipeline would run through both British and American Army sectors.

In the early 1960s, Saudi Arabia, Iran, Kuwait and Iraq all demanded that the foreign companies who extracted their oil increase their rate of production in order to generate a higher income for each state. President Kennedy's administration was also eager that corporations in Middle Eastern states should ramp up their output, for the higher revenues would help bolster local regimes against popular opposition, and thereby halt the spread of Soviet influence. This logic was most clear in Iran, where the shah vociferously demanded higher production from BP, which held a commanding stake in Middle Eastern oil and 40 per cent of the Iranian oil company.

Between 1960 and 1969, crude extraction rocketed and the flow of oil into Western European markets increased dramatically. In Saudi Arabia, production jumped from 1 million to 3.5 million barrels; in Iran, from 1 million to 4 million. In the same decade, Baku's production rose 22 per cent to its Soviet peak of 450,000 barrels, but the output of the region of the Middle East and North Africa grew by nearly 400 per cent, to 13.5 million barrels. Faced with this vastly increased flow of crude, the Western oil companies needed to stimulate consumption. In the same way that the Rothschilds, facing saturated European markets in the late 1880s, drove up kerosene consumption in the Far East, so the oil majors in the 1960s strove to reshape demand and restructure transport routes in order to sell their products. West Germany was a key area of potential growth, but the companies needed infrastructure to bring oil to future customers – infrastructure such as the Transalpine Pipeline. In 1963, the American engineering company Bechtel was hired to assess and plan a pipeline across the Alps.

The choice of Trieste as a starting point for the Transalpine Pipeline was a deliberate move in the power play between the West and the USSR, for the city was a symbol of Cold War politics. In his famous speech of 1946, Winston Churchill proclaimed: 'From Stettin in the Baltic to Trieste in the Adriatic an "iron curtain" has descended across the continent. Behind that line lie all . . . the populations . . . in what I must call the Soviet sphere.'[1] According to the post–World War II peace treaty, the Free Territory of Trieste was to be run by the United Nations. As in Berlin, the Free Territory was divided into zones – Zone A to be administered by Anglo-American forces, Zone B by Yugoslavia. When, after seven years, the UN was still unable to agree on a governor, the Territory was abolished. Zone B became part of Yugoslavia, including the town of Capodistria/Koper, while Zone A was taken by Italy, including the city of Trieste and the town of Muggia.[2]

---

1   M. A. Kishlansky, *Sources of World History*, Harper Collins, 1995, pp. 298–302.
2   P. R. Magocsi, *Historical Atlas of Central Europe*, Thames & Hudson, 2002, pp. 159–61.

The sense of political tension is still clearly present in the pipeline's geography: the heart of the TAL system, the vast SIOT tank farm, lies only 450 metres from the current border with Slovenia, which in 1967 was behind the Iron Curtain. If it seems curious that such a vital piece of infrastructure was placed so close to a potentially hostile power, the pipeline itself was an assertion that Trieste fell within the Western sphere. Its political role was similar to that played in Georgia by BTC and Baku–Supsa, which function as bridgeheads of Western power-projection.

Indeed, the Transalpine Pipeline, built forty years before BTC, in many ways prefigures it. Both projects ran across three states. Both were heavily influenced by the American State Department and the British Foreign Office. Both were owned by a consortium of companies, though BP was central to their commissioning. Both were in part designed by the same corporation, Bechtel. At its opening in June 1967, the 465 km Transalpine Pipeline was hailed as a heroic engineering achievement, travelling to altitudes greater than any pipeline had gone before.

Four decades later, TAL is still jointly owned by eight companies,[3] though the membership of the original consortium has changed. Austria's OMV oil company now owns the largest stake, with 25 per cent, while BP holds 14.5 per cent.[4] The pipeline is operated by the Transalpine Pipeline Company, which has three different subsidiaries in the three countries, with SIOT the operator in Italy.

Two decades after the fall of the Berlin Wall, TAL continues to hold geopolitical relevance, albeit in a radically different context. As SIOT's general manager, Adriano Del Prete, notes, 'TAL is a very important source of supply, because we cover 75% of the needs of Austria, 100% of Bavaria, 50% of Baden-Wurttemberg and 27% of the Czech Republic's oil.'[5] The precise origin of this crude changes from day to day, depending on the tankers that arrive in the Gulf of Trieste. In the year 2010, 30 per cent of TAL's load had been brought to Muggia from the oilfields of North Africa, but over half of the tankers shipped crude from the states of the former Soviet Union. The vast majority of these came from Ceyhan.

The exact percentage of oil that comes from the Azeri–Chirag–Gunashli field offshore from Baku is always shifting, but the political significance of this trade route is constant. This oilfield was once part of the USSR. If its crude reached Central Europe in the 1960s, it did so via the Soviet Druzhba

---

3   OMV (25 per cent), Royal Dutch Shell (24 per cent), ExxonMobil (16 per cent), Ruhr Oel (11 per cent), Eni (10 per cent), BP (9 per cent), ConocoPhillips (3 per cent), Total SA (2 per cent).

4   BP owns 14.5 per cent – 9 per cent directly as BP, and a further 5.5 per cent as 11 per cent of TAL is held by Ruhr Oel, which BP jointly owns with Rosneft (tal-oil. com).

5   H. Guliyeva, 'The Incredible Journey', *BP Magazine* 2 (2006), p. 26.

pipeline. Now this field is in Azerbaijan, and its crude is carried via pipelines and tankers that completely avoid the territory of Russia, just as intended by the Clinton administration and its servants, Sandy Berger and Richard Morningstar. TAL remains the jugular vein running to the heart of Central Europe, and the liquid it carries is still heavy with the political tensions between the West and Russia.

TAL KP 1 – 4,609 KM – SAN DORLIGO DELLA VALLE (DOLINA), ITALY

Marzia has kindly rung the public relations officer of SIOT. They have agreed that it might be possible for us to have an interview with the administrator, but a written and signed request would need to be delivered to the tank farm. So, weaving her Fiat through the traffic with speed and grace, Marzia takes us past the industrial zone, under the flyovers to the SIOT approach road. Beyond the sign that says 'entrance is forbidden without work papers', the grass verges have been clipped with precision. They are overshadowed by a high mesh fence topped with barbed wire and backed by a metre-wide tangle of razor-wire. We can see the great white bulk of the crude tanks, with their natty red trim. Each one has a large number painted on its side.

The guard in the entrance cabin peers through the slid-back glass, as Marzia proffers the fresh white envelope. He takes the letter, and it flops into a tray in a desultory manner. He looks at us with an expression that says 'You'll be lucky', and there is a flash of anger in Marzia's doleful eyes. We never receive a response. Our phone calls are not returned; an appointment cannot be fixed.

It is surprisingly difficult to find anybody in Trieste who will talk about the pipeline. Marzia had asked around persistently on our behalf, but was met with a resounding silence. Her partner Simone knew a man who worked at the terminal until recently, but he too refused to say anything unless we paid him 'a lot of money', because he thought he would be sued for talking. Then Simone hit on the idea of contacting Captain Bruno Volpi Lisjak, who lives in Slovenia. Bruno had spent his entire working life involved with the sea, from crewing cargo ships to the Port of London in the 1950s to being a pivotal figure in the docks of Trieste in the 1970s and 1980s. Now retired, he spends his time writing books on the history of Slovenian fishing.

The road to the Italian border takes us from one world to another: from the thronging city by the shore to the wide open, high plateau of the *carso*. This realm of limestone and underground rivers gave its name to a geological formation: karst landscape. The international border between these two EU states is now hardly marked, and the highway takes us speedily to Kriz. On the outskirts of the village is a newly built bungalow surrounded by a pristine vegetable patch. Bruno, who answers the door with his wife, is an energetic seventy-year-old. Together with Simone, we settle down for coffee.

When we mention TAL, he plunges straight into the history of Trieste itself. The city's fate was decided at the Yalta Conference of 1945. Although Stalin was eager that it become part of the new Yugoslavia, Churchill was adamant that Trieste come under Western influence: the city, he felt, was vital in supplying Vienna, thereby ensuring that Austria was Western-aligned. To keep the citizens of Vienna warm, the harbour of Trieste was turned into a coal terminal for the railway that fed the Austrian capital, carrying fuel across the *carso* and the Alps. The dockside became a mountain of Welsh anthracite, but without the Atlantic drizzle to damp it down, black dust was blown across the city. The Triestini at their café tables on the piazzas grumbled about the British.

The docks of Trieste languished, shorn both of the Austro-Hungarian Empire that had given birth to them, and of Mussolini's Empire that had briefly revivified them. Now Trieste was no longer on a great trade route but, like Berlin, was almost stranded on the fault-line between the West and the Soviet bloc. Perhaps the city would become a shadow, like Venice, but without her allure and beauty? This challenge was particularly acute for Bruno who, by the late 1960s, was the manager of the shipbuilding yards whose livelihood came from the construction and maintenance of vessels.

Bruno explains with delight how he solved the conundrum. In the 1960s the Soviet Union was experiencing its boom under Khrushchev. But, while the Black Sea merchant fleet quadrupled its tonnage, the Russians did not have adequate shipyards and dry docks to service their vessels. Without regular maintenance the ships were unable to meet the standards required for them to gain insurance from Lloyds of London.[6] This one shipping insurer provided the internationally recognised certification that allowed merchant vessels from one state access to the ports of another state. While most of Europe skulked under an anti-Soviet embargo, Trieste threw open its arms to the USSR and the refitting of her ships. Soon vessels bearing the hammer and sickle on their funnels thronged to the Gulf of Trieste.

'I have been to Baku. Twice. To the Ministry of Oil and Gas', Bruno tells us. He explains how, after the Soviets found oil in the depths of the Caspian during the 1970s, they wanted drill ships. They had ordered two such vessels from the French, but these needed spare parts which, under the West's embargo, the USSR could not obtain. So the ships were brought to Trieste and repaired as Italian vessels, before making their way to the Caspian via the Don–Volga Canal. It was these drill ships, exploring off Baku, that worked the mammoth 26 Commissars oilfield, today called Azeri–Chirag–Gunashli.

Bruno's analysis of the building of the SIOT oil terminal in the mid-1960s is precise and critical. Many people in Trieste were against it: 'They knew about the ecology of the area and they could see what was coming.' It was a political project driven by Rome and foreign governments, he says. 'The oil companies

---

6   The same paperwork as required by the *Murex* and *Dugi Otok*.

worked as a cartel and lied about the positive effects it would have on the city. They claimed that the terminal would give many jobs, and that the crews of the tankers would come into town and buy things. But in fact they were cheating. From my experience as a seaman and a manager of a yard, I knew well that tankers at a terminal will only stay about twenty-four hours for discharging, that nobody from the crew would come into town, that even the sex-workers would not make a dollar.'

A shadow of sadness settles on Bruno's face as he says, 'I didn't want to speak about this – but you pull out my tongue.' Gently, he explains that for over 1,000 years this has been a Slavic area. The Slav villages just inland from the coast developed distinct traditions in order to fish on the harsh, rocky shores of the eastern Adriatic. 'This region was 100 per cent Slovenian. It was the only place where Slovenes connected to the sea . . . and so they developed a particular culture.'

Bruno describes how, ever since the part of Istria that lies around Trieste was brought into Italy in 1919, the Italian state has been trying to displace the Slovenian population. The building of the oil terminal and the pipeline played a role in this process, for it would have made far more sense, logistically and economically, to send the tankers to the port of Monfalcone further to the north, at the very tip of the Adriatic. Monfalcone was better suited as an oil port than Muggia, far more sheltered from the *bora*. Choosing Muggia meant that the pipeline had to be buried in the *carso*, and many kilometres of solid rock had to be excavated. But selecting this route allowed the Italian state to expropriate the land of Slovenian farmers under the guise of a national project. He says the mayor of the Commune of Duino refused to agree to this plan, but was summoned to Rome and bullied until he signed the requisite papers. Many villages lost their connection to the sea: the distinct Slovenian fishing culture began to die with them.

The site for the SIOT tank farm was expropriated from the villages of Dolina and Bagnoli. The compound was built on the floor of the valley, on the flatter and well-watered land. In comparison, the small fields that the villages retained were on the *carso*, where the soil is poor and acidic. The land has to be backbreakingly cleared of rocks. It reminds us of how the best land at Gölovası, was taken by the Ceyhan Terminal.

Bruno explains that Rijeka is a good port for oil tankers because the water is deep. On the north-western side of Istria, however, the sea is shallow, so the shipping channels in the Gulf of Trieste and Vallone di Muggia have to be dredged. 'When they built the terminal they brought excavators from Holland, and for two years they had to dig. At Porto San Rocco and Punta Ronco there were big fights with the fishermen as their fishing grounds were destroyed.' Traditionally the Vallone had provided exceptional catches. Oysters were so prolific, and of such quality, that the Slovenian fishermen from the village of Servola, opposite Muggia, exported them to Vienna. When the Aquelina refinery was built in the 1930s, the seabed became polluted and was later dredged for the shipping channel.

This tale of a pipeline built forty years ago has many resonances with the BTC project. Here, too, the route was conceived in the ministries of distant powers – men in Washington and London in a struggle with Moscow. The states through which the pipeline would pass used the project to pursue ethnic and political agendas. And the oil companies pursued their own profit by playing off different sides against each other.

We have spent all morning with Bruno by the time he waves us goodbye from his vegtable garden: 'I will be interested to see the politics of the book. You have to be careful of the oil companies . . . they have long arms, like the arms of an octopus. Now I want nothing to do with the world. I have my tomatoes and my cabbages.'

We drive back across the border into Italy and head to Dolina, stopping in the blistering sun near the church tower. Behind it is the small village square, dominated by a war memorial: a grey marble cenotaph topped with a red star, newly repainted. Hung from pegs are small discs of pale beechwood suspended on yellow ribbons. Carefully incised on each disc are the name and dates of one of the dead:

LJUBOMIR SANCIN 9.7.1919–18.3.1944

There are three rows of these discs, and every name is Slovenian. At the base of the cenotaph a couple of new laurel wreaths are swathed in red ribbons, each inscribed with gold lettering, with the word *Communisti* prominent. A poster pinned to a sheltering tree has a 1940s photo of a band of liberating motorcycle riders, with the title 25th APRIL ARRIVANO I PARTIGIANI. Someone has carefully added the Slovenian word, in broad red felt-tip: PARTIZANI.

The symbolism underscores what Bruno told us. Here, in Italy, is a Slovenian village determinedly loyal to its Yugoslav Communist roots. The war memorial looks out over the former lands of the community, now dominated by the white tanks of SIOT. Two tankers unload at the piers beyond. Far out in the blue sea of the Gulf of Trieste, another tanker waits its turn.

We walk down the hill, past neat vegetable patches of peas and onions, through the cool woods, onto the lower land strung with vines and ranks of young olive trees which run right up to the green mesh fence and the tangle of razor-wire that marks the perimeter of SIOT. The vineyards and olive groves seem to contest the land that was expropriated. Perhaps one day they will return to their former soil, or maybe the site will be left barren like the old refinery on the shore. Nightingales sing from the oak woods; a redstart chatters somewhere in the compound. Coming from Tank number 32 is the hum of an engine – the sound of its belly being filled with the crude from the ship in the bay.

4,612 KM – TRIESTE, ITALY

4. We affirm that the world's magnificence has been enriched by a new beauty, the beauty of speed. A racing car whose hood is adorned with great pipes, like the serpents of explosive breath – a roaring car that seems to ride on grapeshot is more beautiful than the Victory of Samothrace.

11. We will sing of great crowds excited by work, by pleasure and by riot, we will sing of the vibrant fervour of arsenals and shipyards blazing with violent electric moons, greedy railway stations that devour smoke-plumed serpents, factories hung on clouds by the crooked lines of their smoke, adventurous steamers that sniff the horizon, deep chested locomotives whose wheels paw the tracks like the hooves of enormous steel horses bridled by tubing, and the sleek flight of planes whose propellers chatter in the wind like banners and seem to cheer like an enthu-siastic crowd.

Filippo Marinetti, *Manifesto of Futurism*, 1909[7]

It was in Trieste that the poet Filippo Marinetti and his colleagues created the first Futurist Evening, on 10 January 1910. The event was held in the Politeama Rossetti, a vast theatre, in honour of General Assinari Di Bernezzo, who had recently caused a scandal by expressing irredentist views. To hold such an event in an Austrian city, as Trieste was then, was a deliberate provocation.

Marinetti gave a public proclamation of the *Manifesto of Futurism*. The packed audience listened as he celebrated the city as *la nostra bella polveriera* – 'our beau-tiful powder-magazine'. Trieste, the Mediterranean port of the Austro-Hungarian Empire, was a hotbed of irredentism – the Italian Nationalist movement that strove to bring the lands of Trieste, Istria, Fiume, Zadar and the Trentino into Italy.[8] Modernity and the machine, as tools of liberation, were harnessed to the cause of nationalism, just as the Bolsheviks later harnessed them to Communism, and Atatürk harnessed them to the new Republic.

That first Futurist Evening ended exactly as the Futurists had hoped: in a mass brawl. A similar evening in Milan followed a month later: when Marinetti cried 'Long live War! Sole hygiene of the World!', the audience exploded with rage.

7　F. Marinetti, *Manifesto of Futurism*, 1909 – reproduced in U. Apollonio, ed., *Futurist Manifestos*, Thames & Hudson, 1973, pp. 21–2.

8　J. Morris, *Trieste and the Meaning of Nowhere*, Faber & Faber, 2001, pp. 55–6.

Marinetti was arrested on stage. The next day, the Austrian and German consuls delivered formal protests to the Italian authorities.[9]

Sitting in a café on a narrow street overshadowed by the theatre, we talk of the *Manifesto*. Just as Captain Bruno Lisjak came to live in a world of *irredentismo*, it seems we find ourselves in the world that Marinetti and his colleagues hoped to bring about, whose lifeblood is oil. Coincidentally, the Anglo-Persian Oil Company, now BP, was founded six weeks after the *Futurist Manifesto*'s publication on 20 February 1909. Marinetti's ecstatic description of speeding cars and sleek aeroplanes prefigured the advertising posters of the oil companies. Many of the images created to sell fuel in the 1930s incorporated the style of Futurist paintings.

Before World War I, Trieste was a cradle of modernist thought, home to Freud, Joyce and Rilke. As one of the most industrially advanced metropolises in Europe at the time, it was also a mirror of Baku. So it is fitting that the most impressive Futurist-inspired event of all took place in that Caspian city: the performance of Avraamov's *Symphony of Factory Sirens* on 7 November 1922, celebrating the fifth anniversary of the Bolshevik Revolution.

TAL KP 30 – 4,637 KM – SISTIANA/SESLJAN, ITALY

We drive north out of the city to one of the villages up the coast, signposted by both its Italian and Slovenian names, Sistiana and Sesljan. At the wheel is Marzia, who explains that the man we are going to visit is the father of her good friend, Elena Gerebizza. Elena works for the Campagna per la Riforma della Banca Mondiale (CRBM), the Rome-based group that, since 2001, has played such a vigorous role in the coalition of NGOs raising issues about the BTC pipeline. Knowing that she was a Triestina, we had asked Elena for anything she could tell us about TAL. A while passed before she remembered that her father, Paolo, had worked on its construction.

Minutes after we have settled in the living room of Elena's parents' apartment, Paolo proudly produces his workbook from forty-four years ago. It bears the name of the company, his registration number, and the dates of his employment:

CAPAG CH, 7265, 5.5.66, 14.7.66

In the summer of 1966, Paolo worked on the pipeline's construction for two months as a driver, ferrying workers to and from the site, morning and evening. He had been employed by a Swiss company, CAPAG, who were subcontracted to do the pipe-laying from the main engineers, Bechtel of San Francisco, who were themselves hired by the TAL consortium. He never knew where the pipeline was heading, but his memory of that pivotal year is clear.

---

9   See C. Tisdall and A. Bozzolla, *Futurism*, Thames & Hudson, 1977, p. 92.

Paolo is an Italian who grew up in Istria. In 1954, when he was fourteen and the Free Territory of Trieste was abolished and divided by the UN, his family moved from Yugoslavia to Zone A, the Italian part of the territory. Like thousands of others, they were placed in the refugee camp of Padricano, which was one of four settlements created among the Slovenian villages on the *carso* in the hinterland of Trieste.

After twelve years in the camp, aged twenty-six, Paulo was recruited to work on the construction of TAL. 'A newspaper asked specifically for people from Istria to work on the pipeline – they had priority over the Triestinos'. He was employed carrying men from the refugee camps to the various worksites along the 20 km stretch of pipeline that was being buried in the *carso*.

When we ask Paolo why he only worked on the project for two months, he rolls up his right trouser leg to reveal a vivid scar above his knee. Falling from the works lorry, he was badly injured and was laid off. He never received any compensation. Like the landscape scarred by the pipeline at Hacı Ali in Turkey, Paulo's body still carries the marks of the construction.

We leave the apartment and drive through the village of Sistiana towards the hamlet of Mavhinje, further inland. Paulo is keen to show us the place, once a construction site, to which he had regularly driven workers. Up on the hill, among the woods of oak and field maple, we stop the car by pipeline marker post A30. The corridor of TAL is clearly visible, a straight swathe cut through the trees several metres wide. To the south it crosses tight fields of grass; to the north it rises up to the heights of Mount Ermada on the border with Slovenia. Nightingales sing in the warm evening.

This land is in the Commune of Duino, where Rilke worked and where, according to Bruno, the mayor refused to agree to the expropriation of Slovenian fields. Perhaps it was these parcels of grazing that he was trying to defend?

TAL KP 35 – 4,642 KM – GRADISCA D'ISONZO, ITALY

For the better part of twenty kilometres the Transalpine Pipeline runs along the strip of land that lies between the Slovenian/Italian border and the Adriatic. It is like a bone in the limb of territory that joins Trieste to the main body of Italy.

After leaving Marzia, we take the train from Trieste to Mestre, Venice's mainland city. This railway line was built under Mussolini to replace the Sud Bahn that ran from Vienna via Laibach – now Ljubljana – to Trieste. The train skirts the pellucid gulf, mussel farms chequerboarding the sea. Out there on the blue, three tankers are still anchored, silent like the pipeline in the *carso*, coiling its way behind the city. In the heat of the afternoon, the world is asleep. While the Triestinos slumber, the pipeline labours, pumping and pulsing its explosive load. How is it that these projects, so politically potent in their creation, become forgotten?

In May 1915, the kingdom of Italy entered World War I. That spring a number of Futurists performed their final collective action, enrolling in Italy's fastest military division, the Lombard Volunteer Cyclists' and Automobilists' Battalion.

Marinetti, together with the painter Umberto Boccioni and the architect Antonio Sant'Elia, were quickly drafted to the front, high in the Trentino Alps. Boccioni's diary conveyed his passionate delight at seeing action:

Captain Ataneo in spite of orders to retreat, remembering, Buzzi says to Marinetti and me: 'You advance'. We go. Zuii Zuiii Tan Tan. Bullets all around. Volunteers calm on the ground shoot Pan Pan. Crack shot Sergeant Massai on his feet shoots, first shrapnel explodes. We arrive hearing a shout we throw ourselves on the ground: shrapnel explodes twenty steps away and I shout: 'At last'.[10]

A year later, Boccioni and Sant'Elia were dead. Boccioni fell from a horse while training; Sant'Elia was killed at the Eighth Battle of Isonzo. There were twelve brutal battles along the River Isonzo, Italy's Somme. By the time the Eighth Battle began, on 10 October 1916, almost half a million soldiers had died.

Dead at twenty-eight, Sant'Elia had built only one project, a villa near Como. Yet his drawings and the *Manifesto of Futurist Architecture* were profoundly influential on the development of the twentieth-century city, leaving their mark on Republican Ankara, Soviet Rustavi, and today's late-capitalist Baku. Sant'Elia's influence can also be seen at the war cemetery at Redipuglia, a massive piece of fascist architecture, which contains the bones of 100,000 dead. Walking from the nearby train station, we climb the monumental steps that lead up to the three bronze crosses and look out over the *carso*. Five hundred metres from the crosses runs the Transalpine pipeline on its journey to Austria. During its construction in the 1960s, workers from the Istrian camps had to negotiate nearly ten kilometres of trenches and shrapnel, mines and shells, on the battlefields of Isonzo.

TAL KP 60 – 4,667 KM – UDINE, ITALY

Near the city of Udine, TAL passes under the railway upon which we are travelling. Udine is a garrison town, a rail hub and a node on Bratszvo, the great gas pipeline from Siberia. For four centuries, as part of the Venetian Republic's mainland dominions, Udine was key to its control over trade routes across the Alps to Bavaria and Bohemia. Goods from Venice flowed through Udine, over the mountains and on into the German heartlands.

In the seventeenth century, Venice's territories dwindled, sandwiched between two empires: the Ottomans and the Habsburgs. Udine became increasingly

---

10   Tisdall and Bozzolla, *Futurism*, p. 180.

important as a bastion against both threats. Its heavily fortified castle still dominates the town. But with the loss of her colonies and ports, and the rise of Austria, Venice's economic power was waning. Her cloth exports declined by 90 per cent between 1600 and 1715.[11]

Eventually, in 1797, the Venetian Republic fell to Napoleon's armies, which cut a swathe through northern Italy. Subsequently incorporated into Austria, the new territorial acquisitions helped Vienna boom, and out from that city reached the tentacles of its trade system, manifested in due course by railways.

In the mid-nineteenth century, Austria constructed rail lines running across the empire to Laibach, Trieste, Fiume and Venice. By 1858 this entire network had been privatised, with the lion's share purchased by the Rothschild Bank of Paris, drawing in capital from London and Vienna.[12] Like the Baku–Batumi Railway that the Rothschilds financed fourteen years later, these iron roads not only facilitated the transfer of troops, people and goods, but also of fuel – oil in the Russian Caucasus and kerosene from Fiume in the Austro-Hungarian Empire.

The fall of Udine accelerated the passage of Venice into the industrial world. In 1845, when John Ruskin arrived in La Serenissima, the new railway was still under construction.

> The afternoon was cloudless, the sun intensely bright, the gliding down the canal of the Brenta exquisite. We turned the corner of the bastion, where Venice once appeared, and behold – the Greenwich railway, only with less arches and more dead wall, entirely cutting off the whole open sea and half the city, which now looks nearly as possible like Liverpool at the end of the dockyard wall.[13]

Writers such as Ruskin helped to create Venice in the European imagination as a gem to be preserved on account of her art and architecture, and perhaps as a reminder of a pre-industrial world. A pre-modern city revered as utterly civilised, and yet without cars and skyscrapers, shopping malls and undergrounds. She was everything the Futurists reviled. After World War II – in which it was agreed by all sides that she should be left untouched – Venice became a theatre not only for mass tourism but also for the super-rich. Among their number were those who had amassed their fortunes through the building of the hydrocarbon world, such as Enrico Mattei, the mastermind of the Italian oil company ENI, and John Browne, CEO of BP.

The Rialto, at the heart of the city, was the centre of Venetian banking, which in the Middle Ages financed merchants travelling to the eastern Mediterranean

11   C. McEvedy, *The Penguin Atlas of Modern History*, Penguin, 1972, p. 58.

12   N. Ferguson, *The World's Banker*, Widenfeld & Nicholson, 1998, pp. 597–99.

13   S. Quill, *Ruskin's Venice: The Stones Revisited*, Ashgate, 2000, p. 31.

and beyond. Ten minutes' walk through the alleyways from the Rialto lies the Corte seconda del Milion, where in the thirteenth century Marco Polo's family lived and traded. Nearby too is the Riva del Carbon, the 'Coal Quay', a fitting address for Browne's apartment.

Browne first visited the city at the age of twelve with his parents, in 1965, as the trench for the Transalpine pipeline was being excavated across the *carso*. Three decades later, as the project in the Caucasus was well underway, he acquired his property in the Rialto. Soon after the final inauguration of BTC, at the Ceyhan Terminal on 13 July 2006, he came here to rest, as he often did in the summer months. He saw Venice as 'a place that makes me happier than anywhere else, a place to reflect and think. Venice, La Serenissima, creates a curious mix of calm and inspiration. If people are prepared to listen, I believe the stones themselves speak to you.'[14]

Browne's wealth is the product of thirty-seven years of intense and dedicated work for BP. By the time he left the company in May 2007, his remuneration package, of wages and shares, was approximately $35.7 million.[15] He invested some of his wealth in a collection of pre-Columbian art, early printed books and the Rialto apartment.

Some part of this fortune is a direct consequence of his role in driving BP into Soviet Azerbaijan – personal wealth drawn from Baku oil. In this he mirrors a parade of European plutocrats such as Zeynalabin Taghiyev, Ludvig Nobel, Alphonse de Rothschild and Marcus Samuel: Caspian crude transformed into private art collections and libraries, mansions and vineyards.

---

14   Browne, *Beyond Business*, p. 226.
15   There was intensive media speculation around Browne's final pay package, with some estimates as high as $143 million. P. Olson, 'BP: Estimates Of CEO Pay Are Pure Speculation', 13 April 2007, at forbes.com.

19 THE CASPIAN!

We are hunting for the pipeline at Paluzza, north-west of Udine, on the Italian–Austrian border. The River But carves a narrow valley through the Carnia Alps, where the mountains rise sharply from the flat valley floor, so we assume that TAL will be easy to find – even though, as with BTC, there are no publicly available maps of its route. There is a warm wind blowing from the south. In the gardens of the village houses red tulips bend in the breeze. Blankets of pine and oak cover the mountainsides. A few people are tilling plots by hand in the meadowland. The soil is the pale colour of chocolate powder.

Also once under Venetian control, Paluzza was absorbed into the Habsburg Empire after *La Serinissima* fell to the Austrians. Along the valley of the But runs a Roman road, the Via Julia. Its construction was ordered by Julius Caesar to connect the Roman city of Aquileia, on the Adriatic, with the iron- and gold-rich Celtic kingdom of Norium in the mountains to the north. This was already an ancient route. The body of Oetzi, a Neolithic man, was discovered in 1991 exactly where he had frozen to death 5,300 years before not far to the west of here, on his way through one of the Alpine passes.

Crossing the Pontaiba stream into the hamlet of Zenodis, we wonder where the livestock is. Could it be that they are up on the high Alps? But cattle culture has largely gone from here. In its place has come a leisure landscape, the cow byres transformed into holiday homes. There is some forestry work, but most of these villages depend upon tourists from the south or north: walking in summer, skiing in winter. The landscape has been re-created to be viewed. Down the valley passes the Via Julia Augusta, a cycling route named after the Roman road, celebrating a 2,000-year-old feat of engineering. Brochures funded by the EU say the route is designed to 'link the distinct peoples of Europe'. We set foot on the 404 Sentiere de Farinari, an immaculately constructed mountain footpath, an *autostrada* for walkers, mountain bikers and joggers, built with funds from the provincial capital of Udine, and the regional capital of Trieste.

This tourist economy is dependent upon cheap hydrocarbons – fuel for the cars and buses, to build the roads and paths, power the chair lifts, and provide the expected levels of comfort for the visitors in their hotels and *pensioni*. The electricity pylons marched up this valley in the wake of the pipeline. Through this demand for a constant supply of fuel, even the arcadian Sentiere is connected to the Task Force in the Gulf of Aden and the oil platforms off Baku.

Heading back down towards the river, we pass the ruins of an old watermill. Its roof is caved in, rafters collapsed, walls tumbling down. There are twelve such redundant mills marked on the map, once the active engines of the flour millers, the *farinari*.

SIOT ATTENZIONE! OLEDOTO INTERRATO

And there it is. Bold, black lettering on yellow metal; beyond the sign, the red marker posts marching away. We ford the river and walk straight along the pipeline, buried a metre or so below our feet. The ground is easygoing because the pipeline 'corridor' has been cleared of boulders and stripped of large vegetation. It runs naked, slicing through willow saplings and pine woods.

Since the vegetation is cut back, someone must be employed to stop its regrowth, to groom it each year. This pipe has lain in the ground for at least forty-four years now, its route cleared annually. Each marker post is topped with a cone-shaped steel hat and numbered sequentially in white:

$$756 \quad 757 \quad 758 \quad 759$$

The numbers are designed to be read from the air, from a helicopter.

It is strangely thrilling to follow the route unhindered, after all the challenges around the pipeline in the Caucasus. The path, exactly three metres wide, snakes inexorably on – out of the forest, through meadows, across a main road, before plunging once more back into the forest. Underfoot are cowslips and wild strawberry plants.

We can imagine the pipeline's route plotted on a map in some distant office half a century ago; plans drawn up by Bechtel, agreed by the shareholders in TAL, approved by Maurice Bridgeman, CEO of BP, in Finsbury Circus in London. The pipeline lies in the earth, and all the men that fathered it – where do they lie? We know the fathers, visible and invisible, of BTC: Browne, Heydar Aliyev, Shevardnadze, Bagirov, Grote, Morningstar. Who were the fathers of TAL? As with Aliyev and Shevardnadze in relation to BTC, the Transalpine pipeline depended upon the support of the dominant political players in the each of the states through which it passed. In the case of Italy, this meant Aldo Moro, prime minister between 1963 and 1968. As with

Browne in relation to BTC, the TAL required the driving commitment of Maurice Bridgeman. It would be harder to find the fathers of TAL than it was to find those behind BTC, partly because this pipeline is now forgotten. A consequence of this is that there are no guides, such as Mayis, Manana or Ferhat, to help us. TAL, an object still so politically important, carrying so much wealth over such a long distance, is now unseen and known to few people.

Heads down, we follow the route as if it were a sacred line. There is not a sound from the pipe underground. It is silent throughout its length except for the hum of the pump stations. It is a road, but a buried road only used for one commodity; a private road owned by a set of companies, who in turn have millions of shareholders who undoubtedly do not even know that they own this pipeline. Perhaps, one day, this feat of engineering will be celebrated like the Roman road that passes down the valley and gives its name to a tourist route. But today it leaves little mark on the public imagination.

The route of TAL comes to a clearing, or rather rough meadowland between a house and its outbuildings. The pipeline cuts straight across. We stop. Is this semi-public space, or is it private?

We slink back into the woods, and the pipeline fills us with a strange melancholy. What an odd thing to be doing on a Friday afternoon, hunting for something we are supposed to ignore. Then there is a hare, running straight down the 'corridor', cutting through the scrub on the river's bank. The hare lifts us up. Somehow it is laughing at us. It, and its progeny, will outlive all this.

752 751 750 749 748

TAL KP 130 – 4,737 KM – PASS DI MONTE CROCE CARNICO/PLOCKENPASS, ITALY/ AUSTRIA

The valley of the River But narrows to the Canale di San Pietro, which we follow to the base of the mountain. Here is Timau, a village in the shadow of massive limestone crags. Over the houses looms the Creta di Timau, its summit 1,000 metres above the roofs. The vastness of the grey stone is exhilarating and frightening. The mountain feels menacing: perhaps it is the shadow of the long, bitter fight that took place here. As in the Caucasus, this corner of the Alps is a jigsaw of nations and ethnicities – Italian, Austrian, Slovenian, Friulian and Ladin. In the early twentieth century it became a killing ground.

The village still displays rusted field guns, a stretcher frame, barbed wire and spent shells. During the Battles of the Izonso, at the same time that the Ottomans fought the Russians in the Caucasus, World War I brought conflict to these mountains. Supplied with munitions and fuel along road and rail from Fiume or Udine, the Italian and Austro-Hungarian armies struggled over fragments of rock.

Advances or retreats were measured not in horizontal kilometres, but in vertical metres, in altitudes. The Italians called it *il fronte verticale*.[1]

When we travel the road beyond Timau, which follows the Via Julia, we are dazed not only by the altitude but also by the insanity of war. The rock face, 400 metres above the valley floor, is pitted with a myriad of man-made burrows, tunnels carved into the limestone by Italian troops trying to hold ground in the face of Austrian counterparts dug into the rock on the northern face of the mountain. From these *gallerias* snipers on both sides shot at any sign of movement, while explosives were detonated to set off avalanches over enemy positions. We think of Boccioni celebrating the fighting in the mountains. 'Zuii Zuiii Tan Tan' went the bullets. And the roar of the shelling in these valleys rang out as the world of hydro-carbon technology pounded the sheer rock.

We had imagined that the pipeline would follow the road over the pass, but we were wrong. From the middle of the village of Timau we can see the path of TAL running across the wide boulder-strewn bed of the river, picked out by a clear strip denuded of willow saplings. It passes beneath the road and then straight up the mountainside: again, the strip cut through the hazel, oak and fir.

Off the main road, over the crash barrier and into the cleared strip, we follow the line, scrambling up the slope. The first stretch is manageable, but halfway up it becomes almost vertical. We are determined to press on, so we ditch our jackets and scrabble on all fours, bag and camera bashing about. Up and up, out of breath and worried now: 'What if we slip on the small pebbles, fall and break a leg?', 'If we have an accident here, how do we get off, and how do we explain why we were here in the first place?' We are getting to the point of nervous exhaustion, but can see what we think is a small ledge ahead: there, we can rest.

We make it to the ledge – but it isn't one. It is an expanse of flat gravel, with two JCB diggers parked up: a worksite completely hidden from below. The mountain wall ahead rises in a vertical face, but there is a large entrance cut into it, blocked by a pair of bolted, green-painted metal gates. It dawns on us that this is the pipeline plunging through the mountain's heart, far below the summit. It seems extraordinary that the oil companies drilled and dynamited their way through this rock, building the equivalent of a road or rail tunnel, just to shift crude across Europe.

Only after we have taken photos of the pipeline's route up the mountainside, and the tunnel entrance, do we notice the signs saying: 'This place is under video surveillance'; 'This is private property of SIOT'; 'No unauthorised access'. So we follow the roadway that slopes down from the worksite ledge, then cut down through the wood to the main road, trying to look inconspicuous. Half an hour later, at the edge of the village, we see a man coming down the road in blue work

---

1   See M. Thompson, *The White War*, Faber & Faber, 2009.

overalls, the insignia of TAL is on his chest. He is looking out for something on the mountainside. We wonder whether he is looking for us – but we are gone.

A taxi takes us, hairpin after hairpin, up to the high ridge of the mountain and through what is known to the Italians as Pass di Monte Croce Carnico and to the Austrians as the Plockenpass. Swathed in cold mist, the border is marked by a cluster of abandoned buildings and a forlorn-looking wind turbine whose blades are immobile in the stillness. Unlike at Krazny Most in Azerbaijan, or Türkgözü in Turkey, there are no guards here to check our passports or control the movement of people and goods across this international boundary within the EU. Meanwhile, the crude passes through the mountain, far below us.

TAL KP 135 – 4,742 KM – MAUTEN, AUSTRIA

Walking the next morning in a thick pine forest penetrated by lumber tracks and streams that feed the River Gail, we find the pipeline in the Rogaswald. From the entrance on the Italian side of the border, the oil companies tunnelled their way through nearly seven kilometres of rock, passing under the mountains of Gamspitz and Koderhohe, before re-emerging into the Austrian province of Karnten, or Carinthia. From here, the waters that flow into the Gail will eventually reach the Danube, and beyond it the Black Sea. TAL has entered the German-speaking world of Mitteleuropa.

Close to the banks of the Gail stands the hamlet of Wurmlach. A pale green oil tank, rising six metres from the surrounding fields, marks the first pumping station of the Adria–Wien pipeline, the AWP. This branch of TAL runs onwards to the refinery at Schwechat, just south of Vienna, providing the fuel for the Austrian capital that Churchill demanded half a century ago. Like the Transalpine pipeline, this sub-pipeline is owned by a consortium, this time dominated by the Austrian oil company OMV, with 76 per cent of the shares, but also including Shell Austria, Agip and BP Austria.

Beside the TAL oil tank stands another of a similar scale, painted in the colours of the rainbow. This is a biomass plant fuelled with waste from the surrounding farms. On the road between Wurmlach and the nearby town we had seen the sign announcing 'Mauten – Klimabündnis Gemeinde' ('Mauten – Climate Alliance Parish'). Outside the town hall, above the advertisement for the War Museum (1915–1918), is an official notice, 'Energie Autark: Kötschach-Mauten' ('Energy Self-Sufficiency Kötschach-Mauten').

The combined parishes of Kötschach and Mauten are striving to meet their energy needs from local renewable systems. As well as the biomass plant, there is the wind turbine we saw at the Plockenpass, and a number of hydro plants and solar electric systems.

Standing by the green mesh fence topped with barbed wire that surrounds the pump station, we can smell the faintest whiff of oil: the scent of Azeri crude in the Alps. How intimately these two endeavours are entwined. The surrounding communities are striving to draw energy from their own renewable resources, and thereby reduce their carbon dioxide emissions. They are understandably concerned about the impact of climate change on their snow and winter tourism, but nonetheless are dependent upon the petroleum systems that deliver visitors from the cities. Meanwhile, the pipeline, supplying 75 per cent of the oil needs of Austria, runs almost completely invisible, and utterly unremarked upon, across 25 kilometres of the parishes of Kötschach and Mauten.

It would be the same in a parish in England. There is a sense that these international pipelines are not about us and so do not concern us: they are about somewhere else. We think of them as forming part of our national infrastructure, like a bridge or main road, and imagine them to belong to the state. We are not in control of them, we are not responsible for them. They seem unchallengeably vast, a fact of life. Perhaps it is this sense that makes us so blind to them?

LIENZ, AUSTRIA

We trudge along the highway verge, against the heavy oncoming traffic, towards the ruins of Aguntum. The A-road, which we had travelled along by bus from Mauten, cuts straight across this archaeological site on an elevated bridge. Set back a little is a cool postmodern box, the new museum.

Built across the route of the Via Julia, after it had climbed over the Plockenpass, Aguntum was a strategic settlement in the Roman province of Noricum, whose territory covered what is now Central Austria and part of Bavaria. The road carried away rock-salt from the mines at Hallstatersee, gold from Klagenfurt and timber and cheese from the mountains and valleys.

In 27 BCE, Augustus, the first emperor of Rome after his assumption to the position of *principe*, began the consolidation of the empire. New roads were built, the army reorganised. Roman rule was pushed to the *limes*, which were intended to be the empire's eternal limits. The northern frontier[2] ran along the banks of the Danube, while the eastern frontier ran through Theodosiopolis, now Erzurum, on the Euphrates, and Apsarosi, today's Batumi, on the Black Sea.

'Imperatore Domitiano Caesare Augusto Germanico L. Julius Maximus, Legion XII Fulminata', runs the easternmost known Roman inscription. It is carved into a boulder on Boyuk Dash mountain, near the Sangachal oil terminal, memorialising a reconnaissance mission by a centurion during the reign of Domitian. Within twenty years, the Emperor Trajan had extended Roman rule to the shores of the Caspian Sea, absorbing this territory into the province of Greater Armenia. However, stiff resistance from neighbouring states, such as Atropatena, meant the province was relinquished in 117 CE. The frontier retreated back to the Euphrates, the *limes* as determined by Augustus.

---

2   See Tacitus, *The Annals of Imperial Rome*, transl. Michael Grant, Penguin, 1996.

Wandering around the museum, what catches our eye is a map illustrating Aguntum's position in the Roman trade system. It lists the exports that we knew about – gold, cheese, and so forth – and also the imports to this province – lapis lazuli from Afghanistan, pottery from the factories in the Rhineland and oysters from the northern Adriatic. We are reminded of Bruno Lisjak telling us how oysters from the Vallone di Muggia had been sold in Vienna.

Two thousand years on, the mineral deposits of Austria are exhausted, but the agricultural exports – wood and dairy – remain. Throughout these mountains there is timber production on an industrial scale. We see wood yards, stacks of beech and pine, lumber trucks, saw mills, swathes of felled forest. Everywhere we look there are advertisements for the region's cheese – Almkäse. The farming method known as *alm* pastoralism is at least as ancient as the Celtic peasants who lived here under Roman rule. Once the snow melts, the cattle, sheep and goats are driven from the valleys, up to the high pasture, the *alm*. Like the *yayla* pastures in Ardahan province, the *alm* is grazed in the summer. On the summer meadows in the mountains, the animals produce too much milk for the handful of farmers, so it is made into cheese. Protein is preserved in a form that can travel and last into the winter months, like smoked meat or salted fish. Such cheese was once traded down the *via* to cities like Aquilea and Rome; now it is exported onto the world market.

BLOOMSBURY, LONDON

Between 121 and 125 CE, the Roman Emperor Hadrian undertook several journeys by land and ship. He visited the province of Noricum, and very probably the city of Aguntum. He also travelled to the provinces of Britannia; Germania Superior, now Bavaria; Achaea, now Greece; Cappodocia, now central Turkey; and Bithynia and Pontus, now northern Turkey. Remarkably, the pipeline and tanker routes that we are tracing fall almost entirely within the geographical territory of the Iron Age Roman Empire that Hadrian travelled.

In the summer of 2008, Hadrian was celebrated at the British Museum in London, in an exhibition sponsored by BP. The accompanying catalogue featured a sponsor's Foreword, which dilated on Hadrian's remarkable achievements and on BP's pride in backing an exhibition that 'offers a new appraisal of Hadrian's turbulent life and reign through artworks seen together here for the first time'. The Foreword was signed, 'Dr Tony Hayward, CEO BP plc.'[3]

Some of the most celebrated objects in the exhibition were fragments of a colossal statue of Hadrian, excavated the previous year from the ruins of Sagalassos in southern Turkey. The London exhibition saw these items on

3   T. Opper, *Hadrian: Empire and Conflict*, British Museum Press, exhibition catalogue, 2008.

display for the first time. Unsurprisingly, the opening and private view were attended by officials from the Turkish embassy, in the company of Tony Hayward. Also present were representatives of Georgia, as artefacts had been lent from Tbilisi as well. The opening was a significant cultural event; for BP, it was part of maintaining good relations with key governments – critical when dealing with events such as the explosion at Refahiye and the bombing of Baku–Supsa – just two weeks after the exhibition opened.

Like many other corporations, BP has a long history of engagement with the arts. However, in April 1990 the company began a new wave of sponsorship, as the then CEO, Robert Horton, echoed a practice that had been successfully conducted by corporations in the US since the early 1980s.[4] It signed five-year contracts with the Tate and the National Portrait Gallery. Deals with other prominent cultural institutions across London followed soon after: the British Museum, the Royal Opera House, the Natural History Museum, the Science Museum, the National Theatre and the National Maritime Museum. And the ties between BP and these institutions go deeper. Orxan Abasov, our guide at Sangachal, was trained at the Natural History Museum; John Browne joined the board of the British Museum and, on retiring from BP, was appointed chair of the trustees of the Tate.

BP's annual sponsorship budget is not mere philanthropy. It helps build what the company refers to as its 'social licence to operate', which means the company having the support, or at least acquiescence, of the key communities in whichever state it conducts its business. Sponsorship helps create a favourable impression of the company among what are called in the public relations business 'special publics': journalists, academics, civil servants, diplomats and politicians. The aim is not to encourage people to buy more petrol, but to persuade them that BP is a socially responsible organisation, and that they should either actively support the company's interests or accept that, on balance, BP is a force for good and therefore should not be questioned. Just as the company was able to mould 'civil society' according to its interests in Baku, so it intervenes in London's body politic. In this way the opening night of *Hadrian: Empire and Conflict* helped draw both of these strands together, underscoring BP's influence not only in the culture of Turkey and Georgia, but also that of the UK.

The industrial colossus of this Oil Road along which we are travelling is constructed in many phases – in politics, in law, in public and private finance, in engineering design, in impact assessments, and then in physical reality. During this process, before the pipes are laid in the ground and throughout the operational lifespan of the pipeline, the support for the project has to be maintained in the 'special publics' within the states through which the oil

---

4   See C. Wu, *Privatising Culture: Corporate Art Intervention Since the 1980s*, Verso, 2002.

passes and in the capitals of the key international powers. The construction of the 'social licence to operate' is the constant engineering of this support.

After a quick tour of the ruins of Aguntum, we return along the main road. Trucks roar past, buffeting us with their backdraught. We head towards the centre of Lienz, the main town of the province of Osttirol. In the outskirts we pass shopping warehouses, a couple of garden centres, a drive-in sex shop and several giant supermarkets: standard features of high-energy consumer society, but they look curiously out of place, strangely temporary, in this extraordinarily beautiful land-scape of bright green meadows, towering pine forests and snow-capped peaks.

The Roman legions withdrew from this area in about 340 CE. Aguntum was utterly destroyed and lost by 600. This Roman civilisation lasted 300 to 600 years and was buried for 1,400 years, yet so much is invested in excavating and exhibiting it. Perhaps we are drawn to this Iron Age culture like a mirror, taking pride in a bold beauty that we can understand, as we draw from it intellectual and political models for ourselves. We also see our own death in its mirror. The collapsed and vanished exchange systems of Bronze Age Greece seem distant from us, but the complex trade routes and military structures of the Roman Empire – like the Venetian Empire that came long after – seem strikingly simi-lar to our own world. So the evidence that that system unravelled and was lost provides a vision of our own frailty. These car showrooms, supermarkets, sex shops and garden centres may vanish just as completely when the Oil Road ceases to function.

TAL KP 150 – 4,757 KM – HUBEN, AUSTRIA

Our bus takes us north of Lienz, up the narrow valley of the Iseltal, in which river, road and pipeline are squeezed into a space never more than 500 metres wide. The marker posts of TAL are easily visible from the road.

We catch a glimpse of what we are searching for – the dark green bulk of an oil-storage tank, identical to the one at Wurmlach: another pump station. We descend from the bus at Huben. This is a tiny hamlet, about twenty houses crammed into the Iseltal gorge, with a church, a police station, a fire station, an Esso petrol station, and two guesthouses. On the rocky slopes above the village, areas of pine have been carefully felled. The export economy of timber is busy here.

Four more buses arrive as we look around, disgorging troops of school students, satchels on their backs. These teenagers are returning home from the secondary school in Lienz. Huben, on the main road, is the hub for the villages that lie beyond in the Kalstal and Deferggental – vertiginous glacial valleys hemmed in by the towering mountains of the Hohe Tauern. This is the remotest and highest region of Austria, whose pinnacle is the Grossglockner, a national icon. The majority of the area is preserved as the Nationalpark Hohe Tauern, the largest nature reserve in Central Europe, nearly 2,000 square kilometres in size.

The encroaching tide of the industrial world barely lapped at the upper reaches of the Isel and Tauern valleys until the 1960s. The Roman road never penetrated here, while the railway stopped at Lienz, far below. The natural wall of the Hohe Tauern made the road impassable to motorised traffic: the way north was by foot or pack animal, crossing the summit at Tauern Kreuz. This was a world of horses and wood stoves, cattle and kerosene lamps. How similar this hamlet must have been, only fifty years ago, to Dgvari and other villages around Borjomi that we visited in Georgia.

Not only was the Tauern valley a dead end for motorised traffic, but this whole province of Osttirol was largely separated from the main body of Austria. After the defeat of the Austro-Hungarian Empire in 1918, the Sudtirol became the Trentino, part of Italy – just like Trieste, Istria and Fiume – as the irredentists achieved their war aim. In consequence, Osttirol was cut off from many of its lines of communication with the main body of Austria.

So the government in Vienna drew up a plan to build a road tunnel through the belly of the Hohe Tauern mountain range and, alongside it, a tunnel for the TAL pipeline. The two projects grew like twins. Without the road tunnel, perhaps the pipeline would not have taken this route. Without the pipeline tunnel, perhaps the pressure for the road would not have been sufficient to realise this massive engineering project. Together, they altered life in all the region's valleys and villages. Now the Tauern valley and the Felber valley, on the north side of the mountains, are no longer dead ends, but throughways for traffic and oil. Just outside Huben, by the pump station, are the offices of the Transalpine Ölleitung in Österreich, which, like SIOT, is one of the three subsidiary companies of TAL. Here staff administer the Austrian section of the pipeline, and oversee its maintenance and security as it passes through a land of freezing winters and scorching summers. The pipeline's future depends upon the people of this region, and vice versa.

On 11 April 1964, the Austrian chancellor, Josef Klaus, came here for the ceremony that marked the beginning of construction. Land was purchased for the pump station; an army of workers and trucks arrived, widening the roads, laying the pipeline and blasting the tunnel. An intense concentration of labour and capital expenditure, and a million tonnes of TNT, heralded a new world and changed the life of this hamlet that is now on the Oil Road.[5]

5   Dr Walter Fritsch, 'Speech at the Celebration of the 1 Billionth TAL Ton', 14 March 2006, Duino Castle, Trieste.

TAL KP 180 – 4,787 KM – FELBERTAUERN TUNNEL

Our next bus takes us plunging through the wall of the Hohe Tauern. We are 1,600 metres above sea level: the highest point on TAL's journey, and the mountain summit of Reigel is still over 1,000 metres above us. The bus bursts out of the northern side of the mountain, into sunlight. Out of the Osttirol and into the province of Salzburger Land, we follow the pipeline markers down the Felber valley.

The Transalpine pipeline is a system to move crude from Italy through Austria and into Germany. However, just like BTC, it had deep strategic and financial importance for both the US administration and the British government. TAL connected two European Economic Community countries by passing through a third neutral state, Austria. The pipeline also performed an important military function by supplying the refineries in Bavaria, which provided fuel for NATO troops, such as the US Armoured Infantry divisions at Regensburg.

For the British state, the pipeline's economic significance derived in large part from the government's role as the majority shareholder in BP. The company owned a controlling stake in TAL, and the Vohburg refinery it would supply. In 1914, on the eve of the war that broke across Europe, Winston Churchill, first lord of the Admiralty, coordinated the British government's purchase of 50 per cent of the shares of Anglo-Persian Oil Company – later called BP – in order to ensure a secure supply of oil for the Royal Navy. This purchase gave the government the right to appoint two of the company's non-executive directors, who reported to the chancellor of the Exchequer.[6] The intertwining of Anglo-Persian and British foreign policy from that point on would be amply illustrated by the wranglings in the War Cabinet over British intervention in the Caucasus in 1918.

By the late 1960s, the now-renamed BP still functioned almost as a branch of the Foreign Office. John Browne, CEO of BP, described starting his first job, a contract to work in Alaska, as getting 'posting orders', as if he were a civil servant.[7] The company was unable to take major investment decisions that did not assist the objectives of its largest shareholder, the British government. The combined projects of TAL and the Vohburg refinery required the investment of substantial sums of capital by BP between 1963 and 1967. This had to be sanctioned by the board, with the two Whitehall appointees reporting to Reginald Maudling, the chancellor of the Exchequer in the Conservative government of Sir Alec Douglas-Home.

BP's decision to invest in refineries and pipelines in Central Europe was a bold strategy driven largely by three men within the company's executive: Maurice

---

6   J. Bamberg, *British Petroleum and Global Oil, 1950–1975: The Challenge of Nationalism*, CUP, 2000, p. 325.

7   Browne, *Beyond Business*, p. 24.

Bridgeman, BP chairman; Maurice Banks, managing director of refineries, engineering and research; and Alaistair Down, managing director of finances. During the 1960s they oversaw a radical expansion of BP's refining and marketing capacity, opening ten refineries across Europe and another seventeen further afield.[8]

Each decision to sanction a project, made in the BP board room at Finsbury Circus in London, required an allocation of capital. Between 1960 and 1965, BP's annual capital expenditure almost doubled, from £109 million to £207 million, with much of the growth occurring in the refining and marketing division.[9] The company's debt ratio climbed to an uncomfortably high level for a business working in politically risky states. Consequently, Down coordinated an issue of ordinary shares in 1966. Following a decision by James Callaghan, chancellor of the Exchequer, the majority of this equity was purchased by Harold Wilson's Labour government. This increased the British state's holding in the company to 68 per cent. BP was now effectively a nationalised industry.

The route of BTC would not have been determined without constant support from Bill Clinton's administration. The route of TAL would not have been agreed without the approval of Sir Alec Douglas-Home's government. In a neat counterpoint to Khrushchev's promotion of the Comecon pipelines, Druzhba and Bratsvo, the British exchequer left its mark in these Alpine valleys and villages through its co-financing of the TAL pipeline and its tunnel.

TAL KP 195 – 4,802 KM – MITTERSILL, AUSTRIA

We walk to the edge of the town of Mittersill and the Nationalpark Welten, the Hohe Tauern's main visitor centre. Recently opened, it is a beautiful piece of postmodern architecture, like the museum at Aguntum. The exhibition inside is elaborate. In the 'Schatzkammer' 3-D cinema, the benches shake and judder as images of the landmass of Africa batter into the landmass of Europe, forcing up the 'rock curtain' of the Alps. The massive 'Eagle Flight Panorama' video sweeps us across the peaks, and we lie back on the recliners in the 'Alm Summer' audio installation, listening to the sounds of crickets and cowbells. Much is made of the uniqueness of the Hohe Tauern and its links with other national parks worldwide: Yellowstone, the Serengeti, the Galapagos Islands, Mount Everest.

The displays explain in detail the farming life of the Hohe Tauern, 5,000 years of *alm* agriculture. The cows and sheep, the Noric horses – still named after the Celts who introduced them – the cheese and speck. The park goes to great lengths to protect and support the remains of this cattle culture – encouraging rare breeds, restraining the penetration of diesel-fuelled mechanisation. In the café, the plastic cartons for the single portions of cream explain that it comes from the Hohe

---

8   Bamberg, *British Petroleum and Global Oil*, pp. 282–4.
9   Ibid., p. 304.

Tauern. In the shop we buy Milka white chocolate bars whose plastic wrappers assure us 'Garantiert 100% Alpenmilch': they bear the legend 'Official sponsor of the Nationalpark Hohe Tauern'.

'The Caspian!' cries Ferdinand Rieder, the spokesperson for the national park. He is in his early sixties, dressed young in Joop jeans and a checked shirt, his face a picture of astonishment as we tell him that the oil pumped through TAL is partly from the Caspian. He is amazed that the crude flowing through the mountains comes from so far away. We had hoped that he would inform us about the pipeline, but his lack of knowledge and the fact that he has never enquired into TAL confirm once again how this infrastructure is ignored.

The national park was created in 1981, fourteen years after TAL started pumping, in the same year that Mika was born. On the maps printed for visitors, the pipeline is nowhere to be seen. The park is about 1,000 kilometres long, and 40 kilometres wide at its broadest point; it includes many mountain groups and several glaciers. It is divided into two blocks: the western section is a third of the whole area; the eastern section the other two-thirds. Between them runs a narrow strip of land, cutting the park in half. This, we realise, is the route of the oil pipeline and access roads. But nowhere in the exhibition or the literature is there a reference to the constant flow of crude through the middle of this European Yellowstone. Perhaps we shouldn't have expected anything different. Somehow we had thought a museum about the environment would include the pipeline in its lens. But in this idealised vision of nature, the Oil Road is rendered invisible.

We ask Ferdinand about the relationship between the park and the pipeline. He says there is none. But didn't the park come about because of the building of the road tunnel and TAL? No, he replies: it was proposed in the 1970s, in response to plans to build a large hydroelectric plant further up the Salzach valley, and because of the increasing amount of skiing on the glaciers. He further explains that there was a battle to establish the park: there was a demand for the jobs that the power station would bring, and people were concerned that the park would not deliver employment. 'We had to show that it would create jobs.'

'Is there ever a conflict between the road and park?'

'No, the road is not in the park. It helps link the two parts and helps visitors to come. In the first decade there was a traffic problem, with a heavy usage in the summer as Germans and Austrians headed for Italy. But then in the 1980s they built the autobahn running south from Salzburg, passing through Spittal and Villach, bound for Udine.'

The pipeline has been airbrushed out of the local geography. TAL played a part in making the road tunnel possible. And the road also partly made the park possible, bringing the visitors in their cars and coaches, providing the income that employs the staff. Mika's parents brought their young family here, travelling by car down the E45 from Darmstadt via Munich, with Mika dreaming of catching a glimpse of an eagle or, better yet, a Steinbock. So many imaginations have been inspired by these mountains, they have in themselves driven forward ecological understanding. Perhaps things would have been different if the national park had been created in the early 1960s and the pipeline and road tunnel proposed in the 1980s. The European environmental movement might then have been strong enough to resist this industrial project. Or would the Hohe Tauern have gone the way of the Borjomi National Park, with BTC passing through it?

A caption in the exhibition reads: 'Should the current warm trend continue then the Hohe Tauern will be largely glacier-free in the course of the century'. We talk with Ferdinand about the impacts of climate change on the Hohe Tauern. He explains that the permafrost is now heavily affected, which threatens the flow of the River Inn and ultimately the entire Danube river system. In Anatolia we had thought about how BTC and the Euphrates were like sisters: now it seems that TAL and the Danube are similarly entwined.

The species of the Hohe Tauern, adjusting to the changing climate, have begun to migrate further up the mountains. The Hohe Tauern's ecosystem is essentially an island of tundra left over from the Ice Age, surrounded by the 'sea' of a temperate bioregion. As the global climate warms, that sea rises, and the species of the tundra climb higher and higher. Eventually those plants and insects, those birds and mammals, will be able to ascend no further, and will become extinct. The entire ecosystem of the Alps, and with it the culture of the *alm* – millennia of habits and languages, skill and song – will go under, preserved and packaged only in the visitor centre.

TAL KP 250 – 4,857 KM – ROSENHEIM, GERMANY

Our train whistles over the Austrian border, and finally we enter Germany. After World War I, the markets of these two defeated countries were opened up to the business of the victorious powers. The Anglo-Persian Oil Company looked closely at growing demand in the new Weimar Republic, at the same time as it was advancing into the market of fascist Italy and having to accept defeat in Soviet Baku. In 1926 it bought 40 per cent of OLEX, an Austro-Hungarian marketing operation with over 1,000 filling stations. Within four years, its stake had increased to 75 per cent, and it began to promote its products with a trademark shield: the emblem of its marketing arm, British Petroleum. By 1938 the Anglo-Persian Oil Company was the third-largest supplier of fuel to the Third Reich. The company's sales more than doubled in the five years after Hitler came to power.[10] The product that saw the largest increase was aviation spirit: fuel for the growing Luftwaffe.

---

10 J. Bamberg, *The History of British Petroleum Company, Vol 2: The Anglo-Iranian Years, 1928–1954*, CUP, 1994, pp. 131–4.

At the outbreak of World War II, Royal Dutch Shell, Standard Oil and Anglo-Persian shared 57.8 per cent of the German market. All three companies provided fuel to the Nazi state as it rearmed, re-industrialised and established its structures of terror. There is a statistical likelihood that one of these three supplied fuel for the trucks that transported prisoners to Dachau near Munich after 1933. Though many foreign businesses supported the Nazi state in the 1930s, today the links between oil companies and the Nazi regime are a palpable source of embarrassment. The web-published history of BP Germany is thorough, but leaves a blank between 1932 and 1948.

Like the Soviet Union and Mussolini's Italy, the Nazi government worked to build a national oil industry to counterbalance the strength of the Western companies. From September 1936, its second Four-Year Plan provided subsidies for research into synthetic fuels, producing gasoline and aviation spirit from coal, of which Germany had a plentiful supply. When war broke out, many of the refineries in the Reich, such as the plant at Schwechat near Vienna, switched to synthetic production. Foreign oil companies had their assets seized. Anglo-Persian was locked out of its second-largest market. If it had not been for the special circumstances of war, and the fact that its competitors were similarly affected, the corporation would have faced a commercial disaster.

TAL KP 270 – 4,877 KM – STEINHÖRING, GERMANY

Beyond the windows of the train are the pine forests and green meadows of Upper Bavaria. The villages and towns look ordered and affluent. We find ourselves talking of the contrast between this sedate world and the hurricane of war that passed through here only two generations ago – tanks in the villages, bombers in the skies, and refugees on the roads. Time hides the violence.

The markers of TAL are clearly visible against the dark mass of the woods. The houses and fields exist within one of the EU's 'energy corridors', like those at Hacalli, Tsikhisdvari, Hasköy or Gölovası. But the contrast between the Caucasus and Bavaria is marked. Here there is no Azeri MTN, no Georgian Ministry of Interior troops, no Jandarma, no NATO sea patrols. Yet this tranquil scene before us depends upon the violence – or the threat of violence – in another stretch of the same 'corridor'. The more our journey enables us to see these pipelines, tankers and wells as part of one continuous structure, the more the apparent peace before us seems an illusion. Maintenance of this peace on the Oil Road requires a lot of guns.

Between Trieste and here, in the wealthiest regions of the 'corridor', we have seen no police presence – no need to guard the billions of dollars of crude that pass beneath the fields. In contrast, those places that are most militarised are those where the population in the 'corridor' is poorest, and where it has the least access to fossil fuels – on the Ardahan plateaus, in the mountains around Borjomi.

The words of the Colombian writer Hector Abad Gomez come to mind: 'We are living in a time of violence, and this violence is born out of inequality.'[11]

Just north of the village of Steinhöring, east of Munich in Upper Bavaria, is a familiar array of four oil-tanks, their white bulk standing out from the green of the crops. This is a key node on the Transalpine pipeline. Here, a pump station redirects some of the crude east, along a sixty-kilometre spur, to a refinery on the German–Austrian border. That refinery is the lynchpin of the 'Bayerisches Chemiedreieck', the Bavarian Chemical Triangle, where a series of interconnected factories produce everything from plastics and fertilisers to silicon for solar panels.

The pump station at Steinhöring is of strategic importance to the German economy, but there is no Jandarma base like the one in the snow by the Posof pump station. The violence necessary to bring oil to Bavarian industry is hidden. If there were a Jandarma base at Steinhöring, or bombs on the pipeline, sentiment in this part of the 'corridor' might change.

> *It was a small inn (in Upper Bavaria) . . . we sat on benches tightly packed together. It is impossible now to convey the atmosphere. The worst moment was when at two o'clock in the morning of 1 May, the news of Hitler's death came through on the radio. I remember it precisely, but I can't describe the stillness of that instant which lasted . . . for hours. Nobody said anything, but very soon afterwards people started to go outside, first one – then there was a shot. Then another, and yet another. Not a word inside, no other sound except those shots from outside, but one felt that that was all there was, that all of us would have to die. My world was shattered; I couldn't see any future at all.*

The son of Hitler's secretary, Martin Bormann[12]

In the last year of World War II, the British, Soviets and Americans were determined that Germany, having initiated two conflicts in the space of twenty-five years, should never again be capable of such action. They committed themselves to obtaining Germany's unconditional surrender and to dividing it into three – and later four – zones of occupation. Prior to the Yalta Conference, US Secretary of the Treasury Henry Morganthau drafted a plan to convert a defeated Germany into an agricultural economy with a minimum of basic industry – a plan signed off by Churchill and US President Roosevelt. In 1938 Germany had been the largest consumer of petroleum products in Europe, and the second largest in the world. Now, seven years later, the victors of the war planned to reduce it to being an importer of only tractor fuel and kerosene.

---

11   H. Eyres, 'Brave Men of Their Word', 18 February 2011, ft.com.

12   G. Sereny, *Albert Speer: His Battle with Truth*, Picador, 1995, pp. 543–4.

When Berlin fell on 2 May 1945, Upper Bavaria, near the Austrian border, was still in German military hands. This was the last redoubt of the Nazi regime. The landscape to the north was a scene of utter devastation. There was an epidemic of suicides, like that described by Martin Bormann's son, and not just within the ruling elite. The psychological impact on German society of the war, and the sudden loss of the entire social vision of the Third Reich, was immense. As elsewhere in Europe, Bavaria's cities and towns had been destroyed by bombing. Germany and Austria's oil infrastructure was devastated. The refinery at Schwechat had been laid waste by the US Air Force 15th Command, flying out of Foggia in Italy. In the last months of the war Hitler tried to implement a scorched-earth strategy. Albert Speer, Nazi armaments minister, described later how he had been ordered to destroy 'all the railway systems, the waterways, the whole of the communications system, telephone, telegraph and broadcasting, and all masts, antennas and stocks of spare cable and wireless parts. Equally, all switching and cable diagrams – and drawings which could assist in repairs.'[13]

By May 1945, along the route that we have been travelling, great swathes of industrialised society lay in ruins. The oil wells in Baku had been abandoned; the pipeline across the Caucasus unearthed; the ports of Rijeka and Trieste bombed. The Reich was a sea of rubble. Germany had arrived at what it now calls 'Stunde Null' – Zero Hour.

---

13   Ibid., p. 456.

Part V THE FACTORY

MAP VI INGOLSTADT

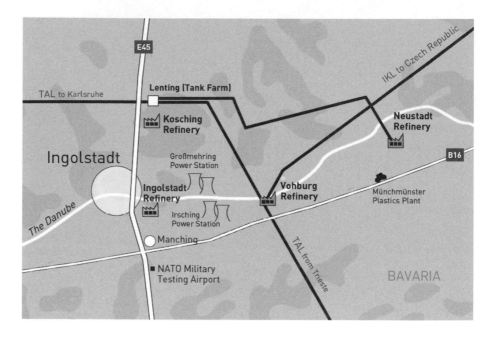

20 THIS IS THE AUSCHWITZ GENERATION, AND THERE'S NO ARGUING WITH THEM

TAL KP 435 – 5,042 KM – GEISENFELD, GERMANY

Night at the village of Geisenfeld, up on the Hallertau ridge. The traffic is a constant roar on autobahn E45 between Munich and Regensburg. In the darkness beyond, we can make out the valley of the River Ilm falling away to the Danube plain and, directly north, the lights of the oil refinery at Vohburg. Orange flames of gas flares against the Köschinger forest on the Frankische Alb, the range of hills between us and Nurnberg. There is a glow in the sky to the east from the lights of the Neustadt refinery, and the low clouds to the west are lit from beneath by the glare of another plant at Kösching. The flames call to mind the photographs of the flare on the Central Azeri platform out in the Caspian.

We are standing in the middle of a region that is effectively one vast Factory. Spread out below, and far beyond the horizon, are the constituent parts of this great industrial machine that echoes the network of platforms in Azeri waters. Most of the crude from beneath the Caspian leaves the offshore fields in a handful of pipelines bound for Sangachal, and this industrial enterprise is largely supplied by one line coming from Trieste. TAL feeds 100 per cent of the crude demand of Bavaria, 75 per cent of Austria's, 50 per cent of Baden-Württemberg's, and 27 per cent of the Czech Republic's needs.

Around the city of Ingolstadt, the Transalpine Pipeline delivers oil to the Vohburg refinery, then runs on to a tankfarm oil depot at Lenting in the rolling hills across the Danube valley, from where crude is distributed to the nearby refineries at Kösching and Neustadt. From Lenting, a further pipeline runs west to a refinery at Karlsruhe on the Rhine, while from a subsidiary tankfarm at Vohburg, yet another pipeline runs north-east to refineries at Kralupy and Litvinov in the Czech Republic.

The battery of refineries running east to west across the belly of central Europe – Schwechat, Kralupy, Litvinov, Burghausen, Neustadt, Vohburg, Kösching and Karlsruhe – are like eight mighty furnaces fed by crude from TAL. In turn, they provide energy for a myriad of machines within an area that stretches from Vienna in the east to Strasbourg in the west; from Prague in the north to the Alps in the south: a zone of production some 700 kilometres long by 300 kilometres wide; a zone one and a half times the land area of Azerbaijan.

When gazing at Azerbaijan, the interested viewer from Western Europe will imagine its oilfields, although they are far offshore and inaccessible. The same eyes tracking media coverage of Georgia will soon perceive the BTC pipeline, although it is buried and only the marker post and pump stations are visible. Yet while these eight refineries that are fed by TAL dominate the landscape and are a familiar sight to millions of people, the plants and the pipeline are not perceived as one system, one machine.

TAL and its eight refineries are part of the skeleton of Central Europe. Gasoline for cars and trucks; heating oil for factories and hospitals; feedstock for chemical works and plastics plants; fuel oil for power stations and river barges; bitumen for roads and roofs. The list continues. According to our basic calculations, approximately 27 million citizens live in the area provided for, and these inhabitants, particularly in Germany and Austria, have some of the highest consumption levels of any people on the earth.

What comes from the refineries fuels the consumption not only of those who live within this zone, but also those who pass through it. At Geisenfeld the night sky is dotted with the flashing pinpricks of aircraft lights: jets arriving and departing from Munich's Franz Joseph Strauss Flughafen, forty kilometres to the south. This is a 'hub airport': the fuel from the Neustadt refinery will take a 747 to Calcutta or New York. The same is true for the other international flight destinations that lie within this zone, such as Prague, Frankfurt and Stuttgart. The refined crude from TAL carries people and machines to every corner of the globe.

The zone is criss-crossed by eleven autobahns covering thousands of kilometres:

E35, E41, E43, E45, E50, E52, E53, E54, E56, E58, E60

These transport corridors within the Factory, carrying vast quantities of traffic, echo the pipelines below ground. A family filling up its Volkswagen Golf at the Aral petrol station at Schollstrasse in Ingolstadt, just before they pull onto the E45, can travel for over 500 kilometres, as far south as the Adriatic or nearly to the Baltic in the north. In this way the shadow of the Factory extends far across the landmass of the continent.

This is one of the car-building heartlands of Europe. From early and forgotten inventors of the Austro-Hungarian Empire, such as Vaclav Laurin and Vaclav Klement near Prague, to those whose names still evoke the industry – Karl Benz in Mannheim, Gottlieb Daimler in Stuttgart and Rudolf Diesel in Augsburg – the automobile was in large measure born in this area. There still remains within the zone a remarkable array of car plants, including Skoda at Mlada Boleslav, BMW at Regensburg, Audi at Ingolstadt, and Daimler Chrysler near Stuttgart. The TAL refineries provide the backbone of this industrial realm.

We have decided to explore one part of this great Factory: the discrete area around Ingolstadt, stretching ten kilometres across the Danube floodplain and thirty kilometres along it. Within this valley lies the heart of the region: three refineries, arms manufacturers, a car plant and several petrochemical works. This is what lies before us at Geisenfeld.

INGOLSTADT, GERMANY

The Danube plain, still so far from the sea, is immense. Across it, fields are neatly squared out, hedgeless; dark with furrows, or rich green with winter wheat. Here and there is the bright yellow of oilseed rape. Between the fields, streams cut their way north from the Hallertau.

Just to the east of Ingolstadt lies the small nature reserve, Lebensraum Donau-Auen. A wondrous jungle of trees, the undergrowth full of cuckoos and chiffchaffs, buzzards and black woodpeckers – this is a glimpse of the wild, waterlogged forest that ran along the Danube before the river was channelled. It would have presented a formidable barrier: no wonder this was the Roman *limes*. Facing the empire across the floodland were the unconquered German tribes, the barbarians. This border was the sister to that running just south of Batumi through the Caucasus, at the other edge the empire.

Since the end of the Ice Age, settlements in this area had been part of what archaeologists call the Middle European Corridor – a convergence of routes that could run from the Caspian, over the saddle between the Greater and Lesser Caucasus, around the coast of the Black Sea, up the Danube and then down the Rhine to the North Sea or the Loire to the Atlantic. Trade took place as objects were exchanged, carried for a distance, exchanged again, and carried further. There is a remarkable continuum of human and material traffic along this river valley, from hunter-gatherer communities to the present day: a span of over 10,000 years.[1]

Ingolstadt grew up on high ground, close to a point where the Danube could easily be crossed. As a place of strategic importance, the King of Bavaria surrounded it with massive fortifications in the 1850s. Hulks of stone bastions still guard the approach to the Danube Bridge and dot the surrounding farm-land in a protective ring. The transport of goods by barge grew substantially in the nineteenth century, and the river was straightened and embanked, raising the water level several metres above the floodplain. After the development of oilfields in Romania in the 1870s, crude and kerosene were carried up this waterway. In 1997 the first crude from the Azeri–Chirag–Gunashli oilfield

---

1   Cunliffe, *Europe Between the Oceans*, pp. 38–41.

arrived, via pipeline, at the Black Sea ports of Supsa and Novorossiysk. At that point it would have been possible for that Azeri oil to have been shipped across the Black Sea up the Danube by bunker barge to the refineries of Ingolstadt. But the drive to construct BTC precluded this idea.

After *Stunde Null,* or 'Year Zero', while the fate of Germany was unclear, Ingolstadt housed a huge refugee camp. From 1945 to 1947 the four occupied zones – British, French, American and Russian – cooperated through the Inter-Allied Control Commission. But in 1947 hostility between the Western powers and the Soviet Union grew, and the British and the US created a joint area, called 'Bizonia', in which they developed the kernel of a new West German state. In June that year, US Secretary of State George Marshall unveiled plans for a European Recovery Program, in which a reindustrialised Germany was to hold the line against Soviet expansion. The Marshall Plan ran for four years, dispensing $12.5 billion to European states from Britain to Turkey, and was significantly biased towards increasing oil consumption.

As Germany shifted from the possibility of the agrarian Morgenthau Plan to the implementation of the industrial Marshall Plan, the Anglo-Iranian Oil Company, as BP was then called, ramped up its position in the occupied state. In an echo of the process that took place after Germany's defeat in World War I, the company purchased large chunks of the country's oil infrastructure, including the Eurotank refinery in Hamburg, and a Bavarian and Austrian distribution company. Anglo-Iranian's fuel sales in the country doubled in three years.

The French Sector had soon joined Bizonia, creating an economically united entity, while funds from the Marshall Plan were used to relocate a car plant from Chemnitz in the Soviet Sector to Ingolstadt in the US Sector. It was renamed Auto Union Deutschland Ingolstadt – Audi. Similarly, Anglo-Iranian moved the head-quarters of its subsidiary OLEX permanently from Berlin to Hamburg, within the British zone. All Anglo-Iranian's new German assets were merged into BP Benzin und Petroleum GmbH.[2]

John Browne was born in Hamburg on 20 February 1948, barely a month after Anglo-Iranian purchased the Eurotank refinery down by the dockside of the same city. His mother, a Jewish Hungarian from the west of Romania, had – remarkably – escaped the Holocaust. In Hamburg she married Edmund Browne, an officer in a British Army tank regiment stationed in the city. In 1957, Browne senior took a job with Anglo-Iranian. Soon, together with this wife and son, he was posted to Iran. So began the intertwining of John Browne's life and that of the company.

On the final day of the Berlin Airlift in May 1949, the *Grundgesetz* – the Constitution – for the Federal Republic of Germany was established. In the elections that followed, Konrad Adenauer, of the Christian Democrat Union,

---

2   Bamberg, *British Petroleum and Global Oil*, p. 299.

campaigned under the slogan: 'No Experiments'. His programme explicitly refused to promise dramatic changes, as a counterpoint to the German experience of both Nazism and, in the east of the country, Soviet Stalinism.[3] In July 1949, Adenauer was elected chancellor, with Ludwig Erhard as his finance minister.

Adenauer and Erhard are seen as the giants of the West German 'economic miracle', the *Wirtschaft Wunder*, which produced an 8 per cent annual growth rate throughout the 1950s and, by the end of the decade, had made the Federal Republic the most prosperous country in Europe. Oil consumption soared in Germany, growing even faster than the rest of the economy: it increased on average by 19 per cent every year between 1960 and 1965. Soon BP's largest market outside the UK was Germany.

And yet, as a consequence of its origins, BP's sales of refined petroleum products, such as petrol and aviation fuel, lagged far behind its competitors Shell and Standard Oil. The founding myth of Shell lay in the *Murex* tanker's journey from Batumi through Suez to the Far East arranged by Marcus Samuel, while the legend behind Standard Oil was that of Rockefeller's ruthless control of the pipelines in the US. These stories of origin emphasise that both corporations had prioritised their ability to refine and sell products. BP's roots lay in drilling and extraction. The Royal Navy was its primary buyer of crude. BP's weakness in actually selling refined products was exacerbated in the 1950s when Iran, Iraq, Kuwait and other host governments demanded ever higher extraction rates. The company was forced to sell crude in bulk rather than refining it first, thereby undermining BP's overall profitability.[4] Maurice Bridgeman, CEO of BP, knew that in order not to lose even more ground to its rivals, the company had to grow its shipping and refining operations. An increase in consumption of BP products in key European markets was seen as essential.

By the 1960s, Bridgeman was seriously concerned that BP could lose its strong position in Germany and other EEC countries. France was following a dirigiste policy, its government backing French oil companies by placing restrictions on foreign corporations, preventing them from dominating the domestic retail market. The French government, together with state-owned French and Italian oil companies, was trying to persuade Germany and the other EEC member states to adopt similar policies. BP being based outside the EEC, it faced the alarming prospect of losing much of its retail market in Europe.[5]

---

3   N. Davies, *Europe: A History*, Pimlico, 1997, p. 1,072.

4   The disparity between the companies was still markedly evident by the mid-1960s. In 1965 Shell produced 2,750,000 barrels of crude oil a day, not much more than BP's 2,250,000 barrels a day. But Shell refined 3,500,000 barrels and sold 6,000,000 barrels – i.e. it refined and sold more than it produced; whereas BP refined a mere 1,500,000 barrels and sold only 2,000,000.

5   Bamberg, *British Petroleum and Global Oil*, pp. 224–5.

Bridgeman was convinced of the need for urgent action. Seeing West Germany as pivotal in the fight against the French-led push for state-directed economies, BP carried out an intensive lobbying campaign in 1967. German ministers were targeted, together with British politicians believed to have influence in Germany. Deminex, the German state-backed oil group, was even offered the prospect of a share of BP's access to crude oil in Iran and Abu Dhabi. In May 1968, the company engaged in European parliamentary hearings, arguing 'in favour of a liberal international economy, free from discrimination against the oil multinationals whose integrated international supply systems were . . . the best guarantee of security and cheapness in oil supplies'.[6]

BP used its financial capital to force more of its products into Europe and drive up demand for oil. Thus the company locked itself into a mutual dependency with certain markets. As Germany's economy expanded and demanded more petroleum, BP helped provide it. As BP needed to increase the sales of its products, it pushed to expand the German economy.

BP, then, had a role in creating the West Germany it needed – just as, decades later, it had a hand in shaping the Azerbaijan, Georgia and Turkey it needed. In all these cases, and in many other states around the world, it has helped form economies and societies in a manner that enables its maximisation of profit, in places of both extraction and consumption.

Our guidebook to the landscape of Ingolstadt is *Eine Stadt baut auf* ('A city is built'). Published by the municipality in the 1960s, it walks us through the transformation of the town between 1960 and 1965: the planned new zones of housing; the massive new Audi works; the sites of the five new refineries; the locations of the new schools and churches. The photographs celebrate the opening of the new Danube Bridge and capture the autobahns from the air. This is the city that in due course gave the world the Audi slogan, *Vorsprung Durch Technik* ('Advance Through Technology').

Standing on an autobahn bridge above six lanes of traffic speeding through the urban fabric, we can see, in all directions, a horizon dominated by smoking power stations and refinery chimneys. Back in 1949, Chancellor Adenauer had promised 'No Experiments', yet here we are in the midst of a great experiment, a piece of social market engineering that echoes the industrialisation of Sumqayit and Rustavi. The 1960s photographs in the guidebook are suffused with the same spirit of technological optimism that flowed through Hikmet's poems and Khrushchev's Soviet Union: the vision of the city as a model of harmony, with the machine as an essential assistant to the citizen.

---

6   Ibid., p. 245.

We were lent this book by Rudi Remm, an environmental campaigner with decades of experience on local issues and a deep knowledge of the industrial history of the region. Over beer and sausages in a Munich bar, talking long into the night, he explains his understanding of Bavaria's development since the war.

Unlike the provinces of Sachsen or Nordrhein-Westfalen, Bavaria had a relatively small coal resource. Consequently the region was comparatively unindustrialised for the first half of the twentieth century, the majority of its population engaged in agriculture. Fuel came from wood and hydropower, known locally as *weißkohl* or 'white coal'. Rudi elaborates how the River Inn, north of Rosenheim, had the largest hydroelectric plant in Germany, generating 400 megawatts: 'That's huge, half a nuclear power plant!' Until 1960, most of Bavaria's energy came from renewable sources: 'Houses were heated by wood and a little coal, but now they are heated by oil, or gas or combined heat and power – most of the latter coming from gas-fired power stations'.

The prime minister of Bavaria, Alfons Goppel, and the Bavarian minister for economy and transport, Dr Otto Schedl, dominated the post-war politics of the region, echoing Chancellor Adenauer and Finance Minister Ludwig Erhard on a national level. As minister from 1957 to 1970, Schedl closed down the few Bavarian coalmines and delineated areas around Ingolstadt and Burghausen as petrochemical hubs. We ask Rudi if the changes that came about were entirely the work of Schedl and Goppel. 'You can't be sure. I feel it was also about the policy of the European oil companies. There's a film that was made for schools by the *Landesfilmdienst*. It portrays the refineries as the "new age" for Ingolstadt'.

Within a year of taking office Schedl had found a key ally: Enrico Mattei, the charismatic general director of the Italian state-owned oil company, ENI. Schedl and Mattei together sketched out the plan that led to the building of a pipeline from Genoa – the Central European Pipeline System. At Ingolstadt a new refinery was to be built, operated by ENI, but 50 per cent owned by BP.

Construction of the pipeline and the refinery began, but these projects neither satisfied Schedl's vision nor quenched the appetite of the oil companies. Long before the first plant opened, plans were well underway for the construction of further refineries at Vohburg and Neustadt, and for a new route to increase the pumping of crude from the south – the Transalpine pipeline that we have been following.[7] Listening to Rudi, we realise we have discovered three more fathers of TAL: Mattei, Schedl and Goppel.

---

7   The CEPS was completed and the refinery opened in 1965 – by which time Mattei was long since dead, killed in a mysterious plane crash in October 1962. To celebrate the completion of CEPS and the refinery at Ingolstadt, ENI commissioned Bernardo Bertolucci, the celebrated Marxist film director, to make a film about the journey of oil from Iran, via Genoa, to Ingolstadt. It was released in 1966, coincidentally entitled *Il Via Petroli* ('The Oil Road').

As the book *Eine Stadt baut auf* rolled off the presses in the late 1960s, the area around Ingolstadt was in a ferment of change as the experiment was given form. A city was built that the Futurists – indeed, Marinetti himself – might have dreamed of.

TAL KP 452 – 5,059 KM – VOHBURG, BAVARIA

Fourteen kilometres east of Ingolstadt, we stand on the precipitous ramparts of the small medieval town of Vohburg and survey the great sweep of the land around. All about is the fertile plain – ploughed fields of black earth, lines of poplars and green swathes of pasture. Vohburg feels like an island in a sea of farmland.

Walking the town ramparts, we can look down at the youth hanging about at the bus station outside the walls. Beyond it, the refinery spreads out to the west, a titanic chemistry set with its distillation units, crude storage tanks, spherical gas holders, chimneys and perimeter fences. All this is recognisable from the aerial photograph in BP's 1977 staff handbook, *Our Industry Petroleum*.[8]

On its completion in 1967, the refinery at Vohburg was owned outright by BP, its construction an expression of the company's drive to maximise product sales in the German market. Vohburg was one of the five refineries around Ingolstadt built in the five years between 1962 and 1967. Their location illustrates a significant shift in the geography of industrialism.

From the mid-nineteenth century, most industrial plants had been built closest to the point of fuel-extraction. The iron- and steelworks of the Ruhr, South Wales and Pennsylvania were constructed in the shadow of coalmines. Similarly, refineries had often been built close to oilfields. However, the fate of BP's Abadan plant in Iran dramatically illustrated the risks of location. In the early 1950s the Iranian government challenged decades of foreign exploitation by semi-nationalising not only its oilfields, but also BP's refinery at Abadan. Oilfields are of course immobile, but as long as the crude can be exported, it can be refined anywhere. Consequently, the Western oil corporations, such as BP, responded to the threat of nationalisation by shifting refineries to places of consumption.

In 1950 BP had shares in four refineries in primarily oil-extracting countries, and ten in primarily oil-consuming countries. Twenty-five years later, the company had no refineries in oil-extracting countries. However, it fully or jointly owned forty-one refineries in oil-consuming countries. This change illustrated a shift in political power, with oil-extracting states no longer turning the bulk of their raw materials into manufactured products before exporting them.

The first delivery destined for passage through the Transalpine pipeline reached Muggia on 13 April 1967, on board the Shell tanker *Daphnella*. It was a shipment

---

8   *Our Industry: Petroleum*, BP, 1977, pp. 248–52; *Bilder aus der Welt des Erdöls*, BP Austria AG, 1994, p. 12.

of crude from Iran, from oilfields partly owned by BP. This oil was not refined by Iranian workers in Abadan but, once it had been piped over the Alps, processed by Bavarian workers in Vohburg. This relocation of refining capacity weakened the hands of oil-producing states, and at the same time strengthened the hands of the oil companies. While construction of the refineries did bring a concentration of capital and employment to Bavaria, it also made Germany dependent on foreign oil supply – thereby forcing it further down the Oil Road.

Seven weeks after the *Daphnella* docked in Italy, the shah of Iran, Mohammed Reza Pahlavi, arrived in West Berlin on a state visit to the Federal Republic. At the Berlin Opera House, where the shah and his wife, Empress Farah Diba, attended a performance of Mozart's *Magic Flute*, large crowds gathered to protest the brutality of his regime.

In the weeks leading up to his visit, the German press had devoted much coverage to the Federal Republic's support for the shah's rule. One journalist, Ulrike Meinhof, had written an 'Open Letter to Farah Diba' in the magazine *konkret*:

> You tell us: 'The summer is very hot in Iran, and like most Persians, I went to the Persian Riviera on the Caspian Sea with my family.' Like most Persians . . . aren't you exaggerating? Most Persians are peasants with an annual income of less than 100 dollars. Most Persian women see every other child die of starvation, poverty and disease . . . And do most of those children who work fourteen hours a day making rugs go to the Persian Riviera on the Caspian Sea in summer too?[9]

As the Iranian entourage arrived at the opera house, protestors shouted 'Shah charlatan!' and 'Murderer!' After the shah and empress entered the building, the crowd began to disperse, but the police and Iranian Savak secret service members charged forward, swinging their batons. In the ensuing chaos a number of demonstrators were beaten and collapsed. One protester, twenty-six-year-old Benno Ohnesorg, was chased by police and beaten with a truncheon. Then, from a distance of less than half a metre, a detective from the Berlin Political Police shot Ohnesorg in the head. At a gathering of students later that night a young woman, Gudrun Ensslin, crying uncontrollably, declared: 'This fascist state means to kill us all. We must organise resistance. Violence is the only way to answer violence. This is the Auschwitz generation, and there's no arguing with them!'

The murder of Ohnesorg ignited a new wave of German radicalism. It catalysed the anarchist 2 June Group, the leftist Revolutionary Cells, and the Red Army Faction, called the 'Baader–Meinhof Gang' by the media. This latter included at its core both Gudrun Ensslin and Ulrike Meinhof, the journalist.

---

9   S. Aust, *The Baader-Meinhof Complex*, Bodley Head, 2008, pp. 24–7.

Four months later, on 3 October 1967, the first shipment of oil to pass through the Transalpine pipeline arrived at Vohburg – Iranian crude ready for refining. BP, itself majority-owned by the British state, now controlled 50 per cent of the three refineries constructed in the Upper Danube valley. Consequently, these plants – one of the densest concentrations of refining on the planet at the time – were effectively UK government assets and highly strategic pieces of infrastructure. Much of their product was going to the US Army and Air Force, based in US Sector Southern Germany – a military then heavily engaged in the war on Vietnam.

By the late 1960s, a generation of young Germans, alienated from their parents, was in a ferment of desperation – even before the murder of Benno Ohnesorg. Born after the war, they had grown up with elders who refused to speak about their experiences during the Third Reich. Their parents were part of the 'Auschwitz Generation', as Gudrun Ensslin had shouted in Berlin. This younger generation was also alienated from the Federal Republic, which had wholeheartedly embraced an American social model, partly to assist the collective amnesia. It was a model not only of Cold War politics, with its arms race and outlawing of the Communist Party in West Germany, but also of a culture of consumerism and technological modernity, of which the vision for Ingolstadt was a prime example. The Factory was becoming a place of struggle.

Six months after the opening of Vohburg, on 2 April 1968, Gudrun Ensslin and Andreas Baader of the Red Army Faction drove from Munich to Frankfurt. Their plan was to carry out the group's first action against symbols of consumerism – the firebombing of two department stores, Kaufhaus Schneider and Kaufhof. The buildings were burned, but no one was hurt.

On 8 May 1972 President Nixon announced that the US would mine harbours in North Vietnam, so the Red Army Faction determined to respond. Days later, three pipe-bombs wrecked the officers' mess of the Fifth US Army Corps in Frankfurt. Thirteen soldiers were injured and one killed. Claiming responsibility, the RAF's communiqué explained: 'West Germany will no longer be a safe hinterland for the strategists of extermination in Vietnam. They must know that their crimes against the Vietnamese people have made them new and bitter enemies, and there will be nowhere in the world left where they can be safe from the attacks of revolutionary guerrilla units.'[10] The group was responding to what it perceived as the hidden violence underlying the Western political and economic system.

Soon these political struggles were targeting the Oil Road itself. Back on the quayside in Muggia, we had asked Fabio the fisherman about the SIOT terminal. He looked up from his nets and said immediately, in broken English, 'Terrorist organisation September Black'. Paolo Gerebizza, who had worked on the

---

10   Ibid., p. 160.

construction of TAL, had also remembered seeing 'the columns of smoke far off, through the window'. His daughter, Elena, sent us the contemporary front page of the provincial newspaper, *Il Piccolo*, which read 'Sea of Fire: Trieste oil pipeline targeted by bombers in the night'.

On 4 August 1972, three oil-storage bunkers at the extensive SIOT tank farm were simultaneously blown up, igniting 140,000 tonnes of crude. The fire burned for four days. Even though the area was crawling with troops – this was a front-line of the Cold War, with Yugoslavia less than a kilometre away – militants had managed to break into the oil-storage site, set up explosives and charges, and escape without capture. The explosion shut down the pipeline, with ripple effects felt at the refineries such as Vohburg and Schwechat, and in corporate offices in Vienna, Bonn, Washington and London.

The Palestinian Black September organisation claimed responsibility, explaining that it had targeted the TAL terminal because it supplied crude to Germany, which had armed and supported both Jordan and Israel in the past. Black September itself was named for King Hussein's 1970 military assault on the Palestinian refugee communities in Jordan.

A month later, Ulrike Meinhof of the RAF explained why Palestinian and European anti-imperialists were blowing up infrastructure in Europe, bringing the struggle 'back to the supplier who provided Hussein's army with panzers, assault rifles, machine-pistols, and munitions. Back to where everything possible was done – using development aid, oil deals, investments, weapons, and diplomatic relationships – to pit Arab regimes against each other, and to turn all of them against the Palestinian liberation movement'.[11]

By the early 1970s it was evident that the growing dependency of the social market economies of Western Europe on regions of extraction in the Middle East had brought its own challenges. The political conflict in the periphery was fuelling conflict in the oil-consuming centre, and vice versa. The violence associated with the growth of European economies was fuelling acts of violence by the very generation who were supposedly enjoying the benefits of that growth.

TAL KP 462 – 5,069 KM – NEUSTADT, GERMANY

On a cold, damp morning, the train from the Ingolstadt Hauptbahnhof runs east, out through red-roofed suburbs, underneath the autobahns and electricity pylons, and into the farmland of the Danube river plain. On the half-hour passage through the Factory towards Neustadt, we take our bearings from the red-and-white-striped chimneys of the power stations at Grossmehring and Irsching, and the cluster of silver pipe-work that marks the refinery at Vohburg.

---

11   U. Meinhof, *Black September: Regarding the Strategy for Anti-Imperialist Struggle*, Red Army Faction, 1972.

We pass long lines of rail oil tankers. Rudi had explained that much of the refined product is sent to industrial customers along these tracks. A line of fifty-one tankers carrying aviation fuel travels every two days to Munich airport. These clunking wagons are like their counterparts on the Baku–Batumi Railway rattling across the Azeri desert.

At length, beyond the bright green leaves of a copse of silver birch, rise the grey chimneys and towers of our destination, Bayernoil. Dismounting from the train, we catch the scent of crude in the air. Perhaps 40 per cent of the oil refined here comes from beneath the Caspian. At the gates of Neustadt refinery we wait in the entrance cabin while the security guard rings through. We have an appointment with Kirsten Pilgram, head of Öffentlichkeit – literally 'openness'. Workers coming on or off shift, in blue baseball caps, blue boiler suits and boots with scuffed toecaps, cast us quizzical looks, reinforcing our sense that visitors to this industrial underbelly are rare.

On the waiting room table lies an array of corporate literature, including a brochure proclaiming the refinery's relationship to the factories and industry around it:

> Bayernoil fits smoothly within the chain of key industries in the high-tech location that is Bavaria: automotive, chemical, medical-technical and other industries place Bavaria ahead in Germany and in Europe. The motor of this development and the base for its growth was and is a guaranteed and affordable supply of motor and heating fuel and other mineral oil products.[12]

Leaving the security cabin, we are confronted by cliffs of steel pipe-work. We are struck by the sheer weight of this thing, rising up from the floodplains: a gargantuan structure, alive with cracking and distillation, settling and separation. It is only four decades old, but its scale conveys a massive permanence.

Immaculately dressed in a white, gold-buttoned blouse, Kirsten brings us into a conference room whose calm cleanliness reminds us of the boardroom at Villa Petrolea in Baku. It is here that the shareholders of Bayernoil might meet, three times a year, to discuss progress and hear future plans. The long table and chrome-and-leather chairs contrast with the heaving megamachine outside. As on every stage of this journey, the raw dirt of the river of liquid geology remains out of sight.

Kirsten is friendly but efficient as she hands us a neat pile of printouts that she has kindly prepared. Talking us through them, she explains how Bayernoil works. The schematic diagram that she lays before us is like a plan for the heart of the Factory.

---

12 *Bayernoil gemeinsam erfolgreich: A Refinery for Bavaria*, Bayernoil, July 2009, p. 2.

Here are the refineries at Neustadt, Vohburg and Kösching. Here is the TAL pipeline arriving at Lenting 'from Trieste' and running 'to Karlsruhe' and 'to Neustadt'. Another, more detailed diagram shows the links between Vohburg, Neustadt and the petrochemical works at Münchsmünster. There are lines in yellow, green, black, pink and purple, each denoting fourteen distinct pipelines, each carrying a different substance – this carries liquid gas, and that ethylene. Pipelines everywhere.

Examining these diagrams and finding our way through Kirsten's blizzard of statistics, we slowly extract a narrative. As we had already come to understand, shareholdings have shifted back and forth, but for thirty-six of the past forty-five years, BP has held the largest stake in the Bavarian refineries.[13] It all bears out the company's commitment to be a long-term player in the German market, and how important BP has been to the region in the post-war period. Despite this prominence, these German assets – unlike those in Azerbaijan – hardly feature in annual reports issued from BP's head office in London. Their existence almost never registers in the metropolitan financial media, partly because the sale of refined petrol products generates far less profit than the extraction of crude, and partly because the refining business is not as glamorous as the drama of drilling for oil far out at sea.

Although Kirsten has worked here for decades, her service does not reach as far back as the refinery's darkest months, during the 1973 Oil Crisis, when the flow of tankers to Muggia and crude through the pipeline temporarily ceased. In a book of nostalgic Ingolstadt images, there is a photo with the jaunty caption: 'During the Oil Crisis it was possible for the Sunday family outing to be a stroll along the autobahn.'[14] The image shows eight characters walking down one of the city's motorways – utterly devoid of traffic. In this picture, the dreams of Marinetti, Schedl and Khrushchev have ground to a halt.

Beyond the material impact of those few months, when the supply of crude from the Middle East effectively stopped, the Oil Crisis had a long-lasting effect on BP, including changing the ownership structure of the company. The spiral of inflation that arose from the crisis meant that, in 1976, the chancellor of the

---

13   In 1967, BP owned 50 per cent of Ingolstadt and 100 per cent of Vohburg. Just over twenty years later, in 1989, the two refineries were merged into one company, and BP held a 62 per cent stake in the combined Raffineriegesellschaft Vohburg/ Ingolstadt (RVI). Nine years later, RVI merged with Erdolraffinerie Neustadt GmbH to make Bayernoil, now controlling three refineries, with BP holding a 42.5 per cent stake. By August 2008, Ingolstadt Refinery had closed and BP's ownership had shrunk to its current 22.5 per cent holding. Bayernoil is owned by OMV of Austria (45 per cent), Agip of Italy (20 per cent), BP (10 per cent) and Ruhr Oel (25 per cent). The latter belongs to PDVSA of Venezuela (50 per cent) and BP (50 per cent).

14   K. Zirkel, *Aufgewachsen in Ingolstadt in der 60er und 70er Jahren*, Wartberg Verlag, 2008, p. 31.

exchequer, Denis Healey, had to go to the IMF for a £3 billion loan. This was the largest application that had ever made to that body. The price demanded by the IMF was £2.5 billion of cuts in UK public-sector spending, and the disposal of 14.5 per cent of the British government's shareholding in BP.[15]

The sale took place the following year, in what was then the world's largest share offering.[16] The whole process was coordinated in two 'operations rooms' – one in the Finsbury Circus offices of BP, under the guidance of the company's financial controller, Quentin Morris; the other in the Moorgate offices of the government broker Mullens & Co., under James's father, Richard Marriott.[17] He worked closely with a number of private banks, the most important being Rothschild.

The share offer was 4.7 times oversubscribed. It not only broke the British government's hold on BP, but also showed the way for future state privatisations under the coming Thatcher government. By 1977, a decade after TAL and Vohburg had started operating, the financial relationship between BP and the UK government was beginning to alter dramatically. Sixty years after Churchill's initial investment, the government was forsaking its controlling stake. A new structure of shareholding – dominated by pension funds, insurance companies and banks – was coming into being. Yet despite this shift from public to private shareholding, the British state and this corporation remain intimately entwined, as we saw in their close collaboration in ensuring BP's advance into Azerbaijan.

A further development stimulated by the Oil Crisis was the growth of a new European political movement. In 1973 'ecology' candidates stood for the first time in elections in France and Britain. The same year a new party was founded in Germany: Die Bauern Congress (the Farmers' Congress), forerunner of Die Grünen (the Green Party).[18] This was a movement committed to radical change, but, in contrast to the strategies of groups such as the Red Army Faction, through parliamentary means. Within six years the Green Party had succeeded in gaining representation in two regional parliaments. Twenty years later, after a long march through the institutions of the state, the party joined the federal coalition government. The Green Party leader, Joschka Fischer, who had once been a member of the 1970s Revolutionary Cells, was appointed German minister of foreign affairs in 1998. He would become the longest-serving post-war foreign minister and take Germany to war for the first time since 1945, at a time when the EU was expanding its influence over energy issues in the Caucasus and the Caspian.

---

15   J. Moran, 'Defining Moment: Denis Healey agrees to the demands of the IMF', 4 September 2010, at ft.com.

16   D. Kynaston, *The City of London, Vol IV: A Club No More, 1945–2000*, Chatto & Windus, 2001.

17   D. Wainwright, *Government Broker: The Story of an Office and of Mullens & Co.*, Matham Publishing, 1990, pp. 102–3.

18   Tony Judt, *Postwar*, Heinemann, 2005, p. 493.

As our meeting is drawing to a close, we ask one last question: 'What of the future of Neustadt?' Kirsten shrugs her shoulders. They plan ten to fifteen years ahead. After that, who knows? 'And what about alternative energy?' She laughs a little, and says: 'This is for *kindergarten* – there is no security with it. But of course, it's a political question. You should ask the Green Party.'

The train to the centre of Ingolstadt takes us back past the plant of Münchsmünster, to which the ethylene pipeline from Neustadt delivers feedstock for the manufacture of plastic. The factory here was once part-owned by BP, but now belongs to the US corporation Lyondell Bassell, one of the largest plastics producers in Europe. Since the 1930s, and particularly from the 1950s, the plastics industry grew rapidly from the infrastructure of oil refining. In Bavaria this development was concentrated around Ingolstadt and Burghausen. At Münchsmünster a range of products is made, including coatings of pipelines – similar to the substance that caused such consternation over BTC in the Caucasus. It also produces polypropylene resin, Clyrell EC340R, which is marketed as being resistant to low temperatures and ideal for food containers, such as the one-litre tubs in which ice-cream is sold. Clyrell EC340R is trucked from Münchsmünster to plants where the tubs are moulded, and the tubs themselves are then transported to ice-cream factories. Eventually consumers buy their favourite brands and carry them back to their freezers. A litre of Carte D'Or vanilla ice cream bought in London might be cradled in a tub made from crude drawn from the Caspian and refined in Neustadt.

What is remarkable about these seemingly mundane processes is not only the space that the crude moves across, but also the time it takes. Although used in every crevice of our lives, plastics are too new for us fully to understand how long they will last. The ice-cream tub may eventually find its way to a landfill site, but it is unlikely to degrade for hundreds of years – far beyond the future plans of Neustadt or the lifespan of the ACG oilfield.

After just a few decades of widespread industrial use, plastic, in the form of litter, is already an acute problem on land and in the oceans.[19] Of the crude that the *Dugi Otok* carries, perhaps 10 per cent will be used to manufacture plastics. In her hold lies an unformed wealth of hip replacements, toothbrushes, laptops, sweet wrappers, and so on. But as she ploughs through the Mediterranean the tanker is passing through a soup of plastic. Every square mile of ocean is estimated to hold 46,000 separate pieces of plastic litter.[20]

---

19   See G. Howard, 'Polyethylene Terephthalate: Making an Economically Informed Material', and R. Thompson, 'Plastics, Environment and Human Health' – both papers at Accumulation: The Material Ecologies and Economies of Plastic, Goldsmiths, University of London, 21 June 2011.

20   United Nations Environment Programme, 'Action Urged to Avoid Deep Trouble in the Deep Seas', 16 June 2006, at unep.org.

21 A LIQUID DISTILLED FROM A FOSSILISED ECOSYSTEM

GROSSMEHRING, GERMANY

The following day the weather is fine, so we hire bikes and set out to explore some of the places we had been alerted to in our conversations with Rudi Remm. From the centre of Ingolstadt we cross the Danube Bridge and head east along the river-bank. We soon find what we are looking for, as we peer at a metal sheet fixed to the top of a two-metre steel pole just by the cycle path. We read off the letters and numbers:

Ol – /Gas Leitung

Schilderpf.Ts 03

VR km 0.533

Mk 9

BO 12

BO 14

Over the next three-quarters of an hour we jot down the details of thirteen such marker posts. Using the diagram that Kirsten gave us, we begin to figure them out: over there is TAL, running out of the Vohburg refinery and passing under the great river as it heads for the Lenting terminal. And here lies E.ON's gas line, which feeds the power stations at Irsching and Großmehring. The first marker we found detailed a pair of pipes, belonging to Bayernoil – indicated by BO 12 and BO 14 – which ran between Vohburg and the now redundant Ingolstadt refinery. This network of pipelines runs under just one small part of the Factory, but the area that it occupies is of a similar scale to the Hohe Tauern National Park. It is as though we are cycling in an 'Industrial National Park', a zone established a decade before the one in the Alps, and similarly dedicated to just one central activity.

As we cycle along, we tease out a riddle we created at the beginning of this journey: What has its roots in the sea, its trunk in the mountains, and its branches in the cities? The roots of the tree are in the Caspian, the trunk is

BTC and TAL, and here in the Upper Danube are the branches. All of these industrial sites, these towns, these people, live in the branches of the system – high up, feeding on the fruits, rocked by the breezes, lulled to sleep. This is the tree at the centre of the world, and it bears a strange fruit that is part life-giving, part poison. 'Rock-a-bye baby on the tree top, when the wind blows your cradle will drop.' Storms often beset the tree, but once in a blue moon it is hit by lightening, the sap that flows up the trunk falters, and the leaves begin to fall. The Oil Crisis of 1973 was such a moment, but another storm threatened far more recently.

Through the trees we catch constant glimpses of the red-and-white chimneys of Großmehring power station on the Danube's northern bank. In the book about Ingolstadt that Rudi lent us, there is a photo of Großmehring soon after construction in 1965, waiting to fire up. The visionary city of Ingolstadt, with its attendant factories, was to need copious supplies of electrical power. Like water, roads and schools, electricity was provided by the state in the social market, and Großmehring was run by a publicly owned company. Electricity provision for everything from homes to hospitals shifted from hydro-power – or *weißkohle* – to fossil fuels. These engines of the Factory were built to burn oil rather than coal, unlike in the rest of Germany. Public power supplies were therefore to be dependent on an energy source in the hands of private multinationals, the most prominent of which was BP.

In post-war Germany, as throughout Europe, a national grid system was created for electricity provision. It remains the same today, with a number of interconnected power stations feeding in energy. At times, certain stations might be shut down for repairs. Others might be mothballed when the price of their fuel is too high. This was the fate of Großmehring and Irsching, which are only switched on to generate power at times of peak electricity demand. Built originally as public utilities, they are now in the hands of a private German multinational, the Hannover-based E.ON. It is this company that judges whether or not to operate them, according to the profitability of electricity sales into the grid.

FERNGAS

E.ON Ruhrgas

RHR 660

MK nr 167

Out here in the wildness and wet of the alder and willow, we find further posts that mark natural gas pipelines belonging to E.ON Ruhrgas, another subsidiary of E.ON. They illustrate a shift in the power supply of the Factory that took place in the 1970s.

The advance of the German Army into Russia in 1941, and the threat of the Nazis seizing Baku, led to the Soviet petroleum industry rapidly shifting from the Caspian to Western Siberia. In the heat of war the Soviet engineers were pursuing oil, but in the following two decades it became clear that Siberia had vast deposits of natural gas. Soon this was being piped across the USSR and beyond its border to Comecon allies. By 1967, as TAL was coming on-stream, the Bratsvo pipeline was completed, bringing Siberian gas to Schwedt, just north of East Berlin: fuel for what had been the Soviet Sector of occupation, but was now the German Democratic Republic – East Germany.

Fundamental to Chancellor Konrad Adenauer's vision was a belief that the Federal Republic alone represented legitimate Germany. Its government would not recognise the East German GDR, nor would it have formal relations with any state that did so. This inflexible position changed after nearly two decades, when the Federal Republic's foreign minister, Willy Brandt, opened diplomatic relations with Romania in 1967, and with Yugoslavia the following year.[1] After his election as Chancellor in 1969, Brandt began to develop his strategy of *Ostpolitik* – the building of a dialogue with the GDR and other Eastern European states. This political shift was mirrored by an increase in trade between Germany and the Soviet bloc, in particular the trade in natural gas.

The first agreement for the supply of gas from the USSR to West Germany was signed the following year, with importation by the private corporation Ruhrgas. BP had a 25 per cent stake in the company.[2] As we cycled from the centre of Ingolstadt, we passed by the houses in the suburbs. These homes, as elsewhere in Germany, were connected to a national gas grid developed in the 1970s. Rudi had explained that the Bavarian state subsidised the laying of gas pipes to all towns and villages, helping shift domestic heating for the vast majority from wood to fossil fuels – exactly as had taken place in Soviet Azerbaijan a decade previously.

West German imports of gas from Siberia increased rapidly after the end of the Soviet Union. Fifteen years after the reunification of Germany, 41 per cent of the new state's gas came from Russia. In 2006, Ruhrgas, now wholly owned by E.ON, celebrated over three decades of imports by signing a new deal with the Russian company Gazprom to continue taking gas from Siberia until 2030. E.ON was by now Germany's main gas import company, and was using it to drive privatised gas-turbine electricity power stations. In the 1970s both Großmehring and Irsching plants had switched from generating electricity by burning heavy fuel oil, and were now running their turbines mainly on natural gas. Consequently, today they are more dependent on the E.ON Ruhrgas pipeline beneath our feet than on the nearby refineries.

---

1   Judt, *Postwar*, p. 497.
2   Browne, *Beyond Business*, p. 199.

But the shift from oil to gas as the central means of domestic heating and electricity generation only entrenched dependence on the importation of fossil fuels, and led to a mirror of the Oil Crisis of 1973. Twenty-seven years later, in January 2006, it seemed that lightning had struck again: this time, it hit not TAL, but the Bratsvo pipeline. It was triggered by Gazprom losing patience with the national gas company of the Ukraine, which was failing to pay bills for the fuel that it was importing from Russia. Gazprom unilaterally shut off the flow of gas at the Russian–Ukrainian border, and threatened to maintain the shutdown until the financial matter was settled. Given that the pipeline also carried gas through Ukrainian territory to customers further west, there was consternation in Slovakia, Hungary, the Czech Republic, Poland and Germany. The European media thundered that, as long predicted, Russia was utilising its 'energy weapon' against the West.[3]

Although, in comparison to the 1973 shock, the 2006 crisis over Russian gas supplies was economically insignificant, it nevertheless had a considerable political impact. In particular, it was used by the oil industry and government circles in Washington, London and Brussels to strengthen a discourse of 'energy security'. By framing the issue as a right to guaranteed imports of fossil fuels, the EU and US justify the projection of power over oil-extraction regions, pipelines and tanker routes. These are the arguments used to bolster the militarisation of BTC and SCP as they pass through the Caucasus, and the West's turning a blind eye to the authoritarian nature of the Aliyev regime. The crisis in 2006, coming only months before the opening of BTC, fed the rhetoric that oil routes from the Caspian must bypass Russian territory.

Three years on, as we cycle along the banks of the Danube, concerns over Russian control of the gas supply to Western Europe are used to further demands for a 'Southern Energy Corridor'. This 'corridor' would contain a number of pipelines running from Central Asia and the Middle East via Turkey towards Greece. These lines would feed the Trans-Adriatic pipeline – part owned by E.ON – or the Interconnector Turkey–Greece–Italy pipeline, both planned to run under the Straits of Otranto. The grandest of these projects is Nabucco, which would take gas from the Shah Deniz field and pump it via Bulgaria, Romania and Hungary to the central European hub at Baumgarten an der March, near Vienna. The political importance of Nabucco to Germany was highlighted in July 2009, when Joschka Fischer, the former foreign minister of the Federal Republic, became an advisor to the project. [4]

---

3   See, for example, A. Blomfield, 'Putin Sends a Shiver through Europe', 2 January 2006, at telegraph.co.uk.

4   Radio Free Europe, 3 July 2009, 'Germany's Gas War? Nabucco vs South Stream', at rferl.org.

Over the tops of the trees we can see that no smoke is issuing from the chimneys of Großmehring or Irsching. It is the middle of a warm spring day: there must be low electricity demand in Bavaria. The turbine's staff will be waiting for a directive from E.ON headquarters, at which point gas from Siberia will be burned on this riverbank among the willows and the alders. Soon gas from the Shah Deniz field in the Caspian, having passed by the villages of Rəhimli and Çalabaş, will be pumped from Turkey into the European grid system, and may make its way to these power stations of the Factory around Ingolstadt.

MANCHING, GERMANY

Cycling south, we pass through further suburbs of the city, clean and orderly with 1950s and 1960s housing blocks, out into the fields and woods. In due course we come to the dormitory village of Manching, with its winding lanes of detached houses and bungalows, converted farm buildings and neat gardens.

On the village's edge, by the banks of the River Paar, lie the remains of what was the largest settlement north of the Alps for 300 years. Manching was a Celtic *oppidum* settlement from the third century BCE until 30 BCE. In an area of 380 hectares enclosed by a high wall, a population of between 5,000 and 10,000 lived in houses on a grid of streets. Extensive ironworks used local ores to smelt and forge swords and jewellery. Manching was one of a network of over a hundred *oppida* that stretched from what is now England in the west to Hungary in the east. From Manching ran lines of exchange, undertaken by foot, by boat or by horse, such as the route over the Plockenpass, bringing wine in Roman amphora from the Mediterranean.[5] This Celtic economic system collapsed after the Roman armies, under Julius Caesar, conquered Gaul. The lines of trade were redirected, some of them to the distant metropolis of Rome, and with this collapse came the demise of Manching. It seems that this town met its end not through sack and pillage, but through the destruction of a continental economic system that is now almost forgotten.

We come to a section of the ancient ramparts. But we cannot reach most of the surviving wall, as it lies on the other side of the perimeter fence of an airport. The archaeological site was partly destroyed by the construction of a Luftwaffe airbase in the late 1930s, as the Nazi government rearmed. Badly bombed during World War II, the base became an Allied facility. Today it is a test-site for NATO weapons development, run by European Air Defence Systems. Rudi had told us that pilot-less planes, 'drones', are currently being designed here: it is strictly off-limits, a 'forbidden zone' behind the high fence and a bank of pines. This, then, is one of

---

5   Cunliffe, *Europe Between the Oceans*, pp. 371–5.

those 'other industries' mentioned in Bayernoil's brochure, 'which place Bavaria on top in Germany and in Europe' – part of NATO's industrial complex.[6]

The Morgenthau Plan would have stripped the German peoples of any army. However, the Cold War facilitated the Federal Republic's rearmament and inclusion into NATO in May 1955, three years after Turkey. Ingolstadt became a West German garrison town, with barracks strategically placed around the rapidly growing city. By 1989 the US Sector South was supported by at least five divisions of Wehrmacht troops and armour.[7]

Today, the ancient site at Manching is involved in the manufacture of military drones, similar to those paraded across Azadliq Square in Baku on 16 June 2008, and the Reapers tracking oil tankers and stalking Somali pirates.

TAL KP 477 – 5,084 KM – LENTING, GERMANY

'DEUTSCHE TRANSALPINE OELLEITUNG GMBH', proclaims the sign on the chain-link gates of a compound just north of the city limits of Ingolstadt. This is the property of DTO, based in Munich – the third of the three companies that own the Transalpine pipeline, along with SIOT in Italy and Transalpine Ölleitung in Austria. The seven massive oil tanks of the Lenting depot were visible from some distance, as we had cycled here, nestled alongside the area's third refinery, known as Kösching and owned by the Swiss company Petroplus.

The sun is hot on the surrounding fields of winter wheat. Despite the rumble of the nearby E45 autobahn, the noise of passenger jets passing overhead and the roar from the gas flare of the refinery just behind us, we can hear skylarks singing.

The terminal at Lenting is the most important node on TAL since the tank farm at San Dorligo, for it is the remote control centre for the entire pipeline. Surprisingly, there are no guards on the front gates, so we ignore the signs that declare, 'Warning! This area in under video surveillance', and skirt the perimeter fence on foot. We climb the gentle ridge on which the tanks are situated. At the summit the view opens up. To the north, out beyond the Danube valley, is the dark mass of trees that forms the Köschinger Forest. To the west, we can see the marker posts of TAL running towards Karlsruhe. This stretch of pipeline was originally called the Rhein-Donau Ölleitung, and carried crude from Karlsruhe to the refineries at Ingolstadt. But in 1967 the line reversed its flow and became part of TAL. Today it feeds the refinery at Karlsruhe, the largest plant in Europe, in which BP holds a 12 per cent stake.

---

6 *Bayernoil gemeinsam erfolgreich: A Refinery for Bavaria*, Bayernoil, July 2009, p. 2.
7 R. Overy, ed., *Times Atlas of 20th Century History*, Times Books, 1996, p. 113.

This final arm of the Transalpine pipeline carries the oil from Muggia out of the Danube valley, and into the valley of the Rhine, flowing towards the North Sea. Some of what is produced at the refinery is used to fuel the industrial barges that ferry goods up and down the river from Basel to Rotterdam. The crude from Azerbaijan has been piped through the catchment area of five seas – the Caspian, the Black Sea, the Persian Gulf, the Mediterranean, and finally the North Sea.

We continue around the compound, and look out at distant ploughed fields and wooded hillocks such as Kalkberg and Kleiner Weinberg. The Transalpine pipeline from Vohburg to Lenting passes beneath them. Not all the crude carried by TAL comes this way. Some fills a set of four new tanks at the Vohburg plant. We had seen their white bulk from the walls of the town: they are monuments to the end of the Cold War.

In October 1990, less than a year after the Berlin Wall came down, negotiations began for the construction of a new pipeline to run north-east from Vohburg, across the former Iron Curtain and into the ex-Comecon country of Czechoslovakia, which itself was soon split into the Czech and Slovak Republics. In a mirror of the long negotiations that occurred in the early 1990s in Baku, a set of – far less fraught – discussions took place in the government ministries of another country in the former Eastern Bloc.

Construction started on 1 September 1994. The trench was dug and the pipes were laid east along the Danube valley, past the city of Regensburg, and up into the Bavarian Forest. Rudi had explained that there was a great deal of opposition to this project, and that the Bavarian government had to create a new law to enable it to appropriate private land. Rising to 1,000 metres as it crossed the Sumava Mountains, the new pipeline moved from Germany into the Czech Republic, reaching the banks of the Vltava River, just north of Prague. Just as the pipeline westwards to Karlsruhe carries crude out of the Danube valley into that of the Rhine, this pipe running to the east moves oil from the Danube into the Elbe watershed flowing north towards the North Sea. The crude is destined for two refineries, one close by at Kralupy, and one at Litvinov on the north-western border with Germany. These final destinations gave the new structure, inaugurated on 13 March 1996, its name: the Ingolstadt–Kralupy–Litvinov pipeline (IKL).

As a refinery town, Litvinov has long been a geopolitical pawn. Construction work on a plant first started there in 1939, after the region had come under Nazi control as part of the 'Protectorate of Bohemia and Moravia'. From 1965 it had been an end-stop for the Druzbha pipeline, built under Khrushchev to bring Soviet oil to satellite states. A mere six years after the Cold War's end, the refinery was being supplied not only from Russia, but also from the West. Like the development of the ACG oilfield and the construction of BTC, the pipeline from Ingolstadt is another example of new Western infrastructure that pulled states out of Russia's former sphere of influence.

This realignment of crude supply coincided with a shift in petrol provision to Czech motorists, as BP and other Western companies advanced into a previously inaccessible Eastern Europe. BP bought gas stations in the Czech Republic, Slovakia and Poland. These garages, with their *Helios* sunflower logos and attendant mini-supermarkets, were bright icons of Western consumer products, and played a part in the reorientation of their states' economies.

We complete our walk around the perimeter of the compound and return to the front gates. Across the road, at the Kösching refinery, tankers arrive to collect their loads. Around 1,000 lorries a day leave the three refineries around Ingolstadt, to supply gas stations and domestic oil tanks up to 100 kilometres away in any direction. A similar number of trucks roll out from each of the other plants supplied by TAL, – at Kralupy, Litvinov, Schewechat, Burghausen, Vohburg and Karlsruhe.

Meanwhile trucks and trains fill the storage tanks of Air BP at airports in southern Germany. This complex process of deliveries – perhaps 250 road tanker movements a day – is coordinated by the Amsterdam-based computers and controllers of BP European Logistics.

There is still no one at the entrance cabin of the Lenting depot, but somewhere on this site somebody is watching one of the meters that register the flow of the river that runs from the middle of the Caspian to southern Germany. At precisely this time, as we idle on the roadside, other people are watching meters in other control rooms in Sangachal, Ceyhan, San Dorligo, Karlsruhe and Amsterdam.

It takes minutes for pressurised oil from the Pliocene sandstone layer to move up the riser to the drill deck of the Central Azeri platform in the Caspian. Within the next few hours the oil has passed through the pipe across the seabed to Sangachal; a further ten days sees it pumped through the BTC pipeline to Ceyhan. Four and a half days aboard a tanker brings thousands of barrels from Turkey across the Aegean, Ionian and Adriatic seas. If this load is not delayed at the tank farm of San Dorligo, it takes three days for the heavy liquid to travel over the Plockenpass and through the Hohe Tauern to Lenting. From the depot in front of us the crude passes to a refinery. Over a period of two days it will be broken down into heavy heating oil, petrol or diesel – products that are then pumped and trucked onwards to power plants, factories and petrol stations. Some of the crude is refined into aviation fuel and supplied to airports such as Munich, where it might fill the tanks of a 747 bound for India.

It takes twenty-two days for this process to run its course – for the oil to travel over 5,000 kilometres across the Earth's surface, and for it to move from 5 kilometres below sea level to 10 kilometres above sea level; twenty-two days for geology laid down 4 million years ago to be incinerated into gas. The energy of those rocks takes minutes for the engines to burn. It is as though we are consuming time itself.

This machine drives forward minute by minute, hour by hour, a vast system transferring carbon from the lithosphere to the atmosphere.

INGOLSTADT, GERMANY

We cycle back across the city to the entrance of Ingolstadt's abandoned refinery. Weeds grow around the gates. Through the fence we can see a great expanse of concrete. There are still some crude storage tanks and a couple of tall chimneys, stripes of red and white against the sky. The scene reminds us of Gəncə and Rustavi.

On Monday 18 August 2008, the refinery closed after forty-three years of operation, with the loss of many jobs. Once, it symbolised the transformation of the Upper Danube into a petrochemical futurescape; but now that vision has faded.

On the day Ingolstadt closed, no crude was being exported from the ACG oilfields. The previous Tuesday, as Russian tanks crossed the Baku–Supsa pipeline, BP had stopped pumping. Meanwhile, BTC was still out of action following the explosion at Refahiye two weeks before. But, whereas the 1973 Oil Crisis profoundly shook the towns and cities of Bavaria and elsewhere, the political earthquake in the Caucasus hardly registered as a tremor in Ingolstadt. By the time the vibrations of the crisis in Sangachal and Ceyhan reached the control rooms of Lenting and Amsterdam, the events were easily navigated.

Western refineries found other short-term sources of supply beyond Azerbaijan, and tankers from other ports besides Ceyhan could be directed to Muggia, to maintain the flow of oil through TAL. The lack of significant impact from the temporary stoppage on BTC belies the project's importance. The pipeline played a crucial role in both the US and EU attempts to pursue energy dominance by asserting long-term influence over oil-extracting and transit regions, diversifying their sources of crude and asserting the pre-eminence of the energy market. BTC itself represents a significant 1 per cent of global oil supply, and, crucially, transports crude from states outside the Middle East and OPEC.

The summer 2008 closure of the Ingolstadt refinery is full of political symbolism. The joint owners of Bayernoil sold the plant to the Indian company CALS Refineries, which then proceeded to move the entire structure, from control rooms to pipework, all the way to Haldia in West Bengal. Kirsten at Bayernoil had spoken excitedly about this development. She explained that the cracking towers and distillation plants had been loaded on to river barges and floated north along the Main–Donau Kanal to the River Main, and from there down the Rhine to the North Sea. At Antwerp the plant was transferred on to ships and taken via the Suez Canal and the Arabian Sea to the Bay of Bengal. Kirsten seemed delighted – all the more so because the old refinery site was soon to be transformed into a stadium for her beloved FC Ingolstadt.

We stare through the gates, thinking about how such a massive industrial plant, covering 106 hectares, can be packed up like a toy set and sailed across the oceans of the world to a new home in the Indian subcontinent.

The fate of Ingolstadt sums up a much wider, changing picture. Consumer demand for petroleum products in Europe appears to have peaked. Just as, in the

1890s, when the Rothschilds found that the European market for oil was saturated and turned instead to the markets of Asia, so in the early twenty-first century the region of growth in global oil demand is East Asia. BP, like all its rivals, has been working hard to break into the Indian and Chinese markets.

Bayernoil is a consortium of four companies, but in the sale of the Ingolstadt refinery, it was BP that gained most.[8] Five months prior to the closure, the chief executive of BP refining and marketing, Iain Conn, signed a memorandum of understanding with CALS Refineries to supply crude to the Haldia plant. The agreement stipulated that BP would deliver 5 million tonnes a year to the newly reconstructed refinery, and that BP would purchase all the refined petrol and diesel that the plant would produce.

Having effectively outsourced the running of the refinery, BP will still be able to supply customers in Asia and Europe with products refined from the oil that it sells to Haldia. The closure of the plant on the banks of the Danube will not lead to any reduction in BP's worldwide crude sales; nor will the relocation of the refinery mean any reduction in the amount of crude being processed. It does, however, mean a shift of employment to West Bengal, where labour is substantially cheaper and workers' rights substantially weaker.

When it is operational, the refinery at Haldia will supply aviation fuel and liquid petroleum gas to the Indian domestic market – in particular to the nearby mega-city of Calcutta and its international hub airport. The rebuilt plant will be a centrepiece of the Haldia Petrochemicals Ltd complex, the HPL – a new industrial zone at the head of the Bay of Bengal. HPL's website speaks of a golden future: 'A symbol of industrial resurgence in West Bengal, HPL has led the economic growth of the region by propelling significant investments in downstream processing industries . . . HPL has played a role as a catalyst . . . generating more than 1,500 employment opportunities in the process. With dedicated efforts, HPL truly symbolises its motto – "Come Grow With Us". How similar the proclamation feels to Schedl's vision for Bavaria back in the 1960s.

BP both drives and rides the geopolitical shifts of our age relentlessly. The dismantled refinery shipped up the Main–Donau Canal on river barges echoes the sections of the ACG offshore platforms that passed down the Volga Canal to the Caspian a decade before. The opening up of the Indian economy by, and to, the multinationals is a next step after their push into the former Soviet Union and the Comecon countries.

We turn away from the gates and pass the bus stop that once delivered workers on shift, but now stands without its sign.

* * *

---

8   'BP to Spice Up Refinery', *Telegraph*, New Delhi, 24 March 2008, at telegraphindia.com.

We have one more place to visit before our departure. In the Old City of Ingolstadt is a Baroque building painted in Hapsburg yellow: the Alte Anatomie, an eighteenth-century medical school that was part of the University of Bavaria, and famed throughout Europe. The building is far less dramatic, far less Gothic, than we had imagined. For it was here that Mary Shelley set the scenes in which the student Victor Frankenstein constructed his creature.

Her novel, *Frankenstein: Or, The Modern Prometheus*, told of the cursed existence of a man driven forward by his ambitions and his desires towards the unwitting destruction of his fiancée, his family, his friends, and ultimately himself. Prefiguring the bravado of the architects of modernity, Frankenstein refused to 'consider the magnitude and complexity of my plan as any argument of its impracticability. It was with these feelings that I began the creation of a human being.'[9]

The building takes us back to the Caucasus and the original story of Prometheus, chained to the peak of Mount Kazbegi as punishment for giving man the technology of fire. Our journey has enabled us to see more clearly how the gift of crude has been used.

In the first instance, oil from around Baku was exported for medicinal and building purposes, as fuel for the hearth and as a weapon of war – the raw material for Greek Fire. The trade in this oil, by sailing ship and camel train, ran for at least 2,300 years, from the Achaemenid Persian conquest of what is now Azerbaijan in 500 BCE until the 1870s.

For barely a generation, from the 1870s to the 1900s, the crude was refined to produce one central commodity: kerosene. It was exported across the world via the tankers of the Caspian and the River Volga, the railway to Batumi, and the ships across the Black Sea and beyond. It provided light for homes, farms and factories, from the villages of the Far East to the cities of Europe. Baku had a globally dominant position in kerosene, with half the world's crude extracted from its wells.

In the following generation, from the 1900s to the 1940s, oil was utilised above all for motive power – fuel for trains and ships, cars and trucks, tanks and planes. The engines of the Red Army tanks in Georgia, D'Annunzio's car entering Fiume, and the Allied bombers over Nazi Germany. It was this fuelling of the combustion engine that raised the Oil Road to its pre-eminent position in industrial societies. The pace of the oil trade itself was accelerated by the shift from coal to oil in the means of transportation – from the engines of tanker ships to those of tanker trucks. This forty-year period saw a massive expansion in global oil extraction; and though the output of Azerbaijan grew, Baku declined in importance relative to other provinces.

---

9   M. Shelley, *Frankenstein: Or, The Modern Prometheus*, Penguin Books, 1992, p. 54.

The period since the 1940s has seen the rapid development of the oil-based chemicals that came to underpin every aspect of daily life, from plastics to fertilisers. The manufacture of these products gave rise to entire towns and industrial districts, such as Sumqayit and the environs of Ingolstadt. Meanwhile the use of oil as a motive fuel has grown exponentially.

The presence of crude in the body of society since the 1870s has fuelled a kaleidoscope of visions for future social orders. From the Bolshevik speeches in the slums of Baku to the Futurist manifestos in Trieste; from the tank regiments of the Nazi Reich to the socialist techno-utopia of Khrushchev's USSR; and from the orderliness of Social Democrat Germany to the armed nationalism of the Aliyevs' Azerbaijan. Above all, as planes and cars burst into our consciousness, it has fuelled 'modernity' – the imagination of the machine age.

All of this cornucopia has been powered by a liquid distilled from fossilised ecosystems, from plants and animals that lived from the Jurassic to the Tertiary era. These visions of the future have been dependent upon the ceaseless combustion of ancient rocks, just as Victor Frankenstein constructed his dream from the organs and limbs of the dead.

The high-speed train glides through Upper Bavaria, bound for Augsburg and Stuttgart, as we head towards London. Beyond the windows, the villages are shrouded in mist. We see them in their Sunday morning sleep heated by oil; houses kept warm by rocks from beneath the Caspian.

In the midst of the pine forest, west of Munich, we spot a vast array of photovoltaic panels, ranks of silver-blue surrounded by barbed wire and CCTV cameras. Soon we pass another field of panels, then a third. A hare runs across the nearby plough-land in the bright first sunlight.

Rudi had explained how renewable energy systems in Bavaria have flourished in the last decade – a reassertion of the age of *weißkohle*. He told us that 80 per cent of the Deutsche Bahn trains in Bavaria run on electricity, and that 80 per cent of that energy comes from wind, water or solar power. The hydro-plants on the Danube alone generate 140 megawatts of electricity, the majority of which is delivered to the railways – including the very train that we are travelling on. The take-up of non-carbon energy systems across Germany has been remarkable. In 2008, 17 per cent of all Germany's energy was provided by renewables. So much for Kirsten's comment on alternative energy: 'This is for *kindergarten* . . . there is no security with it.'

With this level of renewable energy production generated locally, it is possible to conceive of a radical shift in the relationship between places of hydrocarbon extraction and places of consumption; a shift in the 140-year pattern exemplified by Bibi Heybat, ACG, the Baku–Batumi Railway, the *Murex* tanker, the *Dugi Otok* and TAL. Currently, non-carbon systems are augmenting the energy that continues to be provided by imported fossil fuels. But if renewable energy generated from within Germany and her immediate neighbours were to replace the power drawn from oil and gas, such a change would substantially contribute to the demise of the Oil Road.

Rising up now into the Schwabian Alps, the train crosses the border into Baden-Württemberg, leaving Bavaria. Ahead are forests of fir and larch, meadowlands and wheat fields, three wind turbines peeking over the horizon. Soon we will tunnel under the Stromberg and leave the Danube watershed, returning home to the North Sea.

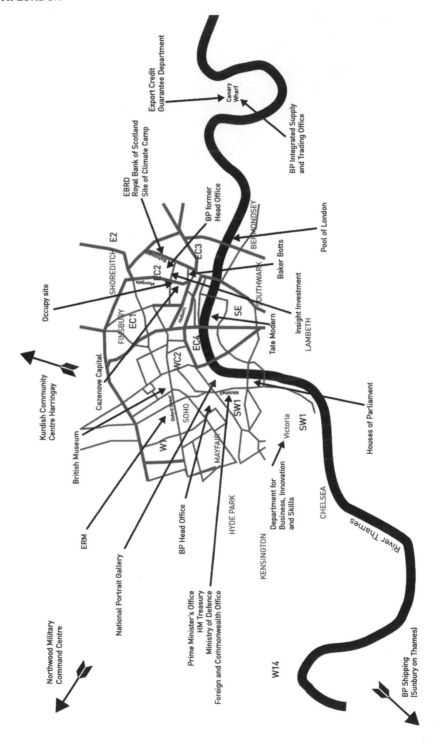

EPILOGUE: THE OIL CITY

THE CITY OF LONDON, ENGLAND

The Oil Road does not end in Bavaria. Apart from oil and gas, what floods back and forth through the channels of these 'energy corridors' is financial capital and political influence. Whereas the crude from the Caspian may ultimately power a car in southern Germany, the profit generated mainly flows to London and New York. While the governments of Azerbaijan and Georgia were involved in the creation of the pipelines, the ultimate political drivers were in Washington, London and Brussels.

On a crisp winter morning we gather a group of friends and allies outside a marquee on Finsbury Square, in London's financial district. It is January 2012, and Platform is hosting a guided tour of our city. To shelter from the cold, we meet in one of the tents at Occupy London's second site. The small canvas structure stands in contrast to the glass-and-steel buildings that surround the square.

The walk will be an exploration of the oil city that we live in. For London is not only the headquarters of those companies and government departments that build oil infrastructure like the TAL and BTC pipelines. This city is also the home of many who oppose such ventures. Our walk aims to reveal the Carbon Web and London's impacts on distant peripheries, as well as the struggle over the future of London itself. How long will it remain an oil city?

Bundled up in scarves and hoods, we head down Moorgate to the offices of Cazenove Capital, one of the major institutional shareholders in BP. A couple of men, busy in conversation, step around us and pass through the revolving glass doors into the lobby. We describe a presentation we gave, in one of the wood-panelled rooms inside, in which we highlighted the risks inherent in deepwater drilling to a group of asset managers, including Wade Pollard, equity income fund manager. Shortly after we began our PowerPoint presentation about the implications of the Deepwater Horizon disaster, Wade explained how he and colleagues had followed the event with a sense of horrified fascination. 'We all watched it on our screens. We had it on for months.' The computer terminals had shown a grainy yellow and grey image of what at first glance appeared to be smoke billowing out of a chimney. It was the leak on the seabed of the Gulf of Mexico – the catastrophic spill that ran for eighty-seven days; a mesmerising plume of crude oil blooming into the ocean.

We describe how we too had watched it in the Platform office. There was something sinister about its mute roar, 1,500 metres under the waves: a force of nature, viewable only with the aid of a remote-controlled submarine. It reminded us of Alexander Mishon's *The Oil Gusher at Bibi-Heybat*. Shot in 1898, this sixty-second silent film documents an enormous blow-out that shrouded Baku in a heavy deluge of sticky crude. It celebrates a cornucopia of oil as a wondrous gift from the rocks to the well's owner. But the contrast between the two is also striking, the nineteenth-century film of Bibi Heybat set against the twenty-first-century streaming video of the Macondo disaster. The first was made out of pride, celebrating newfound fortune, whereas the second was forced upon BP by the US authorities. The footage of Macondo, transmitted live on the internet for most of the duration of the spill, helped maintain the pressure on the company. Rather than making the well owner's fortune, the force of this gusher brought BP to a point where it was only three days away from bankruptcy.[1]

Within weeks of the Deepwater Horizon rig exploding, BP's share price had fallen by 40. per cent. Its credit rating was downgraded, banks refused to lend the company money and suppliers demanded payment up-front and in cash.[2] Staff morale at BP crashed. Employees shifted from a silent belief in the company to an off-the-record questioning of the board's capabilities.

On both sides of the Atlantic, public outrage grew at BP's failure to respond adequately, its repeated downplaying of the disaster and its perceived arrogance. New campaigns demanded accountability and justice. Globally, protestors blockaded petrol station forecourts and company offices. In London, Greenpeace 'rebranded' BP, scaling the company's headquarters and replacing the corporate flag with one that bore the words 'British Polluters'. Liberate Tate mounted actions at the Tate Modern and Tate Britain, questioning why public bodies should take corporate sponsorship from the company. In Washington, senators stood up to the oil industry in a way rarely seen before, and President Barack Obama was caustic in his criticism of Tony Hayward, CEO of BP. The latter only exacerbated the situation with a series of infamous public relations gaffes.

The Macondo disaster revealed not only the perilous nature of BP's daily operations, but also the frailty of the entire company. Even after the corporation managed to secure renewed political backing from both the British and US

---

1   'BP: $30 Billion Blowout', BBC Two, 9 November 2010.
2   Ibid.

governments, there was constant speculation in the financial sectors of London and New York that the company would not survive.

With investors clamouring for reassurance, Hayward embarked on a whirl-wind tour – to Moscow, Baku, Abu Dhabi and Luanda. Each visit consisted of a round of meetings in which the CEO tried to reassure governments key to the company's future. In Baku, Hayward briefed staff in Villa Petrolea before meeting Ilham Aliyev. The Azeri president emerged from their discussions stressing the 'successful long-term cooperation between BP and Azerbaijan' and 'confidence that this partnership will expand more in the future'.[3] The two parties signed an agreement for the new Shafaq and Asiman offshore gas fields, committing them-selves to a thirty-year project.

In order to claw back the company's credit rating and pull the share price up from the depths to which it had sunk, BP had to raise over $22 billion as quickly as possible. Demonstrating the severity of the crisis, oilfields and pipelines in Egypt, Colombia, Vietnam, Pakistan and Venezuela were sold off. In Azerbaijan, the company mortgaged its share of the output from the ACG field, setting it against a loan of $2.5 billion provided by the Royal Bank of Scotland (RBS).[4]

At that, we halt this section of our story and guide our group along Moorgate and into Finsbury Circus. Dominated by the bare branches of tall plane trees, the square is sedate and away from the traffic. We arrive at an imposing office block of 1920s neo-classicism, Britannic House. Designed by Sir Edwin Lutyens and festooned with carved heads, some in Middle Eastern headscarves, this was the headquarters of the Anglo-Persian Oil Company and BP until 2003. It was in this building in 1932 that company chairman Basil Jackson fretted that the Soviets were undermining APOC's European sales through cheap exports from Baku. Maurice Bridgeman, Maurice Banks and Alastair Down worked here in the 1960s and planned the expansion of refining and marketing that led to the financing of TAL and the Vohburg refinery.[5]

We get the group to stand at the foot of the steps made of Portland stone, imag-ining the comings and goings of all the actors in the company's drive into Azerbaijan: John Browne arriving as the new head of BP's Exploration and Production division, bringing with him his lieutenant Tony Hayward; Rondo Fehlberg, reporting back with his findings from Moscow and Baku; all the presi-dents of BP Azerbaijan, from Terry Adams to David Woodward; and those from lesser ranks such as Şükran Çağlayan and Tamam Bayatly, reporting to head office.

---

3   *Monthly Economic Bulletin*, Republic of Azerbaijan: Ministry of Foreign Affairs, July 2010.

4   'Double Trouble', *International Financing Review*, 2011, at ifre.com.

5   J. Bamberg, *British Petroleum and Global Oil 1950–1975: The Challenge of Nationalism*, Cambridge University Press, 2000, pp. 282–4.

On the morning of 4 January 1999, John Browne, by then promoted to the position of BP's chief executive, walked out onto these steps with Larry Fuller, the former head of Amoco – 'former head' because Amoco had just ceased to exist. The two men posed for the press, holding the new 'BP Amoco' logo that would replace the BP shield. Browne, rather shorter than Fuller, stood one step higher. This was a significant day for Azerbaijan. For the previous eight years, BP and Amoco had been the fiercest of rivals in Baku, competing with each other for key contracts. Now, the combined company became the undisputed master of the Western Caspian oil scene. The corporate merger announced on the steps of Britannic House dramatically weakened the hand of Azerbaijan. It also tied the foreign policy of Britain, the US and the EU closer still to BP. This building changed the Caucasus and the Caspian, yet the vast construction project has left no mark on this building; there is no plaque here to commemorate it.

Had BP gone bust in summer 2010 as a result of the Deepwater Horizon disaster, its bankruptcy would have been accompanied by a sale of assets. Who would have purchased BP's holding in the ACG oilfield, the BTC pipeline, the Shah Deniz gas field and the SCP pipeline? While BP was struggling, Russia's Gazprom intimated that it was keen to buy the company's share of Shah Deniz. Such a purchase might have meant that Azeri gas exports to Western Europe would fall under Russian control. Alternatively, if a Chinese national oil company had bought BP's stake in Azeri oil production, could such an acquisition have led to the piping of crude eastwards, away from BTC? And even if they did not alter the material flows of the Oil Road, substantial Russian or Chinese investments in Azerbaijan would have redirected the flow of finance and politics, of profit and influence.

Had BP declared bankruptcy, the sale of its tanker fleet, its percentage share of the TAL and AWP pipelines, or its stakes in Bayernoil and the Karlsruhe refinery, would have had a far smaller geopolitical significance than the sale of its Azeri assets. A shift of Azerbaijan into Moscow or Beijing's sphere of influence is something governments in London, Washington, Berlin, Paris and Brussels are keen to avoid. The collapse of BP would have created a political earthquake in Azerbaijan, shaking the foundations of the Aliyev government.

From the calm of the square, we lead the group towards Broadgate. The scene is busy with city workers carrying ipads, hurrying this way and that, the dark colours of their suits and skirts making the plaza a sombre place. By contrast, the melee in Liverpool Street Station is vibrant with colour. We pass through the crowds on the concourse and emerge into Bishopsgate. Immediately on our left lies the entrance of RBS. A walkway that runs along the front of the building is gloomy, but it shelters us from the cold wind of the street. Somewhere above us, the Oil and Gas division are hard at work. Perhaps Baba Abu, who received the notification of the drowning of Kubilay and Nurullah in the pipeline trench at Yaylacı, is here. Standing in the passageway, we explain that RBS is still in the

Lender Group for BTC, that the loan agreements signed in February 2004 were set to last for twelve years. So the bank is still generating interest off this debt, which will not be fully repaid until 2016.[6]

We point out the European Bank of Reconstruction and Development, occupying the same block of offices as RBS, just a little further along the walkway. We describe our meeting with Jeff Jeter when we came to speak with him about Mansura Ibishova's home in Qarabork, how Manana and Mayis also visited bank officials here, and how Friends of the Earth built a mock pipeline running down Bishopsgate and back along to the headquarters of BP in Finsbury Circus to highlight the threat to Borjomi.

It is a struggle to get our group through the crowds on the pavement of Bishopsgate. Beside us the traffic is, as so often, at a standstill. A lane has been closed off for building work again. Construction is constantly underway here, as another skyscraper rises up, driven by a property company working on the assumption that the City will keep growing as a centre of global finance. We stop at the unmarked place in the street where the Camp for Climate Action set up its tents during the G20 Summit of April 2009. The Credit Crunch had hit, and RBS and several other banks had been rescued from collapse with money from the state. Widespread public anger led to protests such as the Camp, which described a vision of an alternative future for the City – not as a hub for the world's oil industry, but as a place where the limitations of the climate and needs of the planet's population would be prioritised. Thousands had filled the streets outside the European Climate Exchange and the Bank of England, demanding that a better world was possible. Mehmet Ali was in the crowd that night. Frightened, penned in by the police, he was almost arrested, but yanked his arm away and ran. As evening set in, the riot police charged the crowd repeatedly, battering hundreds and killing Ian Tomlinson.

We turn west and make our way to no. 33 Old Broad Street and the offices of the Lloyds Banking Group. This is where Rory Sullivan of Insight Investment told us in January 2009, prior to our journey, that the BTC pipeline was 'finished now... it's a done deal'. Three years on, Insight Investment has gone, sold by Lloyds to the Bank of New York Mellon. Along with 200 other staff, Rory was made redundant. We explain that this change echoes broader shifts in the financial industry, and suggests that the socially responsible investment sector is being particularly affected by the long recession that has followed the Credit Crunch.[7]

6   A. Dufey, *Project Finance, Sustainable Development and Human Rights: The Baku–Tbilisi–Ceyhan Pipeline*, International Institute for Environment and Development, 2009.

7   For example, the SRI team at Henderson's Global Investment, leading players in the London sector, was entirely laid off in December 2012.

Climbing on board a number 15 bus, we escape the hectic bustle of the City and head towards Trafalgar Square. Diesel exhaust issues from the back of the vehicle. In response to a question from one of our group, we explain that it is possible that this fuel was refined from crude extracted in the Caspian. Some of the tankers that depart from Ceyhan do deliver their loads to refineries such as Coryton in Essex or Fawley in Hampshire. But the amount of physical oil delivered to the UK from the Caspian is, and will remain, fairly insignificant. Rather than crude, it is financial and political capital that is extracted and transported to London.

Sitting on the top floor of the bus, we get a good view of St Paul's as we travel down Cannon Street. At the foot of the main steps to the Cathedral, some fifty tents are huddled tightly together. The Occupy London protest camp has survived much of the winter and is in the final throes of an eviction battle with the Corporation of London. The Occupy movement has been constantly criticised for failing to provide 'answers' or 'solutions' to the financial crisis, as if this was the only way to approach the problem. Despite this dismissal, it has sparked imagination and forced a renewed questioning of capitalism into the mainstream media.

Recently, Liberate Tate began their latest unofficial performance here, 'Floe Piece'. Four veiled figures dressed in black lifted a heavy chunk of polar ice, brought to London by an Arctic researcher, onto a sledge. Walking in silent procession, they carried the 55-kilo block across the Millennium Bridge and into the Tate Modern's Turbine Hall. The frozen block was then left on the gallery floor to melt slowly, accompanied by a plaque with the performance title. The piece highlighted BP's sponsorship of the Tate and the latter's role in helping to build the profile of the company. But its intention was also to proclaim that a time is coming when it will no longer be publicly acceptable for so many of London's cultural institutions to be sponsored by the oil industry – that a shift is taking place, that the metropolis is moving away from its long stasis as an oil city.

Our group jumps off when the bus pulls up by Trafalgar Square. Large icicles are hanging from the fountains, and the basins are partially frozen over. Banners adorn the square. Egypt and Syria solidarity activists have joined to call for the downfall of long-lasting regimes. There are placards demanding that Britain drop Egypt's debt and build support for the grassroots uprisings.

Passing down Whitehall towards Westminster, the wide pavements are far easier than the City to navigate with the group. Civil servants dart in and out of the imposing building while tourists saunter past. After the frenzied construction on Bishopsgate, this avenue has an air of calm continuity, overlooked by statues of imperial figures such as Nelson and Earl Haig.

Over the past hundred years, the buildings here – the Ministry of Defence, the Office of the Prime Minister, the Foreign and Commonwealth Office, the Treasury – have hosted many of the key scenes in the history of the Oil Road.

From the government of the Marquess of Salisbury agreeing to the passage of kerosene through the Suez Canal to Lord Curzon's deliberations over the British expeditionary force in the Caucasus; from the chancellor of the exchequer agreeing to BP's investment in the refineries of Bavaria to the Foreign Office's assistance to Mrs Thatcher's visit to Baku. Behind the high gates of Downing Street and its heavily armed police, decisions were made that assisted the interests of oil companies and asserted Britain's dominance over the energy resources of other countries.

We round the corner of Parliament Square and stop outside Portcullis House, full of offices for members of parliament. Over the roar of the traffic on the Embankment, we tell of the World Bank's plan to finance BTC and the popular campaign to stop the Department for International Development from supporting this move. We explain how civil servants were put on the back foot, and how the president of the bank rang John Browne, CEO of BP, at home, worried that the deal would not go through, as the decision went down to the wire. Battles like these show how the British government's alliance with the oil corporations is repeatedly challenged. Behind this lies a deeper questioning of what role London should play in the world, and whether its long reign as an oil city is coming to a close.

We guide the group across the road and down to the calm of Westminster Pier, jutting out into the River Thames. A passenger ferry soon arrives and we step aboard. Once we are heading downstream towards Greenwich, we close the morning's exploration with a final story.

In the wake of the fall of the Berlin Wall, as Azerbaijan, Georgia and other states asserted their independence, there was a wave of articles and discussions as to how the great, and seemingly eternal, monolith of the Soviet Union could suddenly melt into thin air. The German writer, Hans Magnus Enzensberger, wrote about the figure of President Gorbachev. He declared him to be a modern hero: 'A hero of a new kind, representing not victory, conquest and triumph, but renunciation, reduction and dismantling.'[8]

Enzensberger explained that the most difficult of all manoeuvres was retreat – the art of withdrawing from an untenable position. Gorbachev had assisted the process of withdrawing from the untenable structures of the Cold War, of two opposing nuclear armed blocs, and of Mutually Assured Destruction. The head of the USSR had understood that the only way forward was by retreating.

He went on to write that the West must undertake 'the most difficult retreat of all, from the war against the biosphere which we have been waging since the Industrial Revolution. Certain large industries – ultimately no less threatening than one-party rule – will have to be broken up'; that this task would require cour-

---

8   H. M. Enzensberger, 'The State of Europe', *Granta* 30 (1990).

age and conviction.

On the boat there is something timeless about this winter day: the tide pouring out towards the sea; the brown river so unruffled, so unanxious, unstriving.

We talk about the state of the Thames itself – one of the cleanest ex-industrial rivers in the world, with over 115 species of fish. The river is a metaphor of what can be done, and a reminder that things can change. A survey of the Lower Thames in 1957 found no sign of life except for eels, which can breathe at the surface of the water. Downstream of Tower Bridge, the river was entirely devoid of oxygen. Salmon had been extinct for over a century. The seventy miles of the tidal Thames had been given up for dead – a position of devastation. And yet a retreat in that war against the Thames has taken place, through a myriad of small and large acts. Some for the best of reasons and some not. The decline of industry on the banks of the river probably means that these factories have been transplanted to other, cheaper, less regulated places in the world.

And yet a retreat has happened: the Thames has come back to life. We watch a flock of terns, brilliant white, flying over the Pool of London. We proclaim that we can retreat from our untenable position in the war against the biosphere and the atmosphere. With enough bravery, we can retreat from the Carbon Web and enable a different future for this city.

A smart-phone is passed around the group. The screen shows a map with the current location of the *Dugi Otok*. Her position is indicated by a red arrowhead in the northern Adriatic, heading for Muggia. She is a climate bomb, partly commissioned by our city. We can defuse her.

BIBLIOGRAPHY

BOOKS

Abdullayeva, Arzu, Novella Jafarova, Saida Gojamanli and Saadet Bananyarli, *Report on Monitoring During the Protest Rally Held by Opposition Parties on May 21, 2005*, Monitoring Group of Human Rights Organizations, 2005.

Aitstadt, Audrey, *The Azerbaijani Turks: Power and Identity under Russian Rule*, Hoover Institution Press, 1992.

Alieva, Leila, ed., *The Baku Oil and Local Communities: A History*, CNIS, 2009.

Amnesty International UK, *Human Rights on the Line: The Baku–Tbilisi–Ceyhan Pipeline Project*, 2003.

Ascherson, Neal, *Black Sea*, Hill & Wang, 1996.

Asfaha, Samuel, *National Revenue Funds: Their Efficacy for Fiscal Stability and Intergenerational Equity*, International Institute for Sustainable Development (Canada), 2007.

Aust, Stefan, *The Baader-Meinhof Complex*, Bodley Head, 2008.

Babak, Vladimir, Demian Vaisman and Aryeh Wasserman, *Political Organization in Central Asia and Azerbaijan: Sources and Documents*, Psychology Press, 2004.

Bagirov, Sabit, *Azerbaijan Oil: Glimpses of a Long History*, Perceptions (Ankara), 1996.

Bagiyev, Taleh, and Tale Heydarov, *Azerbaijan: 100 Questions Answered*, Anglo-Azerbaijani Youth Society (Baku), 2008.

Bamberg, James, *The History of British Petroleum Company, Vol 2: The Anglo-Iranian Years, 1928–1954*, CUP, 1994.

——*The History of British Petroleum, Vol. 3: The Challenge of Nationalism, 1950–1975*, CUP, 2000.

Barry, Andrew, *Political Machines*, Athlone Press, 2001.

Bayernoil, *Bayernoil gemeinsam erfolgreich: A Refinery for Bavaria*, Bayernoil, July 2009.

Berger, John, and Jean Mohr, *A Seventh Man*, Penguin, 1975.

Bergin, Tom, *Spills and Spin: The Inside Story of BP*, Random House, 2011.

Bergreen, Laurence, *Marco Polo: From Venice to Xanadu*, Knopf, 2007.

Bey, Essad, *Blood and Oil in the Orient*, Simon & Schuster, 1932.

Bozdogan, Sibel, *Modernism and Nation Building: Turkish Architectural Culture in the Early Republic*, University of Washington Press, 2001.

BP, *Our Industry: Petroleum*, British Petroleum Company Ltd, 1977.

——*Bilder aus der Welt des Erdols*, BP Austria AG, 1994.

Brom, Shlomo, and Anat Kurz, eds, *Strategic Survey for Israel 2010*, Institute for National Security Studies, 2010.

Brosius, Maria, *The Persians: An Introduction*, Routledge, 2006.

Browne, John, *Beyond Business: An Inspirational Memoir from a Remarkable Leader*, Weidenfeld & Nicolson, 2010.

Buchan, John, *Greenmantle*, Penguin, 1916.

Carroll, Toby, *New Approaches to Opening Markets: The Baku–Tbilisi–Ceyhan Pipeline and the Deployment of Social and Environmental Risk Mitigation*, Political Studies Association, 2010.

Cornell, Svante, ed., *The Guns of August 2008: Russia's War in Georgia*, M. E. Sharpe, 2009.

Coppieters, B., ed., *Contested Borders in the Caucasus*, VUB Press, 1996.

Cunliffe, Barry, *Europe Between the Oceans: 9000 BC to AD 1000*, Yale University Press, 2008.

Davies, Norman, *Europe: A History*, Pimlico, 1997.

Dekić, Velid, 'The Oil Refinery in Rijeka: A story of Survival', in *The Rothschild Archive: Review of the Year 2004–2005*, Rothschild Archive, 2005.

——*Crude Oil Processing in Rijeka: 1882–2004*, INA Industrija nafte, 2004.

Deutscher, Isaac, *Stalin: A Political Biography*, OUP, 1967.

Dufey, Annie, *Project Finance, Sustainable Development and Human Rights: The Baku–Tbilisi–Ceyhan Pipeline*, International Institute for Environment and Development, 2009.

Dunsterville, L. C., *Adventures of Dunsterforce*, Edward Arnold, 1920.

Eads, Christopher, and Anders Tunold, *Progress Report 2007–2009: Establishing Resource Transparency*, EITI Secretariat, 2009.

Ebel, Robert, and Rajan Menon, *Energy and Conflict in Central Asia and the Caucasus*, Rowman & Littlefield, 2000.

Effendi, Rena, *Pipe Dreams*, Mets & Schilt, 2009.

Ferguson, Niall, *The World's Banker: A History of the House of Rothschild*, Weidenfeld & Nicolson, 1998.

Frelick, Bill, *Pushed Back, Pushed Around: Italy's Forced Return of Boat Migrants and Asylum Seekers, Libya's Mistreatment of Migrants and Asylum Seekers*, Human Rights Watch, 2009.

French, Paul, and Sam Chambers, *Oil on Water: Tankers, Pirates and the Rise of China*, Zed Books, 2010.

Fuller, Elizabeth, 'A Triumphant Year for Shevardnadze', in *Building Democracy: The OMRI Annual Survey of Eastern Europe and the Former Soviet Union*, Open Media Research Institute, 1996.

Gahramanli, Mirvari, Vidadi Rajabov and Alexander Kazakhov, *Report on Corruption in Azerbaijan Oil Industry Prepared for EBRD and IFC Investigation Arms*, CEE Bankwatch/Committee of Oil Industry Workers' Rights Protection, 2003.

Gillard, Michael, *The Con-Tract of the Century: A Special Investigation*, Spinwatch, 2004.

Hemming, Jonathan, *The Implications of the Revival of the Oil Industry in Azerbaijan*, Centre for Middle Eastern and Islamic Studies (Durham), 1998.

Hendrix, Paul, *Sir Henri Deterding and Royal Dutch-Shell: Changing Control of World Oil 1900-1940*, Bristol Academic Press, 2002.

Henry, James Dodds, *Baku: An Eventful History*, A. Constable, 1905.

Hikmet, Nazim, transl. Randy Blasing and Mutlu Konuk, *Poems of Nazim Hikmet*, Persea Books, 1994.

Homer, transl. Robert Fagles, *The Odyssey*, Penguin Classics, 1996.

Hopkirk, Peter, *On Secret Service East of Constantinople: The Plot to Bring Down the British Empire*, Oxford Paperbacks, 1995.

Howarth, Stephen, *Sea Shell: Story of Shell's British Tanker Fleets, 1892–1992*, Thomas Reed, 1992.

Hudson, Miles, *Intervention in Russia, 1918–1920: A Cautionary Tale*, Leo Cooper (Barnsley), 2004.

Koller, Rudolf, *Eine Stadt Baut Auf*, Stadt Ingolstadt, 1966.

Institute for Democracy in Eastern Europe, *The Azerbaijan 'Elections', 15 October 2003*, Baku, 2003.

Internal Displacement Monitoring Centre, *Azerbaijan: IDPs Still Trapped in Poverty and Dependence*, Norwegian Refugee Council (Geneva), 2008.

International Crisis Group, *Azerbaijan: Vulnerable Stability: Europe Report No. 207*, 2010.

International Trade Union Confederation, *2007 Annual Survey of Violations of Trade Union Rights: Azerbaijan*, 2007.

Jawad, Pamela, *Europe's New Neighborhood on the Verge of War: What Role for the EU in Georgia?*, Peace Research Institute (Frankfurt), 2006.

Joseph, Jofi, *Pipeline Diplomacy: The Clinton Administration's Fight for Baku-Ceyhan*, Woodrow Wilson School of Public and International Affairs, 1999.

Judt, Tony, *Postwar*, Heinemann, 2005.

Kemal, Yashar, *Memed, My Hawk*, Panther Press, 1998 (1955 in Turkish).

——*They Burn the Thistles*, William Morrow & Co., 1977 (1969 in Turkish).

Khvostov, Mikhail, *The Russian Civil War, Vol. I: The Red Army*, Osprey, 1996.

King, Charles, *The Ghost of Freedom: A History of the Caucasus*, OUP, 2008.

Kleveman, Lutz, *The New Great Game: Blood and Oil in Central Asia*, Atlantic Books, 2004.

Kynaston, David, *The City of London, Vol. IV: A Club No More, 1945–2000*, Chatto & Windus, 2001.

Ledeen, Michael Arthur, *D'Annunzio: The First Duce*, Transaction, 2009.

Levine, Steve, *The Oil and the Glory: The Pursuit of Empire and Fortune on the Caspian Sea*, Random House, 2007.

Macdonald, Kate, *The Reality of Rights: Barriers to Accessing Remedies when Business Operates Beyond Borders*, Corporate Responsibility Coalition/London School of Economics, 2009.

Maclean, Fitzroy, *Eastern Approaches*, Jonathan Cape, 1949.

Madden, Thomas, *Enrico Dandolo and the Rise of Venice*, JHU Press, 2006.

Magocsi, Paul Robert, *Historical Atlas of Central Europe*, Thames & Hudson, 2002.

Mansley, Mark, *Building Tomorrow's Crisis: The BTC Pipeline and BP*, Platform, 2003.

Marriott, Alfred Lyttleton, 'Persian Journal', unpublished manuscript, 1901.

Marriott, James, and Greg Muttitt, *Some Common Concerns: Imagining BP's Azerbaijan–Georgia–Turkey Pipelines System*, Platform/KHRP/Corner House/Friends of the Earth, 2002.

Marvin, Charles, *The Region of the Eternal Fire: An Account of a Journey to the Petroleum Region of the Caspian in 1883*, W. H. Allen & Co., 1884.

Meinhof, Ulrike, *Black September: Regarding the Strategy for Anti-Imperialist Struggle*, Red Army Faction, 1972.

Ministry of National Security, *Heydar Aliyev and the National Security Agencies*, 2009.

Mirbabayev, Miryusif, *Concise History of Azerbaijani Oil*, SOCAR-AQS (Baku), 2010.

Montefiore, Simon Sebag, *Young Stalin*, Weidenfeld & Nicolson, 2007.

Morris, Jan, *The Venetian Empire: A Sea Voyage*, Penguin, 1990.

——*Trieste and the Meaning of Nowhere*, Faber & Faber, 2001.

Muttitt, Greg, *Evaluation of Compliance of the Baku–Tbilisi–Ceyhan (BTC) Pipeline with the Equator Principles*, Platform, 2003.

——*Fuel on the Fire: Oil and Politics in Occupied Iraq*, Bodley Head, 2011.

Navaro-Yashin, Yael, *Faces of the State: Secularism and Public Life in Turkey*, Princeton University Press, 2002.

Nove, Alec, *Economic History of the USSR*, Penguin Books, 1991.

OSCE/ODIHR, *Election Observation Mission Report: Republic of Azerbaijan, 15 October 2003*, Warsaw, 2003.

Overy, Richard, ed., *Times Atlas of 20th Century History*, Times Books, 1996.

Pirani, Simon, ed., *Russian and CIS Gas Markets and Their Impact on Europe*, OUP, 2009.

Polo, Marco, transl. William Marsden, *The Travels of Marco Polo*, Wordsworth Classics, 1997.

Quill, Sarah, *Ruskin's Venice: The Stones Revisited*, Ashgate, 2000.

Reiss, Tom, *The Orientalist: Solving the Mystery of a Strange and Dangerous Life*, Random House, 2006.

Said, Kurban, transl. Jenia Graman, *Ali and Nino: A Love Story*, Robin Clark, 1990 [1937].

Sereny, Gitta, *Albert Speer: His Battle with Truth*, Picador, 1995.

Shelley, Mary, *Frankenstein; Or, The Modern Prometheus*, Penguin Books, 1992 [1818].

Shevardnadze, Eduard, *The Future Belongs to Freedom*, Sinclair-Stevenson, 1991.

Stalin, Joseph, 'The December Strike and the December Agreement', in *Works*, Foreign Languages Publishing House (Moscow), 1954.

Steavenson, Wendell, *Stories I Stole*, Atlantic Books, 2002.

Stokes, Doug, and Sam Raphael, *Global Energy Security and American Hegemony*, Johns Hopkins University Press, 2010.

Stone, Norman, *Turkey: A Short History*, Thames & Hudson, 2011.

Stoneman, Richard, *Across the Hellespont: Travellers in Turkey from Herodotus to Freya Stark*, Hutchinson, 1987.

Suny, Ronald, *Revenge of the Past: Nationalism, Revolution, and the Collapse of the Soviet Union*, Stanford University Press, 1993.

——*The Making of the Georgian Nation*, Indiana University Press, 1988.

——*The Soviet Experiment: Russia, the USSR, and the Successor States*, OUP, 1998.

Swietochowski, Tadeusz, *Russia and Azerbaijan: A Borderland in Transition*, Columbia University Press, 1995.

——*Russian Azerbaijan, 1905–1920: The Shaping of National Identity in a Muslim Community*, Columbia University Press, 1985.

Thompson, Mark, *The White War: Life and Death on the Italian Front, 1915–1919*, Faber & Faber, 2008.

Tisdall, Caroline, and Angelo Bozzolla, *Futurism*, Thames & Hudson, 1977.

Tolf, Robert W., *The Russian Rockefellers: The Saga of the Nobel Family and the Russian Oil Industry*, Hoover Press, 1982.

USAID, *Multilateral Development Bank Assistance Proposals Likely to Have Adverse Impacts on the Environment, Natural Resources, Public Health and Indigenous Peoples: September 2002–October 2004*, USAID, 2004.

Venn, Fiona, *Oil Diplomacy in the Twentieth Century*, Palgrave Macmillan, 1986.

de Waal, Thomas, *Black Garden: Armenia and Azerbaijan through Peace and War*, NYU Press, 2004.

——Thomas, *The Caucasus: An Introduction*, OUP, 2010.

Wainwright, David, *Government Broker: The Story of an Office and of Mullens & Co.*, Matham Publishing, 1990.

Warner, Koko, Charles Ehrhart and Alex de Sherbinin, *In Search of Shelter: Mapping the Effects of Climate Change on Human Migration & Displacement*, United Nations University, May 2009.

Wiel, Alethea, *Venice*, Kessinger Publishing, 1894.

Willett, John, *The New Sobriety: Art and Politics in the Weimar Period, 1917–33*, Thames & Hudson, 1978.

Winrow, Gareth, 'Protection of Energy Infrastructure', in *Combating International Terrorism: Turkey's Added Value*, RUSI, 2009.

Wu, Chin-Tao, *Privatising Culture: Corporate Art Intervention Since the 1980s*, Verso, 2002.

Zirkel, Katja, *Aufgewachsen in Ingolstadt in der 60er und 70er Jahren*, Wartberg Verlag, 2008.

Zonn, Igor, Andrey Kostianoy, Aleksey Kosarev, and Michael Glantz, *The Caspian Sea Encyclopedia*, Springer (Heidelberg), 2010.

Zurcher, Erik, *Turkey: A Modern History*, I. B. Tauris, 2010.

JOURNAL ARTICLES

Abilov, Shamkal, 'Historical Development of the Azerbaijan Oil Industry and the Role of Azerbaijan in Today's European Energy Security', *Journal of Eurasian Studies* 2: 3 (2010).

Alakbarov, Farid, 'Baku's Architecture', *Azerbaijan International* 9: 4 (2001).

Andersen, Andrew, and George Partskhaladze, 'Soviet–Georgian War and Sovietization of Georgia 1921', *Revue historique des Armées* 254 (2009).

Aslanli, Kenan, 'Oil and Gas Revenues Management in Azerbaijan', *Caucasus Analytical Digest* 16 (2010).

Babali, Tuncay, 'Implications of the Baku–Tbilisi–Ceyhan Main Oil Pipeline Project', *Ankara: Perceptions*, Winter 2005.

Bayulgen, Oksan, 'Foreign Investment, Oil Curse, and Democratization: A Comparison of Azerbaijan and Russia', *Business and Politics* 7 (2005).

Biello, David, 'World's Top 10 Most Polluted Places', *Scientific American* 17 (2007).

Blagov, Sergei, 'Russia's Sakhalin II Project Remains Under Pressure', *Eurasia Daily Monitor* 3: 232 (15 December 2006).

Blair, Betty, 'Who Wrote Azerbaijan's Most Famous Novel, Ali and Nino? The Business of Literature', *Azerbaijan International* 15: 2–4 (2011).

Campbell, Helen, 'Scale of the Century', *Horizon* 1 (2009).

Dam, Win, and Siew-mung Ho, 'Unusual Design Considerations Drive Selection of Sakhalin LNG Plant Facilities', *Oil and Gas Journal*, 10 January 2001.

Enzensberger, Hans Magnus, 'The State of Europe', *Granta* 30 (1990).

Eviatar, Daphne, 'Wildcat Lawyering', *American Lawyer*, November 2002.

ten Hoedt, Rudolf, and Karel Beckman, 'For Nabucco It Is Now or Never', *European Energy Review*, 4 November 2010.

Javadi, Masoud, and Nasser Sagheb, 'Caspian Caviar in Peril', *Azerbaijan International* 2: 3 (1994).

Knickerbocker, H. R., 'The Soviet Five-Year Plan', *International Affairs* 10: 4 (July 1931).

Mir-Babayev, Mir Yusif, 'Azerbaijan's Oil History: A Chronology Leading up to the Soviet Era', *Azerbaijan International* 10: 2 (2002), pp. 34–40.

Naughton, Martin, 'Teams Unite to Manage Tough Times', *Horizon: The Global Publication for BP People* 7 (December 2008).

Nincic, Donna, 'Maritime Piracy: Implications for Maritime Energy Security', *Journal of Energy Security*, 19 February 2009.

Sadigzade, Ummugulsum, 'Our Eyes Full of Tears, Our Hearts Broken', *Azerbaijan International* 14: 1 (2006), pp. 46–7.

Sagheb, Nasser, and Masoud Javadi, 'Azerbaijan's "Contract of the Century" Finally Signed with Western Oil Consortium', *Azerbaijan International* 2: 4 (1994).

OFFICIAL DOCUMENTS AND SPEECHES

Adams, Dennis, 'Memorandum Submitted by Dennis Adams', *Implementation of ECGD's Business Principles*, House of Commons Trade and Industry Select Committee, 2005.

Aliyev, Ilham, 'Opening Speech at the meeting of Cabinet of Ministers', 20 October 2010, at president.az.

Alvera, Marco, *Security of Supply: Does the Future Lay on Gas Pipelines/ Infrastructure?*, European Energy Forum, 6 October 2008.

Barroso, José Manuel, 'Speech: The EU and Azerbaijan: A Shared Vision for a Strong Partnership, 14 January 2011, at europa.eu.

British Embassy, Tbilisi, 'Digest of Email from British Embassy Tbilisi Meeting with BP, Subject: "Meeting with BP"', 19 September 2008, obtained through FOIA from FCO on 12 April 2010.

BP, 'Email from BP to ECGD with Subject "RE: News 141108"', ECGD, 17 November 2008, obtained through FOIA from Export Credit Guarantee Department on 26 March 2010.

——'Email from BP to Société Générale with Subject "RE: BTC Shutdown Lender Update 15 August 2008"', 15 August 2008, obtained through FOIA from Export Credit Guarantee Department on 26 March 2010.

——'Email from BP to Societe Generale with subject "RE: BTC: explosion"', 8 August 2008, obtained through FOIA from Export Credit Guarantee Department on 26 March 2010.

——'Email to Société Générale with Subject "RE: BTC: Fightings in Georgia"', 12 August 2008, obtained through FOIA from Export Credit Guarantee Department on 26 March 2010.

——*Appendix II to Turkey HGA: Turnkey Agreement between BOTAS and BP*, BP, 19 October 2000.

BP Azerbaijan, *BP in Azerbaijan: Sustainability Report 2007*, BP, 2008.

BTC Co., *The Baku–Tbilisi–Ceyhan Pipeline Project: DSU Update*, October 2008, obtained through FOIA from Export Credit Guarantee Department on 26 March 2010.

——*BTC Project Environmental and Social Annual Report (Operations Phase) 2008*, 2009.

——*BTC Safety Communication*, 2004, obtained through FOIA from Export Credit Guarantee Department by Corner House.

——*Lessons Learned: Non–BU Reportable Fatal Incident*, 2004, obtained through FOIA from Export Credit Guarantee Department by Corner House.

——'Letter to Societe Generale with subject "Force Majeure Event on BTC Pipeline"', 6 August 2008, obtained through FOIA from Export Credit Guarantee Department on 26 March 2010.

——*Resettlement Action Plan: Azerbaijan*, November 2002.

BTC Co. Finance Manager, 'BTC Notice to Société Générale and Lenders', 12 July 2004, obtained through FOIA from Export Credit Guarantee Department by Corner House.

BTC Co. Investigation Team, *Investigation Report: BTC Pipeline Project – Botas EPC Contractor (Punj Lloyd/Limak JV – Lot C), 3rd Party Fatality Incident – Turkey*, 2004, obtained through FOIA from Export Credit Guarantee Department by Corner House.

European Union Select Committee, *Combating Somali Piracy: The EU's Naval Operation Atalanta*, House of Lords, April 2010.

FCO, 'Letter: The Baroness in Baku – AGI/FOI 10', 24 September 1992, obtained through FOIA from FCO.

——'With the Baroness in Baku – AG1/FO1 9', September 1992, obtained through FOIA from FCO.

——'Minutes: Call on the Secretary of State by the Chairman and Chief Executive of British Petroleum – HF/FOI 68', 2 December 1993, obtained through FOIA from FCO.

Morningstar, Richard, *Address to CERA Conference*, Washington, DC, 7 December 1998.

——*Testimony: Commercial Viability of a Caspian Sea Main Export Energy Pipeline*, Senate Subcommittee on East Asian and Pacific Affairs, 3 March 1999.

Mortimore, Derek, 'Appendix 4: Response from Derek Mortimore to ECGD Submission', House of Commons Trade and Industry Select Committee, March 2005.

Red Baron, 'Anonymised Statement of Subcontractor Manager', in *Submission to the House of Commons Trade & Industry Select Committee*, Baku Ceyhan Campaign, 2004.

SOFAZ, *Annual Report 2008*, State Oil Fund of the Republic of Azerbaijan, 2008.

US Embassy, Baku, 'Azerbaijan Income Takes a hit as Now Short-Term Fix', Wikileaks/*Guardian*, 26 September 2008, released 15 December 2010.

US Embassy, Turkey, 'Cable 08Ankara1983: Turkey takes BP to court', Wikileaks, 14 November 2008.

Vacheishvili, Merabi, and Eleonora Digmelashvili, 'Complaint to the IFC Compliance Advisor/Ombudsman, CEE Bankwatch, 16 March 2004.

Vinois, Jean-Arnold, *Security of Gas Supply in the EU*, European Energy Forum, 6 October 2008.

WorleyParsons Energy Services, 'Appendix 2: Desktop Study Final Report Field Joint Coating Review', UK Parliament Select Committee on Trade and Industry, March 2005.

Index